THE POLITICS OF MOTHERHOOD

PITT LATIN AMERICAN SERIES

John Charles Chasteen and Catherine M. Conaghan, Editors

The Politics of Motherhood

MATERNITY AND WOMEN'S RIGHTS IN TWENTIETH-CENTURY CHILE

Jadwiga E. Pieper Mooney

UNIVERSITY OF PITTSBURGH PRESS

Published by the University of Pittsburgh Press, Pittsburgh, Pa., 15260
Copyright © 2009, University of Pittsburgh Press
All rights reserved
Manufactured in the United States of America
Printed on acid-free paper
10 9 8 7 6 5 4 3 2 1

Library of Congress Cataloging-in-Publication Data

Mooney, Jadwiga E. Pieper.
    The politics of motherhood : maternity and women's rights in twentieth-century Chile /
Jadwiga E. Pieper Mooney.
        p. cm. — (Pitt Latin American series)
    Includes bibliographical references and index.
    ISBN-13: 978-0-8229-6043-0 (pbk. : alk. paper)
    ISBN-10: 0-8229-6043-5 (pbk. : alk. paper)
    1. Motherhood—Political aspects—Chile. 2. Women's rights—Chile. I. Title.
    HQ1547.M67 2009
    305.420983—dc22

2009024322

To Fanny and Lorena,

with greatest appreciation for your friendship and support

CONTENTS

Preface   ix

Acknowledgments   xi

Introduction   1

Chapter 1. Public Health, Managed Motherhood, and
Patriarchy in a Modernizing Nation   13

Chapter 2. Local Agency, Changed Global Paradigms,
and the Burden of Motherhood   44

Chapter 3. Planning Motherhood under Christian Democracy   71

Chapter 4. Gendered Citizenship Rights on the Peaceful Road
to Socialism   102

Chapter 5. From Mothers' Rights to Women's Rights in
a Nation under Siege   134

Chapter 6. International Encounters and Women's
Empowerment under Dictatorship and Redemocratization   163

Postscript   193

Notes   203

Bibliography   249

Index   285

PREFACE

THE RESEARCH for this book was inspired by experiences on location during my first stay in Santiago in 1993, during almost two years in Chile between 1995 and 1997, and on about nine trips to Santiago between 1998 and 2007. Enrolled in a summer course on "shantytown health care" on my first trip, I was taught by a terrific group of physicians and health-care activists of the Colectivo de Atención Primaria de Salud in Bellavista. I also learned from doctors, policymakers, and female patients who shared their experiences with me and spoke of the problems they encountered in their daily lives. Moved by some of these realities and angered by the lack of power many women have to make autonomous, healthy, and even potentially life-saving decisions about reproduction and motherhood, I decided to examine what I referred to as the "political dimensions of motherhood." I intimated the analytical questions at the heart of this book in response to my ongoing encounters with different groups of Chilean women, with physicians and health officials, and with policymakers—all of whom have contributed to the shaping of the politics of motherhood in Chile.

In addition to traditional historical research methods, formal and informal interviews have been central to my work. The most frequent, regular meetings took place with Dr. Benjamín Viel Vicuña over the course of more than a year. He shared countless stories of his personal and professional life as a physician and tireless crusader for family-planning programs in Chile. Interviews with other doctors allowed me to see that there is hardly a viewpoint of one single "medical class," but that, rather, physicians brought varied interpretations of women's health and rights that contributed to the meanings and politics of motherhood. Dr. Jaime Zipper, for example, focused on medical research and experiments. Drs. Tegualda Monreal, Soledad Díaz, Marisa Matamala, Mariano Requena, and many others prioritized women's rights to (re)productive) health and offered multiple views on the most pressing problems in different moments of Chilean history. And in my meetings with Dr. Arturo Jirón Vargas, I learned that for many doctors an important mission of medicine —that of saving lives and providing equal services to people of all different backgrounds—is still alive.

Interviews also taught me that feminists' views reflect a wide spectrum of interpretations of the obstacles to gender equity in Chile. Teresa Valdés, Alicia Frohmann, Amparo Claro, and many others shared their insights on Chilean and international feminisms. Legal scholar and activist Lidia Casas Becerra was readily available and willing to discuss my questions on the nature of women's rights (and violations) in Chile. And many other women and men have generously allowed me to learn from their experiences. I am grateful for their willingness to share their views.

ACKNOWLEDGMENTS

In Chile, my friends Fanny Berlagoscky Mora and Lorena de los Ángeles Núñez Carrasco have supported me when I needed them most, and they have continued to share insights on questions of life, large and small. Special thanks to my dear sister, Bernhild B. Pieper, for making time to travel to Santiago to help me through troubles I could not have foreseen. Throughout my on-site research my great friend, the distinguished historian María Angélica Illanes, has offered support, invaluable professional advice, and stimulating, creative exchanges at her *tertulias* and other social gatherings. Historian Cristián Pérez has helped me gain a better understanding of the Chilean left even as he, at times, disagrees with my analytical conclusions. I am also grateful for the helpful information by Lidia Casas, Alejandra Faúndez, Josefina Hurtado, Francisca Pérez Prado, Teresa Valdés, and many other feminists, academics, and activists who were willing to share insights and concerns.

I would like to give special acknowledgments to the advisers and colleagues who have taught me the skills of professional research, have shared insightful critiques, and have encouraged me to write and rewrite my analysis of Chilean history and women's rights. I am grateful for the kind and convincing advice of Samuel L. Baily, and for the guidance Mark Wasserman, John Gillis, June Nash, Rayna Rapp, and Peter Winn provided in the early stages of my work. Nancy Carnevale, Noah Elkin, Mary Poole, Stacy Sewell, and Jeremy Varon have been great readers and peer critics. Karin A. Rosemblatt generously guided me in my first research experiences on location. I also thank other historians who research and write about Chilean history, especially Elizabeth Q. Hutchison for her constructive critical assessment of my analytical approaches, and Margaret Power and Corinne Pernet for the comments, confirmations, and critical views they provided to help me move along.

In the stages of writing the manuscript and completing the seemingly impossible task of presenting the complexities of a gendered history of twentieth-century Chile, Stephen Neufeld and Michael Rembis provided insightful, clever, creative, constructive comments that helped me stay on track and made me continue thinking and writing. Donna Guy provided perceptive professional encouragement to keep me going. Joseph Benham has allowed me to use his photographs and kindly allocated time to share some experiences he acquired as a journalist in South America. And Cathy Lyders generously volunteered her professional skills, edited chapters, and provided first-reader responses that proved invaluable.

Many generous colleagues in the Department of History at the University of Arizona have helped as well: thanks especially to Katherine Morrissey for helping me define the project early on; to Kevin Gosner for reading chapter drafts; and to Karen Anderson, Bill Beezley, Bert Barickman, Susan Crane, Martha Few, Alison Futrell, H. Michael Gelfand, and Steve Johnstone for helping me along in different stages on the way. I deeply appreciated the comments and constructive critiques by Christopher Schmidt-Nowara and George Reid Andrews, who also supported my selection of the University of Pittsburgh Press. Susan Besse's generous reading of close-to-final drafts helped me present a more coherent argument—and her observant critiques were, as usual, right to the point. Thanks also to James Douglas Lockhart for helping me proofread the manuscript before submission. Last, but not least, I truly thank all the anonymous reviewers for the constructive tone of their critiques and for their efforts in helping to make this a better book. The University of Pittsburgh Press's acquisitions editor, Joshua Shanholtzer, and freelance editor Amy Smith Bell provided reliable and timely support. All flaws that might persist in the book remain my own.

In the process of research and writing, I also benefited from significant institutional support. While still active as a group, the Colectivo de Atención Primaria de Salud in Santiago's Bellavista neighborhood allowed me to participate and learn in meetings and conferences. They gave me not only office space, but also a friendly place to work. The academics and staff of the Facultad Latinoamericana de Ciencias Sociales (FLACSO) in Santiago provided an intellectual "home away from home," library and computer access, and contacts to fellow researchers that were priceless. A grant from the Social and Behavioral Sciences Research Institute (SBSRI) at the University of Arizona awarded me with much needed time to write. I am also thankful for a Rockefeller Grant and the option to consult the rich archival collections at the Rockefeller Archive Center in Tarrytown, New York. Finally, I thank the colleagues and staff at the Center for the Education of Women (CEW) at the University of Michigan for a research professorship that allowed me to conclude my work with the book. I was able to learn from the scholars and activists at CEW, who are wholeheartedly dedicated to improving the lives of others and to work for gender equity and women's rights. I will do my best to support this mission in my work.

The gratitude I would like to express for the company and partnership of Thomas G. Mooney, great husband and loyal supporter, cannot be expressed adequately in a few words and goes beyond the space provided here. He knows that he means the world to me.

THE POLITICS OF MOTHERHOOD

INTRODUCTION

In 1872, Chilean writer Martina Barros Borgoño made it her personal task to translate into Spanish the acclaimed *On the Subjection of Women,* a work by Englishman, moral philosopher, and political theorist John Stuart Mill.[1] In a provocative prologue that gave her a name as a respected voice among Santiago's intellectuals, Barros Borgoño introduced what she considered Mill's most important contributions to a critique of gender roles at the time, and added her own conclusions regarding the role of women in society.[2] She argued that Mill rightfully exposed some of the fundamental contradictions of societies where men used references to women's "natural qualities" to justify women's limited access to social and political rights.[3] Mill had rightly identified a contradiction at the heart of patriarchy: men believed that they had a legal obligation to force women to engage in their supposed "natural vocations": marriage and motherhood.[4]

Barros Borgoño viewed these contradictions not as an invitation to ignore all "natural differences" among the sexes, but instead as a call to question the seemingly unavoidable consequences of what men termed "women's nature." Why would men in Chile consider it their obligation to force women to choose between marriage and the convent? In her critique, she defended a woman's right to make motherhood a choice and she requested women's access to "social rights," to an education, and to a career. Barros Borgoño provoked her readers by asking questions that had not yet been asked in Chilean society: "[W]ho would accept the tremendous responsibility of forcing you to become a wife or a nun if you had not been born with the ability to be a wife or a nun? In the name of what obligation [could anyone] . . . command such useless sacrifice for society or for God?"[5]

She demanded a new take on the "natural rights" of men and women, in the spirit of Mill's liberal feminism. Both genders should have the right to select their paths based on individual "natural" abilities to avoid "useless sacrifice for society or for God."[6] Barros Borgoño dared to question women's "natural," supposedly predetermined path and argued that women's reproductive capacities should not define their roles in society. Her concerns did not meet a widespread response during the 1870s. They did, however, provide an ideological foundation for her compatriots in the twentieth century, who passionately debated women's "natural" roles and "natural" vocations. Mothers and motherhood became the central concerns of different groups of women and men in Chile, including feminists, reformers, policymakers, doctors, and legislators.

Motherhood and Women's Rights

Barros Borgoño's call to question the seemingly unavoidable consequences of "women's nature" is part of the historical trajectory of women's rights in Chile that can be seen through the lens of the changing social constructions and political uses of the concept of motherhood. Motherhood, as the most important signifier of womanhood in Latin America, has been at the heart of the gender system and critical for defining women's responsibilities throughout the nation. As such, different meanings assigned to motherhood have stood for different qualities associated with the supposed "essence" of femininity. The image of the sanctity of motherhood continues to shape Latin American realities. "Sacar la madre" (to bring out the mother) and question her virtue is still one of the worst possible insults.[7] But motherhood has also stood for women's submissiveness and dependency, justifying the lack of women's individual rights.

Stories of "mothers and machos," of dependent women and controlling men, have often dominated interpretations of historical change in Latin America. But the gendered access to citizenship rights was much more complex than the hierarchies reflected in these simple dichotomous definitions.[8] My lens of motherhood builds on the historian Marysa Navarro's critique of the *marianismo* model by showing that *marianismo* remains insufficient to explain even the persistent reliance on motherhood as a political tool.[9] Referring to an ideal of womanhood modeled after the Virgin Mary oversimplifies the realities of women's lives and wrongly suggests that women have been passive recipients of roles assigned to them by men. Women, just like men, mobilized the category of motherhood, and thereby challenged the stereotype of passive, dependent mothers. In Chile, different groups of women reconfigured the understandings of motherhood throughout the twentieth century and made clear that gender relations exceed the binary concept of identities labeled *marianismo* and *machismo*.

Neither gender politics, nor gender roles, were shaped by men alone— and motherhood has not been a role simply imposed on women by men. In the Latin American Southern Cone, even outspoken feminists embraced motherhood as a vital part of their early political mobilization and celebrated their feminism as a natural extension of their maternal role. The historian Asunción Lavrin has shown the centrality of motherhood to feminism in the Latin American Southern Cone and asserted that "[f]eminism oriented toward motherhood was more than a strategy to win favorable legislation, it was an essential component of their cultural heritage: a tune that feminists not only knew how to play but wished to play."[10] Scholars have also demonstrated how Chilean women have used references to motherhood to increase their political weight. The historian Ericka Verba, for example, has illustrated how elite and middle-class women in Santiago addressed what they saw as alarming by-products of urbanization, industrialization, and modernization. Concerned about lower-class behaviors, these women made it their mission to "uplift" poor women.[11] Other groups of Chilean women have mobilized the category of motherhood in quests for more radical change and for political rights. They used motherhood not only as a "tune they knew," but as an effective tool that could extend the reach of their political campaigns. Feminists of the Movimiento Pro-Emancipación de la Mujer Chilena (Movement for the Emancipation of Chilean Women, MEMCh), for example, drew on the discourses of the parties on the political left—communists and socialists—that framed their quests for workers' rights as mothers' and families' rights.[12]

The Politics of Motherhood shows that the social construction of women's roles, as mothers and as individuals, lies at the heart of gender systems and patriarchal structures and argues that the lens of motherhood offers revealing new insights into specific histories of women's rights. Gender is fundamental to the construction of political power and to hierarchies between men and women, and analyzing the changing social constructions of motherhood allows us to follow and draw conclusions about the changing state of women's rights over time—and in particular environments.[13] The work of the historian Marcela Nari, on political motherhood in Argentina, for example, illustrates that doctors, educators, and legislators attempted to "naturalize" women's maternal roles between 1890 and 1940. Unlike the Chilean case, the Argentines' maternalization of women was greatly inspired by the quest to populate the country, and religious considerations helped doctors to defend a pro-natalist policy early on.[14] In both countries, nonetheless, doctors helped support state policy, and medical debates helped naturalize women's maternal identities. In Chile and Argentina, health officials and politicians created feminine ideals and prescriptions for "proper" mothering that some women found impossible to attain and that other women rejected in their quest for full and equal citizenship.

The focus on motherhood as a privileged lens reveals its uses in debates over women's rights and obligations.[15] The competing uses of motherhood by state officials, physicians, and different groups of women show the frontiers and fault lines of women's place as citizens. While professionals have deployed motherhood as a means of social control and a justification for female dependency, different women have contested and appropriated disempowering stereotypes of motherhood throughout the twentieth century. Diverse groups of women have also profited from and contributed to the reshaping of a global paradigm of women's rights, most prominently in the postwar period.

Motherhood and Chile's Path to Modernity

The fast-paced changes of industrialization and urbanization in the twentieth century provoked unprecedented debates on the meanings of motherhood. Doctors, policymakers, and male and female reformers voiced concerns over "unfit mothers," and contributed to modifications of the politics of motherhood throughout the past century. Women from all class backgrounds made varied quests for women's rights that have surged and resurged. In Santiago, the capital city, residents experienced firsthand the changes that transformed the country from a predominantly agrarian nation to an urban one, where doctors, politicians, and different groups of women continuously negotiated the meanings of motherhood and women's rights.

Ambivalence toward modernity accompanied the economic, political, and social changes brought about by industrialization and urbanization in the changing nation. Industrialization reshaped everyday life, first for Santiago's urban residents, then slowly and steadily for most Chileans who witnessed the rise of new technologies, the transformation of the nature of work, and the changing needs and characteristics of the labor force. Modernization stood for a break with the past in the lives of both those who abandoned their rural homes to come to the capital and those who saw their urban neighborhoods expand and transform. Many Chileans might have felt the "nostalgia of things that had passed" and "sorrow for the *barrio* that had changed," as expressed by those who played the tango known as "El Sur." Many have tried to forget their pains in the bars of Santiago, where rising alcohol consumption provoked great concern among reformers and health officials.[16]

Authorities also addressed the anxieties they felt about change by insisting on protecting the continuity of such gendered responsibilities as women's role as mothers. A 1908 editorial in Santiago's newspaper *El Mercurio* exemplified what was at stake from the perspectives of policymakers and reformers for much of the first half of the twentieth century. It dwelled on the image of a helpless woman-mother who "wears herself out in the workday and wages are insufficient to bring the restorative and sufficient food to her lips; . . . the mother is destroyed as she surrenders herself to work, and . . . [her child] bears the marks of the miserable 'terrain' where the first roots of its life were sown."[17] Indeed, working-class mothers in particular provoked concern and prompted legal changes as women became wage earners in industrializing cities.[18] The image of mothers in need of help revealed the burning concerns that were on the minds of legislators and social reformers: how could mothers be protected from the dangerous consequences of work, and how could they be sheltered from the impacts of urban life that would compromise their maternal mission?

The lives of these "vulnerable" Chilean mothers unfolded in a "male republic," in the midst of a political setting where women still had access only to limited citizenship. In 1822, the first Chilean Constitution addressed citizens as naturally gendered males. And a century later, the 1925 Constitution confirmed the political disenfranchisement of women.[19] Even after women had gained the right to vote in the national elections in 1949, they remained politically, socially, and economically marginalized. Few women held political office, and only a limited number of women were admitted to institutions of higher education. A case in point was medical education: from 1910 to 1960, fewer than five hundred women were permitted to study medicine at the

University of Chile.[20] The Medical School limited women's enrollment by adhering to the low end of its quota—a maximum of 10 percent of total enrollments—thereby ensuring women's limited professional advancement in the field.[21] Added to this was the enduring prejudice against female professionals. Officials, alleging that women professionals might neglect their domestic roles, excluded women from medical careers and other fields of higher education and specialized professions.[22]

Nonetheless, different groups of women and feminists contested "official" constructions of motherhood, with varying degrees of success. In the 1920s, Elena Caffarena, for example, earned a law degree, became a labor inspector, and mobilized for the political rights of women and workers. In 1935, she became a founding member of MEMCh. When interviewed about the negative influence political activism or work could have on a woman's femininity, she replied: "If work influenced femininity, then, believe me, there would not be any femininity left in the world."[23]

Local Women in a Global World

From the poor women who visited Santiago's health clinics, to the political activists who protested dictatorship or joined the emerging debates on reproductive rights, women's lives illustrate the concrete effects of seemingly abstract policy changes and economic transitions. The nature of women's political involvement changed dramatically and varied according to class, age, experience, and the political climate of the time. In the 1930s, middle-class and elite women tried to reform poor women they deemed in need of help. In the same decade, MEMCh mobilized women from all classes to support women's political rights. The group also addressed the problem of abortion and high maternal death rates in its journal *La mujer nueva* (The new woman). Lower-class women, meanwhile, were dying in alarming numbers as a result of resorting to backstreet abortions, when the burden of motherhood became too heavy to bear.

Twentieth-century Chilean history is marked by striking changes in political leadership. Those reveal a different intensity when addressed from the perspective of Chilean women in the global world. The anthropologists Faye Ginsburg and Rayna Rapp have illustrated the importance of adopting a global lens to examine the intersecting interests of states and international institutions as they construct the contexts within which local reproductive relations —and the politics of motherhood—are played out.[24] In Chile, physicians like Benjamín Viel exemplify one dimension of the intricate connections among these levels. A key figure in the foundation of both the Chilean Public Health System in 1952 and the first family-planning programs in poor Santiago neighborhoods, Viel was Harvard- and Johns Hopkins–trained and secured support from the Rockefeller Foundation and other U.S. sources for birth control programs in Chile. His outspoken support of a neo-Malthusian position typified the global alliances among physicians and politicians in the Americas. All agreed on a politics of fertility regulation that prioritized population decline and ignored local women's voices. The impact of the doctors' work and the political changes that resulted from contests over motherhood were both symbolic and materially real. Doctors' global connections and national policies profoundly changed local women's lives.

Chileans did not merely respond to changing global paradigms, but actively participated in their construction. A new understanding of international relations in the Americas comes from examining the ties among medical practitioners of the United States and Chile, for example. These ties are frequently misunderstood within imperialism's narrow theoretical framework.[25] In the history of U.S.–Latin American relations, scholars have often portrayed imperialism as a one-way imposition of ideas between unequal representatives of more and less developed nations. The politics of motherhood, however, show a world of collaboration among doctors and scientists across national economic and political boundaries. Physicians and politicians created understandings of motherhood within a fluid global world of scientific concepts. The hierarchies between nation-states remained secondary, after health officials across the Americas agreed on a neo-Malthusian paradigm and subsequently pushed control over women's reproductive lives to the center of global attention.

Chilean women also acted as agents of change, and different groups of women challenged doctors and policymakers who attempted to control the meanings of motherhood. Female reformers—concerned about health, welfare, and the future of children in the Americas—built international networks early on and often set the agenda of international conferences.[26] Diverse Chilean ties to international feminisms were most pronounced in the 1970s, inspired also by the United Nations Decade for Women (1975–1985) and by global and regional feminist meetings. Globally, feminism (and the different regional and local manifestations of feminisms) became a legitimate vehicle for change—accompanied by a thriving discourse in defense of women's rights. In Chile, diverse feminist groups helped translate motherhood into a new political practice and mobilized for gender equity. Women from different class backgrounds, with varied ties to feminism, transformed the understanding of motherhood as a fixed, essentialized identity, and set in motion new quests for women's citizenship rights. But through the lens of motherhood, we also see unexpected turns and regressions in the history of women's rights that have often been unacknowledged in narratives that follow traditional political chronologies.

This book further complicates recent challenges to the widely accepted belief that democracies expand the rights of the populace and that dictatorships restrict these rights. In a comparative study of Argentina, Brazil, and Chile between the 1960s and the 1990s, the political scientist Mala Htun has analyzed how these countries reformed discriminatory laws and demonstrated that an expansion of women's legal rights did not result automatically from particular types of government. Surprisingly, women secured unprecedented legal rights under dictatorships in Argentina and Brazil.[27] Although I concur with Htun's assessment that legislators and feminists saw women's rights as less pressing under democracy than under dictatorship, the case of Chile, where women saw unprecedented restrictions to their rights under the military, shows very limited evidence of legal changes in favor of gender equity. While some women gained new rights, women in general were subjected to new rigid regulations that compromised their health and reproductive rights. On the eve of democratic transition in 1989, the military eradicated the legal power of a husband to control and administer his wife's moves, but left intact the property rights that gave him sole control over all resources. The regime also made another last-minute change that affected women's lives: it criminalized abortion under all circumstances.

Fertile Meanings and Barren Truths

Chilean history elucidates the primacy of gender in the process of urbanization and industrialization, as argued by the historian Susan Besse in her foundational study on the restructuring of patriarchy in Brazil.[28] Male policymakers, intellectuals, and Church officials acted upon their fear of the destructive effects that a change in women's roles could have on the very foundations of society. In the process, they explored new means of limiting women's agency in a changing society. Gender-based hierarchies in patriarchal societies have continuously assigned a disproportionate amount of political power to men and have set limits to women's rights as citizens. Simultaneously, women have contested, challenged, and expanded the boundaries of patriarchal restrictions in the course of the twentieth century.

Chapter 1 exposes the tensions over women's proper roles in society and pits the construction of "unfit motherhood" by health officials and policymakers against women's struggle for political rights. It shows a new politics of motherhood, justified by public concern for the terrible hardships of poor mothers and their children, especially the high rates of infant mortality. An analysis of public health and managed motherhood concurs with the proposition of historian Ann Zulawki that "no other issue . . . more clearly demonstrates the connection between medicine and politics than the debate about women's health, because it was at base a debate about citizenship and women's roles in the nation."[29] In Chile, doctors in alliance with the state vowed to support the nation's path to modernity by controlling and educating women they designated "unfit mothers." In the process, they cast mothers as the progenitors of new citizens and new workers, and inserted the issue of maternal health into broader discourses on modernity and citizenship. Different groups of women contributed to these debates and often challenged claims about women's "nature" and mothers' obligations to the nation. Early feminists united women from various classes to demand political rights.

Chapter 2 addresses the agency of women who gained special attention as mothers whose lives were at risk. Doctors documented high maternal mortality rates as a result of induced, illegal abortions that had reached epidemic levels. Health officials and policymakers resorted to a specific version of a Chilean "pro-life discourse" that justified pioneering family-planning programs as a means to save women's lives.[30] Women's demands from below led to changes in health policies from above, and doctors responded to women's desperate desire to space their pregnancies. Although women gained access to expanded medical services and saw some improvements in their lives, they also experienced limits to their freedoms. There were few options to making motherhood a woman's individual choice in the context of her own life. When doctors and health officials connected the local politics of motherhood in Chile to the global politics of reproduction, they also contributed to the emergence of a new population control paradigm and to fears of "uncontrolled motherhood." This led to the construction of responsible mothers as "saviors of the nation."[31] In this view, mothers themselves should promote national development by controlling their pregnancies and supporting small, modern families for the modernizing nation.

In the 1960s, doctors addressed mothers as "bearers" of an excess of motherhood, producing families that were too large. Chapter 3 reveals the consequences of rising fears of population explosion, especially in developing worlds. Chilean and global population planners viewed women's unguarded reproductive capacities as detrimental to political and economic stability. Doctors used both the global paradigm of population control and national concerns about maternal mortality to institutionalize family planning with the support of the Catholic Church. Strikingly, the first Christian Democratic government in Latin America, guided by Christian Social doctrine, was also the first to support a nationwide family-planning program in Chile. These developments resulted from the interaction among different historical actors—population planners, doctors, politicians, and representatives of the Catholic Church. Many women found new ways to use family-planning services they deemed appropriate. Nonetheless, officials simultaneously connected these services to obligations they expected women to fulfill. Mothers were now held responsible for limiting family size for the sake of modernization.

Chapter 4 draws on debates over motherhood and birth control to explore the obstacles to women's rights and gender equity under a leftist government that was crippled by sexism. President Allende's Unidad Popular (UP), a coalition government under socialist leadership, promised to secure full and equal citizenship rights for all Chileans. However, in the course of its short tenure (1970–1973), the government failed to deliver on its promises to women and placed even further restrictions on the option of voluntary motherhood. Historian Sandra McGee Deutsch has maintained that the UP was guided by "[a] simplistic faith in socialism as the automatic solution to Chilean problems, including that of discrimination against women."[32] Indeed, men who led the "Peaceful Road to Socialism" in Chile ignored, even reproduced, gender-based discrimination in Chilean society. But the global lens must also be considered—for example, the international political fronts shaped by the Cold War—to understand the difficulties of promoting gender equity at this time. Women's rights as citizens were severely restricted, as they were squeezed between the right wing's appropriation of the discourse of motherhood and the left's anti-imperialist stance. Suspicious of ties between Chilean family planners and foreign birth control initiatives, UP policymakers constrained family-planning programs against the wishes of many women eager to regulate motherhood. The blame thus lay not only on Allende's administration, but also on the deep sexist consensus across international political lines.

Chapter 5 shows the complexities in women's roles as "subversive mothers" who protested right-wing violence and political oppression. Women invoked traditional obligations of motherhood as they entered the public arena and demonstrated against the political leadership in the name of protecting their families. Although some subversive mothers had protested Allende's government and set the stage for a new politicization of motherhood, a different militant motherhood inspired the political restructuring under dictatorship. These women contributed to the end of military rule and created a fresh understanding of citizenship rights: in the process of navigating repressive conditions under dictatorship, women transformed a rights discourse from *mothers'* rights to *women's* rights. Both middle-class and poor women mobilized and helped transform motherhood as a political tool to demand full citizenship rights. Women's movements in Chile contributed to the remarkable reconfiguration of a women's rights discourse. Their international ties supplied key contributions to these developments.

Chapter 6 examines the specific circumstances of Chilean women's international ties and explores their empowerment through connections to global feminisms. It explores the strengths and the limits that a new global discourse of women's rights had on women's local empowerment. With the celebration of International Women's Year in 1975 and the beginning of the UN Decade of Women (1975–1985), women also participated in the creation of an innovative global discussion on women's rights. Chilean women used global connections during the 1980s and 1990s to empower themselves, and used these international connections to demand gender equity back home. Many women became knowledgeable about international feminist movements through returning exiles; others traveled to participate in international conferences and used a global paradigm on women's rights to make demands under the new democracy. Back in Chile, they addressed specific obstacles in their ongoing struggles for rights, especially with regard to health and reproductive rights. In the 1990s and into the new millennium, Chilean women felt the consequences of ideological and economic legacies remnant of military rule. These legacies would manifest in, for example, more difficult access to health care in a neoliberal competitive market as well as the illegality of therapeutic abortion. Adapting feminist political strategies to contemporary realities, Chilean women have continued to rely on transnational and national feminist ties as sources of collective empowerment to contest these and other violations of women's rights.[33]

A culture of feminist mobilization around changing conceptualizations of motherhood has served as a driving force for diverse patterns of women's activism in the 1930s as well as throughout the 1990s. Chilean women have increased their interpretive power, have assigned new meanings to motherhood and womanhood, and have created space for a reconfiguration of women's rights in Chile. From the benevolent maternalist women who protected the traditions of motherhood and the family in the early twentieth century, to the militant mothers who demanded new rights in subsequent decades, women have been agents of change. This trajectory shows that from the perspective of local women, the periodization of Chilean national developments and the meaning of global connections appear in fresh light. Global paradigms of population control, international ties of Chilean health officials, and the global ties of feminists mattered greatly to the construction of gender equity in Chile.

PUBLIC HEALTH, MANAGED MOTHERHOOD, AND PATRIARCHY IN A MODERNIZING NATION

[T]he woman in her role as creator is a public servant who has the right that society assure her the same status as the soldier who defends his land.

Social worker Luisa Fierro Carrera, 1929

IN THE 1920S, when social worker Luisa Fierro Carrera expressed her thoughts on "woman in her role as creator" in society, Chile was in the midst of a profound transformation. New political movements, especially among middle-class reformers, contested the powers of the old oligarchy and promoted, as the historian Patrick Barr-Melej has termed it, a "mesocracy" marked by widespread political participation.[1] This mass politics emerged from economic and social change, as a fluctuating copper industry in the north and stagnating agricultural production elsewhere in the country stimulated urban industrialization and rural migration to cities like Santiago. Chilean industry struggled during the Depression, but the crisis also stimulated state-led economic development and innovative social policies. By the mid-1930s, the number of workers employed in manufacturing had soared once again while the pace of urban growth continued to accelerate.

Many of the workers and rural migrants who came to Santiago in the midst of these transformations were women. Their experiences revealed that in reality, a woman's plea for her rightful place in society was complex and variable, and her status was hardly secured merely by her "role as creator" and "public servant" evoked by social worker Fierro Carrera. Poor women often suffered the devastating effects of infant mortality, and maternal mortality rates were high. Some urban reformers and physicians blamed poverty for "bad" mothering and showed great concern for the health of mothers and their children. Yet, in the process of addressing women's misery and shaping public policy, doctors constructed and deployed the notion of the "unfit mother," claiming she was responsible for the high rates of infant mortality considered shameful in a modernizing nation such as Chile.

Between 1900 and the 1950s, a set of parallel yet intimately related historical developments shaped by doctors, politicians, and different groups of women exposed a new politics of motherhood. Doctors' policy-initiatives became more influential when the Popular Front governments (1938–1952) opened new political spaces, thus permitting them access to state power. The ensuing debates surrounding this politics cast women as the progenitors of the new citizens and workers of the modern Chilean state. The image of the so-called unfit mother became a powerful political tool in the broader discourse on modernity, citizenship, and the role of women in the nation. It helped mostly male physicians carve a space for themselves as skilled professionals and secure a central role in Chilean politics. Doctors' political influences culminated with the establishment of the National Health Service (NHS) in 1952 and helped so-called unfit mothers consult health-care services. Although this alleviated the pains of some female patients, health officials' concerns over motherhood produced multiple effects and meanings for different groups of women.

While the exaltation of "proper" (bourgeois) mothering stigmatized poor women as unfit and in need of instruction and supervision, they, as well as middle-class or elite women, could still use this rising concern over unfit motherhood to better their lives. Poor women profited from selected protective legislation and from the responsibility the state assumed for public health. Simultaneously, middle-class and elite women who engaged in either secular or Church-related beneficent maternalism exploited some Chileans' concern over unfit motherhood to empower themselves. Thus they asserted their voice in the politics of a modernizing nation. Beneficent maternalism—defined by the historian Karen Mead as "any organized activism on the part of women who claim that they possess gendered qualifications to understand and assist less-fortunate women and, especially, children"—characterized a substantial range of women's political engagement.[2]

Not everyone accepted women's "natural" role as mothers uncritically, however. Some women challenged the notion of biologically determined traditions in their writings and in public critiques of the Chilean gender system. In the early decades of the twentieth century, diverse women's initiatives paid allegiance to a feminist cause, some of them with international ties. Women mobilized to improve their lives and to gain new rights that they deemed appropriate and attainable. Yet neither the women who relied on maternal activism to defend their cause nor the women who defied tradition effectively ended the patriarchal arrangement that assigned most power to the agency of men.

The debates of unfit motherhood also framed the strengthening of patriarchy in Chile under the changing conditions of a modernizing nation.[3] Physicians, politicians, and health officials reconfigured the meanings of motherhood and the responsibilities assigned to women toward their children, striving to preserve gender hierarchies that located women in the domestic sphere, assigned political power to men, and protected the gendered social order that, in their view, granted stability in a changing nation. Unfit motherhood became a tool to combat urban misery and to make a case for the promotion of state-sponsored public health. The construction of the model mother required close supervision and control, and while doctors' efforts to save unfit mothers ameliorated specific problems in the lives of poor women, they also restricted poor women's agency. To this end, physicians sought support not only from Chilean power brokers, but also from international sources. Doctors participated in international conferences and cultivated relationships with foreign philanthropists, most notably the Rockefeller Foundation in the United States. At home, they asserted their role in the politics of nation building with bills sponsoring maternal and child welfare programs and socialized medicine.

The Early Path to Modernization

Santiago residents in the early twentieth century witnessed the initial stage of dramatic changes, whereby an overwhelmingly agricultural society began to transform into a predominantly urban one. The population nearly doubled during the first decades of the new century, reaching 712,533 by 1930.[4] Workers from the rural areas poured into the city, responding to the demand for labor. The majority of the recent migrants from the countryside were women, who

Figure 1.1. "El ebrio siembra lágrimas, miserias e infortunios: El ebrio es mal hijo, peor esposo i padre criminal" (The drunkard sows tears, misery, and misfortune: The drunkard is a bad son, an even worse husband, and a criminal father). Poster against alcoholism. *Colección Museo Histórico Nacional, Santiago, Chile (Pfa–000 829).*

took up menial jobs in domestic service, industrial sweatshops, and food and clothing industries.[5] Although city living held its attractions, the resultant hardships of rapid urbanization and increased industrialization were keenly felt by occupants of overcrowded and unhealthy tenements.[6]

Many workers found neighborhood bars a welcome diversion from home and work. Alcoholism became such a problem that public campaigns warned the population of the dangers of alcohol abuse (figure 1.1), and that Congress enacted an alcohol law that made public drunkenness a criminal offense.[7] In addition to the bars, in 1916, 543 licensed brothels operated alongside thousands of *casas de tolerancia* (unregulated houses of prostitution).[8] Between 1925 and 1931, prostitution was declared illegal, to combat the spread of venereal disease, but the limited effect of the measure brought back regulation in the 1930s.[9] In their efforts to regulate public health and national development, officials addressed men and women, as well as their problems, differently. Attempts to regulate prostitution focused on female prostitutes, who had to register with the police and pass health examinations. Officials did not regulate the movement of male clients, however, or test their health.

With industrialization and urbanization, the nature of women's work changed dramatically: it reached far beyond the realm of domestic service and involved new forms of exploitation. In 1912, 35 percent of Santiago's factory workers were women; in clothing, textile, and tobacco production, the number of female workers surpassed the number of men.[10] Employers justified wage discrimination by addressing women as part of a family unit in which they would merely supplement their husbands' incomes. Frequently, women could not count on basic benefits. Although industries needed both men and women workers, they remained unwilling to support pregnant women or new mothers, even when legally required to do so. Although female workers remained attached to the domestic sphere in the public imagination, in reality many women had long become individual earners under difficult circumstances. For many working-class women, the male breadwinner who could support a small nuclear family existed only as a myth, used by employers to justify lower wages paid to women. In the early decades of the twentieth century, more than half of Santiago's children were born to unmarried mothers and family types varied widely. Women often lived with their parents, with other relatives, or with men outside of marriage.[11]

Political turmoil and restructuring accompanied the economic and social changes in Chile. Even as urban aristocrats leisurely walked Santiago's exclusive shops and purchased imported luxury items from Europe in the late Parliamentary Republic (1882–1920), the crumbling of the old oligarchic order became increasingly visible. By the 1920s, old elites could no longer secure sole and uncontested access to state power or control the patterns of economic development. Between wealthy elites and the urban and rural poor rose urban middle sectors, such as small businesspeople and skilled professionals. Social change begat political change, but change did not come smoothly. On occasion, the military interrupted democratic political processes and intervened to impose social order, as happened on September 11, 1924. This military intervention brought about the Constitution of 1925, ending the age of the parliamentary regime and increasing presidential powers. The Constitution also separated church and state, guaranteed individual rights, and opened the door to the passage of an unprecedented number of new social policies.[12]

The transition of power to an innovative political class signaled the decline of power of the old oligarchy. In a first phase of twentieth-century politics, General Carlos Ibáñez's (1924–1931) undemocratic intervention, ironically, helped democratize state institutions. When the government of President Arturo Alessandri Palma (1920–1924) failed to push through his much anticipated social reforms, Ibáñez helped ratify the Constitution of 1925, thus sanctioning the labor and social legislation first proposed by Alessandri Palma. After a short period of unrest and an even shorter Socialist Republic (1931–1932), Alessandri Palma's second presidency (1932–1938) succumbed to Popular Front governments between 1938 and 1952. Led by presidents Pedro Aguirre Cerda (1938–1941), Juan Antonio Ríos (1941–1946), and Gabriel González Videla (1946–1952), these governments dealt with the needs of the population, including workers and women, through social welfare policies and by laying the foundation for the mass politics of the future. In the process, policymakers and medical elites succeeded, and assumed new responsibilities to address the problems of growing urban populations that directly affected the lives of women, specifically mothers.

A case in point was the 1938 presidential election, which Pedro Aguirre Cerda won with the slogan "To govern is to educate." Once in power, an extended version of his motto—"To govern is to educate and to give health"— drove policy measures. The physician, socialist leader, and newly appointed minister of health Salvador Allende Gossens began to promote a call for action. After qualifying as a physician in 1932, Allende entered public life with his book *La realidad médico-social chilena* (The Chilean socio-medical reality), which outlined the policy bases for the creation of a public health system. It would take another twenty years before his vision became a political reality. Physicians like Allende, as well as medical and political elites in Chile and abroad, helped shape the debates on health and the nation and, with these discussions, the role of women in Chile.[13]

In response to the urban tensions, Chile became one of the first Latin American countries to initiate social programs for its entire population and to create a system of obligatory sickness and maternity insurance.[14] Yet Chilean policymakers instituted social security and health policies gradually, often as special benefits for key political and social constituencies: workers, civil servants, the military, and women.[15] The debates and implementation of social services raised questions regarding the roles of men and women and the gendered responsibilities policymakers and health officials assigned to citizens of a modernizing nation. What inspired protective maternalist legislation and managed motherhood? How did policymakers expect women to improve their children's chances to survive? How did physicians help state leaders cope with modernization, and what were the benefits and restrictions to gendered citizenship rights women experienced as a result? Looking through a lens of public health and managed motherhood provides insights into the renegotiation of state responsibilities and of women's roles and rights in a modernizing nation.

Infant Mortality, Unfit Mothers, and Managed Motherhood

Urbanization picked up pace, and an ensuing public health crisis led doctors and state officials to assume new responsibilities to rescue the dying population and thereby end what seemed to be a "barbarism" in a modernizing nation.[16] Health officials prepared to replace private programs, religious charities, and mutual aid societies that had preceded state-led welfare services and government initiatives.[17] Doctors responded to gruesome realities. By the turn of the century, official statistics had documented infant mortality rates of 342.5 for every 1,000 live births. By 1920, the rate had declined only minimally, to 263.4 deaths per 1,000 births, placing Chile among the countries with the highest mortality rates in the world and revealing the shortcomings of domestic health and welfare systems.[18] In general, doctors felt overwhelmed by institutional shortcomings, by lack of personnel, and by the many needs of new mothers in maternity wards. In particular, they developed their own strategy to address the soaring rates of infant mortality and resolve the crisis.[19]

When doctors asserted their public role and offered professional guidance to control infant mortality, they focused attention on mothers, now deemed unprepared to cope with the process of modernization (figure 1.2). In 1912, at the First National Congress for the Protection of Childhood in Santiago, doctors noticed that residents of the capital and in other smaller cities had formed groups for the protection of young children. Yet participants like the physician Víctor Körner insisted that a cure of the "social disease" of infant mortality could hardly be resolved through uncoordinated initiatives. Problem solving, in his words, needed "scientific direction" to "obtain a decrease of

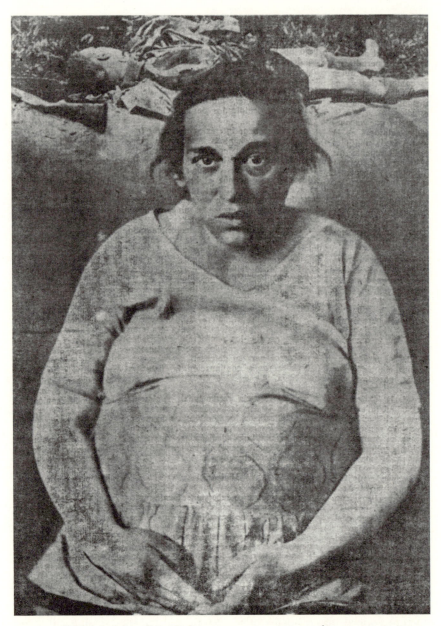

Figure 1.2. "¿Qué será de mi hijo? Es la pregunta angustiosa que dirigen a si mismas todas las mujeres proletarias en este país" (What will happen to my child? That is the distressing question many working-class women ask themselves in this country). From *La mujer nueva* 1, no. 5 (1936): 1. *Archivo Fotográfico, Biblioteca Nacional de Chile (MC002317).*

this plague that threatens the foundations of our society."[20] The development of strategies for the scientific guidance of seemingly unfit and often impoverished mothers became the central objective of the meeting. Health officials depicted the unfit mother as a poor, uneducated woman who had to learn to follow scientific instruction about proper hygiene and nutrition that would save her child. Doctors acknowledged that the "unfit mother" was poor but pledged their commitment to teach her proper resourcefulness: she would overcome poverty not by accepting paid employment in industries, but rather by relying on networks of other women that would help her maximize resources such as breast milk to save her child. Finally, doctors expected the "unfit mother" to postpone all individual needs and agency as she obeyed scientific advice and assumed the proper place assigned to her in support of national progress.

In constructing the unfit mother, doctors equated poverty with ignorance and with the inability of poor women to cope with motherhood on their own. At the Santiago Congress, physicians identified mothers' lack of education as the cause of their children's illness or death, and pediatricians insisted that most infants brought to clinics "got sick due to the mother's fault" as she had not given proper care to her newborn.[21] Chilean doctors such as Robert Simon underscored the blame mothers should take for the shameful state of Chilean civilization and for their infants' deaths: "much more than any epidemic disease, the ignorance of the mothers and the absence of supervision of the newborns are the factors that contribute to the lasting high mortality rates." Correlating poverty with a lack of education and passivity, physicians decided to "concentrate all efforts on assisting pregnant women." But poor women could not be trusted to ask for help, and doctors decided that "in matters of assistance, it [was] necessary that aid be offered to the poor and ignorant, instead of waiting for a call."[22]

Unfit mothers and their dying children threatened the nation's path to progress and prosperity, a threat that justified efforts to supervise women at home. The Institute of Small Infant Care, founded in 1906, had begun to assist women during pregnancy and birth and had documented some improvements of infant health. Nonetheless, doctors insisted that the severity of the problem required additional steps.[23] They assumed responsibility for "finding pregnant women long prior to childbirth, supervising and assisting them before birth, in the process of giving birth, and until the end of child-raising."[24] In short, poor women's lack of education justified the measures to control and manage their lives through teaching and increased surveillance.

Doctors expected mothers to improve as they were guided by experts and learned to obey specific instruction. At the 1912 Congress, participating physicians conveyed a more explicit message to women, defined in an open letter entitled "What women need to know in order to raise their children well," prepared by Luis Calvo Mackenna, the well-known founder of the National Children's Protection Agency. In the detailed directives, he provided scientific medical guidance that he expected mothers to follow attentively: "if the mothers proceeded [as told], their children would grow up healthy." Appealing to mothers' sense of civic duty, Calvo Mackenna encouraged them to help control the problem of infant mortality that "constituted an embarrassment for our country."[25] The open letter specifically addressed nutrition, immunization, and cleanliness. Women's lack of "culture" presented a problem, but their ability to listen and learn provided a solution. Physicians agreed on the option to make women learn, because, in the words of the physician Arturo Baeza Goñi, "any woman in our nation, even the most unfortunate, is perfectly able to make use of the good advice she gets."[26]

Doctors envisioned that mothers' resourcefulness would help them overcome poverty and transform unfit mothers into valuable citizens—modeled after middle-class or elite mothers who raised healthy children for the nation. Physicians such as Baeza Goñi, who enthusiastically pronounced that all women "possessed the qualities that would make good mothers out of them, if they only had [proper] models," expected inventiveness and network building by the poor.[27] Model-mothers nourished their children well, attended their children at all times, and provided proper health care and hygiene. Few doctors addressed the limited tools poor women had at their disposal to fulfill such model expectations. Calvo Mackenna's open letter encouraged breastfeeding as women's most effective weapon against malnutrition and for the protection of their newborns' health. Should women run out of milk, physicians encouraged them to "look for any friend or neighbor with a healthy infant, so that she could help out with raising the newborn," instead of dangerously feeding them cow's milk as a substitute.[28]

Indeed, health officials obliged good mothers to breastfeed: these officials addressed wet-nursing as a crime and argued that the child was entitled to the mother's milk.[29] In his study of the birth of a children's rights discourse in Chile between 1910 and 1930, the historian Jorge Rojas Flores has shown that novel constructions of mothers' obligations thrived.[30] Breastfeeding remained one such obligation, manifested in different and ever more urgent ways. After

1929, couples who received their marriage certificate also got a child-care manual which specified that "'every mother can and should breastfeed her child as long as possible.'"[31] Rojas Flores shows that in 1931, the Sanitary Code even declared "mothers milk . . . the 'exclusive property of the child'" and ordered mothers to breastfeed their newborn for the first five months.[32] Breastfeeding was a tool poor mothers could use to improve their children's health —even while their poverty prevented improvements of their children's lives that only money could buy.

The structural causes of mothers' poverty remained a topic that few people were prepared to address. Even Social Catholics and the Church prioritized the need to teach moral responsibilities to poor mothers over the need to address their material deprivation. Church representatives at the 1912 Congress, such as Monseñor Rafael Edwards, recognized the structural causes of poverty and declared the need to help poor mothers who had to raise children under difficult conditions.[33] In line with a position taken by Catholics who promoted Christian social action, he encouraged benevolence as a path to alleviation: the charity of wealthy elites should lessen the plight of the poor. Father Edwards blamed ill-performing fathers for poor mothers' misery, but nonetheless gave more weight to the moral causes or "bad habits" leading to bad mothering: "The question of the price of goods constitutes, without a doubt, one of the factors [contributing to the discontent of our working classes]; but, if one looks closely, this discontent also stems from more profound causes, more serious ones that have their roots in the peoples' own habits. In this way my personal conviction is that this crisis, as much a moral one as a material one, which is borne by the working class, comes from the bad state that dominates the constitution of the family."[34] Edwards reflected the position Social Catholics took at the time: charitable donations—rather than drastic social, political, and economic change—should lift the burden of poverty and lower its weight on poor mothers.[35] Social Catholics, like doctors, showed concern for unfit mothers and simultaneously tolerated the existing class and gender systems in their effort to help.[36]

The 1912 Congress revealed not only the first steps in the construction of unfit motherhood, but also a number of important premises that would mark the relationship between women and physicians in the future. Physicians developed health policies based on the mother-child pairing: health advice to women was centered on their inseparable ties with children.[37] By leaving fathers out of the equation, physicians and policymakers failed to make infant mortality a family responsibility. This maternalization of health policies demanded that women alone should control infant mortality and thereby contribute to national progress by following scientific prescriptions for prenatal care, nutrition, breastfeeding, and the proper care of small children. In the process, health officials often decontextualized poor mothers' lives from the structural conditions that forced them to seek employment outside the home and limited their choices.

The Inseparable Mother-Child Unit and
the Institutionalization of Public Health

In constructing mothers' obligations to the nation, health officials made a case for their own vital participation in the creation of a public health system as well as their own access to state power. Dr. E. Croizet, addressing an audience at the University of Chile in 1912, lamented the lack of medical standards among private charities. He demanded new state-led sanitary measures and legislation. Chileans, he said, "want to see robust children," and he insisted that it was therefore "necessary to strengthen the mold in which they are 'forged.'"[38] Doctors' persistent efforts to control health management gained a sense of urgency over the following decades. When Chilean delegate Dr. Lucas Sierra reported to Pan-American colleagues on the state of health care in Chile in the 1920s, he made clear that the centralization of a public health system and the reform of motherhood went hand in hand. He explained that Chileans agreed that "everything related to the attendance of the sick can not simply be addressed by charity, but needs to be done scientifically . . . under the control of trained men."[39]

Initially, the institutional changes proposed by the "trained men" of science developed at a moderate pace, but they took a sudden, speedy leap forward with Chile's first military coup of the twentieth century on September 11, 1924.[40] Innovative social legislation was the outcome of doctors' initiatives, the ill state of public health, and the eagerness of the newly installed junta to implement changes that would move the nation out of crisis. General Ibañez's authoritarian leadership overruled the old oligarchy that had prevented legislative reform. A new Ministry of Hygiene, Health Care, and Social Security took charge of health-care regulation under the direction of the country's first health minister. The large majority of the working class began to rely on the 1924 Workers' Compulsory Insurance Law and the Workers' Compulsory Insurance Fund, which guaranteed a range of health-care services for male and female workers as well as access to care in public hospitals.[41] Doctors' interests in state-directed public health were heard loud and clear on the state level.

The campaign to save unfit mothers solidified the alliance between the state leadership and a coalition of professionals who advocated social policy reform and facilitated the integration of such professionals in official government positions. Most of the latter were physicians, prepared to identify and address specific challenges to modernization. Infant mortality and the ill health of the mother-child unit were ongoing indicators of the troubled state of public health. In addition, physicians such as Dr. Alejandro del Río convincingly claimed that the lack of a healthy population not only limited economic production, but also represented an obstacle to national defense. When General Ibañez helped establish the Ministry of Hygiene, Health Care, and Social Security, Dr. del Río became its first minister. In their promotion of centralized health services under state control, health officials continued to address the problem of unfit mothers and incessantly expressed concerns about working-class motherhood.[42]

Physicians' call for a system of public health and the supervision of motherhood by specialists also led to the passage of protective legislation for working women. From the mid-1920s on, concerns about working-class motherhood opened the way to an unprecedented consensus among policymakers about the state's obligation to regulate industries and labor relations, evident in legal debates on protective legislation for working women.[43] By 1931, the Chilean Labor Code gave working women a total of six weeks of maternity leave with reduced salary. Employers who hired more than twenty female workers had to provide breastfeeding and child-care facilities, and women could feed their newborns in two half-hour sessions each workday. Medical attention during pregnancy, birth, and the postpartum period was to be free of charge for working mothers. Women were prohibited from accepting employment in unhealthy work environments and could not be in a job that required great physical strength, among them being the mining, construction, and agriculture industries. Lastly, new labor regulation also required enforcing equal pay for equal work.[44] Protective legislation aimed to ease the burdens of female workers, especially working mothers, but its benefits remained limited at best because of poor regulation and inadequate oversight.

Managed motherhood and the legal protection of working mothers often failed to address the specific characteristics of women's lives. Contemporary observers lamented that official claims about the legal protection of mother-child welfare only concealed a different truth—namely, that the lack of gender equity at the workplace persisted despite protective legislation, and employers did little to meet women's needs. Many child-care facilities remained unused. Few mothers agreed to bring a child to work under conditions they considered risky and inadequate. Working mothers often depended on overcrowded public transportation with little space for children. Others were single mothers who feared public censure if they brought their infants to work. Much to the chagrin of medical personnel, mothers often arranged alternative child care and substituted baby food for breast milk. Some even resorted to working at night, exhausting themselves with double shifts that negatively affected the well-being of both mother and child. Women's salaries remained far below those of their male counterparts, often justified by the limited scope of tasks women—mothers and nonmothers alike—were allowed to engage in at the workplace. Unequal pay for unequal work was, after all, legal and justifiable. But control and protection of women were closely linked. Some doctors continued to demand increased regulations to secure that mothers followed protective legislation, even if this meant closing higher-paid occupations to women.[45]

In public celebrations under government auspices, policymakers, health officials, and educators aimed at incorporating the attention to mothers and children into the national culture. In May 1928, a Santiago parade of three thousand high school students kicked off the "Week of the Chilean Child." Schoolteachers presented information on the rights and obligations of children. One day was dedicated especially to questions of health and hygiene at home, enhanced by conference presentations on cleanliness, nutrition, and specific health problems that affected the nation. The nation's first exposition on health was inaugurated at a Santiago library to honor the occasion, and the city's largest theaters contributed with film screenings. Finally, a contest to determine the healthiest and most robust children enjoyed popularity. Chilean doctors were at the forefront of the institutionalization and expansion of these activities; the following year, the campaigns to educate the public about infant health were larger than ever.[46] The 1929 "Week of the Chilean Mother" reminded Chileans that the responsibility for creating robust and healthy offspring lay on the shoulders of mothers, not fathers. Sponsored by the Society of Pediatrics, this event spread information on health and hygiene, infant care, and, once again, "proper" mothering. According to the pediatrician organizers, the "Week of the Chilean Mother" was meant to be "an intense information campaign . . . to educate women about every aspect related to the upbringing of their children."[47]

In the 1930s, the government-sponsored Office for Family Education (OFE) picked up the quest for sex education as a tool to help the single mother and her "illegitimate" child. Physician-educators argued that sexual misconduct was closely connected to antisocial behavior and criminality. Documenting the lack of supervision of children who roamed Santiago's streets, and adding chilling details of the characteristics of overcrowded living quarters that led to individual misconduct and rising criminality, doctors showed that unfit mothers, again, were at the root of the problem. According to the physician-educators, poor, single mothers wrongly exposed children to information on "the phenomenon of reproduction" and thereby inspired "a premature awakening of their sexuality and a whole series of practices ranging from masturbation to homosexuality."[48] Doctors noticed that small homes without much privacy exposed young children to dangerous details about sex and reproduction. They believed that inappropriate learning experiences, in turn, encouraged multiple sexual misbehaviors among the young.

Dr. Alberto Bahamonde, who had long spearheaded the work of the OFE, participated in the development and distribution of an elaborate manual on *The Regulation of Sexual Education* and initiated classes on sexuality offered to physicians and parents in 1935. Freudian sexual theories laid the groundwork for the curriculum. In fifteen sessions, course participants learned about topics ranging from sexuality and its connection to delinquent behavior, to the stages of sexual development, to the challenges of adolescence. Nonetheless, all progressive debates on sex education were restricted by the widespread fear of immoral and dangerous consequences such instruction could have on female sexual behavior. Even public health concerns, like doctors' warning of the threat of syphilis, were not convincing enough to promote new educational strategies.[49]

Ideas of sexuality and reproduction were based on moral-religious paradigms that also rejected the regulation of reproduction, a possible consequence of sex education. Even medical professionals feared that sex education could potentially change the reproductive behavior of couples—leading to an increased understanding of birth control and to a decline in mortality rates in the nation.[50] In the words of one doctor, an understanding of sexuality could give couples the option to practice "voluntary sterility," his term for birth control.[51] These fruitless debates on sex education confirmed the centrality of motherhood in women's lives. It also showed the strength of a religious-moral understanding of women's sexuality, to be expressed only in marriage and inseparable from reproduction; this understanding of female sexuality would persist for decades to come.[52]

Mother-child pairing—not women's individual health—remained an effective political tool doctors used as they mobilized to "repair the human machine, and to reclaim it as a factor of economic development for society."[53] Continuing high infant mortality rates of 209 deaths per 1,000 live births encouraged cooperation among doctors and policymakers to develop new approaches to public health.[54] Under the first Popular Front coalition led by President Pedro Aguirre Cerda, doctors helped ratify the 1938 Preventive Medicine Act. Dr. Eduardo Cruz Coke affirmed that their efforts to protect the mother-child unit made Chile "the first South American country to establish a compulsory national scheme of sickness and maternity insurance."[55]

In their ongoing mission to build an effective public health system, some physicians evoked the threatened maternal body to challenge the political economy of the time. In 1939, Health Minister Allende's widely read book *La realidad médico-social chilena* addressed the issues of infant and maternal mortality within a more radical vision of Chile's future.[56] A section on "medical problems" opens with a chapter on the "mother-child unit," elucidating the problem of single motherhood, addressing high infant mortality rates but looking at poverty rates for explanations.[57] Strikingly, the image of a poor boy holding a younger sibling provides the opening to the text.[58] The children look abandoned, destitute, and the younger child in his brother's arms appears without much hope for a healthy future. In stark contrast to this urban poverty, the picture also captures an image of the polished shoes of a wealthier passerby, calling to mind the "other side" of Chilean life. The black and white photograph brings attention to the gap between rich and poor and connects the health of infants to the challenges of poverty and economic maldistribution. Childhood mortality and impoverished mothers, according to the message, were not the isolated problems of individuals who had "failed." Rather, they remained social issues within the larger economic and structural challenges facing the nation and therefore could be remedied only through state intervention.[59]

In a classic expression of social medicine, Allende's political conceptualization emphasized class divisions as the primary obstacle to the health of all members of Chilean society. It encouraged the construction of a new world of medical care that would reach beyond the "original" medical mission to care for the sick and extend it to economic and political domains. Health-care improvements, he wrote, "had one single essential goal: to improve and defend the human capital, the fundamental basis of the greatness and prosperity of a nation." Mothers were central to the reproduction of human capital, and from this perspective the mother-child unit was central to the future of Chile.[60]

As health minister, Allende combined his concern for the mother-child unit with a call for attending to *all* sectors of the population. In his view, only a new strategy, interventionist and equalizing, would overcome class-based differences in access to health-care services. Allende set out to reform the social security system and proposed to change Law 4054 that had originally set up the Workers' Compulsory Insurance Fund, still at the center of the health system at the time.[61] His project involved the centralization of all public health services under one agency. Yet when health-care debates entered the provinces of political economy and state responsibility, they provoked mixed reactions. For some, Allende's call for changes in income distribution, housing, and industrial reforms were too far-reaching, too revolutionary. His proposal was ultimately rejected by Congress, and it would take more than a decade to secure support for a centralized national health service.[62]

Between the 1910s and the 1950s, doctors' enduring insistence on the protection of the mother-child unit, their support of the legal protection of working-class mothers, and their call for the supervision and management of so-called unfit mothers fulfilled multiple functions for the modernizing nation. These efforts justified increased surveillance of women in the name of protecting mothers and children, thereby inspiring passage of protective legislation and unprecedented measures of public health. Simultaneously, the construction of unfit mothers, the calls for the protection of the mother-child unit, and the image of the mistreated maternal body contributed to the growing professional clout of doctors. The notion that unfit mothers needed supervision and control limited women's agency, strengthened the role of male decisionmakers, and contributed to the ongoing institutionalization of patriarchal privilege—even as some women questioned their "natural" roles.

Despite the legal constraints placed on women's political participation, on their professional choices, and on their access to education, women engaged a wide range of political activities. Diverse women's groups addressed social problems, defended the importance of motherhood, or mobilized for what they considered a worthy political cause. Female workers unionized and developed strategies to improve their plight, even if the politics of male workers provided a hostile climate for female initiatives.[63] The union activism of female workers and their participation in strikes in the first decade of the twentieth century caused concerns over "proper" female morality and inspired elite women to teach working-class women about the importance of Christian marriage and motherhood.[64] Women of the political right (and left) mobilized in what the historian Sandra McGee Deutsch has called the "era of the ligas" (between World War I and the mid-1920s) and the era of fascism (between the late 1920s and 1939). Conservative elite women, often connected to the Catholic Church, fought what they considered dangerous leftist and feminist inroads in national politics; they attempted to organize female workers and tried to ground them in the Catholic faith.[65] But Chilean feminists on the political left initiated changes of more groundbreaking dimensions: they successfully mobilized women of different classes to get the right to vote—and even overcame some of the prevalent class barriers at the time.

In the first decades of the twentieth century, Chilean women of the upper and middle classes were at the forefront of beneficent activism in urban settings. In Santiago, Catholic women addressed what they saw as alarming byproducts of urbanization, industrialization, and modernization.[66] Pioneer groups like the Liga de Damas Chilenas united elite women who located the roots of society's problems in the misguided behaviors and consumption patterns of the poor, both men and women. The Damas Chilenas saw women's work in factories as a threat to traditional domestic norms and to working-class morality. Other secular and autonomous organizations of elite and middle-class women were equally concerned about lower-class behaviors and got involved through benevolent commitment. The Círculo de Lectura de Señoras (Ladies' Reading Circle) and Club de Señoras (Ladies' Club) organized around gender-centered goals and made it their mission to "uplift" poor women— sharing concerns about working-class motherhood.[67] Beneficent maternalism, located in the informal political sphere, drove the activism of these upper- and middle-class women in their efforts to protect poor mothers and children. Referring to the moral qualities Chilean reformers saw as natural components of women's public engagement, neither social reformers nor politicians nor the women themselves questioned the naturalized maternal identities of the time.

In the first wave of "motherist" mobilization, when the women's movement took shape primarily in the informal sphere, women relied on what the political scientist Susan Franceschet has termed the "politics of difference."[68] Motherhood and women's traditional role in the family held a central place even within the feminist fight for rights. According to Elsa M. Chaney's classic book, *supermadres* (women in official positions) often saw themselves as presiding over the "domicile" of the national "family." They viewed their tasks as extensions of domestic duties, differing only in scale from the nurturing tasks they traditionally performed.[69] In fact, their choices for political participation were limited by legal codes that denied women political, economic, and cultural rights until they gained the vote in municipal elections in 1934 and unrestricted suffrage in 1949. Married women were especially disadvantaged. The Chilean Civil Code secured uncontested legal authority of male heads of household to administer the lives of their wives and children. Proposals to reform the Civil Code to return to women the rights they had lost in marriage were rejected by political leaders as serious challenges not only to the authority of the *pater familias*, but also to social order.[70] In this legal setting, many women held on to the strategy of maternalist mobilization to increase the impact of their political influence.[71] Other women, nonetheless, openly defied traditions and challenged the restrictions placed on their lives—even beyond the boundaries of the Chilean nation-state.

In the 1930s, Chilean feminist and leftist Marta Vergara showed that not all women prioritized the defense of motherhood, and that cooperation with other Latin American women and connections to transnational political quests were part of the feminist landscape in the Americas. Vergara and the Columbian feminist Maria Pizano, for example, headed the Inter-American Commission of Women (IACW) of the Pan-American Union and lobbied the League of Nations in defense of citizenship rights of married women worldwide.[72] They also helped document and monitor the legal and political rights of women in the region and promoted women's property rights, the right to education, and suffrage.[73] The historian Francesca Miller has drawn attention to the "persistent participation and valuable contributions of Latin American women to internationalist movements," especially as informal initiatives developed into organized, effective networks of Pan-Americanism between 1890 and the creation of the Inter-American Commission of Women in 1928.[74]

As in Chile, global politics were dominated by men, and women's participation in international dialogues required inventiveness and audacity. In the course of their international appearances, women adopted a particular take on Pan-Americanism. First, they organized independent, parallel meetings to official international gatherings that excluded them on the basis of sex. Next, they won the support of male physicians and lawyers across the Americas for goals they had defined on their own. Latin American feminists organized the first Pan-American Child Congress held in 1916. In this and other congresses that followed, they presented strategies for the legal protection of working women, the protection of children, civil and political equality for women in the region, and other matters.[75]

In Chile, some feminists made a number of sweeping demands for women's rights—with considerable success not in their effort to redefine the meanings of motherhood, but in their quest for the right to vote. In 1935, a group of Chilean feminists founded the Movimiento Pro-Emancipación de la Mujer Chilena (Movement for the Emancipation of Chilean Women, MEMCh). In the words of founding member Elena Cafferena—herself a feminist, lawyer, and communist—it was meant to be "an institution for struggle, one that would mobilize, be militant."[76] Vergara, one of MEMCh's tireless activists, spelled out the greatest strength of the organization: its cross-class mobilization and the wide scope of its extraordinary program. It was attractive to "women of the bourgeoisie and the proletariat," and it covered subjects ranging from "the right to vote to the spread[ing] of methods of contraception among the destitute."[77] At the first MEMCh Congress in 1936, participants made clear their radical position when they proposed to "emancipate the woman from compulsory motherhood by means of spreading contraceptive methods."[78] While feminists' call for voluntary motherhood remained unanswered at the time, MEMCh participants (known as Memchistas) scored high in their fight for suffrage.[79] They arranged regional conferences and exhibitions, held weekly assemblies, and offered a lecture series. Members closely followed political developments and legislative proposals. They also submitted proposals of their own.

The MEMCh journal *La mujer nueva* (The new woman) documented the broad range of the Memchistas' concerns and political goals—goals that exceeded mere "motherist" concerns. Multiple articles addressed the needs of working women with particular urgency and emphasized "equal pay for equal work" as a central ingredient of women's emancipation.[80] *La mujer nueva* reflected Memchistas' progressive stance when presenting women's responsibilities as *individual* wage earners who wanted not only to improve their access to the labor market and their working conditions, but also to secure the well-being of their children. Women lamented the double exploitation they suffered as women and as workers—and bemoaned the fate of their hungry children.[81] High rates of infant mortality and the increased general interest in public health helped Memchistas promote additional items on their agenda. They defended the protection of pregnant women and new mothers and provided strong arguments for maternity leave as a woman's *right*, not as a privilege.[82]

MEMCh activists did not entirely break with the motherist argument for women's political rights when they made a case for motherhood, not womanhood, as a justification for the extension of women's rights.[83] Nonetheless, they broke new ground when they used the concept of motherhood in unconventional ways. The historian Corinne Antezana-Pernet has shown the amazing range of Memchistas' demands that included not only the economic and legal emancipation of women, but also made a case for women's right to birth control and to legal abortions when women had no other means to escape poverty and misery.[84]

La mujer nueva used vivid imagery and language to expose the realities faced by poor mothers and challenged readers to see this as the "wound of crucified motherhood." One 1937 photograph of a homeless woman outside on the sidewalk depicts her desperately embracing her child. The caption read: "Here is the poor Chilean mother holding her small son in her arms. It has been said that she is the one guilty of his death; however, it should be said that this woman understands that nothing, not even the courage she acquires through her motherly love, would change her destiny."[85] The caption is accompanied by an appeal to respect motherhood and to take pity on the heroic self-sacrifices of poor mothers like the unfortunate one in the photo who, as much as she might try, could not save her child. According to the text, the overworked and overwrought woman had given birth to a child who was, upon entering the world, almost as tired as his mother. And the baby's undeveloped stomach just could not accept what little his mother was able to feed him.[86] The devastating effects of poverty on mothers and their children became the focus of debates not only in Chile, but also throughout Pan-America, in large measure inspired by activist women and by doctors with global ties.

Women's mobilization improved their access to political rights and social services—yet changes were woefully inadequate to give most mothers the resources needed to fulfill their socially assigned responsibilities. Literate women older than twenty-one could vote in municipal elections in 1934 and were granted full suffrage in 1949. Social services were sometimes acknowledged on paper but hardly enforced in reality. Although women employed in the industrial labor force, as well as a select group of female white-collar workers, had legal rights to maternity leave in the 1930s, employers often either laid off pregnant workers despite regulations or failed to deliver on maternity subsidies. The large majority of female workers could not rely on support from the nation's elites. In the class and gender system that limited the political power of poor women, they would have to rely on public health initiatives and the efforts of a new professional medical class for some time to come.

Transnational Technologies, Traveling Doctors, and Professional Power

Physicians who assumed a leading role in the restructuring of public health in Chile had long been global travelers, building international ties, especially to health officials in the United States. Chilean doctors were frequent participants at international conferences, received study grants for medical training abroad, and invited foreign technical assistants and advisers to support their work in Chile. As Chilean doctor Lucas Sierra put it in a 1927 meeting in Washington, D.C., the international exchange among physicians had become "a great opportunity to learn in a climate of democratic cooperation."[87] Sierra and others regularly shared their experiences through events and publications of the Pan-American Health Organization that had begun to dedicate specific sections of its journal to *puericultura* (small infant care) and *maternología* (the science of motherhood) in the 1930s. Chilean contributions ranged from statistics on mortality to details on domestic policy change.[88] At an international meeting in 1940, Dr. Salvador Allende, then Chile's Minister of Public Health, Welfare, and Social Assistance, evoked the lasting spirit of American partnership in public health, reminding audiences that "the American countries, meeting in medical and public health conferences, have undertaken a broad social policy of international cooperation in the struggle against the evils which most deeply affect . . . society." He confirmed that "Chile hopes that the American Governments, with the always effective and enthusiastic cooperation of the Pan-American Sanitary Bureau, will continue in this direction, to make [the] continent the example for the world in public health and social medicine."[89]

Allende and other health officials negotiated new approaches to public health in the context of Chile's own historical trajectory. European approaches to public health had become influential by the turn of the century, evident in French ideas of small infant care, in German and English models of public health financing, and in the presence of European social medicine practitioners at Chilean academies.[90] U.S. approaches, too, especially gained significance in the early decades of the twentieth century. Throughout Latin America, the impact of medical philanthropists from the United States grew with the arrival of the Rockefeller Foundation's "missionaries of science," who sought to eradicate yellow fever in Brazil and Mexico and to support agriculture and health initiatives throughout the region.[91] The Rockefeller Foundation's International Health Division awarded a first fellowship to Dr. Benjamín Viel in 1939 and broadened its activities in Chile in the 1940s.[92] U.S. physician John Long served as a long-term adviser in the development of health legislation in Chile and, in 1941, Allende invited Oswald Stein, then head of the Social Security Division of the International Labor Organization and a collaborator with William Beveridge, to assist in Chilean health reforms.[93]

U.S. influences were most pronounced in Chile's embrace of certain "modern orientations," including functional approaches to problem solving on the local level, greater reliance on new technologies, and more efficient division of labor among medical personnel.[94] One significant example was the reform of medical education in 1945, which "modernized" national medicine in the areas of public health and hospital assistance.[95] In the 1940s this understanding of "modern" public health began to compromise the more holistic view of social medicine of the 1930s. Through the skillful initiative of physicians in Chile, the International Health Division of the Rockefeller Foundation provided financial and technical assistance in the development of "modern public health practices" throughout the country. It supported the preparation of personnel and gave technical advice to health officials at the highest level. Training strategies included the setup of a technical school of public health and the goals to improve and modernize the training of nurses.[96]

Between 1939 and 1947, fifty-eight Chileans, receiving sixty grants from the Rockefeller Foundation, went to the United States for training in public health, nursing education, and medical sciences.[97] According to the Rockefeller Foundation's J. H. Janney, who continuously reported back to the foundation from Chile, returned and active fellows began to constitute "an important factor in the changes which are taking place in the training of health personnel, medical students, and nurses, and in the administration of public health institutions in Chile."[98] They helped break up the inefficient bureaucracy of an "old régime" in the Santiago Health Department and directed a new type of health unit first tested in one city district at Quinta Normal.[99] Another crucial centerpiece of Rockefeller support became the School of Public Health at the University of Chile.

Chilean doctors remembered the 1944 opening of the School of Public Health as a product of the "Good Neighbor Policy" with the United States and with the Rockefeller Foundation.[100] Most physicians who developed the curriculum and gave classes had indeed received part of their medical training in the United States, notably at Johns Hopkins University. The School of Public Health was nicknamed "Little Hopkins" in its early days. Chilean physicians also received multiple study grants from the Rockefeller Foundation and brought experience from Harvard, Columbia, and Princeton back to Santiago.[101] Physicians like Hernán Romero, Onofre Avendaño, and Benjamín Viel coordinated public health education and also addressed infant mortality and motherhood in light of their public health training abroad. The nature of change in Chile and the characteristics of doctors' approaches to public health were best exemplified by a novel form of public health unit aimed at inspiring community organizing, impossible without territorially based health care.[102] Quinta Normal, a poor section of Santiago, became a testing ground for an innovative cooperation among physicians, nurses, and midwives, who worked closely with local populations. Local leaders were included in the technical coordination and organization of the project, thereby enhancing outside professionals' understanding of the community's needs as well as facilitating their interaction and communication with patients.

From its beginnings in 1943 and throughout the decade, Dr. Viel and others led the Quinta Normal project with technical and financial support from the Rockefeller Foundation. Public health statistics confirmed its success, specifically in caring for low-income families and lowering mortality rates.[103] Its success, nonetheless, depended on the increased supervision of mothers, begin-

Figure 1.3. "La visitadora social recoge datos de una madre, 1928" (Social worker collects data from a mother). From "Servicio social: Órgano de la escuela de servicio social," *La escuela* 2, no. 1 (1928): 62. *Archivo Fotográfico, Biblioteca Nacional de Chile (MC0023731).*

ning with a preliminary house-to-house survey to improve maternal and infant hygiene and sanitation. In the three initial years of the program, a nursing service was committed exclusively to the mother-child unit, with nurses surveying 14,632 families of a total population of 66,942 in the first year alone.[104] A Rockefeller field officer noted that "improvement is evident, mothers are more interested, more request service, [and] babies are better cared for."[105] The vision of doctors and their approach to controlling and healing the social ills of society became an accepted part of Chilean nation building in the twentieth century. Medical professionalism legitimated a high degree of autonomy for physicians, who lobbied to secure professional and political power. The need to manage motherhood eased doctors' access to women's homes and their control of family life. But in their controlling mission, physicians also relied on the support of female professionals.

The Policing of Mothers and Families
through an "Army of Women"

Doctors, nurses, and midwives built intimate connections to women's lives in their most private settings.[106] In the decades after Dr. Allende's book *La realidad médico-social chilena*, the power of physicians as a professional class paved the way for the medicalization of problems related to modernization.[107] In the process, predominantly male physicians relied on support systems provided by predominantly female health-care workers to find entry into intimate worlds. Female social workers (*visitadoras*) created these connections early on, accompanied and followed by certified midwives and nurses (figure 1.3).[108] Physicians helped define the healing mission of the state and shaped state policies; social and health workers, who were all state educated, carried out the state's mission for mothers.

Managed motherhood and the policing of women and families went hand in hand.[109] Chileans health officials supported Lewis Hackett, the Rockefeller Foundation's field officer on location in Chile, who insisted that the family should be "under constant solicitous and efficient surveillance. We need to keep the family clean, healthy, and well nourished, and thereby we will secure our race and our future."[110] After all, nuclear or extended family units served as an essential point of reference in all national settings in the Americas and were central to the ideal family of the nation. Chilean nation builders and physicians developed a specific foundational narrative in which the policing of families and mothers was clearly defined. Physician educators, also relying on an army of women, headed for household settings, aiming to connect to mothers and families. Their strategies differed, but their goals of controlling and reforming mothers overlapped. Whereas physicians relied on the power of their profession, female social workers relied on the personal bonds they formed through their moral mission.

The professional relationship and specific tasks of doctors and social workers emerged from the Chilean gender system and simultaneously buttressed some of its foundational myths. *Visitadoras*—all female, unable to escape the paternalism of charitable work and themselves part of a patronizing hierarchy —fulfilled an important part in the persistence of essentialized womanhood.[111] Many educated women who visited the homes of the poor easily equated their new tasks with the traits of self-abnegating mothers and their families, prepared to abandon their homes and sacrifice themselves as they extended their love to the nation's abandoned children. In this process they represented "model mothers" who helped poor, indigent women to attain their own moral standards—all in the name of doctors and the state. *Visitadoras* supervised proper mothering and also supplied definitions of proper sexual mores to their less fortunate compatriots in need of help.[112]

Physicians utilized and respected these female services as part of the first efforts to curb high infant mortality rates in the early decades of the twentieth century. At a professional gathering, a representative of the Patronato Nacional de la Infancia (National Council for Protection of Childhood) honored the support of female social workers, indispensable to the male medical mission: "We have assembled the women to request their assistance and we have fully recognized their abilities; in the context of the role of our institution, we plan to rely on these [abilities] to solve a problem of major importance. It is to the woman that we assign a central role in the execution of this task. Without her selfless cooperation, our own labor would have the coldness and solidity of marble."[113] Indeed, selflessness as an essential quality of the woman-mother served as a justification to place the female social workers at the center of professional tasks directed by men and motivated them to leave their middle-class homes and reach out to poor mothers in need of assistance. Motherhood, at the heart of their womanhood, served as the connection among women of different class backgrounds, with different educational levels and diverse challenges of everyday life. Social workers, in their visits, brought the first instructions of managed motherhood to the poor women, whose lack of training could challenge Chile's progressive path to lower mortality rates through a modern public health approach.

When doctors and leading government functionaries inaugurated the National School of Sanitary Nurses in February 1927, they celebrated the improvement of a project long in the making. Women who registered in the University of Chile's nursing school had to be between eighteen and thirty years old and had to have completed a basic education. The school's purpose was to prepare visiting sanitary nurses (*inspectoras visitadoras*) to work with new mothers. Visiting women included certified nurses as well as the visiting social workers, who were sent to homes to study the social conditions in the lives of the poor.[114] In 1928, the nurses' importance increased, when the Department of Sanitary Education took measures to assign all children born in the maternity wards of Santiago's public hospitals to the control and supervision of sanitary nurses. The nurses assured "that the mothers who once left [the hospital] on their own were now attended professionally from the start." Between April 1 and November 30, 1928, almost every one of the 3,714 newborns discharged from public hospitals remained under the supervision of sanitary nurses.[115]

With the changed focus of public health well on its way by the 1940s, an army of women continued to "invade" mothers in their homes, and the role of the visiting nurse practitioners remained as prominent as ever.[116] Addressing an audience of Chilean health officials, Rockefeller field officer Hackett insisted that the eradication of disease began in the household, with the help of "young women of character and adequate education, with devotion and the professional training of a nurse."[117] The social worker, for Hackett and the health officials he worked with in Chile, served as the intermediary between the household and the many social services provided by the state. The nurse practitioner, in turn, took on the important function of a direct bridge between the family and the public health service in charge.[118]

With a new emphasis on team work, a division of labor among medical personnel, and the functional, technical orientation of modernizing health services, women's role as nurses was also redefined, consolidating the gender-specific tasks of the women workers and their female qualities. Nurse practitioners became general practitioners with training broad enough to recognize and report problems as well as give primary care to patients. Supervising doctors assured that "the general nurse-practitioner does not act alone: she is part of a large organization, guided by her superiors," who would be able to make decisions based on the information she had collected during her home visits.[119] Under specific supervision, female health workers would therefore fulfill the expectations of male medicine. Some female health workers, however, perceived their role differently and attempted to challenge or democratize the system that relied on their assistance. Most of their efforts, unfortunately, were unsuccessful. The historian Karen Rosemblatt has articulated the complex political relationships and the gendered and class-based characteristics of social work, when social workers of well-to-do origin filled the niche left by female aristocratic reformers who once built philanthropic bridges to the poor.[120] Some were women whose families hesitated to allow them to pursue more scientific (male) careers and thus relied on the professional characterization of social work as nonscientific, made for women's emotional (that is, "natural") qualities.

Although increased professional training did distinguish the *visitadoras* from traditional social workers, they possessed limited tools to change the conditions they documented in poor women's and families' homes. In the 1940s, some social workers, inspired by the Communist Party and other progressive women's groups, tried to redefine the profession, but their efforts coincided with women's mobilization for political rights on a larger scale and remained largely ineffective. The top-down missions of the "army of women," even if questioned from within, failed to stimulate the collective mobilization of women and a critique of the male-dominated medical projects in the patriarchal setting.[121] The ongoing politics of the Chilean medical elite revealed the failure of Allende's 1938 quest for a redistribution of wealth and his support of social medicine, and the success of a conservative program that left class and gender systems intact and would determine the relation between patients and doctors, and women and men.

Gender, the Power of Professionals, and Nation Building in Twentieth-Century Chile

In the early part of the twentieth century, health officials employed the image of the unfit mother as a powerful tool to assume a voice in shaping public policies. Their engagement helped a new professional elite carve a place for themselves in the modernizing nation and simultaneously ameliorated specific problems affecting the lives of poor mothers without increasing the power of women's agency. The regulation of public health became central to the redefinition of obligations and rights in the relation between male and female citizens and the state. The strengthening of patriarchal control by controlling women's maternal bodies took some curious steps and surprising turns. Infant mortality provided the first issue for public debates on the need to secure the health of the nation's population, but meanings of motherhood became lasting foundational constructions.

Health-care projects by physicians were both medically inspired and socially oriented, and important to the construction of hegemony in Chile.[122] Through their increased access to state power, medical professionals supported the state in its mission to conform civil society to the economic structure. Physicians became both agents of and actors within the state: the improvement of public health under their auspices helped secure the conditions for the economy to function and grow in the capitalist system. Attention to health concerns that hampered productivity and the supply of a labor force became natural extensions of the state's role in the promotion of economic modernization. Women workers, valued both for their participation in the (industrial) labor force and for their reproductive labor, needed attention, guidance, and control.

Chilean women experienced the contradictions between the competing demands of modernization. Employers needed female workers as part of the growing urban labor force. Women's domestic roles consequently changed—modernized—and thus became more demanding, as mothers had to show competence under new instructions. Public health, infant mortality, and motherhood were at the center of the discursive and political responses health officials, politicians, and feminists adopted to fulfill the seemingly irreconcilable demands of modernity. Their emphasis on women's inseparable ties to children and their conflation of womanhood with motherhood were manifestations as well as "solutions" to the contradictions of modern life in the making. The pairing of mothers and children in an indivisible mother-child unit became the dominant reference to women; as part of this unit, mothers were expected to support the modernizing nation and overcome the most troubling challenges of the time.

The approach of physicians to infant mortality through the construction of unfit motherhood and mother-child pairing marked the formative period of public health in Chile, concluding with the creation of centralized, state-led medical care in 1952. Building on their domestic engagement and international ties, doctors of the School of Public Health of the University of Chile had significant doctrinal and technical impact on the health system. Their active participation in health-care debates in the Americas forever changed the outlook of Chilean practitioners and the practice of medicine. By 1950, more than a decade after Allende's original proposition for change, physicians and politicians initiated health and social security reforms in a new political climate in which Health Minister Dr. Jorge Mardones Restat successfully advocated for the creation of the National Health Service. Health-care services were now separated from the vast body of social legislation, and the medical technocrats in charge of the system oversaw thirty thousand employees. Closely cooperating with the faculty of medicine, physicians continued to work on improving health programs specifically geared toward the mother-child unit and mothers in need of advice.[123] And, evident also through public health policies, motherhood remained the most important signifier of womanhood from the perspective of medical and political elites.

In 1952, First Lady Rosa Markmann de González Videla accompanied her husband, the last of Chile's Popular Front presidents, on a journey to the United States, where she was granted the honorary title "Madre Universal" (global mother).[124] In Chile, a turbulent period of restructuring would end with economic inflation, government suppression of strikes, and ongoing tensions between labor, employers, and the state. The same year, Carlos Ibañez del Campo won the election and led a second presidency between 1952 and 1958. He presided over a country in which matters of class relations, citizenship rights, and motherhood remained central to political struggles. Women's roles had changed with the enactment of national female suffrage in 1949. Women had contributed to the transformation of gendered citizenship rights in Chile, and some had a public voice. Yet the constraints placed on women in a patriarchal society were enhanced by physicians' and policymakers' efforts to uphold gendered hierarchies and claims of female dependency.

Connections between health, modernization, and the medical-political discourse on motherhood that had shaped early twentieth-century developments gained new relevance after World War II. The link between the public outcry over infant mortality and the insistence that unfit mothers be professionally managed did not work in favor of gender equity. Medical elites and politicians employed the rhetoric of mothers in need of protection to defend their politics of modernization. Instead of liberating women from what were perceived as the burdens of motherhood, politicians and physicians obscured some of the complex realities of women's lives. The efforts led to increased control over women's bodies, justified through the need to protect the health of the body politic.

In the 1930s, some Chilean physicians had addressed the problem of self-induced abortion, maternal mortality, and even acknowledged women's need to control pregnancies, but it would take more than two decades to mobilize widespread initiatives to tackle the problem. Physicians and policymakers would address the threat unwanted pregnancies posed to proper motherhood only by the 1950s. Women themselves pushed doctors to reveal the neglected darker realities that often took their lives: they moved "unwanted motherhood" to the forefront of public health concerns—and induced abortion and maternal mortality became the focal point of medical initiatives.

LOCAL AGENCY,
CHANGED GLOBAL PARADIGMS,
AND THE BURDEN
OF MOTHERHOOD

[J]ust imagine the discovery of a drug, of a device, simple, easy to handle, that would prevent conception; and [imagine] that we would have, from that moment on, the only requirement still needed today so that a woman, convinced that her role is not to bring one child after another to this world, would have her children when she desired to have them.

Dr. Víctor Manuel Matus, 1938

A few pioneers of public health . . . started to talk about the topic [of family planning] early on . . . because they read a lot and had international connections. They introduced, sort of, the idea that a woman had the right to control her fertility. The reason why the gynecologists addressed the issue [of family planning] was because we treated abortions . . . and the deaths as a result of abortions. [Our family-planning initiatives were] not the result of the need of women to fulfill their lives as wives, as mothers, as workers . . . or the needs of women to not have many children for economic reasons. Those were realizations that did not reach us back then, I remember it well.

Gynecologist Gildo Zambra, remembering his involvement
in family-planning programs in Chile in the 1960s

IN 1964, a woman we know only as Cristina, from the municipality of Conchalí in Santiago, found herself pregnant, desperate, and unable to face the challenge of raising another child. She tried to make a home of a shack in a neighborhood invaded by squatters. At thirty-one, she and her four children lived in poverty. Even though her hardworking husband sold bread door-to-door for up to sixteen hours a day, the family's limited resources made feeding them a difficult task. Cristina worked in a textile factory by day and studied dressmaking at night. She had had seven abortions. Her eighth took a near-fatal turn after an unlicensed abortionist poured water into her womb through a rubber tube. Signs of a life-threatening infection forced Cristina to seek help at the J. J. Aguirre Hospital, where physicians found her in a perilous condition and barely saved her life.[1]

Cristina was just one of thousands of Chilean women with similar stories. These women's experiences reveal the painful realities of illegal abortions, a practice that, according to studies by public health officials in the 1950s, had risen to epidemic proportions. Women like Cristina forced new questions concerning the meanings of motherhood to the forefront of public health concerns and policies. The view that motherhood could be a burden too heavy to bear, especially for poor women, had been addressed as early as 1930 by progressive doctors who had tried to provoke measures to limit women's self-induced abortions. Dr. Víctor Manuel Matus, for example, dreamed of "a device, simple, easy to handle, that would prevent conception," and acknowledged women's need to regulate pregnancies. Indeed, in 1938 Matus envisioned a new paradigm of voluntary motherhood when he referred to contraceptive technology as "the only requirement still needed today so that a woman, convinced that her role is not to bring one child after another to this world, would have her children when she desired to have them."[2] But when effective contraceptive technologies became more accessible in the 1950s, the opportunity for the widespread acceptance of such a paradigm was frustrated by new developments.

After World War II, Chilean doctors supported family planning with a sense of urgency in response to national and global events that, in their view, left little space for concerns over women's autonomous choices and individual rights. When doctors first promoted birth control, they set out to diminish the horrendous maternal mortality in Chile. Dr. Gildo Zambra and fellow gynecologists addressed family planning because they saw that many of these maternal deaths resulted from induced abortions. Zambra recalled that doctors, driven to end this public health crisis, did not think of individual women's rights or of "the need of women to fulfill their lives as wives, as mothers, as workers . . . or the needs of women to not have many children for economic reasons. Those were realizations that did not reach us back then."[3] Chilean health officials responded to what they saw as a global crisis and supported family planning as a tool to prevent what they considered excessive population growth. Consequently, many doctors either ignored or openly rejected paradigms of voluntary motherhood and women's reproductive choice. Their sense of population problems that needed to be resolved left no space for the preferences of individual women.

This historical trajectory inspires a cautious reassessment of Chile's path toward gender equity in the context of women's reproductive and sexual rights. While health officials and politicians have often claimed a steady improvement in the lives of mothers and have depicted a continuous increase in access to health services and women's reproductive freedoms, the notion of linear progress is misleading at best. Instead, changing national and global alliances as well as paradigm shifts that inspired policy design in Chile could either enhance or hinder gender equity and had multiple effects on mothers' and women's lives.[4] Connecting the local politics of motherhood in Chile to the global politics of reproduction exposes these processes. It also expands our understanding of the boundaries of women's choices regarding motherhood, which persisted even after effective contraceptive technologies became available.[5]

On the global level, the availability of more effective birth control technologies had revolutionary implications, but the meanings of efficient birth control were contested from the start. In the 1950s, when the first contraceptive pills were tested in Puerto Rico and the United States, health officials and women worldwide began to discuss human reproduction in new ways.[6] Some argued that developments in contraceptive technology could provide a material basis for gender equity, given that control over pregnancy and motherhood could expand women's life choices. Others emphasized what they saw as unprecedented options to manage population size. Contraceptive technology did indeed provide an important basis for gender equity, but women's choices were tied to the ongoing negotiations over the meanings of motherhood in patriarchal settings. Male physicians, after all, were only one of several groups attempting to control women's access to motherhood as a choice. They were joined by politicians and economic modernizers in Chile and abroad who promoted economic and political progress by regulating women's reproductive decisions. Political leaders also feared "overpopulation" as a source of political unrest and revolution, a fear fueled by increasing Cold War tensions.[7]

In Chile, health officials claimed to respond to both global and national emergencies when they adopted two parallel discourses that justified controls over women's fertility and reproduction.[8] First, doctors addressed abortion as a medical problem, to be prevented through birth control, and adopted a pro-life discourse to defend their measures. My use of "pro-life" speaks to particular Chilean realities, quite different from the pro-life/pro-choice dichotomy of the political battles in the United States. Here it describes a new stage in the public discourse on fertility regulation in which physicians justified technological solutions and the use of contraceptive devices to save their patients' lives. Doctors' justification of birth control revealed a second objective, tied to global fears of overpopulation. Chilean physicians participated in the construction of a discourse that promoted birth control and smaller families for the sake of modernization and economic development in Chile. When they connected birth control to population control, doctors further contributed to the silencing of the notion of a woman's right to make decisions on her own.

Many women sought to make motherhood a choice, and their demands from below led to changes in health policies from above. When women expressed their desperate need to prevent pregnancies by inducing abortions under life-threatening circumstances, they pressured doctors to help them remove constraints from their lives. In the process, women stretched some of the barriers Chilean society had placed on their agency: they pushed the illegal practice of abortion into the medical realm and instigated a shift from criminology to epidemiology. This shift led to a medicalization of abortion, the treatment of women as patients in hospitals instead of as criminals with possible prison terms. Simultaneously, it reveals the strengths and weaknesses of local women: their display of agency did not grant them autonomous choices regarding motherhood. Medical interventions eased the lives of some women. But the nature of medical intervention also exacerbated many women's vulnerability, as they became the "human material" for new experimentation.

Post—World War II Modernization, Urbanization,
and Cold War Politics

After 1945, Cold War politics severely influenced Chilean history. Indeed, all of Latin America became contested ground. Many Latin Americans viewed U.S. interventions, such as Guatemala in 1954, not as anticommunist actions but rather as imperialism and as threats to their sovereignty. Latin Americans' responses to this interventionism ranged from small-scale, localized protests to outright revolution. Fidel Castro and Ernesto "Che" Guevara deposed U.S.-supported Cuban dictator Fulgencio Batista in 1959. Eventually, Castro's revolutionary government broke all economic ties with the United States and made the Soviet Union its major trading partner. Cuba, feared by the United States as a pro-Soviet communist stronghold and as an exporter of guerrilla warfare, created lasting tensions concerning the threat of revolution in the Americas.

Chile, meanwhile, continued to move on the path toward participatory democracy. Two presidents oversaw the nation-building process of the era: Carlos Ibáñez del Campo (1952–1958) and Jorge Alessandri Rodríguez (1958–1964). In 1952, Ibáñez counted on women, who participated in the national elections for the first time, and presented himself as a "General of Hope" who no longer relied on the authoritarian means that had characterized his earlier presidency, in the 1920s. Using a broom as his campaign symbol, Ibañez promised to "sweep away" political bickering and to end economic stagnation. Ultimately, he would not solve the economic problems his predecessors had left unresolved, even with foreign economic consultants advising him. Just before the end of his term in 1958, however, Ibañez made a move that *did* strengthen the democratic process: he introduced an electoral reform that enforced the secret ballot system, thereby significantly enhancing the electoral system's integrity. Landowners could no longer control rural workers' votes, and Christian Democrats and Marxists found new political support.[9]

Alessandri's subsequent victory as the candidate of a liberal-conservative alliance represented a brief return of right-of-center politics. In the elections, Alessandri barely defeated Salvador Allende, the standard-bearer for more extensive social reform and economic redistribution. Under Alessandri's presidency, Chileans saw a further extension of education and a more organized national labor movement. Yet the president restricted land reforms that would modernize labor relations and production systems in the countryside. Allende's near victory lingered as a first sign of the increased polarization of the Chilean electorate—and the general population. On the one side were those eager to defend old hierarchies and traditional privilege. On the other side, many Chileans defended further democratization and equality.[10]

Santiago's population continued to grow rapidly due to declining mortality and increasing migration. Between 1930 and 1964, the nation's overall population rose from 4.5 million to about 8 million, an increase stimulated by improved public health, longer life expectancy, and an overall decline in death rates primarily as a result of antibiotics and rigorous campaigns to control tuberculosis, the single most frequent cause of death in the nation.[11] The life expectancy of women rose from 37.7 to 53.8 and from 35.4 to 49.8 for men. Nonetheless, infant mortality rates in Chile remained one of the highest in the Americas—

129 deaths per 1,000 live births in 1952.[12] And the rising life expectancy for women offered limited reason for optimism: it was accompanied by high maternal mortality rates of women of childbearing age, caused by women's desperate attempts at birth control.

Immigrants from the northern mining regions and the Central Valley contributed to Santiago's demographic explosion in the middle of the century, with the number of migrating women from the countryside continuing to exceed that of men. From 1940 to 1952, Santiago's population increased from slightly more than 952,000 to about 1.35 million. Between 1960 and 1970, the city's population increased by almost a million, from 1.9 million to 2.9 million in the span of a mere decade.[13] Men and women fled the countryside's limited opportunities—opportunities that remained even less promising for women than for men. Women who did not have access to land and received only limited financial compensation for their work in rural areas hoped to make a living in the city.

Urban conditions forced both male and female migrants to find new ways to survive the increasingly overcrowded cities. Gendered traditions, moreover, created additional hardships for women. Since poor women, unlike poor men, could not live alone, most resorted to domestic employment as *puertas adentro,* residing in the homes of their employers. In 1962, 64.2 percent of female migrant workers in Santiago were domestic workers, while only 15.6 percent worked in sales or manufacturing.[14] For female migrants, the years between 1950 and 1970 were the most difficult. Although these two decades witnessed the largest migration of women from the countryside in search of work in the city, these years saw the lowest growth of female employment rates in Chile's urban centers. More women came to Santiago, but fewer could count on employment opportunities and a living wage.[15] The 1950s also marked the unstoppable growth of new shantytowns, appearing at the outskirts of the capital and serving as overcrowded spaces for working-class housing.

From Persecuting Abortions to Healing Troubled Motherhood

Urban mothers' dilemmas multiplied. Evidence of troubled motherhood had shaped the politics of public health in the early decades of the twentieth century and continuously inspired diverse responses to the plight of urban women. In

1936, Chilean feminists demanded initiatives to "save working women," especially those affected by unwanted pregnancies and abortions.[16] Others, like Dr. Victoria García Carpanetti, replaced calls for protection with accusations, painting grim pictures of working women who not only abandoned their domestic responsibilities by leaving their children unattended while they worked, but also "resisted new motherhood . . . and began . . . a dangerous phase of life, provoking abortions that killed future human beings, and often the mother herself."[17]

Data revealed cases of abortion being performed in public hospitals but provided few details about their circumstances. Medical statistics of the University of Chile's health service documented that medical personnel attended 1,566 live births and 663 abortions in 1931, and 1,481 live births and 591 abortions in 1932, but the numbers did not distinguish between spontaneous and provoked abortion and provided no further information on the aborted pregnancies.[18] Neither doctors nor policymakers were prepared to move the darker side of women's troubles—induced abortions—to the center of public policy debate. They commented on the evidence of unwanted pregnancies, abortions, and maternal mortality in hushed voices and isolated spaces at medical conventions and hospital conferences.[19]

The apparent dangers of induced abortion attracted the attention of physicians, but their statements remained cautious. In 1936, at a medical convention in Valparaiso, a group of physicians proposed relaxing some restrictions on induced abortion and the distribution of contraceptives—and doctors and medical students made a case for improved statistics on abortion in public hospitals.[20] In the same year, Dr. Gazitua, in charge of a Santiago public health service, suspected that 451 (42.8 percent) of a total of 1,068 abortions that were attended to in his health service were self-induced. Only thirty-nine of his patients admitted to having induced the abortion. A colleague, Dr. Rodriguez, found that in the maternity ward of the San Borja Hospital, eighty-four women died in the process of giving birth, compared with the much higher number of 282 women who died as a consequence of self-induced abortion outside the hospital.[21]

In 1949, Drs. Romero and Ugarte revealed preliminary results of the first long-term study on maternal mortality. They showed that the number of self-induced abortions attended in Santiago hospitals had quadrupled between 1931 and 1945, from approximately five thousand to twenty thousand abortion cases. They admitted that the statistics illustrated "a clear expression of birth control, practiced in the worst form imaginable." Nonetheless, subsequent statements revealed the doctors' unease with their findings and attested to their unwillingness to set off widespread reactions to the problem. They insisted on the unreliable nature of their data and pronounced that "the moment of presenting the disturbing and momentous problem of abortion had not come yet."[22] The treatment of sexuality and contraception as private matters, coupled with the illegal nature of abortion, help explain why physicians addressed the abortion epidemic only reluctantly.

Reproductive health specialist Bonnie Shepard's notion of a "double discourse system" helps explain the longevity of public silence on the issue of abortion. This system maintains the status quo through repressive public policies while at the same time tolerating expanded sexual and reproductive choices behind the scenes. Chilean cultural norms perpetuated rigid standards of proper sexual morality upheld in the public sphere, but simultaneously put up with deviance from public norms when deviant acts remained private.[23] The tradition of accepting hidden violations of sexual norms or religious-moral expectations, hypocritical from the perspective of outsiders, followed a logic widespread in Chilean society. It avoids the political costs of espousing a change in norms and traditions and offers loopholes to avoid their repressive consequences. Although its logic accommodates perpetrators who committed minor sins, this tradition punishes those who do not have the means to hide the public consequences of their moral-sexual mistakes. The double discourse system also prevented an honest dialogue on all matters of reproduction, including abortion.

In Chile, open discussions on sexuality, contraception, and women's life cycles were as rare as public references to abortion. Women's options to prevent pregnancies were limited, and health officials treated fertility regulation as largely a private matter. Traditional methods involved periodic abstinence, withdrawal, prolonged breastfeeding, and folk medications. Only a few doctors, like Amalia Ernst and Onofre Avendaño, made spermicides, diaphragms, and condoms available to women upon request in the 1930s and 1940s.[24] Flawed traditional methods, the lack of resources to purchase contraceptives, or the lack of knowledge of contraception resulted in numerous unwanted pregnancies. Women felt the consequences of lacking decision-making power at home, as many methods of preventing births depended on men's cooperation, without which the measures would fail. The official silence on sexuality and the regulation of reproduction represented barriers to making motherhood a woman's choice. The illegal nature of abortion represented yet another barrier.

Religious and secular condemnation of abortion made it a sin as well as a criminal offense. The Catholic Church condemned an abortion as the murder of an unborn child, and Chile's criminal law made few exceptions to this verdict.[25] Although criminality could be circumvented in rare cases involving women's "honor," illegality and silence dominated the reproductive lives of Chilean women. Abortion remained a criminal offense under the Chilean Penal Code of 1874, leaving little space to consider the economic hardships or personal misery of individual women faced with unwanted pregnancy. Articles 342–345 mandated prison terms up to ten years for those who induced an abortion and for the pregnant woman who consented to have the procedure. Yet Article 344 revealed the close connection between a woman's sexual behavior and the honor bestowed on her by Chilean society. Women could reduce their prison sentences if they testified to the need to protect their honor, which was connected to the honor of their families. If a woman had committed the crime of inducing abortion "to hide her dishonor"—and to "diminish" the consequences of what had been the betrayal by a man who had abandoned her—she was defending the proper standards and gendered traditions.[26]

Therapeutic abortion was legalized under the Health Code of 1931, but many women who did not have access to regular medical care continued to rely on illegal and unsafe abortions. The new law required the signatures of at least two physicians to testify that pregnancy threatened a mother's life.[27] Hidden announcements, like the small article in a 1962 Sunday paper entitled "Detained Doctor," showed that the criminalization of abortion and related arrests were infrequent but forceful realities. An obstetrician had been detained for "illegal interventions," and two additional offenders had been captured.[28] Shifting perspectives and women's increasing ability to speak of their experiences began to move such offenses out of the criminal courts and into the medical world, but change came slowly.

A stubborn culture of silence on sexuality and reproduction lasted well into the postwar period. Even women with access to resources and education found it difficult to learn about sex and to secure access to contraceptive devices. In the memoir written for her daughter Paula, novelist Isabel Allende shared her experiences of the 1960s that shaped her own coming of age. She recalled her first encounters with the need to make intimate decisions: "I first heard the women in the office talking about a marvelous pill that would prevent pregnancy; it had revolutionized the cultures of Europe and the United States, they said, and was now available in a few local pharmacies. I investigated further and learned that one had to have a prescription to buy it. I did not dare go to the ineffable Dr. Benjamín Viel, who by then was the guru of family planning in Chile."[29] Isabel Allende remembered how couples of the elite and middle classes rarely talked about the details of sexual relationships: "[I]n those days of collective hypocrisy the subject was taboo."[30] Women of wealthier families would have contact with private physicians and could find family-planning information in more protected environments than the poor could, but many of them knew little about the mechanics of sex. Although the upbringing of poor women might have been less puritanical, their access to contraceptive devices was inhibited by their lack of knowledge on the subject and their inability not only to get prescriptions for contraceptive pills but to pay for them as well. Regardless of their class, many Chilean women learned to fear pregnancy.

Only after World War II did women testify that economic pressures, sexual abuse, anxiety about moral condemnations of children born to unmarried mothers, as well as the sheer inability to control pregnancies had forced many to seek abortions without medical support.[31] Doctors and demographers collected data on abortions in Santiago and revealed that women of middle- or high-income sectors were among the high-risk group of women who sought abortions to limit family size. For example, a woman we know only as Norma, the wife of a taxi driver and relatively financially stable, frequently relied on abortions between pregnancies and after the birth of her second child. She remembered that she "wasn't careful" and that "in the years between the birth of the youngest and the oldest [she] . . . had at least one abortion each year." Norma reported that "most [of her] friends have abortions because of the number of children they have, because they have children against their will and all their life is spent raising children." Some abortions took place in unsafe conditions. Norma recalled how "her sister was critically ill for three months because she provoked an abortion with the *sonda*, . . . a rubber tube with a bulb at one end through which water is squeezed. . . . [Her] sister was turning purple when they took her to the hospital because the dead foetus was still inside of her."[32]

When some doctors initiated systematic field research to study the problem of abortion, they gave women unprecedented space to present their heretofore hidden worlds. In a 2006 BBC special honoring her outstanding achievements as a physician and epidemiologist, Tegualda Monreal recalled her personal approach to the health challenges that gravely affected women: "I visited people's homes and talked to women to learn about the particular circumstances of their lives."[33] She explained that "the originality of the investigation is that it takes place right in people's homes, and addresses a very emotional problem that is extremely complex also on human and social levels."[34] Monreal's research exemplified a more holistic approach to fieldwork that covered everything from documenting the specific realities of induced abortions to assessing measures to prevent abortion and maternal mortality.

Studying the lives of Santiago women of fertile age, doctors combined conventional sampling techniques with qualitative surveys on the women's personal histories, their economic situation, nature of employment, frequency of sexual relations, their relationship to a partner, and the details of their pregnancies and abortions. Based on data from the 1960 census, Monreal and her colleague, the physician Rolando Armijo, drew a random sample of 2,464 homes in the greater Santiago area for a new study.[35] In 1963, the doctor Mariano Requena conducted his survey in a poor section of Santiago's Quinta Normal, the health district that served as a teaching and research area for the Department of Preventive Medicine of the University of Chile. In the second stage of their fieldwork, doctors expanded their scope to include the recording of women's interest in preventing unwanted pregnancies through contraception. In May 1964, Requena, Viel, and others extended the program to a larger Santiago area, to a population of 450,000 people with an estimated 120,000 women of childbearing age.[36]

Women's statements collected during the surveys forced physicians in Santiago to declare that self-induced abortion had reached epidemic proportions and constituted a major public health problem.[37] In 1940, Chile had a population of approximately 1.2 million women of childbearing age. Public hospitals attended to 16,560 cases of abortion, or 13.9 of 1,000 women of childbearing age. By 1965, this rate had increased by 104.4 percent. The documented number of abortions reached 56,130—a ratio of 29.1 of every 1,000 women.[38] In 1961, four thousand interviews of women between twenty and forty-nine years of age showed that one of every four women admitted to having had between one and thirty-five induced abortions.[39] These results reached audiences in Chile as well as attendees of international health conferences in the United States.[40]

Data revealed a common desire among women of different classes to regulate their fertility and a common practice to resort to abortion, but it also showed the striking differences among the environments in which abortions took place. Women's answers made clear that not the sexually promiscuous, but rather married women, from all ranges of urban society and with multiple children, were the most likely to seek abortions.[41] Poor women ran higher medical risks than middle-class women, who could find private medical care or rely on the services of midwives. Furthermore, poor women frequently increased their health risks by delaying their abortions for as long as five months. In response to Requena's question on "why they waited so long," these women invariably referred to financial reasons. If they had the abortion performed in the first weeks of pregnancy, chances were that they would get pregnant soon thereafter. By postponing the procedure, they could therefore get by with fewer abortions and fewer expenses.[42] Finally, poverty forced these women to seek clandestine abortions from backstreet abortionists who operated with limited medical knowledge under unhygienic conditions.

Women's responses also documented the dangerous abortion techniques that led to high maternal death rates. For example, abortionists commonly inserted unsanitary rubber catheters, tubes, wires, sticks, or plant stems into the uterus—a common practice to induce contractions and expel the fetus.[43] In Santiago, the *raspado* (a method that involved dilating the cervix and scraping the uterine walls with a metal instrument) and the *sonda* (the insertion of a catheter or tube) were among the most frequent methods.[44] Patients of clandestine abortion services, like Cristina or Norma's sister, were rushed to emergency rooms with blood poisoning, internal hemorrhaging, pelvic infection, or uterine perforation. Many did not survive the experience. In the early 1960s, physicians found that about a third of the women who sought abortions required immediate medical care. Doctors in public hospitals also found that complications as a result of induced abortions accounted for 8.1 percent of all hospital admissions throughout the country and that postabortion patients made up 27.3 percent of admissions in obstetrical services.[45] Cases admitted to the hospital for complications following an abortion accounted for 35 percent of surgeries in obstetric services and 26.7 percent of the blood used in all emergency services.[46] Emergency rooms were overwhelmed with the demand, and often two women shared a single hospital bed. Only a third of those admitted for postabortion complications left the hospital alive.

Encounters with these realities indelibly shaped women's lives but also prescribed new tasks for physicians and health officials. Listening to testimonial accounts and seeing the deadly consequences of backstreet abortions, they grew acutely aware of women's unmet needs. As a young intern in a Santiago public hospital, Dr. Aníbal Faúndes attended women who sought emergency care because of induced abortions. More than fifty years later, he still remembers his distress in 1953: "Witnessing the physical and psychological pain of women, young and more mature, listening to their stories, seeing them suffer for weeks and watching them die or survive gravely mutilated was a strong motivation to dedicate my professional life to finding a way to mitigate their suffering."[47] Faúndes was not alone. Other physicians felt the need to take action and began to mobilize support for the first family-planning initiatives. In his early pilot projects, Mariano Requena had given more than two hundred lectures to women who lacked knowledge about birth control, while other doctors used his approach to community-centered work.[48] Those who prioritized research and technical solutions to the abortion epidemic remained prominent among the pioneers—and demonstrated that the medicalization of abortion had advantages as well as shortcomings from the perspective of female patients. Physicians at the time argued that "women, far from being criminals, were victims of the organization of society."[49] They helped initiate a shift from criminology to epidemiology that affected women's lives and changed doctors' tasks. Nevertheless, women who desired to plan their pregnancies continued to face limited reproductive choices.

Medicalizing Abortion and Testing Contraceptive Technologies

Chilean doctors familiar with the abortion epidemic developed an eager interest in the progress of birth control technologies. Some undertook trials on their own, independent tests with Chilean "human material" to present results. In October 1968, a representative of the United States Population Council, a private organization founded by John D. Rockefeller III to promote fertility regulation on a global scale, contacted Johnson & Johnson International's representative in Santiago to follow up on data and sample plastic condoms sent to Chile the year before. But when these men discussed the marketing of condoms as luxury products, reusable and extremely durable due to the thickness and strength of their plastic base, they learned that Chilean doctors had long since begun to distribute other types of contraceptives under their own auspices.[50] In Chile, condoms never topped doctors' priorities: their usage required independent initiative, and they therefore seemed much less favorable than contraceptive devices inserted and controlled by medical professionals.

Some physicians, like Jaime Zipper, independently adopted innovative technical approaches to fertility regulation and tested his discoveries on patients from the hospital's neighborhood. "I opened the first Contraceptive Clinic in Chile, and I know that I am still providing valuable services to millions of women who don't even know me," he remarked in a 1997 interview.[51] Zipper looked back on the late 1950s, when he gained fame in the international medical community for his invention of the Zipper ring, an intrauterine device he developed independently from any initial institutional encouragement and supervision, with a sense of accomplishment.[52] Local women of the Barros Luco Hospital community were the first who were used as part of Zipper's unauthorized trials with his own invention.[53] Most of them struggled with the burden of feeding large families with limited resources. The Barros Luco Hospital served a low-income population, also characterized by high fertility rates. Many of the mothers who came to the hospital had no social security or health insurance. About 35 percent of the patients who delivered at the hospital had given birth to five or more children. A high proportion of patients were over thirty-five years of age, had nutritional problems, a high incidence of abortions in the past, and found it difficult to withstand another pregnancy and add yet another child to their impoverished family.[54]

Zipper still recalls how, in 1959, he stumbled across an unexpected research opportunity. Reading an article on experiments with modified metal intrauterine rings, first used by Ernst Gräfenberg in 1929, Zipper learned about the medical problems physicians had encountered with the first intrauterine devices (IUDs).[55] Described as "tailless," they were difficult to remove and their proper placement could not be easily checked. Zipper felt inspired to conduct a series of experiments with nylon thread, material otherwise used for fishing. Winding it several times around two fingers, he made a ring whose loose end could be used as a tail for removal. To validate his discovery, he tried the Zipper ring on patients in his office at the hospital. "Just like that!" Zipper remarked. "I got so excited with the idea! I started with as many women as I could, took them with me into the little room, and fitted them with the ring."

Zipper claimed that he made some information available to his patients. He "told them what he was about to do to them," but, characterizing his typical patient as a poor woman, he added that "of course, within her lack of culture, I don't think that she could have understood much of it. So I said that I would insert the ring, and that she should not worry about it."[56] This personal account of Zipper's first contraceptive services speaks volumes about the chasm that separated medical scientists from their female patients. Women became part of studies for the sake of medical advancement and the development of new technologies. Because informed consent was not part of doctors' research at the time, women were not asked about the risks they were willing to take in support of the progress of medicine.

The initial setup of Zipper's unsupervised experiments avoided restrictions of any kind and allowed him to use the bodies of female patients without restraint. He did not disclose the nature of the trials to the hospital community, and the vague information he made available to his patients came to light only when a woman observed bleeding, sought help, and reported to a physician-colleague at the hospital. In this particular case, the doctor removed the ring from this patient. When he asked her about it, the woman did not have specifics; she could only say that she got it from "a grey-haired guy in the second floor, who put these things into women."[57] The doctor reported Zipper's malfeasance and promptly called a meeting. Upon hearing the news, alarmed colleagues cited the dangers of inserting foreign objects into a woman's body, pointed to the risk of infections, and even expressed fears of uterine-cervical cancer and their lack of knowledge about its causes. Zipper's expulsion from the medical community seemed imminent, but he took a stand.

The reaction of Zipper's doctor-colleagues, and his ability to justify unprofessional behavior in a world of medical professionals, stemmed from the long-standing crises of induced abortions and maternal mortality, as well as the doctors' inability to cope with these problems. Zipper justified his fitting of "600 women . . . with the ring" by comparing the limited risks of the insertions to the everyday realities in the emergency rooms. The statistics backed up his case and helped convince the other doctors to agree on a quick professional resolution. The experiments with the rings and using patients' bodies as "guinea pigs" set off a brief uproar, but in light of their daily encounters with botched abortions and troubled mothers of large families, Zipper's colleagues offered to support the initiation of official clinical trials with the ring. He placed a sign "Contraceptive Clinic" on his office door and between October 1959 and June 1963, an additional sixty-five hundred women were fitted with the contraceptive device.[58] Ongoing experiments revealed that doctors remained concerned about improving medical technologies to address maternal death rates and control women's fertility, and continued to obtain test results of experiments using unwitting subjects.

At a New York medical conference on intrauterine contraception, Zipper chose to speak on the "results obtained with the first 3000 ring wearers" in the Barros Luco Hospital experiment, but he failed to mention the initial unscientific sample-selection of the first six hundred women he had fitted with the ring. His report revealed his priorities, the weight he placed on quantifiable test results, and the limited attention he gave to patient-participants. Zipper had no exact documentation about the insertion process, but "[thought] that most of [the rings] were inserted by medical personnel." His team worked with "two midwives—one of them especially [was] extremely clever and expert in inserting devices."[59] He did not provide exact information about the process used to select female patients for his experiments, either, but he did supply a detailed account of his testing of different metal rings in 709 human subjects who helped him decide to adopt nylon rings in the end.[60] Indeed, Zipper expressed an overall satisfaction with the results of his research, the low expulsion rates, and a total of only 155 unintended pregnancies.[61] Women's desperate need of access to contraceptive devices, combined with the global paradigm of overpopulation, opened the door to new experiments initiated by other Chilean doctors using human bodies for the sake of medical progress and their international reputation.

Obstetrician Juan Zañartu, like Zipper, embodied the persistent desire for scientific breakthroughs on the medical front and encountered only limited resistance to his use of human subjects for his far-reaching medical trials. In June 1963, highly confidential correspondence between Carmen Miró, director of the newly established Center for Demography in Santiago, and Dudley Kirk, of the U.S. Population Council, revealed that human experiments in this field could take a turn for the worst. Miró's letters showed that she had, indeed, reason to be alarmed. Zañartu had sought support for "a pilot programme for fertility regulation research," and Miró had become aware of "certain developments which constitute[d] a source of worry and anxiety" for her and other physicians. Zañartu had shared an "extremely secret" component of his research, which involved "the experimental administration of new drugs to a group of women classified as high fertility" (as they had already given birth to ten to twelve children). Miró went on to report that in Zañartu's plans, "after the administration of the drugs, these women will be sterilized and the surgical intervention which will be performed with this purpose will also be used to make biopsies of the women's uterus and ovaries in order to determine the possible secuelae of the drugs in the women's reproduction organs."[62]

The medical experiments proposed by doctors at this time mostly involved women, but Zañartu's plans also involved men. The proposal included tests on men who would be sterilized, after which their testicles would undergo biopsies following the administration of the drug. These men would receive payment for their willingness to participate in the experiment.[63] Although Miró's letter helped prevent official support for this research and caused alarm among those physicians who rejected experiments without informed consent, her correspondence elucidates the irrefutable fact that Chilean women, and some men, were used as submissive subjects for the medical experiments of many physicians. Medical emergencies like abortions and maternal mortality rates allowed some doctors, like Zipper, to justify the risks of unsupervised experimentation, but the use of female subjects went far beyond eminent emergencies that justified such acts.

Doctors used Chilean women as "human material" for experiments that supplied valuable research results to colleagues beyond Chile. Starting in 1962, and obtaining in May 1964 support from the Ford Foundation, Zañartu directed a pilot fertility-control clinic and set up research laboratories at the hospital of the University of Chile.[64] According to one Ford Foundation evaluation, he provided "the human material for studies on the morphological effects of ovarian steroids by Dr. David Rosemberg from the department of Pathology, for the cytological studies by Dr. Rodrigo Prado of the department of Preventive Medicine, for histochemical studies by Dr. Marcus Pupkin, for the myometrical studies of Dr. Carlos Gomez-Rogers in the obstetrical physiology unit, for the ovarian incubation studies at Worcester Foundation in Shrewsbury, Massachusetts, and for sociological evaluations in cooperation with Dr. Luis Fuentealba of the department of Sociology."[65] Indeed, the sheer amount of references on this list indicates that studies involving Chilean women were hardly unusual occurrences.

The same evaluation concluded that some of the multiple studies were "hampered by lack of follow-up on women receiving medication and by the wide variety of drugs being used."[66] The tone of these professional conclusions almost spoke for itself. Doctors did not question their experimenting with human bodies and showed no concern for the consequences the trials had on the lives of those women who had been exposed to different substances. The wide variety of medications physicians used in the tests were of interest only insofar as they obscured the clarity of some of the outcomes—not as they might have endangered the health and well-being of the human subjects. Medical experiments relied on the female patient's relationship with her physician, a relationship determined by traditional hierarchies between the professional and the patient, as well as between men and women. The women who depended on public health services rarely questioned medical authority—and often found it hard to challenge male authority at home.[67] Some physicians, evaluating women's testimonies, asserted that "we need to educate men as well, because many prevent their wives from using contraceptives; it seems that many [husbands] like to see their wives pregnant 365 days of the year. . . . At the bottom the problem is rooted in the immaturity of men."[68] Nonetheless women remained at the center of programs that often excluded men and single women who had never given birth. Family-planning centers provided contraceptive devices only for women.[69] Women's exposure to reliable information remained limited and, for unmarried women without children who did not visit maternity clinics, often nonexistent.

Women who responded to doctors' inquiries about their use of birth control also revealed that their trust in contraceptive methods and choices was shaped by multiple dynamics. Many women felt suspicious and nervous about unfamiliar technologies. Women in poor neighborhoods most frequently acquired their information on birth control from neighbors, mothers, or sisters. Only 20 percent of a group of 448 women had consulted a physician or midwife regarding contraception. Mariano Requena, working in Quinta Normal, reported an incident that elucidated to what extent rumor could influence a woman's choice of method. At the start of his fieldwork, Requena found that most women listed IUDs as their first preference. When the same women's responses suddenly shifted to the contraceptive pill, surprised interviewers were informed that new information had spread in the neighborhood, warning women that IUD insertion could lead to cancer. Given these fears, many continued to resort to abortion as a way to limit pregnancies and births.[70]

Women who overcame their suspicion of family-planning devices and, in doctors' terminology, became "program acceptors," often adopted the contraceptive method promoted by their local practitioner.[71] IUDs became the most widespread contraceptive method in Chile, popular among doctors because the device was cost-effective, low maintenance, and relatively reliable after insertion. In 1966, for example, in the western health sector of Santiago, with a population of 460,000, gynecologists inserted IUDs at a rate of about sixty devices a day.[72] Dr. Benjamín Viel was in charge of the proceedings and documented the noticeable reduction in both the number of births and abortions that followed. Between 1964 and 1969, birth rates had declined by 33 percent. The number of women hospitalized for abortion had decreased by almost the same rate in the same time period and geographical area. Viel emphasized that these declines were significantly greater than those documented "in countries where the family planning program has been using 'pills' as the major contraceptive" and contributed his success to the effectiveness of the IUD. When Viel suggested that "[t]he greater continuation rate among IUD acceptors" might have been responsible for the difference, he also knew that continuation rates were directly related to doctors' control over IUD insertion, a control they did not have over women's reliance on the Pill.[73]

Chilean "Pro-Life" Missions

The urgency of the need to save lives, combined with the absence of a widespread discourse on women's rights in Chile, summarized many doctors' priorities at the time. Gynecologist Gildo Zambra, a candid advocate of fertility regulation in the 1960s and president of Chile's first official family-planning office from 1972 to September 1973, confirmed that the first initiatives in Chile remained simply void of any notion of women's rights: "A few pioneers of public health, like Benjamín Viel and Hernán Romero started to talk about the topic [of family planning] early on . . . because they read a lot and had international connections. They introduced, sort of, the idea that a woman had the right to control her fertility. The reason why the gynecologists addressed the issue [of family planning] was because we treated abortions . . . and the deaths as a result of abortions." The pioneering initiatives, according to Zambra, took shape in response to maternal mortality, and were "not the result of the need of women to fulfill their lives as wives, as mothers, as workers . . . or the needs of women to not have many children for economic reasons. Those were realizations that did not reach us back then, I remember it well."[74]

Zambra's words also show how medicalizing abortion helped move women out of the criminal sphere, which enabled doctors and others to address abortion primarily in the context of medical procedures and technical solutions. In a 1998 interview, Dr. Soledad Díaz, a physician and researcher of contraceptive technologies long actively involved in working with women and their individual concerns, said that the medical community, indeed, focused on "a big problem with maternal mortality caused by abortions, and started to think of medical procedures to initiate change, . . . yes, abortions were the official motivation" to make contraceptives available to women. She added that doctors' reach into Santiago neighborhoods was therefore "not dedicated to making pregnancy a choice, but specifically to [the prevention of] abortion."[75] Doctors tried to save women's lives.

The national media helped spread the medical community's pro-life position. Popular journals like *Ercilla* picked up the story and paid particular attention to female victims and the doctors who treated them. Chileans learned about Monreal and Armijo's assertion that "the prevention of abortion [wa]s connected to the prevention of unwanted pregnancies via adequate education campaigns that inform[ed] women about the use of contraceptive technologies adopted to their cultural and economic realities."[76] Journalists invited readers to support the "deadly struggle for the sake of life."[77] The fieldwork studies of the 1960s and women's testimonies supplied evidence necessary to support the correlation between access to family-planning devices, the prevention of unwanted pregnancies, and the decrease of self-induced abortions and their gruesome consequences. This evidence in hand, physicians were prepared to take the path to alleviate this epidemic. Women should have the right to live.

Government officials and physicians adopted an official language of family planning and began to institutionalize a fresh approach to motherhood, also counting on global connections to speed up the process. In May 1962, Ofelia Mendoza, technical representative of the International Planned Parenthood Federation (IPPF), traveled to Santiago and set up an open discussion with the Chilean Women's Medical Association to discuss family planning.[78] The meeting sparked a two-step response by physicians who sought increased support from the director of Chile's National Health Service (NHS). First, they established an advisory council of professionals from the medical schools of the University of Chile and the Catholic University for the purpose of studying in greater detail questions regarding abortion, maternal mortality, and fertility regulation. Next, they transformed the council into the Comité Chileno de Protección de la Familia (the Chilean Committee for the Protection of the Family), an independent, private organization with corporate status under the chairmanship of Hernán Romero.

The family as an institution became central to the organization's official promotion of fertility regulation. Its emblem depicted mother, father, son, and daughter within a small triangle and served as the guiding symbol of the first official family planners.[79] By 1965, seven family-planning projects operated in Santiago, most directly linked to earlier fieldwork efforts to control abortion and decrease maternal mortality rates.[80] Chilean doctors had secured ongoing financial and technical support from the Rockefeller and Ford foundations as well as the U.S. Population Council. The committee also negotiated an official affiliation with the IPPF/WHO, the Western Hemisphere Organization of the IPPF with headquarters in New York City, which included technical and financial support, starting with fifty thousand dollars in 1964 and eighty-six thousand dollars in 1965.[81] Support from abroad was invaluable, but there were fears among Chileans that too much foreign involvement could lead to questioning of family planning's legitimacy—perhaps even rendering it disreputable.

The relationship between the first committee of family planners and state officials reveals the subject matter's lasting delicacy. Although state officials supported pro-life initiatives, they remained cautious in their commitment to change. In 1965, a small delegation of the committee visited the new director of public health, Dr. Francisco Mardones, and offered to cooperate with the government in matters of family planning. He readily acknowledged that the National Health Service was prepared to take an "active approach to the problem of abortion and to the explosive growth of the population." In concluding the meeting, he reminded participants that the government had not yet adopted an official policy on family planning but reassured them of "his desire and hope that the National Health Service would adopt a clearly defined policy in support of the goals of the committee."[82] The committee's own Hernán Romero, meanwhile, prepared to join the governing body of the IPPF and negotiated official patronage of Chile to host the IPPF's eighth international conference in Santiago. Through these growing connections, doctors would soon seek to save not only the individual woman, but the national population itself.

Chilean doctors began to connect their pro-life discourse—their efforts to prevent maternal mortality and save women's lives—with a discourse on modernization. Family planning would serve the nation by controlling overpopulation and promoting development through the modernization of the Chilean family. Doctors' initiatives took shape within a private association of family planners, relatively independent from the state. In this niche, they could add less popular rationalizations of family planning, such as efforts to control family size, to the popular pro-life discourse.

Paradigms of Population Control in a Cold War World

In 1966, Dr. Benjamín Viel published his widely received study on the Latin American experience of a demographic explosion. Documenting a "decline in mortality that began in Santiago about 1937," he claimed to see a baby boom of dangerous proportion. Viel warned of the consequences of "[t]he exaggerated growth that every year adds to our region whole nations of infants, each larger than the last," and advocated immediate fertility regulation aimed at limiting population size in response to three dominant threats.[83] He argued that the prevalence of self-induced abortions and their deadly consequences needed to be controlled. He also connected the challenge of underdevelopment to overpopulation, suggesting that too many people competed for limited resources, which stalled economic progress. Finally, Viel supported a neo-Malthusian interpretation by suggesting that population growth would soon exceed food supplies and thereby lead to starvation.[84] His view of a threat posed by overpopulation was popular among scientists, politicians, and economists in the post–World War II era.

The drastic measures proposed to curb population growth in Latin America and the threatening images of some population campaigns were also linked to the tensions of the Cold War. Some population planners disseminated fears of spreading revolutions and communist takeovers to garner support for their mission. In advertisements and information campaigns, they presented "hungry nations" filled with people who could ignite the "population bomb." The poor would "imperil" or "threaten the peace of the world" when their growing discontent would inspire social revolution.[85] Ads warned that "the ever mounting tidal wave of humanity now challenge[d] us to control it, or be submerged along with all our civilized values."[86] Combined with the Cuban Revolution's energy, the threat of revolutionary unrest seemed as real as the lack of food supplies and declining living standards due to uncontrolled population growth. In an open letter to President Lyndon B. Johnson, population planners warned that much was at stake: "The population explosion w[ould] inevitably lead to chaos and strife at home and abroad—to more Cubas and Vietnams—to revolutions and wars, ... All of it grist for the Communist mill."[87]

Speaking at a 1964 conference on contraceptive technology, John D. Rockefeller III gave voice to the growing concerns of postwar population planners and the engagement of private groups like the Population Council, the Milbank Memorial Fund, and the Ford Foundation to address the issue. As leader of the Population Council, he invited the participants to set clear priorities, for "the problem of unchecked population growth is as urgently important as any facing mankind today." Rockefeller went on to explain why the general public needed to understand and face these realities: "Until recently, I believed an even greater problem [than population growth] was the control of nuclear weapons. However, there is a justifiable hope that the use of these weapons can be prevented; but there is no hope that we can escape a tremendous growth in world population. Therefore it becomes a central task of our time to stabilize this growth soon enough to avoid its smothering consequences."[88] New concerns led to innovative policy approaches, as the scientific community and the media helped spread the word and provided appropriate technological support.

At the same conference, participants from Chile testified that they also were deeply troubled by overpopulation in Chile and its impediment to development. The doctors Guillermo Adriasola and Onofre Avendaño acknowledged that many Chileans were still "approaching their population problem the wrong way." Expressing concern about the nation's annual population increase of 2.5 percent, these physicians feared that it "seriously counteract[ed] economic development."[89] At a 1965 international gathering on family-planning programs, Hernán Romero added a critical evaluation of family size, suggesting that it was the family "which suffer[ed] most from excessive fertility. The size of the family [wa]s unquestionably in inverse relationship to material welfare, even though family allowances in Chile [we]re the most generous in Latin America."[90] Studies by Chilean population planners were read widely in Chile and Latin America and further elucidated readers' understanding of how family size could effect a nation's economic and social modernization. Viel linked the demographic explosion to food shortages, urban poverty, crime, and alcoholism. Romero insisted that contemporary society was the enemy of large families. Lawyer and scholar Moisés Poblete Troncoso presented the problem of overpopulation from a global perspective and insisted that Latin America needed to adopt solutions with exceptional urgency. All agreed that modernization demanded a reconceptualization of the family and the adaptation of the small family model.[91]

In light of the need to curb population size, Chilean and international researchers cooperated to improve the effectiveness of contraceptives technologies. From 1961 to 1962, Zipper was a postgraduate fellow in Massachusetts, working in reproductive physiology with Gregory Pincus, best known for his research on the contraceptive pill. In 1964 and 1965, Philadelphia-native physician-researcher Howard Tatum spent his sabbatical year working with Zipper at the University of Santiago. Jointly, Tatum and Zipper aimed at improving Zipper's nylon-plastic IUDs and postulated that T-shaped devices would be less likely to cause bleeding, pain, and expulsion. By 1969, they completed their first tests, and Tatum's new copper-bearing T devices reached the market.[92] The scientific community also pushed research and education for future generations of population planners. In 1964, the well-known U.S. obstetrician and gynecologist John Rock, an outspoken defender of contraceptive technologies and a collaborator of Pincus on clinical trials of the Pill, was enthusiastically received in Santiago. There he addressed medical communities and shared his views on fertility regulation and the contraceptive pill he had long campaigned for in the United States. Rock also taught a postgraduate course on physiology and fertility regulation at the University of Chile Medical School.[93]

Back in the United States, Rock became an outspoken advocate for the scientific community, encouraging political leaders to reallocate "brains and money" to help solve the problems of a crowded world.[94] Impatient prominent scholars insisted that the idea of limiting family size had to "penetrate" people's minds and educators aimed at creating a popular mind-set "that not only shun[ned] the third or fourth pregnancy but brand[ed] them as shameful and antisocial."[95] Population planners like Fairfield Osborn in the United States tirelessly repeated their warnings about the coming decline of the quality of life on "our crowded planet" as a result of population pressures.[96] Many alarmed voices joined in and prolonged the debate: Philip Appleman's *The Silent Explosion* (1966), Paul Ehrlich's *The Population Bomb* (1968), Joseph Tydings' *Born to Starve* (1970), and Lawrence Lader's *Breeding Ourselves to Death* (1971) all dramatized how a "population problem," which had its roots in the developing world, threatened the survival of humankind. Population planners made clear that they expected funds flowing through international channels to spread their sense of urgency and develop techniques for effective fertility control.[97]

In 1965, President Johnson's famous statement that "less than five dollars invested in population control is worth a hundred dollars invested in economic growth" well reflected a consensus committed to preserving political stability through population control, especially in developing regions.[98] In the United States, private foundations such as the Milbank Memorial Fund, the Rockefeller and Ford foundations, and the Population Council played a vital role in setting an agenda that also shaped U.S. foreign policy. Private foundations, U.S. scholars and researchers, as well as different sectors of the U.S. government disagreed about the pace and content of policy changes. Their agendas, however, sprung from similar ideological assumptions and shared the same long-term goals: fertility regulation and small family size would promote economic modernization, secure economic stability, and prevent social unrest or revolution in the developing world. In this context, government and private population planners allocated resources and secured funding for family-planning programs in Latin America as well as in Chile. They provided the international support that Chilean family planners sought to promote programs at home.[99]

In light of the economic and political relevance of family planning, physicians and policymakers decided they needed to be in charge. Doctors like Jaime Zipper, who continued to improve family-planning technologies and present their work at international conferences, pronounced that "the medical profession rather than the patient must ultimately decide on the efficiency of any [contraceptive] procedure in light of the relevant factors."[100] They insisted that the agenda they proposed left little room for women's choices. Women's reproductive behavior had taken on new meaning in its relationship to concerns over development and political stability—and needed to be controlled. In global meetings, population planners conveyed a message of female ineptitude, which was shared by the medical establishment and by the male world of science at large. Some physicians were prepared to ignore women's preferences altogether: too much was at stake to tolerate a "cafeteria-choice" allowing women to choose among several contraceptive methods. Some contraceptives required a high level of motivation and continuous incentive to be effective, so the mass application of such methods was "not advisable from an economic and demographic point of view."[101]

Physicians interested in family planning and population questions could count on growing institutional support in Chile. In a 1965 strategic move, Chilean family planners renamed their first committee and inaugurated the Asociación Chilena de Protección de la Familia (APROFA, the Chilean Association for the Protection of the Family), which continued to operate as a private organization. In this manner, its leaders could strengthen their international ties and cooperate with the National Health Service on the domestic level. The NHS continued to contribute material support and staff, yet APROFA's private status secured family-planning programs under more independent leadership. Financing from abroad, including IPPF subsidies, and ongoing funding by private institutions in the United States helped to equip clinics and expand family-planning programs. APROFA became a full member of the IPPF/WHO and was granted "persona juridica" by the Chilean government in September 1966.[102]

The ongoing support of family planning under the Christian Democratic government of President Eduardo Frei Montalva (1964–1970) confirmed the success of pro–family-planning arguments predicated on both a positive response to the Chilean pro-life discourse and a clear consensus that family planning remained intrinsically connected to economic development and modernization. The tensions of the postwar period and the Cold War provided an ongoing context for neo-Malthusian arguments. Chileans joined these global think tanks from early on and continued to accept or reject international affiliations based on what they deemed the proper path to progress for Chile.[103]

Global Paradigms, State Policies, and Local Women

As part of the population control paradigm that shaped the postwar world, medical and political elites reevaluated the meanings of motherhood for the body politic. Examining the global connections of Chilean physicians, medical elites and politicians in Chile were not passive recipients of an international population control agenda. They actively participated in its creation. They helped reconstruct the meaning of motherhood by debating overpopulation and poverty, and they suggested that family size be controlled by the state. With the overwhelming consensus on the need for population control, physicians increased the impact of public health campaigns, simultaneously assigning new meanings to motherhood and increasing the surveillance of women's bodies and their reproductive lives. Poor mothers with many children thus became potential threats to modern life.

Many doctors, researchers, and population planners agreed that pregnancy, childbirth, and motherhood could not be considered private matters of local women, but were instead connected to global progress, economic development, and political stability. Bernard Berelson, as vice president of the U.S. Population Council, testified to the significance population planners assigned to their work when he praised the "revolution" of IUDs and insisted that "[i]ndeed . . . this simple device can and will change the history of the world."[104] He foresaw economic prosperity, political stability, and "the freedom of mankind," all due to first controlling women's reproduction and then producing smaller families. Countless poor women, meanwhile, tried to solve their problems on their own.

Many women expressed their desperate need to prevent pregnancies by inducing abortions under life-threatening circumstances, and thereby created a public health crisis of epidemic proportions. Their attempt at fertility regulation produced high maternal death rates and encouraged a pro-life discourse aimed at guaranteeing women the "right to live." Doctors began to address abortion not as a crime, but as a medical issue that needed attention. In the process, the medicalization of abortion removed women and health officials from the immediate threat of incarceration and criminal prosecution. This shift inspired new solutions, sought in the promotion of family planning. Driven by concerns about maternal mortality, but also by ambitions to promote Chilean development and modernization, health officials and politicians became key players in the development of national family-planning programs.

Some physicians engaged in fieldwork studies to document the abortion epidemic and to identify the conditions that led to the deaths of so many Chilean mothers. The alarming results, indeed, moved abortion from the criminal realm to epidemiology. But the medicalization of abortion brought with it further medical experiments with contraceptive devices as well as new policies of fertility regulation and family planning that revealed the use of women's bodies for the modernization of medical technology and the economic modernization of the body politic. Chilean physicians fashioned alliances with scientists, policymakers, and social engineers in Chile and abroad, and succeeded in institutionalizing fertility regulation as family planning and in spreading its civic respectability. Many women did profit from gaining access to contraceptives, as made evident by the decline in abortion and maternal mortality rates.

Nonetheless, this keen attention to women's role in fertility regulation left little room for individual choices of female patients who sought medical advice. In stressing women's responsibilities in the prevention of unwanted pregnancies or limiting population size, the program's dynamics maintained the gender hierarchies that restricted women's autonomy. Although some physicians demonstrated genuine concern about local women's needs, family-planning programs did not consider a number of fundamental challenges that affected female patients' lives: their ongoing lack of education about sexuality and reproduction and, significantly, their continuing lack of decision-making rights within family settings and intimate relationships as well as in doctor-patient encounters. While assigning new gendered responsibilities for the sake of progress and modernization, male politicians and health officials insisted on defining the territory within which female citizens were allowed to act.

PLANNING MOTHERHOOD UNDER CHRISTIAN DEMOCRACY

> Throughout the world . . . there are all sorts of men. They look different in different places and have different ways of life. But, basically, all men are the same. So to make things easier, let's put them together into one and let this one stand for all. He's a common man, just like you and me.
>
> *Disney narrator, introducing the "Common Man" in the film*
> Family Planning/Planificación Familiar

IN 1968, CHILEAN doctors received an educational film, *Family Planning/ Planificación Familiar*, from the U.S. Population Council.[1] It was first shown in screenings organized by the Association for the Protection of the Family (APROFA) and quickly gained popularity. Within a year, more than thirty-six thousand Chileans had seen the film.[2] The Disney animation, produced in both English and Spanish, introduced viewers to a cartoon husband, claiming to represent the "common man," and to Donald Duck, who leads the audience from one theme to the next. After describing the dangers of overpopulation and underdevelopment, Donald tells the viewers that family planning, which will bring about smaller families and population decline, is the only way to ward off poverty (figure 3.1). "Common Man's" cartoon wife has doubts, but she is too shy and embarrassed to speak. "Common Wife" only manages to whisper into her husband's ear while he articulates her concerns. The cartoon concludes with a message meant to comfort the worried wife: family planning is not only so-

Figure 3.1. Donald Duck in his role as guide to the content of Disney's film on family planning. Here he is introducing a typical small family. *From the Population Council's* Studies in Family Planning *1, no. 26 (January 1968).*

cially acceptable but also indispensable to the healthy future of a woman's family, her community, and humankind as a whole.

In the film, Donald Duck appropriates the right to guide "Common Man" and professes to fulfill a civilizing mission by introducing modern values and behaviors to far-off lands. Despite claims that he speaks for "everyman," Donald's voice is in fact the voice of physicians and policymakers who promoted population control remedies as a path to modernization. Fertility regulation, the film suggests, would pave the road to modernity by altering reproductive behavior to create smaller families, which would in turn promote the modern values necessary to stimulate economic development and end poverty. Beneath the humanitarian rhetoric of the film lay the economic and ideological goal of limiting population and replacing traditional images of the family with more modern ones. Public health leaders and politicians warned that the prevalence of large families posed a threat to a people's well-being: too many children meant that not all of them could be properly fed, dressed, or educated. They insisted that only small families would craft a healthy, wealthy, and *modern* nation; this burdened women with new responsibilities.

Under Christian Democracy (1964–1970), different historical actors—population planners, doctors, politicians, and representatives of the Catholic Church—reshaped the dynamics of family planning as they negotiated competing positions on Chile's advancement on its path to modernity. Women's options and obligations changed as a result of these negotiations; their tasks now included responsible motherhood through family planning. Family-planning arguments were predicated, first, on the protection of women's lives, and, second, on the promotion of national development and modernization through fertility regulation. On this basis, male physicians and policymakers relied on women's cooperation in their project of modernization and also expanded state-supported family planning with the backing of the Christian Democratic government and the Catholic Church.

As residents in the vibrant capital city, women found novel grounds to make decisions about their lives, but their options carried with them the burden of new responsibilities. As more women gained access to family-planning programs, policymakers remained determined to align women's reproductive choices with the modernizing projects of national and international elites. Gender relations in Santiago were not shaped by the same preoccupation with women's roles that accompanied agrarian reform politics in the countryside, skillfully presented in the historian Heidi Tinsman's study of rural change.[3] In the city, Christian Democratic reformist projects fashioned a modernity that buttressed patriarchal structures and depended on the execution of male professional authority to guide or control women's reproductive behavior.

Doctors and policymakers advanced the cause of family-planning programs and, at the same time, touted their nation as a model of cooperation between the public health system and private family planners. Santiago became a center of demographic research and studies of contraceptive technology. The abundance of population projects in the capital city, the ongoing work of APROFA, and the 1967 Conference of the International Planned Parenthood Federation (IPPF) in Santiago provide ample evidence of the modernizing missions of Chilean doctors and policymakers. Yet the success of their projects relied not only on the dependent role of Chilean women, but also on controlling motherhood and the family for the sake of the modernizing nation. Population planners depicted mothers who limited pregnancies as saviors of the nation. In the process, they would help to reconstruct the meaning of family in an urban, modernizing Chile.

Cold War Realities and Alliances

Cold War anxieties indelibly marked Chilean history. At a 1961 meeting in Punta del Este, Uruguay, the U.S. president John F. Kennedy inaugurated his Alliance for Progress among American nations "to complete the revolution of the Americas, to build a hemisphere where all men can hope for a suitable standard of living and all can live out their lives in dignity and in freedom."[4] This aimed to undermine revolutionary change through democratization and modernization. The Alliance especially emphasized land reform, for example, to weaken landowners' traditional power relative to rural labor while increasing rural production. In theory, the Alliance offered a guided, antirevolutionary path for change within the free market economy's parameters. In reality, however, security and counterinsurgency concerns came to outweigh all others as the 1960s unfolded. Indeed, the U.S. president Richard Nixon sharply increased military aid while virtually eliminating developmental aid after 1969. Some Latin American officials oversaw a few improvements in land distribution, education, and health care under the Alliance's auspices. But Latin American elites tended to resist these changes, and, in the words of its initial sponsor and beneficiary, Chilean president Eduardo Frei Montalva, "the Alliance . . . lost its way."[5]

Frei's personal trajectory, as well as the ascension of Chile's Christian Democratic Party, represented changes under way in Chile and throughout Latin America. Frei had led the National Association of Catholic Students (1932–1933) and had been a member of the youth department of the Chilean Conservative Party in 1935. As a leading proponent of Christian Democracy, he participated in the search for a viable space for Social Christian doctrine in politics. In 1938, he was one of the founders of the National Falange, a party of Christians against fascism, and served as its president and as a minister of public works under two governments in the 1940s. In 1957, Frei helped found the new centrist Christian Democratic Party, in doctrine inspired by the Catholic philosopher Jacques Maritain and European Christian Democratic movements that promoted humanism and social responsibility over radical change.[6] Frei's government followed this moderate pattern of sociopolitical and economic modernization in the midst of more radical quests for change.[7] It also represented the U.S. president Lyndon B. Johnson's showcase for democracy in Latin America. Through the Alliance and through Frei's example, Washington, D.C., hoped to influence the entire Western hemisphere.

Counting on overwhelming middle-class support, the reluctant backing of the Chilean right, and massive financial and propaganda support from the U.S. government, Frei campaigned for a "Revolution in Liberty" and won the election with 55.6 percent of the vote in September 1964. This victory created the first Christian Democratic government in Latin American history. The Christian Democrats proposed substantial economic redistribution through land reforms. They also planned a political program that would empower all Chileans. Frei's *promoción popular* (popular promotion) program promised "the incorporation of the people, not as part of a vague, unspecific power . . . but instead . . . into all the agencies of power that . . . exist (legislative, executive, judicial, and municipalities)."[8] At the heart of this proposition lay a set of policies that mobilized marginal sectors, groups traditionally excluded from the political process. The Christian Democrats aimed to win their support. Mothers' Centers, neighborhood committees, youth clubs, and a wide range of workshops constituted the approximately twenty thousand organizations sponsored by the state.

The 1964 election campaign that brought Frei to power also reflected changes of a different nature: candidates expressly addressed women and women's issues.[9] Legislators had made voting mandatory for all Chileans, and for the first time in history, the registration of female voters increased from 35 percent to 70 percent.[10] Candidates were compelled to please the female electorate in light of a distinctive Chilean form of documenting votes in the nation: men and women cast ballots in separate places, and returns were reported separately. Faced with the precise accounting of women's votes, the Christian Democrats emphasized their family policies and their commitment to furthering women's interests. The Christian Democratic platform, which was the only one to support birth control, promised to make family-planning information available to all Chileans.[11]

The promises of the Christian Democrats—and their efforts to incorporate all Chileans, rich and poor, into their political vision—were frustrated by the unrelenting realities of urban poverty. Even notorious bank robber El Loco Pepe, making his way to the Chilean capital from his home in Argentina in the 1960s, could not help but comment on the horrifying image of "ragged women with little kids, begging for charity in the city center."[12] In 1960, nearly two-thirds of the Chilean population were city dwellers, but more than 30 percent of urban households lacked electricity and over 40 percent had no running water. The nation's infant mortality rate remained one of the highest in the region, at 120.3 deaths for every 1,000 live births.[13] By 1963, more than half of Santiago's workforce was of migrant origin. Recent migrants shared shanty-towns with impoverished city-born populations.[14] Poor women found employment predominantly in domestic work or as washer women or seamstresses. Domestic service had continuously low status, even as the Labor Code, and later Frei, changed the term for domestic servants from the humiliating *criados* (signifying *brought up*) to *domestic employee*, to *household adviser*, and finally to *private home employee* in 1968.[15]

Although many women in Santiago could count on new services provided by Mothers' Centers, the structural transformations necessary to give women full citizenship rights were not forthcoming. As the Christian Democrats assumed power in 1964, they "modernized" the traditional goals of the vastly expanding Mothers' Centers to further the Revolution in Liberty's political and economic objectives. But their actions revealed their determination to achieve modernization without undermining gender hierarchy.

Political Participation, Paternalism, and Mothers' Changing Obligations

The Christian Democratic government encouraged all Chileans to strengthen community ties, support local and national developments, and work for the common good in designated institutions. Half of the organizations at the heart of this *promoción popular* were Mothers' Centers, set up in the spirit of Catholic social doctrine and participatory democracy.[16] New legislation, spelled out in the *Law of Neighborhood Organizations,* regulated the organizational structure of these institutions and defined the agenda of women's activities.[17] The central goals of Mothers' Centers evoked the boundaries of women's domestic obligations, aiming at "the personal advancement of their members, and the solving of problems inherent to their condition and gender, within the local sphere."[18] Likewise, membership was restricted to women eighteen and older, and also to those who were mothers at a younger age. Only women who resided in the community could join "their" Mothers' Center, but each location formed part of a network under the umbrella of government-approved "proper" women's engagement. The guiding motto of all Mothers' Centers promised that "the advancement of a woman also leads to the well-being of her children."[19] It adequately reflected a mission, in which the government also aimed to keep this advancement within the boundaries of a "female" sphere.

The statutes encouraged members to improve traditional female skills and to bond across class lines but discouraged any political activities. In fact, the spreading of political or religious propaganda in local meetings or official activities could lead to the suspension of membership rights.[20] First Lady María Ruiz Tagle de Frei supervised the proper functioning of the organizations. She set out to integrate all centers under one formal structure, the Central Organization for Mother's Centers (CEMA); she defined leadership functions and administrative tasks; and she moved to attract women of poor neighborhoods. Well-off women with time for community work supported the activities of centers in marginal neighborhoods and helped instruct members primarily in manual skills related to domestic tasks, such as sewing. Poor women responded enthusiastically to President Frei's promise to make sewing machines available to all members of Mothers' Centers. The machines allowed them to improve their skills and to earn money. Some women began to produce clothing or stuffed animals for sale; others saved money by making clothes for family members. Women could also attend courses in leadership skills, intended for mobilizing support for Christian Democratic policies in their communities.

The government-sponsored Mothers' Centers enjoyed an unprecedented rate of participation, although gendered practices followed a historical tradition of Chilean Mothers' Centers that tied women's involvement to the domestic sphere. Their origins dated back to the 1930s, when wealthy or middle-class women would make their way into marginal neighborhoods to instruct poor women. Mothers' Centers also shaped the late Popular Front period.[21] In 1947, for instance, First Lady Rosa Markman de González Videla endorsed Mothers' Centers aimed at "preparing women with access to limited resources to fulfill their role as housewives in the best way possible, to encourage women as consumers to fight the high cost of living, and to raise their interests to partake in other aspects of public life in the country, like work and political participation."[22] Rosa Markman did support women's right to vote as a civic duty, but she addressed women as family members, whose political participation fell within the traditional realm of responsibilities to support their families and their country.[23]

In the 1960s, the Christian Democrats put the new Mothers' Centers at the heart of their political campaign and, in so doing, revealed the ongoing tension between tradition and change, between competing justifications for the need to support women's mobilization. Carmen Gloria Aguayo, who became familiar with the Centros de Madres Techo through her mother's charitable engagement during the 1930s, was assigned the task of designing the new Mothers' Centers of the 1960s. She helped the Christian Democrats secure the support of the female electorate without challenging gendered traditions of political participation and citizenship. Aguayo also headed the party's women's department, instituted for the purpose of attracting the female electorate. The party's platform, drafted by a committee of thirty-eight men, well reflected the political direction of the initiatives: it included policies to protect the family while also defending women's right to work, to maternity leave, to equal pay for equal work, and to new opportunities for training and learning in the promised Department for Female Labor Studies.[24] Although Christian Democrats openly sought women's support, they continued to control the nature of women's political engagement and thus kept alive the traditional perception that these mothers were mobilizing primarily for their families.

Both the Christian Democrats' election campaign and their subsequent official policies reaffirmed this pattern of continuity in gendered expectations. The centers aimed at disciplining women, especially the poor. Elite and middle-class women would "instruct" poor women in particular skills and help define what should be their "proper" contributions to their communities. The programs were anchored in traditional gender roles and directed toward the perfection of women's responsibilities as mothers, housewives, and homemakers.[25] Although some husbands found it difficult to accept their wives' engagement outside the domestic sphere, the all-female environment and the opportunity to use newly acquired skills to supplement household income had the potential to convince even the most traditional males to accept controlled changes.[26] Nonetheless, many women discovered innovative ways to address personal problems as well as to find solutions, independently from their husbands and families.

Despite the official traditional bent of the Mothers' Centers and the government's efforts to limit change to a mere "revolution of the sewing machine," members testified to the centers' liberating potential.[27] Some women described their experiences as having "a very positive impact on women's self-esteem and their identities as women." Others remembered the financial advantages and a certain sense of pride for "being direct beneficiaries of a state-sponsored national program directed toward women."[28] Many women who wanted to see change in their lives turned their work at the centers into tools for political participation through communication and networking with other like-minded women.[29] Under the government of the Unidad Popular that replaced the Christian Democracy in 1970, women explored unprecedented ways of shaping political and economic developments according to their needs.

Mothers' Centers also became testing grounds and sites of political contestation when class struggles in Chile were further amplified during President Salvador Allende's "Peaceful Road to Socialism" (1970–1973). Some women in poor neighborhoods used the centers as stepping-stones to fiercely defend their class interest against those of Chilean elites. Others adopted more moderate political views, still guided by the influences of Christian Democratic leadership. Even as the official motto of Mothers' Centers continued to remind members that "the advancement of a woman also leads to the well-being of her children," women expanded their spheres of political participation from their homes, to the Mothers' Centers, and far beyond.[30]

Global Travelers and New Paradigms for the Planning of Proper Motherhood

Meanwhile, politicians and doctors continued to strengthen their political ties at home and abroad. The Revolution in Liberty, as well as Chilean leaders' approach to planned motherhood and population growth, attracted U.S. politicians, philanthropists, and researchers eager to evaluate the vast changes Santiago had undergone on its path to modernization. John D. Rockefeller III, founder of the U.S. Population Council and long active in the health and population programs of the Rockefeller Foundation, visited Chile in October 1966. Private family planners from APROFA followed the visit of the "distinguished philanthropist" with rapt attention, documenting his interest in "Chile's family planning movement" and his recognition of the country's "advanced position . . . on family planning."[31] Rockefeller's mission included visits to public hospitals and brought him to the country house of Dr. Hernán Romero for a discussion of family-planning policies. Rockefeller also took a helicopter to Viña del Mar, where he joined President Frei and health minister Ramón Valdivieso for a luncheon meeting. Following this visit, Rockefeller referred to Frei as "a good man for the job," remembering their conversation on a matter close to his heart: in his diary, Rockefeller recalled that when he promoted the World Leaders' Statement on Population, Frei's reaction was "entirely favorable."[32]

Rockefeller's lobbying for the *Statement on Population* reflected the changing global paradigm on population questions and the politics of motherhood. He

Figure 3.2. The text on the image reads (translated into English from the original Spanish): "The 'demographic explosion' alarms scientists and thinkers who once more turn their eyes to the venerable theories of Malthus. The world population grows at an impressive rate, and every day there are thousands and thousands of [new] mouths that open to order food in each country." *From* Punto final, *no. 7 (December 1965): 6.*

first presented this statement to the United Nations secretary general in 1966. Heads of government were asked to endorse several convictions, among them their belief "that the population problem must be recognized as a principal element in long-range national planning if governments are to achieve their economic goals and fulfill the aspirations of their people; . . . that the opportunity to decide the number and spacing of children is a basic human right; [and] that lasting and meaningful peace will depend to a considerable measure upon how the challenge of population growth is met."[33] This document expressed the need to curb the dangers of overpopulation and aimed to enlist the support of political leaders from around the world.[34] Rockefeller and others saw family-planning services as a first yet moderate step toward population control, which they hoped would eventually lead to the more widespread acceptance of birth control measures and, ultimately, to new limits on population growth.[35]

Contrary to Rockefeller's first impression in the meeting with President Frei, however, the Chilean government's position would not fully correspond

Figure 3.3. The text on the image reads (translated into English from the original Spanish): "It is in shantytowns where the problems flourish that supporters of birth control want to correct. The proletarian woman exhausts herself through successive annual births, or she dies at a young age due to the brutal methods used to provoke abortions and [thereby] prevent the growth of a family impossible to maintain." *From Punto final, no. 7 (December 1965): 8.*

to the vision of the *World Leaders' Statement*. In Chile, concerns over population control were accompanied by concerns over maternal mortality. The private family-planning initiatives of Chilean doctors, researchers, and population planners could thrive within the global paradigm of population control, a paradigm often picked up by the Chilean press and imagined in local contexts (figures 3.2 and 3.3). These private initiatives also paved the way for state-led family-planning programs that upheld the importance of population growth, but would justify family-planning programs, primarily, by the need to save women's lives.

Population Research in Santiago

By the mid-1960s, Santiago had become a bustling center of population activities. It offered seemingly endless opportunities for population planners and global student-researcher-travelers to advance their research through positions at the Medical School and the School of Public Health of the University of Chile, through APROFA and the National Health Service (NHS), as well as the Latin American Center for Demography (Centro Latinoamericano de Demografía, CELADE) under UN auspices.[36] Last but not least, researchers worked with the Latin American Center for Population (Centro Latinoamericano de Población y Familia, CELAP), a religious organization that operated as part of the Latin American Center for Social and Economic Development (Centro para el Desarrollo Económico y Social de América Latina, DESAL). These institutions cooperated with each other, and all received ongoing financial support from the IPPF and USAID, or grants from the Population Council, the Ford Foundation, and other organizations in the United States.[37]

Private population planners, not the official family-planning programs of the Christian Democrats, first developed Chile's international links to population planning, thus establishing Chile's international reputation. CELADE's influence, for example, was so far-reaching that El Salvador's outspoken opponent to birth control, Napoleon Viera Altamirano, deemed it a "genocidal center."[38] CELADE had emerged under the joint sponsorship of the United Nations and the Chilean government in 1957. It counted on ongoing international interest and support. By 1966, the organization had come under the auspices of the United Nations Development Program (UNDP). It also received financial support from the U.S. government through AID as well as grants from the Population Council and the Ford Foundation. It published its research findings in *Demographic Bulletin*, a journal published semiannually since January 1968. CELADE also attracted an international body of researchers and students, who learned or perfected the principles of population studies.

Since its inception, CELADE has been run by an international governing board whose members have included such eminent population planners as Frank Notestein, a representative of the International Union for the Scientific Study of Population.[39] Notestein worked closely with Rockefeller; he was one of the original trustees of the Population Council and became its president in 1959.[40] Rockefeller, Notestein, and Chilean physicians such as Benjamín Viel promoted long-range goals that aimed to decrease maternal mortality while supporting birth control and economic development. They often disagreed with the more cautious yet outspoken position of the Catholic Church represented by CELAP and its influential founder, Father Roger Vekemans. CELAP produced studies guided by Catholic thought, which directly informed Christian Democratic policies ranging from "popular promotion" to family planning.

In 1965, CELAP was founded by Belgian sociologist and Jesuit priest Vekemans, who had resided in Chile since 1957.[41] Intent on studying problems of development and publishing theories of marginalization, CELAP typified the efforts of some sections of the Catholic Church to analyze secular mechanisms conducive to economic and social change.[42] Run by the strong-minded Vekemans and shaped by his own specialization in marginalization theory, CELAP directed research studies on fertility and contraception in widely defined "marginal populations."[43]

President Frei's program of popular promotion was inspired by Vekemans and institutionalized by Christian Democrats. Much like the model of Church institutions and male-dominated politics, it was contradictory in its language and its practice. Its tasks included, first, to end what Vekemans called "passive marginality," by allowing marginal populations to profit from rewards offered by modern society and the state. Second, popular promotion aimed at helping marginal populations overcome "active marginality" by leading them to organize and participate in the political decision-making process under Christian Democracy. Closely supervised participation of marginal groups, similar to women in the Mothers' Centers, reflected paternalism and political hierarchies rather than integration on the basis of equality.[44]

In 1967, Catholic theologians wrote CELAP's highly influential interpretations on "Church, Population, and Family" and addressed the demographic explosion as a spiritual challenge that should allow Catholics to practice birth control.[45] The organization also sponsored seminars throughout Latin America and attempted to guide political leaders in their search for "proper" approaches to population questions from a Christian perspective.[46] In Chile, Christian Democrats relied on CELAP publications and Vekemans's interpretations, which combined a tolerance for birth control with calls for larger structural changes, redistribution of resources, and economic development.[47] Population planners often feared the influence of the Church as an obstacle in their efforts to promote family planning, but Chilean women's contraceptive practice showed that those fears were largely unjustified.[48]

Religious Women Regulate Motherhood

In 1968, Josefina Losada de Masjuan published a fieldwork study on women's contraceptive practice in poor Santiago neighborhoods and affirmed that "religion is not a decision-making factor in reference to contraceptive use."[49] The study confirmed earlier assessments of women's use of contraceptive devices, such as those of Carmen Miró, demographer and head of CELADE, who claimed that "the behavior of Catholic women toward [birth control] does not seem to be different from that of other women."[50] Indeed, religion was not a significant factor either in the decision to practice birth control or in the choice of method. Losada de Masjuan found that Catholic and non-Catholic women alike had relied on methods ranging from the contraceptive pill and IUDs, to diaphragms and condoms, to sterilization. Nonetheless, the Church itself underwent a set of major transformations in its tolerance of birth control. On one level were women, whose decisions were shaped by their interpretation of Catholicism as a set of values. On another level was the Catholic Church as an institution and a hierarchy.[51]

The changes in Church views on fertility regulation were shaped not only by the organizational hierarchy of Catholic thought and action, but also by the emerging preoccupations of the time. The papal *magisterium*, the word of the Pope, has been and still is at the apex of the institutional hierarchy and continues to define a unity of thought in normative Catholicism. Although it is considered infallible and cannot be questioned, bishops, theologians, priests, and laity have often acted according to their own interpretations of the meanings of papal teachings. They frequently have operated with extensive diversity in their practice, stimulated by different environments they encountered and by their personal approaches to challenges like poverty and underdevelopment. In Chile, Church officials supported the pro-life discourse and tolerated family planning. In the 1950s, the Jesuit publication *Revista mensaje* still echoed voices that accused "alarmists, [wrongly] preoccupied with future super-population of the planet" and suggested that they should rather "spread culture and religion instead of propagating birth control methods that degraded the marital union."[52] In the 1960s, priests, bishops, and laity adopted a less accusatory tone.

The Chilean episcopate's position regarding responsible motherhood and family planning took shape at a unique historical moment, when the crisis of high maternal mortality and the resulting pro-life discourse in Chile coincided with a significant restructuring of the Latin American Church. In the Americas, the innovative spirit of the Second Vatican Council initiated a period of introspection for the Church and allowed for more flexibility on the topic of family planning. As a result, the pope and the highest teaching authorities of the Church engaged in a period of prolonged reflection on the topic of contraception, which led to an unsettled state on questions regarding birth control until the publication of *Humanae vitae* (On human life) in July 1968.[53] In Chile, bishops, like doctors and politicians, were influenced by the pervasive sense of urgency arising from the problem of abortion and the need to save women's lives.

Before Pope Paul VI's 1968 encyclical, which rejected all artificial methods of fertility regulation, the Chilean episcopate—and priests—found space to support family-planning programs aimed at decreasing rates of abortion and maternal mortality.[54] Priests who worked in Santiago's poor neighborhoods did not leave much written testimony on their position on birth control but often agreed to tolerate or support family planning in light of their everyday contacts. In the words of a young Chilean priest, "it is . . . difficult to be too strict . . . when you see how [poor people] live."[55] Bishops' comments reached the population through the popular media, confirming that "Church teaching would not replace personal awareness, which should be motivated by human moral sensibility." The journal *Ercilla* cited the bishops' further conclusions: "It is therefore necessary that the individual Christian assumes, on this matter as well as on others, a mature position of personal responsibility, appropriate to human care."[56] In short, the Chilean episcopate did endorse individual decision making regarding a couple's use of birth control, in agreement with the options and challenges families faced.

Nonetheless, the Chilean press commented on ongoing worldwide concerns about the rights and wrongs of what could be a proper "Catholic Pill" and considered the Roman Catholic Church's historical viewpoint on the subject of contraception.[57] Before the 1968 *Humane vitae,* the Catholic position was defined by Pope Pius XI's 1930 encyclical *Casti connubii,* which commanded that "any use whatsoever of matrimony exercised in such a way that the act is deliberately frustrated in its natural power to generate life is an offense against the law of God and nature, and those who indulge in such are branded with the guilt of a grave sin."[58] In 1951, this defining statement on sex and marriage was accompanied by Pope Pius XII's allowance of natural methods under certain circumstances. Traditional moral theologians, drawing from St. Paul and St. Augustine, saw marriage as an instrument for procreation and a remedy for sexual sins. They tolerated only natural or rhythm methods that prescribed the limitation of marital sexual relations to the nonfertile period of the menstrual cycle. In the early 1960s, leading moral theologians began to argue that it was acceptable for women to use the contraceptive pill, and at the Vatican Council a number of bishops urged a decision on this matter.[59]

In the spirit of flexibility and innovation of the 1960s Church in Latin America, some Church leaders asked for a revision of the official Church view of birth control.[60] The 1965 constitution *Gaudium et Spes* revealed the progressive tone that had distinguished the Second Vatican Council; participants expressed concern about population growth and referred to the responsibilities of couples in family planning.[61] In 1964, Catholic clerics and laymen requested a review of the Church's traditional ban on any chemical or mechanical means of fertility regulation, an appeal they justified through modern scientific, social, and demographic conditions. Consequently, Pope Paul VI set up a commission of priests, scientists, and laymen "for the study of problems of birth." The commission was expected to recommend a Roman Catholic policy on birth control in response to "the anguish of so many souls on the issue." The central question that required its response was: "In what form and according to what norms should married couples accomplish, in the exercise of their mutual love, that service to life to which their vocation calls them?"[62] The commission's decision was not quickly or easily reached. In March 1965, fifty-five members attended the fourth secret study session, but participants kept observing the secrecy and remained silent. The Pope referred to the "demographic" aspect of the problem and prolonged his debate with the committee's findings.

The transnational debates on family planning that took place at the highest levels of the Church hierarchy were conduced in the utmost secrecy but were not free from secular negotiations and initiatives spurred by population planners like Rockefeller. After an audience with Pope Paul VI in July 1965, Rockefeller initiated a lively correspondence on population questions with the Pope, in which he underlined the central responsibility he assigned to the Pontiff in this worldly matter. "A clear strong statement from you, from your great Church," writes Rockefeller, "would have tremendous impact in every home and every seat of government in every country where it was received. It would lift the problem of population out of politics and practical expediency and affirm it as a moral question with the welfare of the family as the principal consideration." Rockefeller went so far as to envision a *solution* to population problems as a result of a papal declaration in favor of family planning: "People the world over would be eternally grateful to you and the solution of the population problem would . . . be assured."[63] A letter of October 1965 that Rockefeller wrote in response to the Pope's official appearance in the United States reveals that the call for papal support did not attain the intended results. Although he praised the Pope's message of peace, he nevertheless was dissatisfied with what the Holy Father had left "in regard to the population problem." For, in Rockefeller's opinion, "peace can not be attained without population stabilization . . . and

[therefore the] Church's forthcoming statement on the family and family planning is widely and keenly anticipated."[64]

Sectors of the Chilean Catholic Church adopted multiple responses to the
Second Vatican Council and its call to end poverty and people's suffering. Liberation theology found its expression in, for example, the Christians for Socialism, just as others distanced themselves from all Marxist influences.[65] Some
conservative Catholics rejected all connections to liberation theology as a Marxist
threat, evoked the danger of communist influences, and suspected disorder behind every attempt to promote human equality.[66] In the midst of this diversity,
a progressive tone dominated the Christian Democratic stand on questions of
inequality, exposing the dark side of underdevelopment and poor living conditions.[67] Chilean Church leaders elucidated their views through pastoral documents that preceded President Frei's election and overtly supported Christian
Democratic political principles, balanced reforms to prevent drastic social, political, and economic change.[68] In a 1962 pastoral letter "On Social and Political
Responsibility in the Present Hour," Chilean bishops urged the government to
assume responsibility for the common good. They advocated reforms aimed at
addressing the system of land tenancy, poor living conditions in marginal sectors of urban centers, as well as high unemployment and malnutrition in a context of rapid population growth.[69] Subsequently, the 1968 pastoral "Chile, Will
to Be: The National Community and the Catholic Church in Chile" encouraged
Catholics to work for social justice, to assume responsibility for redistributing
social power, and to embrace marginal social and ethnic groups as equal members of their society.[70]

A key 1967 document, the "Declaration of the Chilean Episcopate about
Family Planning," highlights the unique juncture of Chilean national developments and the global discourse on population control.[71] The bishops introduced their position with a reference to the complexity of the "demographic
problem" and conveyed the Church's willingness to find realistic resolutions to
the problem.[72] Referring to the Second Vatican Council, Chilean bishops acknowledged that solutions to rapid population growth should involve actions
on the global level *and* in the family. Thereby, the declaration confirmed its tolerance for couples' personal decisions to use contraceptive devices. The Chilean
episcopate expressed concern also about maternal mortality and articulated its
willingness to support contraception as a lesser evil. Contraception could be
justified as a possible solution to a more pressing moral and medical burden—
abortion—for which contraception provided the only alternative. In circum-

stances in which a significant number of Chilean women were so strongly opposed to having more children that they were compelled to use a method likely to result in hospitalization or death, they argued, the prevention of abortion was not only a legitimate option but a responsibility that Catholic physicians, priests, and the majority of Chilean bishops would accept. As Cardinal Raúl Silva Henríquez of Santiago said in 1967, the position of the Church should not be considered "pro-natalist at all costs"; instead, it advocated "responsible parenthood."[73]

In 1968, the unexpected conservative tone of the decisive and long-awaited encyclical *Humanae vitae* elicited not only surprise but also provoked initial opposition to the official condemnation of birth control.[74] Some Chilean bishops tried to adhere to their previous position of realism and flexibility. Cardinal Silva Henríquez addressed Chilean Catholics in a television message, stating that the document's chief emphasis was on "responsible parenthood." He suggested that Catholics should not feel alienated from the Church even if they could not fulfill all of its commands—and, more significantly, he made no reference to the prohibition of artificial methods of contraception.[75] Theologians at the Catholic University in Santiago reacted to the encyclical in an open letter, stating that they were divided on the question of contraceptives.[76] They illustrated the debatable nature of the authority of the encyclical and, like the bishops, they left space for individual Catholics to make their own informed decisions.

Clearly, the period of reflection and openness elicited by the time the Vatican took to examine the legitimacy of family planning just before the publication of the *Humanae vitae* provided the necessary space and justification for Chilean women and the Chilean episcopate to maintain a flexible position. The National Health Service and APROFA reported continuity in women's visits to family-planning clinics and insisted that patients' "religious principles did not influence their decision" to adopt birth control.[77] In Chile, the period of postponement of a decision at the highest levels coincided with concerns over maternal mortality and national development. It was marked by extensive debates on the need for family planning by physicians and government officials, and it enabled the initiation of private and public family-planning programs. Eighteen of twenty Chilean bishops interviewed shortly before the publication of *Humanae vitae* permitted couples to use contraceptive devices or sent them to a Catholic physician, assuming that he or she would prescribe contraceptives and allow couples to practice birth control.[78]

Nonetheless, Chilean bishops had to affirm their unconditional agreement with the Pope as dictated by Church hierarchy. The Chilean episcopate's official response to the *Humanae vitae* acknowledged their opposition to the family-planning campaigns developed by APROFA and the NHS in light with the message of the encyclical. They defended the traditional Christian view of marriage and the dictates of natural law, denouncing the use of artificial contraceptive methods as confirmed in the *Humanae vitae*.[79] The *Revista católica* asserted that "the end did not justify the means" and declared the use of contraceptive devices a violation of the natural order.[80]

Although the episcopate's position did not change the behavior of the large majority of Catholic women who, in the words of a journalist for *Amiga,* no longer treated their use of birth control as a "dark secret," it did inspire new caution at the level of state-supported family-planning programs.[81] The encyclical not only was about the meaning of marriage and the official Church view that restricted sexuality without procreation, but it was also about interpretive power. Should procreation be the undisputed goal of marriage and sexual relations as dictated by the Catholic Church? Did women, or couples, have an obligation to consider the threats of overpopulation and to procreate responsibly in the context of modernizing nations? To what extent could women, or couples, claim the right to make individual decisions regarding pregnancy and birth? Conflicts over interpretive power had long shaped competing justifications for family planning in Latin America and in Chile.[82] International conferences, such as the 1967 International Planned Parenthood Conference in Santiago, provided abundant evidence of such competing views.

Planned Parenthood: A Duty and a Human Right

As Chilean doctors continued to improve their educational tools on family planning and responsible motherhood, international family planners packed their bags to meet them in Santiago. Physicians associated with APROFA had successfully lobbied to host the 1967 Eighth International Planned Parenthood Conference, the first such conference to take place in a Latin American nation. The Chilean capital, with its research institutions and active family planners, seemed an especially appropriate site for a gathering of top-level research scientists and physicians in the field of human reproduction.[83] Under the tenet

"Planned Parenthood—A Duty and a Human Right," conference organizers promised that "medical and scientific advance towards cheaper, safer, and more effective contraceptives will be reported by leading gynecologists and scientists from all parts of the world."[84] The two thousand participants from more than eighty countries arrived in Santiago prepared to exchange insights on research results, discuss newly developed birth control methods, and share experiences with family-planning policies. Nonetheless, the attendees and their program made it clear that questions of human rights, or women's rights to make decisions regarding motherhood, would not be the primary focus of the conference. Instead, they gave precedence to competing justifications for family planning and debated concerns over national responsibilities and international cooperation.

In his opening address, Chilean health minister Ramón Valdivieso displayed remarkable familiarity with the subject matter of population control, but the conclusions he offered so unmistakably rejected a neo-Malthusian approach that participating doctors feared embarrassment and conflicts. Valdivieso insisted that "even those who accept without reserve that the excessive growth of the population is the greatest obstacle to securing improved living standards, have had to concede that the seemingly specific remedy of restriction of the birth-rate would have little importance as an instrument of development."[85] He emphasized that his own Ministry of Health would "proceed prudently and . . . analyze the overall effects of the interdependence of the two processes of socio-economic development and of demographic development."[86]

At the time U.S. observers noticed that the address, as well as a list of family-planning norms Valdivieso circulated among delegates, reflected CELAP's influence and suggested that even a casual observer would have noticed the replication of Father Vekemans's own words and his insistence on addressing the multiple needs of "marginal populations" in Valdivieso's presentation.[87] CELAP and its tolerance of family planning, if only within a set of larger political and economic changes, significantly shaped the view of Christian Democratic policymakers and their official justification for family-planning policies. The list of family norms circulated by Valdieso at the April conference became the "Official Norms of Birth Control of the National Health Service" in October 1968.[88]

Following Valdivieso's speech, President Frei himself addressed the conference participants, as he realized the need to provide a balance to his minister's interpretation in light of the widespread support of neo-Malthusian views among the audience. The president expressed that Chileans were "aware that . . . the population explosion is a problem that can not be evaded and that it is necessary not only to study it but to work out solutions to it and face it with courage; that [it is] a problem affecting not just each family and each country, but humanity as a whole." Frei emphasized that he also supported international cooperation on topics of family planning and population control, which "bring men and women from all over the world to seek out the path which [they have to] find and follow."[89] Chilean officials would continue to assume the responsibility of developing national programs in line with global initiatives that addressed the challenge of population growth. Frei did not address the new "duties" of local women, of Chilean mothers, but others made clear that they were expected to play a crucial role in the initiatives.

The closing remarks by Dr. Francisco Mardones Restat, director general of the National Health Service, exalted the path that would lead women to become the saviors of the nation. In spite of the different justifications for family-planning programs that continued to coexist not only in conference presentations, but also in Chilean policies, he evoked unity. "Our people, and especially the women of Chile, feel that your decision [to hold the conference in Santiago] is an homage to them, for if Chile has done anything in family planning and can speak of what it has achieved, it is because [of] the women [who are] generous in fulfilling their tasks as wives, heroines sometimes. . . . For centuries they have accepted all the children heaven sent, but one day circumstances changed. Heavy migration from the countryside to the city meant for them such an accumulated burden that they realized that the victims of the situation, if they went on having children, would be the children themselves."[90] Mardones showed concern about the effect socioeconomic changes could have on women's lives. He imposed a periodization in which "one day circumstances changed," based on larger socioeconomic changes in the nation and on the need to transform women into agents of development and modernization. Placing the responsibilities for modern motherhood on the shoulders of women, Mardones claimed to speak for local women and assigned new duties without addressing the question of individual rights.

The conference brought into the open other lurking matters related to population planning and birth control: for example, sex education and its relation to unwanted pregnancies. In 1965, a journalist writing in *Punto final* had pointed to the negative consequences of the silence on the topic of human sexuality, "the big taboo" that placed obstacles in the way of young people as they became adults.[91] Lamenting that "the mother of yesterday, and still today, did not confront [the urgent task of] educating her daughter about sex, motherhood, and the methods of preventing pregnancy," the article complained of outdated moral concerns. Many mothers feared their daughters would become "fallen women," promiscuous libertines, if sexuality were discussed openly and honestly. And many young women felt they could not ask questions about sex. An incident at a Barros Luco Hospital program for biology students clarified that the *Punto final* journalist had a point. In one of the program sessions, the lecturing physician offered a question-and-answer session. When one of the female students asked about methods of birth control, the sudden silence among fellow students led her to add, hastily, that she did not ask for personal reasons but for general educational purposes. The doctor congratulated the student—and broke the silence with detailed information on birth control.[92]

Medical doctors who experienced the dark side of unwanted motherhood, evident not only in induced abortions but also in teenage pregnancies, demonstrated that they were quite open to supporting sex education programs. At the IPPF conference, they organized a forum on sexuality, explicitly addressing Chilean youth. Demand exceeded all expectations: as the session was about to begin, two thousand participants had taken their seats in the Municipal Theatre where the conference was held. Five hundred disappointed students had to be turned away—and police had to intervene to convince the crowd that, indeed, they could not be admitted into the packed auditorium. Those who could stay learned about topics ranging from the stages of human sexual development, to premarital sexual relations, to homosexuality, to the position of the Church regarding sexuality and marriage.[93]

Press reporting sensationalized this first open forum on sexuality, claiming that "Chilean Youth demanded liberty regarding their sexuality" or that "young people [were] tired of being virgins." Those comments indicated that much was still at stake when traditional silences regarding sexuality were challenged. For some Chileans, "sexual liberties" threatened the survival of the traditional order of the family and of society, since it depended on women's moral behavior and on silence regarding women's sexuality.[94] Doctors like Hernán Romero, meanwhile, addressed the issue calmly and professionally, concluding that "it became very clear to me that a woman and a man could not wait until the age of 25 to do what they desired since they were fourteen years old."[95] Teaching responsible sexual behavior was key. Instituting sex education programs for young people had become an immediate but impossible short-term goal. Other doctors, like Guillermo Adriasola, sought advice on program building abroad. But even the Population Council had not yet developed approaches to sex education and was unable to help. The council's Clifford Pease apologized, explaining that their "involvement in sex education projects in Latin America is under review and involves a number of policy decisions that . . . have not been resolved."[96]

Even as many issues like sex education and women's sexuality remained unresolved or spoken of only in hushed voices, the conference enhanced Chile's cooperation with the IPPF and asserted its global presence among population planners. It also recharged lingering debates on family planning and proper motherhood in Chile. In the journal *Mensaje*, CELAP's Father Vekemans praised the contribution of Health Minister Valdivieso but sharply criticized the content of conference panels. He accused participants of shortsightedness and ideological bias based on medical and technical concepts that denied Latin American realities.[97] The essence of Vekemans's criticism was hardly new: he felt that the Church was wrongly accused of provoking "overpopulation," and he defended his views on family planning within larger structural changes that would address the "marginality" of the poor. Hernán Romero, in his role of executive secretary of the conference and an APROFA member, rejected the accusations hurled at the Church and quoted multiple references to the Church's flexible position.[98] After all, although the conflicts between population planners and religious authorities lingered, flexibility had permitted a coexistence between the two that had allowed for a widespread acceptance of family-planning programs in the country.

APROFA's "Ambassadors" and the Modernization of the Family

Private family-planning ambassadors from APROFA employed diplomacy to advance their cause. They may have gazed with suspicions at CELAP and the Christian Democrats. But they provided continuity in family-planning services despite the Chilean government's hesitations.[99] The NHS's "Official Norms on Birth Control" emphasized three major goals: to diminish maternal mortality due to abortion; to control infant mortality; and, most importantly, to promote the well-being of the family.[100] With these public guidelines, private family planners worked hard to hold on to the "pro-life" discourse, the need to save women's lives, as they secured support for their work. When the APROFA vice president Dr. Guillermo Adriasola shared insights with physician-colleagues

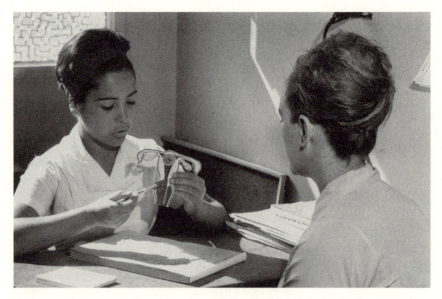

Figure 3.4. Birth control clinic in Santiago, Chile. Photograph by Jim Wallace, March 9, 1965. *Library of Congress, Prints and Photographs Division,* U.S. News & World Report *magazine collection (LC-U9-13462, frame 20 A).*

in Quito, Ecuador, he clarified the organization's official incentives. Reporting on "how we did it in Chile," he described the important role doctors played when responding to the abortion epidemic. "We concluded that family planning was a medical problem and a problem of Public Health, because abortion directly affected the well-being and the health of the family," Adriasola testified.[101] Indeed, abortion and the Chilean pro-life discourse had implications that went further than Adriasola's account suggests. In Chile, the pro-life discourse also secured the ongoing support of the NHS, where doctors had to walk a fine line when justifying birth control. The official contract between APROFA and the NHS was signed in December 1968, to be renewed annually. It formalized and clarified the cooperation and responsibilities these two institutions had shared since the foundation of the first Family Planning Committee.[102]

Women used APROFA services, which were well connected through the network of the NHS and even advertised in radio and television programs (figures 3.4 and 3.5).[103] By 1966, there were 102 family-planning centers nationwide, and more than fifty-eight thousand women received contraceptives free of charge. By 1967, the government allocated funds to provide contraceptive services to

Figure 3.5. Birth control clinic in Santiago, Chile. Photograph by Jim Wallace, March 9, 1965. *Library of Congress, Prints and Photographs Division,* U.S. News & World Report *magazine collection (LC-U9-13462, frame 6).*

an additional one hundred thousand women.[104] APROFA disseminated information on family planning and coordinated seminars and conferences with health educators, social workers, labor leaders, and volunteers. Its monthly news *Boletin* was published at a circulation rate of about four thousand and distributed in hospital communities throughout Chile. Close to two hundred educational film screenings, including the Disney cartoon, had drawn more than fifteen thousand viewers. It continued to disseminate information on family planning in newspapers, radio stations, and television programs, documenting sixty-two printed articles, forty-three radio announcements, and two television programs. In Santiago, female volunteers led sixteen discussion groups composed of 450 members in poor neighborhoods.[105] In short, APROFA became the single most active institution to promote family planning and to make birth control devices available to Chilean women. Its strength lay in its successful combination of a pro-life discourse with population planning for the sake of modernization. Romero of APROFA confessed that he had "grown to abominate the expression 'population explosion,'" but he quickly added that there had been an explosion of a different nature: "an explosion in the 'family microcosm.'"[106] Romero and others helped reconstruct the meaning of family in an urban, modernizing Chile.[107]

While APROFA used the pro-life discourse to secure widespread acceptance of birth control, its family planners' diplomatic methods were more complex and far-reaching than publicly acknowledged. Its reference to the "family" offered clues. Its promise to work in favor of "the protection of the family" evoked a long tradition of nation building and an image of continuity. After all, the family had been the pillar of stability in the changing nation after Chilean independence in the nineteenth century, securing the ongoing social and gendered hierarchical order. Nonetheless, it was a particular family type that now built a bridge between the old and the new. When Adriasola addressed his colleagues in Quito, he referred to the modern world in which "women's answers to surveys, globally, showed their opposition to families larger than three children." He referred to a different type of family, long present in APROFA's projections.[108] Its quiet yet insistent reinvention of the family proved crucial in its appeal to international funding institutions like the IPPF and shed light on women's new role in the modernizing nations.[109]

By helping to comply with the demand of the changing world, in this case by accepting the modern limits to family size, women became saviors of the nation, in addition to saving their own lives. In 1967, the Experimental Film Department of the University of Chile produced the only educational film on family planning and abortion made in Chile, *The Abortion*. Its narrative evokes the harsh realities of Chilean life and the testimonies of women's unwanted pregnancies and induced abortions that doctors had long encountered in public hospitals.[110] Although the images are recognizable, reminiscent of earlier decades in the twentieth century, their interpretations now far exceed the range of familiar approaches to local misery. A black-and-white feature, *The Abortion* bares the grim realities of urban misery and portrays the all-too-common fate of a housewife in a poor neighborhood struggling to survive with three children and finding herself pregnant once again. Unable to feed another child, she seeks the services of an abortionist. The backstreet abortion leads to serious medical complications, which necessitate a trip to the nearest hospital, where she must undergo emergency surgery performed by trained medical care. The final scenes provide the essence of the film's message and an encouragement to learn from the familiar story: in her hospital bed, pale, tired, yet alive, the woman revisits her life's traumatic moments. Through insights presented in flashbacks, she exposes the characteristics of the overcrowded, unhealthy living conditions in her neighborhood that should, clearly, not be the home of yet another child. Obviously, poverty and large families are a deadly combination.

The story had a double message: lack of family planning caused both *individual* misery and *communal* distress. Death was an immediate threat to women who did not practice family planning and, as a result, had clandestine abortions. Without birth control, the woman not only endangered her own life, but also threatened the survival of her family and her community. Either women would increase the misery and discomfort of poor urban life by not limiting the number of children they raised; or women could use family-planning methods, the only way out of individual, communal, and national distress. They had to become the saviors of the nation by planning and regulating births. The tepid tribute of saviors, continuously diminished by women's ongoing lack of rights, was accompanied by the threat of vilification in the national narrative of modernization. Saviors or villains, women did consult family-planning clinics and obtained information on family-planning methods. Chilean program leaders kept alive their global connections while promoting their goals of diminishing maternal mortality and supporting national development.

Multiple family-planning and postpartum programs continued to function with assistance from foreign grants. Under the auspices of the faculty of medicine at the Barros Luco Hospital in Santiago, the San Gregorio project and Benjamín Viel's work in the Quinta Normal district thrived with a Population Council biomedical grant to the University of Chile.[111] The project leaders kept detailed records, aimed at documenting the effect of a family-planning program on the abortion and birth rates of the working-class population in the South Santiago Health District.[112] At the Eighth World Conference of the IPPF in 1967, physicians presented a report that not only demonstrated a reduction in the pregnancy rate but also showed that the drop in the abortion rate was proportionally higher than the reduction in the birth rate.[113] From the perspective of population planners and foreign observers, the postpartum program at the San Juan de Dios Hospital in Santiago under the direction of Benjamín Viel demonstrated ongoing success. It treated women in two hospitals and six satellite clinics. Physicians managed postpartum care at the San Juan de Dios Hospital in Quinta Normal, a large public hospital, which treated about ten thousand obstetrics and abortion cases annually. Doctors also worked with maternity patients at the Félix Bulnes Hospital, once a tuberculosis sanitarium, in the same district, and treated about eight thousand obstetrics and abortion cases a year. In a site-visit report of the program, Population Council staff associate Gerald I. Zatuchni praised Viel "for organizing and supervising the Postpartum Program in the Quinta Normal District of Santiago de Chile." Zatuchni emphasized that "the program is going exceptionally well" and showed the greatest admiration for "Dr. Viel's perseverance and humanitarian interest."[114]

Many female patients did profit from these programs, but their access to unbiased information had changed only minimally. Most women became part of the program and its promotion of family planning when they came to the hospital to give birth; what followed were standard operating procedures. At the San Juan de Dios Hospital, doctors transferred obstetrical patients to a neighboring building, reserved exclusively for maternity patients who were brought in after having given birth or having had an abortion. Over the next four days, on average, trained social workers offered family-planning education. Dr. Viel had developed visual aid material and flip charts for educational purposes, which were used in group sessions and in one-on-one counseling between social worker and patient. All postpartum and postabortion insertions of IUDs took place in the special annex. When women were discharged, they had been exposed to information on family-planning methods, but nevertheless their "choice" still depended on doctors' assessments of efficiency and cost.

Zatuchni's report documented Viel's own evaluation of the program's success. In postpartum and postabortion insertions, physicians, including Viel, had much praise for the Saf-t-coils, IUDs popular at the time. Zatuchni stated that the doctors "like the sterile packaging and feel that the expulsion rate is similar, if not lower than the Lippes loop." Meanwhile, the Population Council helped obtain Saf-t-coils and Lippes loops "for comparison's sake." In Viel's program, most patients could not opt for contraceptive pills "as the costs were too high."[115] He reported insertion rates of about eight hundred IUDs per month. Ninety percent of the abortion patients and 80 percent of all obstetrical patients at the Felix Bulnes Hospital were discharged with an IUD.[116] Viel's statements in the Santiago press made clear that, in his view, poor mothers needed special attention. Insisting that birth rates in Santiago's poor neighborhoods were significantly higher than those in wealthier districts, he praised middle-class women who "secured an acceptable living standard for their families by avoiding birth rates that could destroy their quality of life."[117] This discourse revealed that doctors, once again, expected responsible mothers to be saviors of the nation and of their families without addressing the material shortcomings and personal challenges that informed women's lives.

Persistent Traditions, Women's Agency, and Signs of Change

While doctors discussed family-planning methods and population planners sought to curtail poverty by controlling family size, some poor and uneducated women found new ways to address their misery on their own. Among them were Laura and Hilda, who testified to their experiences in the first *tomas* (land takeovers), which began to interrupt Santiago's urban landscape under the government of President Frei.[118] Both women had to take charge of their lives at a young age: Laura migrated from the southern region of Valdivia in search of work; Hilda was born in Santiago but abandoned by her family after a failed marriage in her teenage years. Both had young children and struggled to keep temporary jobs without a proper place to live. Laura remembered her first encounter with La Pelusa, a political organizer who was "active and motivating" and who used a word Laura had not heard before: "combative." "You need to be combative," La Pelusa repeated, again and again, adding that "nobody will fight for you. . . . You have to resolve your problems by yourself, and claim your rights."[119]

Laura learned how to build barricades and to defend a piece of land against police who came to remove the squatters. Hilda learned that tight organization and an outright refusal to give up the much-needed land could prevent police from coming in to remove them. Laura and Hilda both found new communities, comrades with whom they united in their struggle for a livelihood in the city. Laura began to take charge of her life when leaders like La Pelusa "educated [her] on all levels" and when she participated in multiple fronts to defend the land they took over.[120] Hilda described how she "discovered a new life" in which she not only gained access to a piece of land, but also shared tasks in the struggle for survival with her new community.[121] Like many other women, Laura and Hilda would test the limits of gender equity and class struggle under a government that proclaimed a Peaceful Road to Socialism.

Educated, professional women in wealthier Santiago neighborhoods, meanwhile, lamented that life in Santiago was still shaped by a double standard that assigned different moral codes to women and men. The IPPF Conference demonstrated not only that many Chileans were prepared to address questions of birth control, but that a new generation of Chileans was ready to adopt a more open approach to sexuality. Women's roles remained connected to motherhood, far removed from sexuality, and women's lives seemed inseparable from their families. Men, married or single, were expected to have affairs and sexual conquests that would affirm their masculinity. Women, however, were severely condemned for sexual misconduct. Writer and novelist Isabel Allende made clear to what extent the gendered double standard also shaped public understandings of male and female sexual rights. When she wrote an article about an unfaithful wife, the journal *Paula* gave it front-page coverage, relegating reports on key world news to a few meager lines. Allende remembered that "the November issue of the magazine carried ten lines about the execution of Che Guevera, news that sent a seismic shock around the world, and four pages of [her] interview with the faithless wife that shattered the calm of Chilean society." Chileans could not forgive "that the protagonist of the piece had the same motivations for adultery as a man: opportunity, boredom, dejection, flirtation, challenge, curiosity."[122] Clearly, women in Santiago reassessed their role in the family and nation, even though the official politics of the Revolution in Liberty tried to confine the scope of change to a "revolution of the sewing machine" in the Mothers' Centers.

Changing Political Priorities and Shifting Assignments for Women-Citizens

The first official family-planning program was created under a government inspired by Christian social doctrine. Doctors and politicians were the first to connect family planning to overpopulation and underdevelopment as well as motherhood to modernity. Church influences and Chilean Catholic leaders contributed to the innovative spirit of the time and helped address what they saw as immediate challenges in the lives of women. Contrary to those who have interpreted Church influences as a major obstacle to family planning, Chilean experiences revealed a different reality. Chilean bishops supported the pro-life mission that aimed at promoting family planning to prevent abortions and save mothers' lives; some maintained that large families hindered economic development.

As birth control programs provided the opportunity to make motherhood a choice, doctors and politicians began to perceive and present women as potential saviors of the nation. They thus aimed to limit women's choices. Instead of villains, "bearers" of an excess of motherhood, producing families that were too large, Chilean women could become saviors of the nation by limiting family size and thereby securing the well-being of their family, community, and nation. In the eyes of population planners, only the latter path was right, a path that required the policing of women's bodies and their use of reliable contraceptive techniques. Fears that fertility and conception could threaten modern life assigned new meaning to traditional gendered responsibilities. In this context, male politicians and health officials strengthened their control over women's bodies to realize their mission of modernization.

By the end of Christian Democratic leadership, APROFA director Guillermo Adriasola assessed the success of his organization in numbers, documenting that the number of children born in Chile had declined by thirty thousand between 1965 and 1970. Lower birth rates, he acknowledged, were also a sign of the changing times and new demands placed on women's lives.[123] Many Chileans now interpreted those demands in light of the unfulfilled promises of Christian Democratic political leaders. In his six-year term as president, Frei failed to deliver on his pledge to bring about a Revolution in Liberty. Not only did reforms remain too limited, but many had destabilizing effects. Inflation, economic stagnation, and popular discontent characterized the final years of Christian Democratic government, further polarizing those who demanded radical political change, on the one hand, and those who opted for more conservative political programs, on the other. In this environment, even Christian Democrats began to splinter into factions.

After the 1970 election of President Allende and his Unidad Popular government, Chileans witnessed a fresh approach to revolutionary change and equality. Global fears of overpopulation became a less prominent influence on Chile's domestic policies. Allende's Peaceful Road to Socialism brought new opportunities for and challenges to the achievement of women's rights and gender equity.

|| 4 ||

GENDERED CITIZENSHIP RIGHTS
ON THE PEACEFUL ROAD
TO SOCIALISM

When I say "woman," I always think of the woman-mother. . . .
When I talk of the woman, I refer to her in her function in the nuclear family. . . . [T]he child is the prolongation of the woman who
in essence is born to be a mother.

President Salvador Allende Gossens, 1972

WHEN LAURA, a woman in her early twenties, talked about her experiences
under President Allende's government (1970–1973), she painted a picture
markedly different from the established portrait of women's roles. She recalled
her initial plunge into politics in the late 1960s, at which time she was involved
in struggles for land that led to the foundation of Nueva La Havana (New
Havana), a *campamento* on the outskirts of Santiago.[1] The *campamentos,* she explained, were not like other shantytowns, because those who lived in them
were politically conscious and militant, energized by the land occupations that
had brought them together and by the need to defend their communities. New
Havana was founded in November 1970, when three smaller *campamentos* were
merged together as a result of eight prior land takeovers led by the Movimiento
de Izquierda Revolucionaria (MIR, the Movement of the Revolutionary Left).[2]

Laura knew that, in practice, the political structures in her *campamento*,
and the tasks assigned to men and women, differed from the model of popular
participation proposed by President Allende's coalition party.[3] In New Havana,
an elected high command of members directed a horizontal structure, con-

sisting of both cultural and health fronts as well as defensive militias that addressed the residents' most urgent needs. Often considered as replacements for state services, the fronts were organizations that promoted solidarity and social cohesion as they solved problems for the community.[4] The militias, for example, dealt with threats to the neighborhood and with internal security. Laura asserted that in New Havana "women were prominent in all . . . activities, whereas in other *campamentos* there were special women's sections which precluded participation on equal terms. . . . [T]here was real integration; in the directorate, on the marches, even in the confrontations. . . . This weakened male chauvinism at a very basic level. Of course there was a lot of resistance to this—cases of husbands forbidding wives to go to the meetings, and drinking and beating them up if they did so."[5] Quite different from Allende's vision of the functions of the "woman-mother," Laura envisioned herself as an integral part of the community where her political engagement was unrelated to her role in a nuclear family. Like many *pobladoras,* she also began to shift her sense of collective responsibility toward fellow women.[6]

New Havana became "something of an attraction to intellectuals and artists" after 1970. Laura recalled that these outsiders' interests seemed somewhat detached from local realities and often counterproductive to political collaboration. Intellectuals came to New Havana meetings and, in an effort to enhance the residents' political knowledge, launched discussions on such topics as the global causes of underdevelopment and its implications on the national level. According to Laura, these interactions were uncalled for, since "local people already had a profound political education arising from their own experiences . . . [and], although many of them were politically active, they weren't necessarily interested in political debates by intellectuals."[7] Local problems shaped *pobladores*' activism on the local front, but in practice gender relations and everyday life were not as harmonious as some distant observers assumed. For instance, many women were especially committed to fighting alcoholism, given that drunken confrontations often led to domestic violence. According to Laura's experiences, "alcoholism was also a mainstay of male chauvinism . . . especially [as] . . . many women had social activities outside the home. . . . This new independence caused some really violent scenes, especially on paydays, when drinking was always at its heaviest."[8] Her take on women's initiatives reflected an optimistic view of political participation across gender lines, but it also exposed the arduous realities of women's lives. Clearly, the women who lived in *campamentos* or in other poor neighborhoods struggled with the everyday challenges resulting from class and gender inequalities. Poverty and do-mestic violence did not disappear overnight, but many people felt that the new government offered unprecedented hope for change.

In 1970, President Salvador Allende's Unidad Popular government prom-ised new equality and unprecedented rights and stability to working-class fam-ilies. A traditional left, well represented by Allende himself, envisioned a society of equals as the product of a class struggle; it did not challenge specific inequalities of "natural" gender roles. Allende's position—"when I say 'woman,' I always think of the woman-mother"—mirrored that of the political leader-ship. Many male politicians found it difficult to overcome the notion of women as dependent and domestic.[9] In general, patriarchal politics continued to limit women's citizenship rights and political participation. In particular, women who wanted to make motherhood a choice even experienced the regressive effects of the political ideology of this traditional left. When the government placed ideological limits on programs funded by population planners in the United States, and when the media helped promote family planning as a weapon of foreign imperialism, women found it increasingly difficult to prac-tice birth control.[10]

The Unidad Popular's program of a Peaceful Road to Socialism provoked ample manifestations of women's agency. Pro-Allende women of the left, on the one hand—be they militants of the socialist and communist parties or union activists—expanded their political participation even though they were engaged in a class struggle that remained predominantly a male affair. Anti-Allende women, on the other hand, drew attention to their maternal respon-sibilities to protest UP leadership. The unexpected public assertion of their views paved the way for a new political role of "militant mothers," a term first used by the political scientist Sonia Alvarez to describe women's claims that traditional responsibilities of motherhood justified their resistance to military authoritarianism in the Latin American Southern Cone.[11] Under the UP gov-ernment, the militant motherhood in the making would be strikingly different from the references to motherhood maternal activists had used early in the century. Anti-Allende women established a lasting presence of women on the political arena—and prepared fellow Chileans for a reinterpretation of women's citizenship rights.

Pro- and anti-Allende women mobilized under the UP government, but conservative anti-Allende women who contested the politics of revolution more effectively made their voices heard.[12] There were many unintended consequences of the protests by anti-Allende women, who broke the boundaries of traditional understandings of maternal responsibilities located in the domestic sphere. The nature of women's political activism indeed supplied evidence of the power of militant motherhood that would remain central to the gendered patterns of political mobilization in Chile. Anti-Allende women's militant motherhood had long-term consequences, not desired by them: it further transformed the gendered underpinnings of political participation.

The Peaceful Road to Socialism Meets the Cold War

At the height of the Cold War, and with the forward march of the Cuban Revolution, U.S. fears of communism continued to have a bearing on Chilean domestic developments. The Central Intelligence Agency (CIA) spent three million dollars to support the Christian Democrats in 1964 and invested even more money and effort to control Chilean politics in the 1970s. Through extensive propaganda and the investment of "assets" in Chilean media organizations, the CIA also spread "black propaganda," known by U.S. officials as "material falsely purporting to be the product of a particular individual or group." In the 1970 presidential election, for example, it aimed to sow discord between the communist and socialist parties to undermine Salvador Allende's campaign.[13]

The Cold War in general, and the arrogance of appointed state officials like U.S. National Security adviser Henry Kissinger in particular, consolidated political arrangements and efforts to control Latin America at the time. In the words of *New York Times* correspondent Stephen Kinzer, the "desire of people in poor countries to assert control over their natural resources, . . . which pushed [them] into conflict with the United States during the Cold War, lay completely outside the experience of most American leaders."[14] Indeed, in a conversation with Chile's foreign minister Gabriel Valdés, Kissinger declared that "nothing important can come from the South. History has never been produced in the South. The axis of history starts in Moscow, goes to Bonn, crosses over to Washington, and then goes to Tokyo. What happens in the South is of no importance."[15] Such positions help elucidate the outspoken anti-imperialism of much of the Latin American left and put into context the political strategies of the Unidad Popular.

In Chile, the 1970 election campaign reflected the tension between the political left and right, as well as the ongoing competition for women's votes.

Unidad Popular candidate Salvador Allende ran against the Christian Democrat Radomiro Tomic and the former president and Nationalist candidate Jorge Alessandri. Whereas Tomic promised to deepen the reforms initiated by his Christian Democratic predecessor, Alessandri promised to defend the entrepreneurial sector's privileges. Similar to the 1964 election, competition for women's votes relied not only on drastic depictions of communist threats but also on promises to help women. Alessandri's platform included a separate section for women that pledged to honor them by protecting their traditional role in society. The Unidad Popular, without a separate women's platform, sought to attract women voters by promising a family ministry, equal pay for equal work, and legal changes that would expand the rights of married women and illegitimate children.[16] All candidates evoked the well-being of the Chilean family in their campaigns.[17]

In the 1970 campaign, the political left manipulated gendered messages that affected women, and mothers, in an unparalleled way: it accused family planners of selling out to foreign imperialists for the sake of controlling, and limiting, populations. In August of that year, the Communist Party's newspaper El siglo went to great lengths to accuse Chilean health officials in general, and family-planning pioneer Dr. Benjamín Viel in particular, of "heading a campaign of North-American origin to pressure working class and peasant women into limiting births."[18] El siglo alleged that Viel had exploited the vulnerability of poor Chileans and implemented population control measures to limit procreation among target populations well beyond the reach of the National Health Service. The paper further accused him of manipulating doctors and midwives to promote family planning by paying them with dirty money from abroad. El siglo claimed the Rockefeller Foundation and other U.S. institutions had a political and economic interest in limiting population size in Chile. Another El siglo article even addressed a "Dr. 'Maltus' Viel" in the title and called family-planning initiatives economic and political weapons used against Chileans.[19]

The view of family planning as a foreign plot—instead of a tool that could help women regulate motherhood and diminish maternal mortality—was prevalent among sectors of the traditional left throughout the Americas. Men and women of the left saw birth control as a capitalist strategy employed to control the hemisphere by limiting population size in the developing world. They called family planning a tool of the rich to control the poor and branded "birth control as a weapon of imperialism," a diversionary tactic to silence those who protested against injustice and inequalities.[20] In Chile, this view helped political leaders and doctors redefine the connection between motherhood and women's bodies and the hegemony of the Chilean body politic. New restrictions on family-planning programs were inspired by global competitions and national political campaigns, *not* by local women who wanted to make their own decisions about motherhood. Government preoccupations with national hegemony exposed a political dimension of motherhood, where ideological disputes on national and global levels threatened to silence the right of local women to decide about pregnancy and birth in the contexts of their own lives.

Disagreements over birth control pitted political leaders against health officials on the highest levels. Campaigning in defense of family planning, Dr. Benjamín Viel, a personal friend of President Allende, also a medical doctor, reminded Allende of his professional obligation and argued that his responsibilities as a physician obliged him to secure foreign grants for programs in Chile.[21] Viel used his international ties to prevent foreign donors, who began to consider Chile an unreliable ally under the new government, from cutting off supplies. In a letter to the U.S. Population Council, Viel quoted Allende who insisted that "I am a Medical Doctor, I know the problem of large families, and believe that to decide about the size of the family is a human right, and being the President of a poor country I need to help make it a reality."[22] Foreign observers noted that Allende *did* appoint a few "population pioneers to strategic positions in government," including Mariano Requena, chief planning officer in the health ministry; Anibal Faúndes, adviser to the ministry's Mother-Child program; and Carlos Concha, the program's director.[23] All of them had long supported family-planning programs in their quest to save women's lives— and all knew that the state's rejection of foreign funds doomed their programs. This commitment to family planning, nonetheless, was dangerously narrow in the eyes of doctors who foresaw the disintegration of the programs they had built.

Some family-planning leaders, including Viel, left the country in response to what they denounced as a lack of commitment to family planning by the UP. In 1970, the International Planned Parenthood Federation (IPPF) proclaimed that "an internationally known medical researcher and authority on preventive medicine w[ould] arrive in New York City on December 1 to become Director General of the Western Hemisphere Region of the International Planned Parenthood Federation."[24] That researcher was Viel. Steadfast in his decision making, and dedicated to his cause, this pioneer of family-planning programs in Chile had decided to support programs in his native country from abroad. Having accepted a key position in the hemisphere, Viel traveled to in-

Figure 4.1. Supporters of Chilean president Salvador Allende with a flag depicting Che Guevara, in a bus in the center of Santiago. Photograph by Joseph Benham, September 20, 1971. *Library of Congress, Prints and Photographs Division,* U.S. News & World Report *magazine collection (LC-U9-24948, frame 5). Reproduced by permission of the photographer.*

ternational conferences, met with Chilean delegations to evaluate developments in his home country, and continued to support APROFA in Santiago.[25]

Allende, meanwhile, assured Chileans that curtailing chaos and guaranteeing stability through economic independence were uppermost priorities in his political agenda. The Unidad Popular aimed to liberate Chile from imperialist intervention, put an end to economic exploitation, increase employment opportunities, and offer free education for all Chileans.[26] Campaign ads invited women to support the UP and promised to bring well-being to Chilean families and children.[27] Election results demonstrated the tense competition between the right and left, with Allende becoming president without an absolute majority. In September 1970, the Unidad Popular victory was won by only thirty thousand votes, which meant that the decisive vote was cast by Congress. Allende declared that the Chilean road to socialism would be taken within the

Figure 4.2. Marxists demonstrating in support of Chilean president Salvador Allende, near the Presidential Palace in Santiago, just three days prior to the military coup. Photograph by Joseph Benham, September 8, 1973. *Library of Congress, Prints and Photographs Division*, U.S. News & World Report *magazine collection (LC-U9-28379, frame 18). Reproduced by permission of the photographer.*

legal confines of the constitution: it would be democratic and peaceful. Only in the aftermath of this assurance was Allende inaugurated as the president of Chile in November 1970.

The Unidad Popular thus embarked on a constitutional course to diminish class differences through the redistribution of political and economic power. The government initiated the nationalization of the economy and set out to increase access to political decision making for all Chileans. Although most supporters were optimistic at the onset, euphoria soon gave way to caution (figure 4.1 and figure 4.2). An economic squeeze by international and national adversaries disrupted the nation's production process and prevented the import of basic consumer goods. Divisions among the members of Allende's governing coalition undermined the unified front of the revolutionary process. Workers demanded control of production before the government was ready to comply. Finally, the international economic pinch increasingly contributed to shortages of basic consumer goods, associating the Peaceful Road to Socialism with hunger and scarcity and further undermining Allende's legitimacy. Increased national unrest and growing opposition instigated the military coup, which led to the overthrow of the Unidad Popular government and Allende's death on September 11, 1973.[28] The few years on the path to a new society, nonetheless, offered innumerable insights into the power of old traditions that shaped the role of women in the politics of revolution.

Women as Mothers, Workers, and Comrades

President Allende asserted that social and political liberties depended, first and foremost, on economic equality.[29] Chileans from all walks of life learned about the path to a new society by reading such works as Marta Harnecker's *Cuadernos de educación popular* (Notebooks for popular education). Widely available throughout Chile, Harnecker's booklets explained, step by step, the mechanics of exploitation under capitalism, the relation between the exploited and those who exploited them, and the tools necessary for effective class struggle.[30] The Unidad Popular government strove to limit the wealth and power of the economic elites by creating a working class that would form an alliance with the middle sector. The socialization of the economy was central to the achievement of class equality. Workers, Allende believed, would be exploited as long as they were denied control of the means of production. Quite different from the reformist and developmental impulse of the Alliance for Progress, the government now exposed the destructive influences of global capitalism, economic dependency, and U.S. imperialism—all of which limited Latin American development.[31] All Chileans, men and women, were encouraged to help end this dependency, but men would lead the way. In 1971, President Allende addressed the nation and stressed that "[w]e will triumph when the Chilean woman hears our call, and joins the struggle of her husband, her father, her son, and her brother."[32] He conveyed that male revolutionaries on the Peaceful Road to Socialism expected women to walk by their side, as mothers, workers, and comrades who joined their cause.

In accordance with Allende's reference to women as "the woman-mother . . . and her function in the nuclear family," new measures promised to improve women's domestic lives and secure the protection of their families, but they did not address women as citizens with needs independent from those of their families.[33] Feminists and women of the political left discussed women's participation in the Peaceful Road to Socialism and struggled to set priorities in their political participation.[34] Feminist Vania Bambirra, for example, insisted that the proletariat's struggle for equality needed to address the specific characteristics of the exploitation of women. Quoting U.S. Marxist feminist Margaret Benston, Bambirra echoed her call to end women's economic dependency on the husband-father and to prioritize the struggle for women's material and legal equality.[35] At the same time, Bambirra added a distinction between "first" world and "third" world feminisms. Asserting that "the struggle for women's liberation in dependent capitalist countries . . . has to . . . take a distinct political form," she explained that "in dependent capitalist countries, and in Chile in particular, where the class struggle . . . has acquired a constantly more defined and radical character, it will not make sense to establish movements of specific social sectors isolated from the general context of the struggle of the oppressed classes."[36]

Bambirra pronounced an opinion quite prevalent among men *and* women of the Chilean left: a women's movement had to "be under the direction of the working classes through the revolutionary parties and organizations." In agreement with, for example, the Chilean Assembly of Communist Women, Bambirra prioritized class struggle. Accordingly, women would mobilize: first, as agents of Chile's revolution and, second, as women whose liberation would come with the end of class divisions.[37] For many, this vaguely defined path toward women's liberation offered an easy solution to the threat of competition between male revolutionary leaders and women interested in gender equity. Female authors who published under the auspices of *Quimantú,* the Unidad Popular's national press, exposed some of the discriminatory aspects of the gender system but often lamented the disadvantages of Chilean women without directly challenging that system.

In her book *The Chilean Woman*, Amanda Puz presented women in different work and home environments, fond of their families, interested in fashion, and defending their children "like lioness[es]."[38] Puz praised the Chilean woman's romantic nature, her loyalty, and her faithfulness that stood in stark contrast to the faithlessness of the Chilean man. In her chapter on *machismo,* Puz acknowledged that the gendered double standard she had described went well beyond the dimension of women's broken hearts. Even though Puz lamented that women lacked political rights, economic independence, and legal equality, she offered few solutions. She acknowledged women's active role in the reproduction of a gender system that limited their options and declared that it was "the women [who] raise macho children" and that "good mothers" clearly helped produce the "bad fathers" of the future.[39] Nonetheless, she advised a cautious approach to addressing gender inequities. Puz's solution appeared to be a natural outcome of the linear progress that would "come to Chile," in tune with the revolution, and according to the pace of its own history. She wrote: "The Chilean woman wants to liberate herself, [but] not like North American and European feminists who came close to rejecting men, but instead according to matters that are important to her. Until now, [she] has been the victim of a socioeconomic system that has also trapped her man, and of a whole set of cultural taboos that, luckily, are beginning to disappear."[40] With these assessments, Puz neither challenged nor complicated the Unidad Popular's official view of the course of the revolution and the "natural" benefits it would have for women.

Virginia Vidal, a contributor to *El siglo* and an author with experience abroad in China and Czechoslovakia, offered a more daring critique of gender discrimination but ultimately did not wander too far from the official revolutionary party line to address women's plight independently from the class struggle.[41] In her 1972 *Woman's Emancipation,* Vidal humanized her theoretical reflections by presenting Doña Maria, a "typical" Chilean housewife, who learned about the meaning of and proper path to the "emancipation of women" throughout the course of the book. Vidal described how, for the first time, International Women's Day (March 8) was commemorated as a workers' celebration in 1972, with the Central Unica de Trabajadores (CUT, the National Workers Syndicate) celebrating in state-run businesses and offices. Yet Doña Maria sensed that the times were changing on many other levels as well. Vidal explained that "women's emancipation is inseparable from class struggle," but it must include sexual liberation and the open discussion of women's sexuality.[42] Doña Maria understood the importance of sexual liberation by listening to her daughter and by acknowledging the necessity of birth control. The new generation of women finally would have the chance to address motherhood not as a burden, but as a choice. In the words of Vidal, "Doña Maria begins to understand that women's emancipation is not sexual licentiousness, but instead the responsibility a woman must assume to live in her society, married or single."[43] Underlying the story was a sense of a sexual revolution among Chile's youth and the acknowledgment that young women might make different claims to rights than their mothers.

Vidal's story had exposed the double exploitation of women and demonstrated the ill effects both capitalism and patriarchy had on women's lives. With Doña Maria as her spokeswoman, she broke the silences on women's sexuality and the choice of many women to have sex without procreation. Nonetheless, her vision of the path to gender equality in the revolution remained as vaguely defined as was that of Allende and the Unidad Popular. "Socialism" would ultimately bring "the end of the enslavement of women . . . because society would provide food, well-being, culture, and security to every man, every women, and every child."[44] By liberating women from their traditional household tasks, this message implied, they would miraculously attain citizenship rights equal to those enjoyed by men.

Although women of the left offered theoretical reflections and actively participated in the struggle to build a new society, it became clear that, in the eyes of the UP's male leadership, the men would *lead* the revolution and expected the women to *follow*. Allende commented on his understanding of women's rights but remained vague when referring to the nature of women's oppression and the path they would have to take to freedom. He asserted that a woman's liberation would depend on her ability, first, to join the revolutionary struggle and, second, to participate fully in the construction of a new society. In his words, the UP's task was "to conquer [the woman] so that she would understand that her own future fate depended specifically on those rights that are denied to her." The president admitted that women lacked equal rights, but asserted that the UP would "not just give her [those rights] as a gift, because she herself would earn them by becoming . . . a woman who would construct a different society."[45] Political leaders, for Allende, were gendered male, but men depended on women-followers.

Allende's persistent view that women, of necessity, had to be "conquered" toyed with sexual meaning and with the realities of a gender system that assigned an active role to men, who ultimately won over the passive female. It effectively portrayed a political process in which the male leadership expected to *make* women part of their cause. His ambiguous reference to women's role in the creation of a new society and his insistence on her subsequent "automatic" liberation as a result illustrate the continuity of gendered traditions that rendered women passive, juxtaposed to the active men. It also foreshadowed the failure of Allende's government to address class *and* gender as causes of the inequalities that plagued the nation.[46]

Accordingly, the government proposed a number of policy changes for the benefit of women—and their families. The most extensive proposal was the foundation of the Ministerio de la Familia (Family Ministry), which was presented to Congress in 1971. It stalled, however, and never passed. Despite this proposal's failure, it revealed Allende's goal of increasing legal equality between women and men in the family, taking responsibility for problems like domestic violence and alcoholism within the family and addressing the challenges of working mothers.[47] Through the Family Ministry, Allende hoped to secure the rights of single mothers and their children, acknowledging the double standard that judged men and women's moral behaviors differently. He envisioned legal as well as educational changes to alleviate the problem of discrimination, asserting that these changes were much needed "in a country without an honest sex education, and . . . with a different moral code applied to women than to men."[48] The president also recognized that "children could often represent a burden in homes where the resources were limited" and promised to give special attention to the plight of working women.[49] The proposed ministry aimed at improving the options of working mothers and the social security of all mothers and their children.[50]

Although the proposal to establish the Family Ministry remained stalled in Congress, the Unidad Popular instituted the Secretaría Nacional de la Mujer (the Woman's National Secretariat), an agency dedicated to a much more limited range of what were considered women's concerns. The secretariat focused on such issues as price controls, food supplies, family health, and child care. In an effort to promote equality and break new ground, the secretariat also offered information and advice on women's legal rights. It addressed questions of legal equality and invited debates on the legalization of divorce and changes to paternity laws.[51] Nevertheless, the secretariat, limited as it was in its responsibilities, failed to break the division of gendered labor within the government. Instead, it merely reinforced the compartmentalizing of "women's issues" in a separate sphere.

Separate or not, in the eyes of male leaders, Chilean women remained an integral part of the revolution.[52] Allende made clear that "nobody could think of an emancipating, constructive revolution of a new society without the active presence of the woman, friend, sister, and comrade. [The revolution] depended on the woman who would assume responsibilities, next to the man, without inequalities, and in service of the great task they had in common." Allende's confident references to the equal participation of both men and women were, nonetheless, accompanied by allusions to the different characteristics that marked their participation. These differences seemed to originate from the natural, biological differences between women and men. Women would contribute by offering "their tenderness and strength," which were more deeply present in women because of their natural, maternal qualities. After all, it was "the mother who felt more closely the pain caused by the hunger of her child and by the suffering of [her family] caused by the injustices of a regime still marked by imperialist exploitation."[53] In this context, it seemed a woman's biological destiny led her not only to follow her man, but also to improve the lives of all children, not just her own. It was "the woman, who due to her biological imperative to perpetuate her species, [had to] incorporate herself more consciously, and more fervently . . . to the task of giving equal possibilities to all children."[54]

The Unidad Popular also employed the Mothers' Centers to win women's political support. The government built on the tradition of the centers that had brought women together under the previous administration by increasing participation and recasting their functions to reflect current political goals. By 1973, more than a half-million women had joined over ten thousand centers nationwide.[55] Labor minister Mireya Baltra announced that each center "should be a living organism, dedicated to the interests of the working class and the people; . . . it should be connected to the structural transformations that are taking place, coordinating with the appropriate government agencies." Baltra also expected the centers "to exert a watchful position in . . . the [government's] fight against inflation, speculation, and greed."[56] To improve the organization of women at the grassroots level, the centers were placed under a new administration, the Coordinadora de Centros de Madres (COCEMA, Coordinating Office of Mothers' Centers) in 1971. Under the auspices of the First Lady, Hortensia Bussi de Allende, COCEMA coordinated government policies and local-level activities. Still, the women in the Mothers' Centers continued to involve themselves in national political life for their own reasons.

In 1971, the members of a Mothers' Center in the *campamento* Siete Canchas on the outskirts of Santiago presented a play depicting moments of everyday life, showing experiences familiar to actors and audience alike. In the play, a husband takes the freedom to go out and return home late at night, without any consideration for the needs and desires of his wife. He claims the right to limit her freedoms and had earlier prohibited her from attending the meetings at the Mothers' Center "because there, all women did was gossip" and she would neglect her work at home.[57] The play itself, its subject matter, and its direction by women at a Mothers' Center illustrate that some women took independent, creative approaches to the centers' official goals. The guidelines of the Mothers' Centers encouraged women to "find solutions to the problems inherent to their status and their sex"—and the play did just that.[58]

The Unidad Popular's promotion of Mothers' Centers aimed to push women's participation beyond the limits of traditional women's tasks. Even though center guidelines emphasized the importance of both collective responsibility and community work, members also engaged in cultural activities that encouraged personal growth.[59] Elcira Navarro, president of the leaders of Mothers' Centers in the Cisterna municipality, addressed three hundred mothers at a meeting and made clear that women had grown tired of the stereotypes linking them to gossip and petty competitions. She said: "We want to get rid of the image that we get together in the Mothers' Center to knit and quarrel. Enough already. We want to participate in cultural activities, and learn new things. [We want to] know what's going on in the world, in other countries where there are women just like us. We want to learn all that was denied us until now."[60] Ester Veldebenito, presiding over the Mothers' Centers of Santiago's First District, confirmed that women not only desired change but had already taken matters into their own hands by beginning "to participate with enthusiasm in a wide range of activities." The activities Veldebenito mentioned to prove her point included women's discussions of health issues, initiatives to control food prices, and communal lunches to improve the local diet that was often restricted due to families' limited financial resources.[61]

In June 1973, the journal *Paula* published a report on Mothers' Centers as well as interviews with members, concluding that women who had left their homes now "wanted more." A woman, so the consensus among interviewees went, "was no longer exclusively connected to the home, and . . . her intelligence and talent could be of value outside the four walls of her house."[62] Ana, for example, remembered how in the first meetings of her Mothers' Center, she chose to sit in the back of the room, too intimidated to speak. She had seen her fellow participants in the neighborhood, among them the greengrocer and a woman who ran a local store. After only a few meetings, Ana claimed, all the participants became friends, openly sharing problems and discussing solutions. She soon realized that she had found a voice to speak to fellow members and "that her housework took too much of her time."[63] Ana's Mothers' Center had, at last, provided her with a valuable space to share her experiences. *Paula*'s report on Mothers' Centers indicated in no uncertain terms that the female members had entered a new phase in their lives. They were now involved in a world beyond the walls of their own homes and the Mothers' Centers as well.

The nature of women's political participation would change significantly throughout the three years of Allende's rule, as their involvement reached beyond their poor neighborhoods and Mothers' Centers. Women made clear that they were prepared to defend their own political goals, sometimes transgressing the government's narrow understanding of the notion of *poder popular* (popular power). For it was evident that when the Unidad Popular leadership envisioned the construction of a revolutionary culture, it merely alluded to the creation of the "new man" in support of the Peaceful Road to Socialism. Having identified economic dependency and U.S. imperialism as major obstacles to Chilean development, and having nationalized key businesses like the copper industry to end foreign control over national resources and production, leaders also created a national revolutionary culture.[64] Writers and singers called for Chile's cultural independence and the birth of the "new man" who would drive the revolution on the road to its ultimate success.[65] But those who promoted the new culture reproduced old gendered patterns. They failed to include, even imagine, "new man's" counterpart: new woman.

Roasting the Duck: National Hegemony and Revolutionary Culture

Whereas Donald Duck, particularly prominent in Chile through educational films like Disney's *Family Planning / Planificación Familiar*, had still enjoyed a widespread cultural presence in the 1960s, Chilean leaders of the 1970s read-dressed Disney's world from a new political position. In their attempt to abolish the emblems of cultural imperialism, political leaders prepared to "roast the Duck."[66] Disney's cartoons provided a suitable starting point for a critique, aptly launched by novelist, essayist, and human rights activist Ariel Dorfman and sociologist Armand Mattelart's 1971 instructions on *How to Read Donald Duck*.[67] The authors effectively question the innocence of the cartoon characters who present "global" values in seemingly timeless stories of winners and losers. The characters' dialogues and interactions displayed a world of race-, and class-based hierarchies that Allende and his supporters sought to reject. While Disney dispatched "civilizing" ducks to distant lands, Chilean producers created their own cartoons.[68] A new government publishing house, Quimantú, produced a number of limited-edition comic books with *La Firme* (Upfront) becoming the best known among them.[69] In addition, the importance of Chile's national culture was extended to other forms of artistic production, such as music.

New Chilean music, like the Nueva Canción Chilena, reached many corners counter-comics could not, spreading the sound of a genuinely Chilean revolutionary process. Artists, such as folk singer Victor Jara, were adored for their contribution to what became the *nueva canción* movement, a revival of traditional Latin American musical styles and effort to embrace indigenous cultures as part of Latin American identities.[70] Other musicians, like the bands Quilapayun and Inti-Illimani, drew audiences as they paid tribute to the histories of labor struggles in the mines and to exploited rural workers who resisted the traditional hierarchies that placed them at the mercy of the all-powerful *patrón*. Musicians protested through their songs against the economic and political injustices that had brought suffering and poverty to those people throughout Latin America and Chile who faced the harsh struggle for survival with every passing day. The themes of the *nueva canción* movement stayed the old, familiar ones of poverty and abuse. But because the movement encouraged people to listen collectively and to embark on a course of revolutionary change, it was fresh, innovative, and inspiring.

In 1970, Inti Illimani launched an album called Canto al Programa (Song of the program), which put into melody the Unidad Popular's political platform. Its songs were introduced by Peyuco Pueblo, a representative of the Chilean people who, as he told in the tale he shared with listeners, was as much at home in the city as he was in the countryside, on the coast, and in the mines. Peyuco Pueblo first introduced the "Song of Popular Power," which gave voice to the belief that it was "the people who would construct a different Chile," that the people "now were the government" because of their political activism. Other songs included "El vals de la profundización de la democracia" (The waltz of the deepening of democracy), "Canción de la reforma agraria" (The song of agrarian reform), "Tonada y sajuriana de las tareas sociales" (Tune of social tasks), and, of course, the "Canción de la nueva cultura" (Song of the new culture). Inti Illimani's album and the New Song movement strengthened the sense of community among those who supported the Peaceful Road to Socialism in the nation.[71] Contrary to the culture of competitive capitalism, the songs praised collective mobilization for collective needs, instead of praising individual, often material success.

The new icons of revolutionary culture often reproduced the image of women as passive and domestic, however, or they did not mention women at all.[72] Even the popular "Venceremos" (We will triumph), recorded as part of the Canto al Programa, added women only as an afterthought to the glorification of the "male peasants, soldiers, and miners," even though all the people— including the women—were expected to dedicate their work to the success of the revolution.[73] Songs that paid lip service to female workers as they walked behind the men on the path to revolution and counter-comics that challenged the "foreign" cartoon heroes they accused of imperialist ambitions in fact continued to attract audiences through gendered images of strong masculine heroes and weak dependent women. In his study of *La Firme,* the art historian David Kunzle has shown that sexual imperialism was tolerated as a peripheral by-product of the "real" and relevant critique of political and economic domination.[74] *La Firme* presented women, more often than men, who failed to see the proper revolutionary path, for female revolutionaries were often slow to grasp the meanings of anti-imperialist policies. About forty issues of *La Firme* were dedicated to specific topics regarding exploitation. Yet none addressed the particularities of the exploitation of women.[75]

Many cultural productions of the left reproduced the image of women as sex objects. They tempted readers with female nudity, or dressed women as objects of desire in short skirts that showed long legs and in tight sweaters that emphasized large breasts. In 1972, the women's magazine of the Communist Youth, *Ramona,* used a picture of a naked woman wrapped in the Chilean flag to promote what it called the "decisive year of the woman."[76] *Ramona* and *La Firme* steadfastly defended Allende's policies; simultaneously, they replicated the old gendered hierarchies that accompanied the new revolutionary culture.

Foreigners who came to Santiago in support of the Peaceful Road to Socialism, like North American feminist Carol Andreas, noticed the persistence of gendered hierarchies also within the culture of communal living that brought together Chileans and an international group of activists in residences throughout Santiago.[77] While Andreas fought battles over housework, she also wrote and published examples of cultural expressions that exposed class-based oppression but left her "with a powerful revulsion at [their] . . . heavy machismo" that was left painfully unaddressed. Andreas described how revolutionary theater conveyed this tension. One director, for example, adapted a play by Chilean playwright Eric Wolff to the new conditions the Peaceful Road to Socialism had produced. This director had retold a story in which a wealthy businessman had a very personal nightmare of a *toma* (a land takeover). Andreas recounts that whereas Wolff had written the play with a Christian Democratic "bent" and therefore as a "creative encounter between [a] bourgeois family and [a] *lumpen* pair" in which a poor, uprooted couple attempts to take over the businessman's household and engages him in dialogue, the new version depicted the encounter as a prelude to class struggle.

In the businessman's dream, the poor couple, seizing his household, engages him in conversation and slowly but surely breaks "down his bourgeois defenses." The businessman's wife, offended by the *lumpen* pair's crudity, feels compelled to walk out on her husband. The businessman's children, initially toying with the benefits of revolution, suddenly realize that a changed reality could force them to have to work for a living. They quickly follow their mother. It now dawns on the abandoned head of the family that he has been cheated out of his wealth and his family and that he must "arm himself to defend his home and business against the invaders." Although the depiction of the wealthy couple spoke for itself, Andreas remembered that the relationship between the poor couple reflected a gender bias that was left unaddressed.[78] Portrayed as a dependent and downtrodden female, the poor woman utters not one word of protest or rebellion to evoke a critique of her oppressed condition. These cultural expressions showed no prelude of a gender or sexual revolution. And alternative "revolutionary" education in other spheres was often accompanied by new restrictions.

Negotiating Political Priorities and Fresh Politics of Gender, Health, and Sexuality

On March 28, 1972, Chileans were invited to attend the opening of an exhibit, *El cuerpo humano* (The human body), in Santiago. Chile was the first South American country to display the precious pieces brought in from the Dupuytren Museum in Paris. On the first two floors, the exposition presented the latest wonders of technology, among them a robot programmed to answer questions in the fields of biology and medicine. On the third floor, a wax cabinet of life-sized human bodies conveyed themes related to human reproduction. As the daily press reported, the bodies appeared "more real than reality."[79] Visitors could enter the Hall of Sexology, where human development was displayed from conception to birth to the physical development of bodies in different stages of life. Spectators were particularly impressed by a performance of "almost live-childbirths," which took place right before their eyes. Children under the age of twelve could not attend and those under the age of sixteen were admitted only with parental permission. Anticipating the possible shock reactions of the audience, organizers set up a room to administer first aid to all those who might become completely overwhelmed by the mysteries of human life.[80] Organized under the auspices of the Ministry of Education, the exhibit's daring themes offered a taste of the innovative spirit of the new administration, which continued to promote more open discussions on sexuality, reproduction, and motherhood first endorsed by the Christian Democrats.

John Bogolawski, head of the museum's council in Santiago, insisted that Chile largely owed the privilege of displaying the much sought-after collection to the fact that Allende, a physician who had "always been preoccupied with the education and the health of [the] people," was now president.[81] Indeed, with Allende's election, *New York Times* reporter Juan de Onis recalled how Allende had provided a critique of capitalist society as a medical student and that his book *La realidad médico-social chilena* had proposed a revolutionary response to the country's social and economic ills as early as 1939.[82] Most members of the Unidad Popular government shared the optimistic assessment of Allende's influence as a president and as a physician. In 1970, health minister Oscar Jiménez suggested that President Allende's professional training would not only increase the attention given to public health, but also ensure that access to health care would be treated as a right, for "it was the obligation of the State to provide [health care] . . . in an egalitarian, wide-ranging, and efficient way to all Chileans."[83]

As president, Allende continued to believe that health care represented a basic human right. He promised to reorganize public health in conjunction with his administration's reorganizing the capitalist system.[84] In the medical journal *Vida médica* he reiterated that "socialist medicine could not exist in a capitalist system and [that until now] Chilean medicine had been merely a public system with all the troubles that such an organism entails."[85] He built on the changes Frei had initiated, which had created community health councils with an advisory function.[86] Under the UP government, the reorganization of public health care reflected a policy approach aimed at strengthening popular participation and popular power.[87] It reorganized the structure of health-care services and encouraged the input of nonprofessionals and volunteers in neighborhood health councils to increase community involvement in health decisions. Local community involvement meant leadership training and health education of specific local health monitors, who supervised preventive health measures and raised the level of health education among their communities.[88] This arrangement was based on the assumption that local residents were best prepared to address local needs.[89]

The Unidad Popular government also picked up on earlier calls for sex education, especially at the 1967 IPPF Conference in Santiago. Allende challenged fellow Chileans to admit that the need for sex education was not yet openly addressed, and he encouraged them to consider the benefits of speaking "about [human] biology and about human couples."[90] In short, the government promoted the role of the people at the grassroots level to participate in decisions regarding their own health and to help expand the understanding of public health in a framework that included sexuality. It suggested that collectively Chileans could improve the nation's health, stimulate better social organization and social participation in health-care services, and identify major and minor challenges to the health of the body politic.

Inspired by the signs of a new openness regarding health issues, the popular women's journal *Paula* surprised readers with an invitation to join in a debate on the legalization of abortion in Chile. The responses not only reflected a diversity of views on the topic, but also served as harsh reminders of the lasting problem of maternal mortality and induced abortion in the country. Between 1970 and 1972, medical professionals, legislators, and the general public were invited to articulate their positions. *Paula* published statements by doctors Onofre Avendaño and Tegualda Monreal, by such politicians as Gladys Marin, the deputy of the Communist Party, and Wilna Saavedra, the Christian Democratic deputy, as well as by the Jesuit priest Renato Poblete. Not surprisingly, the range of views expressed was wide and varied. As a physician, Monreal had seen too many women die and expressed the simple fact that "with the legalization of abortion the rates of maternal mortality will decline." Poblete rejected the legalization of abortion without restrictions but defended "responsible parenthood" and contraception. Readers sent letters from all over the nation. Their contributions ranged from personal experiences with dangerous abortions to the outright rejection of abortion as a crime against human life.[91]

The debate was fueled by action at the highest levels: Héctor Campos, vice president of the Cámara de Diputados (Chamber of Deputies) prepared an unsuccessful legal proposition that aimed to end the criminalization of all abortions. Even President Allende commented on the topic of abortion in 1971, declaring the need for an "eventual legislation of abortion . . . and more immediately . . . an extension of the indications for therapeutic abortion, as in the cases of contraceptive failure, for example."[92] In the end, other pressing matters of economic and political reorganization, threatening the very survival of the government, occupied politicians and legislators, and no official legal changes on abortion were initiated. The public polemics in the journal stopped in 1972; the threats to mothers' lives did not. On this basis, physicians continued, and temporarily expanded, programs to prevent abortions and save mothers' lives.

In 1971, doctors at the Barros Luco Hospital used this climate of openness and flexibility to implement changes that, in Monreal's words, "saved more women's lives than ever in the history of abortion and maternal mortality in Chile."[93] Long experienced in administering to the needs of women who came to public hospitals for emergency treatment after enduring botched abortions, physicians initiated a revolution on their own. For the first time, they *openly* provided counseling, abortions, and postabortion care for women who felt desperate to find help.[94] Monreal went on to explain how doctors did not break the law but extended the definition of therapeutic abortion to help pregnant women "without a new law, but with a new interpretation of the old law."[95] She noted that in 1972 and 1973 "maternal mortality declined in an extraordinary dimension," which convinced her that the program's success would have justified its expansion to other public hospitals—if it had not been interrupted by the military coup in September 1973.

Women's reactions to the project confirmed that the Barros Luco initiatives addressed their continuing needs. Dr. Anibal Faúndes, one of the physicians in charge, reported an unexpected surge in patients. Word of mouth traveled fast among women in poor communities as "women came not only from all over Santiago, but from all over the country. All attempts to verify their address were continuously foiled. Doctors knew that it was not difficult to obtain a certificate that 'proved' the patient lived at a given address."[96] Female patients told the physicians that they sought these services because the hospital offered conditions "more favorable than the clandestine hiding and the feeling of commercial exploitation of their problem in the hands of an abortionist whose primary orientation was financial and who many times was not technically competent."[97] Under the UP government, some women were fortunate enough to benefit from a greater leniency and services in matters of health.

Others, however, found themselves subjected to a new rigidity that adversely affected their lives. The openness on questions of women's health was accompanied by restrictions on women's rights with respect to their most intimate decisions. From women's perspective, state-led reproductive health programs took a turn for the worse in 1971, when health minister Oscar Jiménez openly challenged what he considered the imperialists' politics of birth control. He rejected family planning and population control, resenting the "false image of underdevelopment as a problem of overpopulation." In his view, Chile would profit from population growth, given that it would bring about an increase in consumers who would stimulate the economy. Jiménez charged physicians with having "inserted IUDs while women were anesthetized, violating their constitutional rights."[98] Jiménez seemed to understand the importance of preventive health measures and dutifully proclaimed that "to govern is to give health"; the Ministry of Health, nonetheless, officially condemned foreign-backed birth control programs as ideological agents spreading a message that economic development depended on population control.

This dismissal of family-planning programs as tools of foreign imperialism demonstrated how the requirements of the new ideology of national hegemony sometimes superseded women's needs. In an effort to control foreign funding of family-planning programs, the National Health Service officially integrated birth control programs into its Program of Women's Health, addressing contraception only as one among the many needs of women-mothers.[99] In an integrated program of maternal and child care, a health team of doctors, midwives, nurses, and social workers would address all the needs of every patient. Health officials were told to provide such services as prenatal care, delivery, and postpartum care just as they would instruct women on birth control. For physicians like Benjamín Viel, financial and technical assistance from the IPPF did not represent a threat to Chile's independence but rather resources Chileans could use to improve public health. For others, including doctors affiliated with the Ministry of Health, both IPPF support and APROFA's family-planning programs forced Chilean doctors to unduly prioritize family planning and to limit their care of patients who sought help in other matters.[100] In 1970, the National Health Service ended all previous agreements with family planners in Chile and stipulated that all birth control services had to be offered as part of the state-controlled program of the Maternal and Child Department.[101]

Dr. Gildo Zambra, leader of APROFA at the time, recalled the state of family planning under the UP and described a widespread sense of dismay. Like Viel, Zambra expressed consternation over not only the leadership's effort to monitor family planning but the restrictions imposed as a result of a new ideology in which it had suddenly become "elegant to be anti–North American." He recalled how doctors confronted unexpected difficulties when justifying birth control, as now they had to "negotiate between family planning for economic reasons without connecting to ideas of population control," now branded an imperialist tool of the United States. All health officials once affiliated with the IPPF were suddenly regarded with suspicion, considered unreliable for their ties to foreign agencies.[102]

For Zambra and others, the solution was obvious: they "had to change the language of birth control." Given that national hegemony was at the forefront of the leadership's agenda, policymakers could hardly reject the right of Chilean families to make autonomous decisions regarding their offspring. On that basis, APROFA developed a new discourse on "family rights," which emphasized that it was "important to allow families to decide about the number and spacing of their children."[103] To keep alive its community connections, APROFA also added a program to train "Leaders of Responsible Parenthood." Between September 1972 and December 1974, it offered 925 specialized training courses that prepared 22,702 community educators to supervise and to offer guidance regarding family-planning services nationwide. Seventy-two percent of the new educators were women.[104] Through the voice of community educators, APROFA not only distanced its campaigns from the accusation of "population control," but also secured continuity in women's access to birth control devices despite the controversies set in motion by the political leadership. Yet even as APROFA's family planners constructed survival strategies in a new political climate, Chileans were confronted with everyday challenges, including food shortages, limited access to basic consumer goods, and, as a result, growing unrest.

From New Beginnings to the Beginning of the End

Chilean women soon confronted challenges more immediate than this threat to their uninterrupted access to birth control: food shortages and the difficulty of feeding their families increased dramatically with rising social tensions. The first two years of the Peaceful Road to Socialism were characterized by a consolidation of the forces of the left under the hegemony of the Unidad Popular and by a number of changes that improved people's lives. In the first year of UP leadership, wages increased faster than prices, and basic consumer goods were subject to price controls and remained affordable. Poor households had milk, bread, and other staples that contributed to a newly improved diet, with special subsidies for children and pregnant women.[105] But the sense of well-being and dignity did not last long.

Chileans experienced the different phases of the revolutionary process, which moved from initial optimism into a period of difficulties that ended in outright desperation and dismay. The government and the people felt the challenge of an ever-growing effort by the political right to consolidate its forces.

The Partido Nacional and the Christian Democrats formed a coalition, the Confederacion Democratica (CODE), hoping to win two-thirds of the seats in Congress in the March 1973 parliamentary elections, so that they would gain the required majority to begin impeachment proceedings against Allende.[106] The opposition controlled the large majority of newspapers and weekly journals and used its influence to enhance the growing insecurity. The media helped mobilize political constituencies and the citizenry, including women. "Apolitical" women's magazines like *Eva* politicized its content, even the recipe sections. French sociologist and Chilean resident Michele Mattelart showed how recipes called for hard-to-find ingredients in an attempt to persuade readers to yearn for the "good old days" before the Peaceful Road to Socialism took its course.[107] Destabilization efforts from abroad contributed to the rise of national unrest, moving the Peaceful Road to Socialism closer to its violent disintegration. Foreign sources underwrote two major strikes that undermined production and cut off the supply of essential goods: miners and truck owners on strike were supported financially by the United States. By 1973, the extreme polarization between the UP government's advocates and its opponents had begun to touch everyone's life.

Disagreements between the leadership and the grassroots levels accelerated the tension. Workers and the urban poor urged leaders to speed up policy changes and to redistribute at a faster pace than the government was prepared, or able, to do. As one women of a poor Santiago neighborhood put it, the people "knew and trusted the strength of the [revolutionary] project, but [they] also knew and trusted [their] own strength." Just as workers seized factories and control over production at a more rapid pace than planned by the government, Chileans at the grassroots level, recently encouraged to voice their needs, wanted immediate and substantial changes in their lives. Many accused political leaders of keeping an undue distance from the very poor they claimed to defend. According to some shantytown residents, the class struggle should have been allowed to take its course and "the government should rely on the workers, because it is they who offer their support and secure their office, preventing the *momias* [right-wing "mummies"] from overthrowing the government because they are afraid of us."[108]

The Unidad Popular tried to increase support from female constituents and asked for their patience and their loyalty. Official calls for women to be patient appeared early on—for example, when the leadership specifically summoned Chilean *women* to a meeting at Santiago's stadium on July 29, 1971.

Thousands showed up and listened to Pedro Vuskovic, the Minister of Economy, Development, and Reconstruction as he pleaded for their support.[109] He asked women to help calm the rising storm and, significantly, he addressed them as both mothers and citizens. It became apparent that leaders felt obligated to explain the crisis and promised to work on a solution that would benefit all Chileans. On multiple occasions, President Allende encouraged women's voluntary work in support of the revolution, inviting young women "who did not study and did not work" to help out in kindergartens and daycare centers.[110] He proposed women's obligatory service, suggesting it was really "not much to ask from the Chilean woman to give three or six months of her life . . . so that she could help support and defend what was most valuable for the future of the nation: the country's children."[111]

The president also pronounced his willingness to listen and learn from women-citizens and emboldened them to "criticize their government, . . . if it did not provide the necessary resources . . . required . . . by women and children."[112] He admitted his dependence on women's collaboration and insisted that a government had to be open to honest assessments made by adversaries and supporters alike.[113] These efforts elucidated the lasting conflict between addressing women as citizens and, at the same time, locating their political participation in the female sphere. Although some of Allende's supporters, men and women, were willing to take time enough to sort out how best to serve the revolution, the women who opposed Allende, heedless of his calls for patience, acted on their own. In the process, they challenged not only the government, but also the gendered terms of interaction between male leaders and female citizens. Thus they provoked new understandings of the roles and responsibilities of mothers and women.

Feminine Power and the Use of Motherhood in Defense of the Patriarchal Pact

On December 1, 1971, more than five thousand Chilean women stunned their fellow citizens in an extraordinary public display of political protest, later known as the March of Empty Pots and Pans. The women first met at Plaza Baquedano, a square at the center of Santiago that many Chileans considered a dividing line, both symbolic and real, between the wealthy and poor sectors of the city. The women who planned the event included representatives of political parties like the Christian Democrat and National parties as well as members of right-wing civic organizations like Patria y Libertad (Fatherland and Liberty). Organizers recruited participants through the networks of these organizations, but also through "unorthodox" strategies, such as their posting flyers in beauty salons.[114] Throughout the recruitment campaign, organizers emphasized the nonpartisan character of their initiative, claiming that women needed to put aside all differences and join forces to challenge, together, the government they said had caused the crisis. These women, from all different walks of life, joined together and participated in the march for various reasons: for example, to oppose President Allende, to protest the growing climate of violence, and to embarrass the government in front of Cuban leader Fidel Castro, who was in Chile for an extended visit.[115]

Elite women were a significant stimulus to inspire the march, yet compromise, cross-party alliances, and cross-class agreements conditioned it. No clear dividing lines separated the protesters. Elite and working-class women had decided that the intolerable shortcomings of Allende's Peaceful Road to Socialism required an active, collective response.[116] Marching through busy downtown areas, they made their objections seen and heard by shouting anti-government slogans and by banging empty pots and pans purchased especially for the occasion. Pounding household tools not only provided the desired sound effect, but it also delivered the message that food shortages and women's concern for their families had motivated their call for military intervention to replace the incumbent government. These sounds raised above urban Santiago's habitual background noise. This and the presence of large numbers of women on the streets of Santiago produced positively provocative effects.[117]

Reactions to the march were manifold. The musical group Quilapayun promptly composed a song that condemned the marching women. This song described "Las Ollitas"(Little pots). It accused right-wing women of "having two pots, a little one and a big one": "the little [pot] was just bought, and used only for banging on," while the "ugly old protester" had kept at home "the big [pot] filled with chicken, potatoes, and meat."[118] But the anti-Allende women's March of Empty Pots and Pans had consequences far beyond the scope of protest songs. Santiago was not the only city to experience the angry din of pots and pans: a similar march was staged three days later in the port city of Valparaíso, while other protests were reported in Rancuagua, south of Santiago.[119] Most important, organizers and participants provoked a revision of the gendered understandings of citizenship rights and notions of women's political participation. Images of thousands of women marching through the streets of Santiago abruptly shattered conventional visions of "secluded" motherhood and domesticity, as imagined by tradition-bound city residents. The march, moreover, initiated a lasting "border-crossing," in which the protesters removed old boundaries that had prevented women's active political participation in earlier decades.

The public reactions to the march, as well as the silences, offer revealing insights into the force of militant motherhood. In the context of traditional gender responsibilities in Chilean society, it was surprising that nobody condemned the women's active involvement as "maternal transgressions." Instead, both left- and right-wing political leaders worked hard to question the autonomy of the women's decision to march against Allende. Leaders of the right made every effort to use the event for their anti-Allende campaign by describing the "superior feminine virtue" of the women "who had seen through the lies of those who wanted to impose a Marxist dictatorship."[120] Leaders of the left, supporting Allende, singled out the working-class mobilizing mothers, describing them as "ignorant, tradition-bound" and "so lulled by deceitful enemies as to ignore their own true class interests."[121] Accordingly, they had become victims of right-wing propaganda campaigns, puppets without their own cause. These critics from both sides of the political spectrum articulated their assessments with a thunderous silence on the challenge such a display presented to understandings of the apolitical woman prevalent at the time. It also pointed to the limits such gender norms had in practice: in times of shortages that threatened the well-being of their families, many women were prepared to break this silence on their own.

Some women, like Communist Party member and UP volunteer Ana Maria, joined the opposition with great reluctance and protested only when the struggle for survival became unbearable. She recalled: "We were exhausted, I mean really wiped out. . . . We were at the end of our rope. . . . You could feel it in the lines for cigarettes and in the bread lines. By then there was no more bread. The people were saying, 'All right, bring on civil war, but at least let us have bread.'"[122] Others considered the outbreaks of violence and the insults they suffered during the March of Empty Pots and Pans as confirmation that protest indeed was the right choice at the time: 150 women from a poor Santiago neighborhood signed an open letter to Allende, affirming that they were "women of the people who have a clear understanding of morality" and were therefore wrongly insulted on the March.[123] After all, they saw it as their mission to reestablish order in the nation for the sake of their families. Some women, like

Ana Maria, did not have children at the time, but witnessed what drove women—as mothers—to join protest marches and fight for change.

For the first time, women from all sectors of society used motherhood and family welfare as principal forces driving them to mobilize in public protest against the incumbent leadership. Women, deemed apolitical members of a civil society, discovered that they could step into the political arena without direct intervention or opposition. They rallied to defend their rights as wives and mothers, rights which traditional gender systems assured them in theory, but which current economic and political realities denied them in practice. Overtly and angrily opposed to Allende's government, they demanded the right to care for their families. As mothers, they experienced the hardships brought about by food shortages and, with it, the helplessness of not being about to fulfill their familial obligations.[124] Anti-Allende women evoked traditional understandings of gendered responsibilities to enter the political arena—and came to stay. Some organizers of the March of Empty Pots and Pans helped create a new organization, Poder Feminino (Feminine Power). They aimed to coordinate the activities of multiple groups of anti-Allende women and recruited members by relying on tradition.[125] Some women were drawn to Feminine Power by its rejection of feminism and by the official allegiance of its members to their obligations as wives and mothers. Others joined because of its non-partisan character. All claimed to be on a mission to save the country from communism—and to save their families along the way.[126]

Women, as part of anti-Allende organizations or as individual opponents to the government, also used traditional understandings of gendered responsibilities to challenge masculinity. Relying on gendered rhetoric and sexist slurs, they often insulted the men who refused to support their cause. Women protesters, including military wives, not only openly challenged the military's ability to do its job, but also questioned the "proper" masculinity of those in the military by calling them *maricones* (fags) in public.[127] On multiple occasions, women went to Santiago's Military Academy and threw grain at the soldiers, thereby "treating them like hens," scolding them for their lack of virility and their supposed weakness for tolerating Allende's government.[128] Other women sent envelopes full of feathers to the soldiers to provoke a military coup.[129] Within Chile's traditional gender system, especially its emphasis on machismo, such insults certainly provoked many.

Before its violent end, the Chilean path to socialism continued to be accompanied by the political engagement of women on both sides of the political spectrum. Female workers, just like their male comrades, seized factories and took it upon themselves to accelerate production. Female protesters held demonstrations throughout the nation even before the massive march of militant mothers with empty pots and pans openly challenged the image of female domesticity. After the 1972 congressional elections, women marched in support of Allende with white doves, symbols of peace, and with banners urging citizens to say "No to civil war" (No a la guerra civil). Anti-Allende women appeared with banners declaring that they were "Combative Women prepared to give it all for Life" (Las mujeres combativas, nos jugamos por la vida).[130] In early September 1973, militant pro-Allende women staged a massive demonstration at the downtown Plaza de la Constitución to protest an anti-Allende women's demonstration at nearby Alameda. "We want to send a message to the women on Alameda," proclaimed one of the pro-Allende women in an interview with the newspaper *Las notiticas.* "If they don't like our [revolutionary] process, they should leave."[131] Many demonstrators did not want an outright civil war, yet neither side prevented the coming military takeover.

In the aftermath of the 1973 military coup, the anti-Allende women reminded fellow Chileans that "if it hadn't been for El Poder Femenino and its allies, the Unidad Popular would probably still be in power today pushing Chile toward Marxism."[132] Anti-Allende women were just one among multiple forces that fatally ended Chile's revolutionary experiment. Nonetheless, they had clearly left a mark, moving columnist David Belnap of the *Los Angeles Times* to remark that "the hand that rocks the cradle rocked the ship of state of Chile's late Marxist President Salvador Allende until it overturned and sank."[133]

From the Peaceful Road to Socialism to the Violence of Dictatorship

Anti-Allende women helped assure the military that it could count on support from within civil society when mobilizing to stop the revolutionary government on its Peaceful Road. The moment came on September 11, 1973, as the Chilean armed forces attacked the presidential palace in the center of Santiago. Within a few hours, President Allende was dead, the palace was in flames, and leading members of the Unidad Popular government were in prison or in hiding. Military tanks and helicopters continued to assault the residents of Santiago's poor neighborhoods, forcing tens of thousands of Chileans from their homes. In the months following the coup, more than a hundred thousand civilians were detained. Many were brutally tortured, executed, or "disappeared." Initiating the nation's economic and political transformation, the Chilean military regime relied on systematic repression to eliminate the left.

In a 2003 homage to Salvador Allende, Marta Harnecker, at the time involved in the mission of public education, published her detailed account of the phases of the Peaceful Road to Socialism and the counterrevolution that led to the defeat of "the struggle of an unarmed people." Her work, which originally was meant to accompany Patricio Guzman's documentary *The Battle of Chile,* reflects the difficulties that Chileans confronted on their Peaceful Road to Socialism. Both women and men, in support of Allende and his mission, tried to keep up economic production even as resources became scarce. They marched in the streets of Santiago, competing with the opposition's demonstrations in a city that became nothing less than a battlefield for change. And just as the political leaders at the time failed to address women's roles, so too does Harnecker's careful documentation of the people's struggle fail to mention the role of women-citizens.[134] Other participants have asserted that in retrospect, from women's perspective, the experience under the UP had varied results.

In 1999, feminist sociologist Teresa Valdés, a college student and active Allende supporter at the time, assessed the impact UP policies had on women with a tone of nuanced optimism. She asserts that "there was an extraordinary increase in women's participation. When you look at all the mothers' centers, [and at] the groups that controlled food supply and prices . . . women participated a lot more than they had before. . . . And there were an impressive number of women in leadership and women doing volunteer work."[135] No doubt, women did participate in politics. But Valdés also admits that "there was no real gender consciousness."[136] Male policymakers did not address gender as a category of revolutionary change—and women, as mothers and citizens, often remained in a separate political sphere when unity, not separation, was needed to initiate change. In their attempt to create a Peaceful Road to Socialism, male leaders saw women's bodies as a natural part of the revolutionary body politic. Their persistent reproduction of patriarchal relations also reproduced gender-based hierarchies in men's and women's access to citizenship rights.

Nonetheless, women's mobilization implied a break with the past. The militant mothers demonstrated that women could seize interpretive power and claim new citizenship rights despite the perspective of male public voices and their attempts to squash the autonomous political decision on the part of women to march for a cause. A society that had long defined motherhood and women's family roles as fundamental expressions of womanhood began to engage in a process of transforming women's identity from private to public. Leaving behind the role of *apolitical* mothers, women were on their way to becoming citizens with new rights and obligations. Conservative women contributed to the end of the Peaceful Road to Socialism and to the rise of the infamous military regime (1973–1989) led by General Augusto Pinochet. Yet regardless of their conservative political convictions and their goal to defend gendered traditions, they paved the way for the militant mothers of the future.

|| 5 ||

FROM MOTHERS' RIGHTS
TO WOMEN'S RIGHTS
IN A NATION
UNDER SIEGE

We reconstructed the story of what had been invisible and we proposed to break with the private; we were very brave: heretics by
dint of shamelessly, openly turning everything around; . . . we discovered, discovered with passion, laughter, tough fights, difficult
reflections, we kept going, we opened the Circle [of Women's Stud-
ies], the House [of the Woman, called "La Morada," the Dwelling],
we opened books, even the Lila Women's Bookstore; we were
crazily daring, I can see it now.

Julieta Kirkwood, Chilean feminist, 1983

IN JANUARY 1974, the French newspaper *Le monde* published a story on Santiago's *campamento* New Havana. Its residents had been the best organized and
most combative *pobladores* during Allende's term as president (1970–1973). In
the course of only three years, they had constrained illegal alcohol sales and
prostitution while at the same time their own defense front had prevented in-
trusion by outsiders, including the national police forces. New Havana residents
had built their own health center and had provided education for their children
in discarded school buses.[1] Now *Le monde* reported that their concerted efforts
to create new lives in the city were destroyed by a single painful blow. After the
coup of September 11, 1973, violence and terror became the order of the day.
A junta, led by General Augusto Pinochet, seized control of everyday life in
New Havana and throughout Chile.

Hilda, at home in New Havana, recalled the fear that overcame her neighbors on that day. They had called an emergency meeting. But when the junta imposed a curfew, such public gatherings became risky and nearly impossible. The people who left their homes despite the prohibition could see military vans as they heard shots and screams. Hilda's descriptions were reminiscent of a battlefield report.[2] Systematic military raids interrupted people's lives, and many in New Havana disappeared. Hilda's experiences paralleled those of others throughout the city. A woman from the shantytown La Victoria, for example, testified: "[E]very day new bodies arrived, nude and headless. They floated in the river. . . . We cried, please no more. They took my husband on the twelfth [of September, the day after the coup]. A police patrol arrived. . . . The wife of my older son was six months pregnant. She was disappeared . . . we learned that anything was possible."[3]

In the days that followed, the regime employed curfews, violence, and censorship to control the lives of women and men. The military spoke in gendered terms as it addressed the responsibilities of Chilean women and men. The new First Lady, Lucía Hiriart de Pinochet, encouraged women to excel in their "inborn" responsibilities and expected them "to serve others" in "self-surrender."[4] Her references to women's roles reflected the leadership's emphasis on the naturalized gendered responsibilities of women as mothers and wives. But in the course of almost two decades of dictatorship, many women found ways to continue to protest and resist, despite the brutality they had to confront. They eventually emerged as leaders of a movement that ended Pinochet's rule. In the words of Chilean feminist Julieta Kirkwood, women "were very brave: heretics by dint of shamelessly, openly turning everything around."[5]

How did these "subversive mothers" mobilize under the dictatorship?[6] When women, as mothers and family members, protested against the regime, their goals differed sharply from the anti-Allende women who had earlier demanded military intervention. Different groups of women contributed to the end of military rule and created a new understanding of citizenship rights. Chilean feminists participated in a range of national and international feminist networks. A remarkable trajectory of a new rights discourse and women's rights practice in Chile shows how middle-class women's feminist organizations and women's groups in Santiago's poor neighborhoods transformed motherhood as a political tool that enabled women to engage politics as *women*—and not mothers—first.

Women with diverse ties to feminism and from different class backgrounds contributed to this novel construction of rights, bringing a wide range of experiences to women's movements under dictatorship. A small number of foundational organizations representing middle-class and popular feminists formed, ranging from one of the earliest feminist organizations, the Women's Studies Circle (Círculo de Estudios de la Mujer), to the most influential groups of *pobladoras*, like the Committee for the Defense of Women's Rights (Comité de Defensa de los Derechos de la Mujer, CODEM) and the Movement of Shantytown Women (Movimiento de Mujeres Pobladoras, MOMUPO).[7] The experiences of these groups helps trace the steps women took to overcome the challenges of living in a society that traditionally had only addressed women in the context of their families. Diverse women's groups found unexpected spaces to reconfigure the sex-gender system that restricted women's rights. But their story also reveals new challenges that would constrain women's reproductive rights: a redemocratizing Chile would inherit a lasting legacy of women's rights violations from the military regime.

Women's movements and their defense of rights under the dictatorship elicited unexpected debates on gender and sexuality. These debates contested the uncompromising, top-down traditional model of gender relations that the military aimed to impose. Just how rigid was the gendered legislation under military governments? The liberalization of women's rights that scholars have found under some authoritarian regimes was limited at best in Chile. In a recent comparative study on legal reforms in Argentina, Brazil, and Chile, the political scientist Mala Htun has argued that laws on gender and the family were liberalized at surprising moments: they often took shape under dictatorships, when legislators and feminists grew more concerned about "modernizing" gender relations and women's rights than they did in democracies.[8] Expert policymaking commissions appointed by military governments modernized, for example, by improving the legal rights of married women, most effectively in Argentina and Brazil. In Chile, the Pinochet dictatorship formed expert commissions as well, but laws remained restrictive, defending a social conservatism that starkly contrasted with the regime's support of economic modernization.

Even though Chile did not follow other regimes' patterns of modernization through the legal liberalization of women's rights, the same modernizing interests helped create "liberal" spaces elsewhere. On the one hand, the dictatorship supported a pro-natalist doctrine and set more restrictive limits on women's engagement beyond the domestic sphere. On the other hand, it tolerated the discussion of gender and sexuality in surprising venues, and to a remarkable degree, in an effort to stay on a modern path toward development.[9]

High maternal mortality rates due to induced abortions and an increase in teenage pregnancies were indicators of underdevelopment and of a failed path to modernity—both of which the military wanted to avoid. Rigid censorship and attempts to control women characterized the deeply conservative nature of dictatorship. Yet the dictatorship's core values also featured a powerful commitment to modernize the nation. Consequently, a growing tolerance of liberalized spaces for debates on sexuality and family planning was inescapable even under the dictates of a military regime.

The Rise of State Terror

Life in Chile changed dramatically under the military. Initially, the four-man junta that had led the coup governed the nation. By 1974, General Augusto Pinochet had seized power and forged a personal dictatorship. The military ordered executions and disappearances to assert its control over civil society after the coup. A former agent of the security forces testified that "the first cadavers began to arrive at the clandestine cemetery in November of 1973, a few months after the military coup. The first executed prisoners were from the National Stadium. In the early hours of the morning the army's . . . trucks would transfer their loads, covered with canvas, to the military installations in San Bernardo. . . . At first, due to the quantity of dead that were arriving, the graves were one meter deep. Later they gave orders that the graves be at least four meters deep."[10] Although leftist politicians and civilians were the first victims of arrests, torture, and executions, state terror soon affected all members of society.[11] An estimated two hundred thousand Chileans sought exile in countries of the Americas or in Europe to escape military control.[12]

The authoritarian regime also imposed a new economic vision, reversing the nationalization of industries and ending land reforms. Its economic doctrine was guided by the "Chicago Boys," University of Chicago economists, who promoted a neoliberal vision of capitalism without price controls and regulations, accompanied by cuts of government expenditures in social spending. Wages were frozen, and a new labor code crippled unions already weakened through military repression. This neoliberal "shock treatment" aimed to increase productivity and Chile's ability to compete in global markets. It also contributed to a financial crisis in the early 1980s, which eased only by the end of the decade.

Some Chileans did profit from renewed prosperity in the late 1980s, but the benefits of this "economic miracle" did not trickle down to the poor. The earlier economic crisis had also coincided with increased protest against human rights abuses. When the voices of the opposition within Chile were accompanied by increased pressure from a global human rights movement, Pinochet, still confident, gambled his power against the weakness of his detractors. Counting on the support of elite and middle sectors, he scheduled a plebiscite in 1988. Chileans could vote "Sí," which would grant Pinochet another term, or "No," which would compel him to schedule elections. A majority of Chileans voted "No," and the plebiscite thus removed Pinochet from office. Military rulers subsequently began transferring power to civilian politicians. The 1989 presidential elections marked the beginning of a new chapter in the nation's history of democracy.[13]

Controlling the Woman Citizen

Sociologist Maria Elena Valenzuela has eloquently described the politics of the military regime as the quintessential expression of patriarchy: "The Junta, with a very clear sense of its interests, has understood that it must reinforce the traditional family, and the dependent role of women, which is reduced to that of mother. The dictatorship, which institutionalizes social inequality, is founded on inequality in the family."[14] The regime also emphasized sexual differences that "naturally" placed men and women in different spheres. Its efforts to control women, reassigned to the domesticity of house and home, were enhanced in institutionalized, gender-segregated communities controlled by supporters of the regime. The surveillance of women by women in new Mothers' Centers and by the Women's Secretariat helped assert gendered doctrines, temporarily.

The military placed public rhetoric on the family and gendered responsibilities center stage—and it created the notion of natural, transhistorical characteristics of family life in service of the nation. First Lady Lucía Hiriart de Pinochet proclaimed that "the family is the basic unit of society. It is the first school . . . , the mold in which the moral character of each citizen is formed, [so that] the Nation is truly the reflection of the hearth."[15] Governmental institutions, like the Women's Secretariat, further strengthened the connection between "patriotic values and family values" and the fixed, unchanging notion of family. Its newsletter asserted that "in its basic trait—the emotional, spiritual, and human bond between the couple and the children—the family has existed always. This proves that the family is an institution based on natural law. In other words, it [the family] corresponds to human nature itself, and is not an invention of specific eras or cultures."[16] Relying on the explanatory power of nature itself, the military dissuaded citizens from questioning not only the natural role of the family, but also the natural role of women.

As part of the natural family, the military expected women and men to take their proper place in the task of "national reconstruction," but it was a new generic natural woman who gained exceptional praise for defending her home against the threat of communism. In the words of Pinochet, "the woman wanted the fall of the Marxist government . . . and sought the protection of a strong and harsh authority to reestablish . . . the order and public morale." Pinochet went on to explain that "in her feminine instinct, [the woman] could clearly tell that what was defined in those dramatic days [of the military coup] was not simply a game of political parties, but the survival or death of a nation." With this he clarified that the woman's anti-Marxist position came not from her understanding of political and economic circumstances, but rather it was informed by her natural instincts.[17] Motherhood remained women's primordial task, and their dignity depended on their accepting this reality, their "superior destiny and . . . vocation to be . . . mother[s]."[18] Generous and abnegating, women, as mothers of the nation, had to collaborate with the government and provide support even if it meant personal sacrifice. Pinochet, in the image of the nation's father, relied on the cooperation and self-sacrifice of patriotic mothers.[19]

Confined to the domestic sphere and, in the eyes of the military, reduced to passive spectators of political and social change, women encountered a rigid routine in restructured Mothers' Centers. Military leaders rewrote the centers' guidelines in the immediate aftermath of the coup and privatized the organization as a foundation with new statutes in 1974, the *Fundación Graciela Letelier de Ibañez, CEMA-Chile*.[20] First Lady Lucía Hiriart de Pinochet presided over the new hierarchy, and more than five thousand select volunteers, often officers' wives or conservative, civilian women, coordinated joint activities or meetings in individual Mothers' Centers. CEMA-Chile had a Division for Social Assistance that offered health services and provided "bare necessaries at a low cost." It had a Division for Labor, instructing women to "work at home, increasing their incomes and not neglecting their duties as housewives." And it also had a Division for Training that counted on the "woman-volunteer" to supervise CEMA activities and instruct members in basic skills. Paid instructors offered additional instruction in classes ranging from cooking and sewing to fashion and cosmetics.[21] The new guidelines asserted "the members of mothers' centers would never again be mere objects of political maneuvering as they had been in the past."[22] Just as the guidelines "promised" the absence of political maneuvering, they also instructed women to refrain from political participation.

Domesticating and controlling apolitical women in service to the fatherland became the dominant theme of CEMA-Chile's activities. The First Lady announced that "with CEMA-Chile, we can be in permanent contact with all women in the centers,"[23] and the army's lieutenant general, Julio Canessa Robert, praised "the organization of the Chilean woman in apolitical groups nationwide."[24] Both confirmed that CEMA-Chile would redirect the mission of Mothers' Centers away from the politics of popular participation encouraged by previous governments and toward a new controlled mission for the nation. CEMA-Chile allowed the leadership to account for women's activities and their lives. Early on, CEMA's new leaders purged their ranks. They erased from the membership lists all of those women with a history of political participation or those considered "dissidents" for other reasons. After these purges, the centers became part of the "national reconstruction" agenda that relied on female role models who engaged in their "natural" duties.[25]

Women in CEMA's communities reacted with desperation or alarm as the First Lady and CEMA volunteers not only controlled their movement and convictions but even prevented their membership in organizations other than those controlled by the military.[26] Some members lamented the destructive effect the military's top-down control had on the sense of community that used to shape women's relations in Mothers' Centers. Raquel, for example, remembered her mother's pain and outrage when conservative or right-wing political beliefs created unprecedented discord in her center's community and, when "after the coup, [the center] got divided . . . and many people blamed it on the communists who were part of the center. The old president was forced out, and decided to leave the country. Those who took her to the airport waved goodbye with red handkerchiefs. They were all arrested as a result. In the end . . . those who were in favor of the government began to run the center."[27] Some women chose to remain because it allowed them access to health-care services or for the discount food items they could receive. Others found the hostile atmosphere impossible to bear. Membership declined nationwide, from about twenty thousand centers with approximately a million members in 1973, to less than half that number of centers and some two hundred thousand members by 1988.[28]

In the process of purging the "old" political woman, the military promoted the "woman-volunteer" who represented the model of proper womanhood and also provided practical support in the surveillance campaigns of CEMA-Chile and the Women's Secretariat. About ten thousand trained volunteers worked for the secretariat alone, defending the values of "family and fatherland" in seminars and lectures throughout the country. Between 1973 and 1983, the volunteers reached out to two million female participants.[29] Women volunteers helped control potential dissidents and the political opposition. A volunteer from the Pudahuel neighborhood in Santiago described how her center dealt with specific neighborhoods identified as "radical" and therefore in need of an adequate strategy of penetration: "A volunteer was assigned between 14 and 16 families. . . . [She had to] make sure that the families received government subsidies, go visit them once a week, all year round. . . . We have 16 houses with a specific plan for each, with its notebook documenting the lives, or rather, the specific information that interests us about the people, to identify the situation."[30]

Clearly, the woman-volunteer extended her "natural" service from the domestic sphere to that of serving the nation. In her "selfless and fruitful work," she devoted herself to educating and controlling her fellow citizens without asking for compensation in return. The role model for all volunteers, according to the secretariat's official assessment during its seven-year celebration, was the example of "selflessness and sacrifice for others" offered by the First Lady herself.[31] Female volunteers, the unpaid army of the regime, even manifested their support in parades for the military: they marched in synchronized, color-coded formation, the colors revealing the nature of their different social tasks.[32] The blue block worked in prisons, the red ones cared for the sick, the women in white addressed the needs of malnourished children, while those in light blue attended the elderly.[33]

Under dictatorship the sense of duty of self-abnegating volunteers meshed with a model of motherhood for the fatherland, the latter endorsed by official venerations of mothers who would bear children for the nation. Celebrations that honored the "Mother of the Year" helped promote this natalism. In 1982, for example, "Doña Doralisa, a fertile woman," was praised for her fecundity. She was lauded for raising and educating seven healthy children, professionals prepared to serve their nation. In an interview, Doralisa Marimbo brought to light her own story, recalling that a large family, "a house full of children," had not been part of her initial dreams. She gained special praise for accepting her natural role and for overcoming hardships to make ends meet. During the day, she fed and cared for her family; at night, she quietly worked to supplement her husband's limited income. She sold clothing knitted by her own hand, sweets and cakes she herself had baked.[34] Other Chilean mothers could derive a valuable lesson from her story: if they did not feel they could feed numerous children, they had only themselves to blame. The work of a mother, a labor of love, could allow any good mother to raise a good family. The nation's leadership, meanwhile, prepared itself to promote natality in a concerted effort to coerce mothers to populate the nation.

Motherhood for the Fatherland

Doctors who supported military rule often supported the natalist doctrine and worked to prevent women from "interfering with nature" through birth control. A woman from Santiago named Leontina Huetel felt the consequences of this change when she was utterly overwhelmed by the news she got in her doctor's office in January 1981. Her doctor repeated what he had just shared with her in a calm, soothing, yet mechanical voice: "What is happening to you, Señora, is that you are pregnant." Señora Huetel did not know how to respond: not that she disliked motherhood, but this was the worst possible moment for her to have another child. She was a single mother with four children and had been a domestic worker since she was eighteen years old. "This cannot be," she replied, "I have protection."[35] She was using an IUD and had recently had its proper placement checked. Indeed, she recalled that during her checkup a few weeks ago the doctor had commented on women's duty to bear all children sent by God—and had asked her to spread her legs to check her device. Only now, too late, Señora Huetel discovered that what that doctor had really done was remove the contraceptive device without her knowledge.

Leontina Huetel was neither the first nor the last patient to lose access to family planning against her will. In 1976, for example, a woman wrote a letter to a Chilean solidarity group abroad, describing how one day the neighborhood women were summoned to their local Mothers' Center, where they were told that "Chile needs soldiers; the pill and IUDs violate religious and moral norms." All women in the neighborhood were then ordered to stop using birth control. When some refused to comply, their Mothers' Center relied on medical records to single out patients and forced all women with IUDs to see their local healthcare practitioner to have the devices removed.[36] The number of IUD removals against the will of patients cannot be documented, but specific policy changes contributed to an environment in which motherhood as a choice became an increasingly difficult task. In 1973, the military began to decentralize the public health system and placed local health clinics under municipal control. The changed health-care regulations impeded women's access to family-planning programs by shifting priorities from preventive care to curative care and from family planning to maternal-child services. Between 1979 and 1985, the regime implemented a temporary pro-natalist population policy and obstructed physicians' delivery of family-planning services. Many doctors in private practice no longer made contraceptive devices available to women. In 1989, the regime terminated women's legal right to therapeutic abortions; this criminalization of abortion threatened doctors and patients with prison terms for illegally induced abortions. In sum, the military initiated a set of parallel and interrelated legislation to yoke motherhood to the interests of the regime.

The restructuring of the health-care system effectively tied women's personal decisions about motherhood to the modernizing mission of the military early on. In the immediate aftermath of the coup, health minister Alberto Spoerer declared that "health care is not given; rather, it must be obtained by the people."[37] Ideological reasons inspired the restructuring. Guided by the economic doctrines of technocrats, the regime pursued a politics of privatization that also reshaped the relation between women and health-care practitioners.[38] Between 1974 and 1983, state spending on health decreased by 10 percent.[39] Patients faced terrible conditions in local health centers, when a new system to municipalize primary health-care clinics gave only limited fiscal autonomy to centrally controlled municipalities and thereby radically changed medical practice. Decentralization compromised the quality of care and hurt patients. In restructured funding systems, health clinics were reimbursed for each *service* provided and began to encourage unnecessary services to make ends meet.[40] In this corrupted arrangement, doctors subjected some patients to unnecessary procedures and sent others away without any treatment at all.[41]

For women who sought information on birth control, the restructuring of the health-care system had devastating effects. Wage decreases and hiring freezes in the public system affected local health clinics, where women now had to wait in line to receive basic assistance. Family-planning services took the brunt as new regulations concerning the order of attendance in health-care centers gave top priority to patients needing emergency care, second priority to pregnant women and maternal-child assistance, and placed preventive care, including family-planning services, at the bottom of the list. With fewer health-care personnel available, women seeking information on family planning often returned from health-care centers without having any of their questions and concerns addressed.[42]

The restrictions placed on voluntary motherhood further accelerated when geopolitical concerns moved to the forefront of military policies. In 1979, even foreign observers noticed the change. Under the headline "Chileans, in Change, Oppose Birth Curbs," a *New York Times* journalist reported that "[a] steady decline in the birth rate since the military's takeover prompts a shift in policy," and commented on a new and dramatic "campaign against birth control."[43] Indeed, back in Chile, physician Dr. Ricardo Cruz-Coke acknowledged that the armed forces had grown "alarmed about the impact natality decline would have on Chile's [national] defense."[44] In the journal *Revista médica,* he provided some of the context that led to the first official pro-natalist legislation in Chilean history by drawing a connection between the declining population size and concerns over national security. The Office of Government Planning (ODE-PLAN) issued the *Population Policy of the Chilean Government,* which pronounced that "a significant increase of our population is desirable" to keep pace with the rapidly growing birth rates in neighboring countries that could supersede population size in Chile.[45] The office also claimed that birth control programs had already taken their toll, and any further decline in the birth rate could seriously undermine not only Chile's national security but its national development as well.[46] Although ODEPLAN acknowledged that decisions over birth control were "free decisions of individual families," it severely restricted access to contraceptive services and endorsed campaigns that "encourage motherhood and dignify the role of the mother."[47] In addition, research and publications on family planning were now subject to censorship. The ODEPLAN decree demanded that the government be notified before doctors published their research, be it nationally or internationally, on family planning in Chile.[48]

The regime attempted to control the meaning of motherhood even when it reversed this population policy in 1985—and spread a new, quite unexpected message. The health ministry not only issued an "Update on Responsible Parenthood," but also addressed questions of family planning in a language that bore little resemblance to its earlier natalist stance.[49] In the document, undersecretary of health Dr. Augusto Schuster Cortes acknowledged that "it had become clear that responsible parenthood contributes to the decline of infant mortality rates and effectively diminishes the number of high risk pregnancies."

The document listed objectives of "responsible parenthood" that included "the decline of maternal and infant mortality" and "the prevention of unwanted pregnancies among teenagers." It even expressed concern over teenage sexuality, when citing the need to study "the reproductive behavior of adolescents and its consequences."[50] In short, the health ministry framed the reversal of its rigid pro-natalism as a much needed boost to the development of a modern nation. The protection of women's health, the control of maternal and infant mortality, and the prevention of teenage pregnancies were necessary priorities on that path to modernization. Although the regime openly acknowledged this reversed position only in 1985, many Chileans who played less official parts in the making of public policies had transgressed the rigid control, censorship, and pro-natalist positions early on.

Addressing Gendered Traditions and Sexuality to Cast a Modern Nation

Parallel to the official steps the military took to yoke motherhood to the regime's interests, multiple events and initiatives helped breach official doctrines and opened the door to alternative realities of life. Women and men opened up new dialogues about such terms as *sexual freedom,* and even sex education for young Chileans would thrive. In 1976, the newspaper *El mercurio* published a study of Chilean views on sexuality, birth control, and abortion. The paper had commissioned a Gallup poll entitled "Chilean Profile," which surprised readers with a range of topics unusual in the censured, conservative press. The "Profile" was based on the participation of 595 people older than fifteen who had been selected to represent a wide range of socioeconomic backgrounds and generations. All were residents of the larger Santiago area, with the majority (56 percent) being male. The views this cohort presented defied some established norms but defended others. Whereas participants were prepared to challenge some of the restrictions on abortion to save women's lives, most were unprepared to grant women any degree of sexual freedom.

The poll concluded that 74 percent of the participants would favor a more tolerant legal position on abortion, and 91 percent declared that they considered birth control a necessary part of every couple's life. When asked about their definition of sexual freedom, 27 percent stated that, for them, the term stood for the right to live a healthy sex life, while 38 percent thought that sexual freedom should have the same meaning for women and for men. A little more than a third of the participants felt that *men* needed more sexual freedom than women, with more *women* than men upholding this view. Not one of the over five hundred participants maintained that women needed more sexual freedom than men.[51] In light of Chile's traditional gender system, the gendered biases of the views expressed in Gallup's findings were less surprising than the actual publication of the study's results. The poll exemplified the unprecedented attention given to sexuality and sex education despite the silence imposed by dictatorship. It also offered a first glimpse of the spaces of transgression Chileans could create to contest the hegemonic views of military leaders. Some people and institutions packaged their transgressions in clever language that made them acceptable.

In 1974, APROFA's family planners published a mission statement that contained a welcome message of peace, coming as it did in violent times. It employed a new language to propose educational campaigns that even the regime could hardly question. Community educators promised "to advance responsible parenthood, the optimal development of children, and the interpersonal harmony of couples." Outreach teams from APROFA designed programs prepared to teach hospital staff, educators in schools and universities, and other groups nationwide in an attempt to address a wide range of topics including the "prevention of abortion, malnutrition, child abandonment, juvenile delinquency, and homelessness."[52] Years of practice had allowed the educators to fine-tune their message. They were prepared to eradicate dangerous misinformation about the human body that often compromised women's health and led to misuse of birth control devices. By the end of the year, community educators had given a documented total of 425 courses and had trained 10,625 participants about responsible parenthood.[53]

Success of educational campaigns soared. In December 1974, Zunilda Pizarro Ramirez, head nurse of the Hospital San Juan de Dios in Santiago, wrote a letter to thank APROFA's educators for the information they had shared with nurses and health-care practitioners throughout the calendar year. Her records showed that a total of seven hundred hospital professionals had attended the courses. Pizarro Ramirez praised the educators for providing the only collective family-planning education in public hospitals in South America. Others, like Lucy Salcedo Rojas, appreciated APROFA's outreach on a more personal level: in her letter, she reported that information on family-planning methods had helped her and her husband "to improve and insure the wellbeing of their children."[54] In the following years, APROFA "kept up its good work." The organization signed an agreement with CEMA-Chile and gave regular talks about responsible parenthood in selected Mothers' Centers.[55] It showed films like *Family Planning, Responsible Parenthood,* and *Human Reproduction* in a total of 615 screenings to an audience of about 217,000 people nationwide in only a year.[56]

The success of APROFA's campaigns even breached national boundaries. Chilean professionals applied their knowledge at home and shared their experiences abroad. In 1975, thirty-six Chilean APROFA delegates traveled to Washington, D.C., to attend a seminar on sex education they helped organize in collaboration with the Pan-American Health Organization.[57] In 1976, *People's Magazine* featured Chilean doctor Benjamín Viel, who shared his views on the success of free family-planning services and the effort to diminish abortion rates and maternal mortality in the Americas.[58] Throughout the 1970s, educators refined and improved their outreach strategies in Chile and discussed responsible parenthood and human sexuality. Importantly, a new language on the meaning of sex shaped these events. Educators moved sex education from a medicalized approach, addressed as an extension of human biology, to a humanistic understanding of sexuality as integral to the development of both women and men.[59]

In training courses for community educators, health officials began to adopt an approach to human sexuality that rejected a narrow treatment confined only to the biological aspects of human reproduction. Instead, sexuality became a positive force, "the instrument of individual wellbeing and partnership, the instrument of communication and love." Sex education, according to APROFA theorists at a 1977 meeting, needed to focus on the relational and emotional qualities of sex.[60] In 1978, a new campaign addressed "sex education and family life," adding an experimental project explicitly geared to teach young people, male and female, outside the narrow setting of their own families. About four hundred teenagers from poor Santiago neighborhoods and from a number of small towns in the Chilean central valley promptly signed up. In groups no larger than fifteen, they discussed sexuality, responsible parenthood, and family life.[61] In ongoing campaigns, the educators of teenage sexuality tested the boundaries of tradition and of tolerance by the military government.

Community educators, eager to bring their theoretical considerations to the field, ventured out to help schoolteachers, parents, and all those willing to participate in a mission to spread "lessons for life." In 1980, the campaign "Education on Sexuality for Students" included twenty-three courses that reached an audience of 402 teachers as well as sixty-seven courses for parents and other educators. A total of 1,498 participated in the latter.[62] The project "Lessons for Life: Focusing on Young People" pioneered an innovative teaching series intended for those "on the margins," who did not regularly attend school and were left "outside the system of formal education." Thirty outreach educators prepared to reach a target population of nine hundred adolescents, male and female, to talk about sex. In the course of the decade, ninety-three meetings opened up new dialogues.[63] Although its work was remarkable, APROFA could not overcome all boundaries on its path. It gained international fame for developing model health clinics and education strategies, designing sex-education components for the curriculum in Chile's largest technical training institute, and taking a pioneering role in the development of discussion groups for young people where they could talk about sex-related matters among peers in a relaxed atmosphere.[64] But although concerns over teenage pregnancies were addressed and acknowledged at international conferences, doctors in Chile found bringing about actual change in this regard to be a much more complicated issue.

People who lived worlds apart, like Dr. Enrique Onetto, APROFA leader and promoter of responsible parenthood, and Leontina Huetel, the aforementioned patient whose IUD had been removed without her consent, noticed that family-planning programs seemed to have come under violent attack. The pro-natalist legislation and the changed priorities in health-care centers created a climate of insecurity and left their scars.[65] Reactions varied: some doctors ignored the polemics altogether; others supported the views expressed in pro-natalist campaigns; and finally some spoke out against legislation they thought would threaten public health. In 1979, Radio Cooperativa invited professionals to comment on the implications of the politics of family planning in the aftermath of ODEPLAN's population policy, and many voiced their concerns on the air. Dr. Ramiro Molina of the J. J. Aguirre Hospital, for example, declared that "the elimination or suppression of fertility regulation would lead to an increase of mortality rates due to abortions, and to clandestine sales of contraceptive devices." He feared a black market in the sale of contraceptives with horrible consequences, especially for poor women.[66] Others voiced concern about the children born to mothers who were forced to give birth. Dr. Fernando Monckeberg lamented nutritional shortages that would adversely affect poor children, further widening the gap between rich and poor. And Dr. Pablo Huneus added that the ODEPLAN document could lead to a world of misery, given that "the unwanted child is not a happy child."[67]

Elsewhere, Dr. Benjamín Viel evoked international resolutions such as the 1977 UN Declaration of Bucharest, which proclaimed "the right to plan children is a basic human right," a right Chile supported with its affirmative vote. According to Viel, APROFA and the UN needed to defend planned motherhood as a basic human right. But Chile, as a modern nation, also had to work to ebb the rising tide of teenage pregnancies in an attempt to rid the country of this "national disgrace."[68] Using the military's interest in advancing Chile's reputation as a modern nation, Viel had, once again, found a path to justify change in the midst of opposition. In the 1980s, Viel, then head of APROFA, tried to promote a campaign alerting fellow Chileans to the public health problem of teenage pregnancy that threatened the nation's path to modernity.[69] The number of pregnant teenage girls in maternity wards caused great concern: in 1960, doctors delivered twenty-seven thousand babies born to teenage mothers, and almost thirty-six thousand by 1987. Alarmed health officials widely addressed the topic in the early 1980s. They showed that many young mothers gave birth before the age of fifteen, dropped out of school at the onset of maternity, and faced a difficult life for themselves and their children.[70] Teenage pregnancies occurred more frequently among the poor, and early motherhood limited young people's options to escape a life of poverty.[71] Between 1970 and 1987, the numbers of "illegitimate" births by teenage mothers had skyrocketed from 30.8 percent to 58.2 percent.[72] Many became single mothers.

Viel and others saw multiple causes for what they considered irresponsible sexual relations and their costs. They blamed the media that encouraged "premature sexual experiences among young people" by presenting provocative nudity and pornography. They found that new understandings of female morality had taken a turn for the worse, as "adolescent girls no longer attribute the same value to virginity before marriage as in the past."[73] But not only girls were to blame. Some doctors held responsible the unfair double standard regarding sex: they lamented that Chilean society encouraged men to have sexual conquests and simultaneously absolved them from facing the consequences of their acts. Indeed, society held only the women responsible for unwanted pregnancies, and mothers and children paid the price.[74] Psychologist Irma Palma added that young women in poor neighborhoods were disproportionately affected. She spoke of high incidents of domestic violence that ranged from rape to parental neglect, and of daughters who were especially vulnerable. Although doctors disagreed over who exactly deserved most of the blame, they all agreed on the importance of education to address the crisis.[75] New doors for action were opened as the growing problem of teenage sex made it increasingly evident that teenagers needed to learn about sexuality and sexual responsibility.

Censorship, book burnings, and purges notwithstanding, individual educators and institutions like APROFA broke some silences on sexuality and reproduction and helped bring about surprising changes for the sake of Chile's development.[76] In 1980, the Ministry of Education readdressed the topic of sexual education that had been silenced in the aftermath of the coup.[77] In that year, Decree 4002 modified the curriculum for elementary schools to include courses on human reproduction, and in 1981, Decree 300 defined new educational objectives for secondary schools. Students at both levels were to be instructed on the principle characteristics of human reproduction and sexual maturity in an effort to convey the message that sexual relations should lead to responsible parenthood.[78] Curriculum requirements, nevertheless, did not call for information on birth control. Subsequent changes in the policies of the Ministry of Health were more explicit about the nature of sex but remained removed from the realities of everyday life.

In 1983, when the Ministry of Health responded to concerns over sexually transmitted diseases (STDs), it called for sex education in the context of preventive care. Decree 362 aimed to enact educational efforts at all levels of the National Health Service as well as to address parents in their role as educators in the family.[79] Sex education also could be offered in work places, prisons, and hospitals and had to fulfill specific objectives defined by the ministry. Legislators expected a "description of sexual anatomy and physiology, and the conceptualization of human sexuality as a heterosexual relationship." The required basis of educational programs on the subject matter was biology and physiology of reproduction. The decree tolerated the regulation of fertility and sexuality in the family setting, but distinctly defined sexual "pathologies" in juxtaposition to heterosexual sexual relations and reproduction. To understand "proper" sexuality, sex education needed to deal with such "pathologies" as "homosexuality, prostitution, rape, [and] incest."[80] Although legislators in service to the military tolerated some leniency in the rigid system of silence on sexuality and birth control they had imposed a few years back, they held on to traditional norms of what constituted "proper" understandings of sex.

For the military, women's sexuality remained intrinsically linked to motherhood and to what Maria Elena Valenzuela has termed a "sexuality-maternity."[81] Conservative women, the regime's "natural allies," helped defend the religious-moral position that defined proper female sexuality. The only suitable manifestation of sexuality was in marriage, where sexual relations between husband and wife became acts of redemption and sacrifice. Wives could redeem the earthly character of sexual desires through procreation, abnegation, and self-sacrifice for their children.[82] In this understanding of moral values, God represented virtue; humans embodied sin. Women had to overcome sexual desires to remain virtuous and pure; they had to decide between the role of Eve or Mary, between rebellion against the word of God or the attainment of perfection akin to that of the mother of God. The history of Chile's first saint reflected some implications of the religious-moral condemnation of female sexuality. In 1987, Pope John Paul beatified Santa Teresa de los Andes, not for her miracles but for her writings that documented her self-flagellation as a means to maintain her virginity and sacrifice herself completely to God. In the same year, a woman wrote a letter to the journal *Apsi* expressing her regret for not being able to achieve purity through sexual abstinence. Her public display of remorse testified to the power of Santa Teresa as a role model for some Chilean women.[83]

For many women, sexuality evoked not moral fulfillment through sexuality-maternity, but trauma and disgust. A woman who only used her first name, Maria, at home in the poor Huamachuco neighborhood in Santiago, shared her personal feelings about the subject matter with a female researcher in the 1980s. She described how she lost her virginity to her boyfriend at the age of thirteen and how the experience made her fear every sexual encounter ever since. "I think I am just very cold," Maria suggested, blaming herself.[84] Another *pobladora* from Huamachuco explicitly made the connection between sex and marriage when she declared, "Let's face it . . . we practically married the first man who raped us; 'cause that's what it is, the first sexual encounter is like a rape. The men take what they want."[85] Psychologist Heliette Saint Jean has offered workshops on sexuality to Chilean women and found that women's lack of sexual knowledge or pleasure, their experiences with sexual violence, and even their outright fear of sex were widespread.[86] She suggested that, especially in poor neighborhoods, women tended to think of sexuality as "made for men," with limited benefit for women. Few women knew of sexual pleasure or held their husbands responsible for their lack of sexual satisfaction. Most thought of their sexuality as not an integral part of themselves, but rather the "terrain of the gynecologist, the midwife, and the husband."[87] Motherhood could be the welcome result of unwelcome sexual relations. Some women felt that children at least gave them something of their own that nobody could take away from them even when husbands were abusive, violent, or absent.

When women *pobladoras* from different neighborhoods discussed their lives under dictatorship, they indicated that a struggle over sexuality was merely one among many other struggles that shaped their lives. Women told of hard work, efforts to feed their children, attempts to survive as a family, and relationships with husbands that sometimes grew tense when resources became scarce. Angela, for example, expressed pride in how she made peace with her husband who used to drink and how she cherished her home life. She worked taking care of an older woman until she had her first child.[88] Others, Ana and Maria, told of husbands who controlled every aspect of their wives' lives, forcing the women to stay home while the men were free to come and go as they pleased and often beating family members to keep them in their place.[89] Yet another woman, Soledad, told of her lasting faith in monogamy and therefore waited for the father of her children to return from other relationships and sexual escapades. She also thought that she had to think of her children first when she considered protesting his choices and taking the risk of losing him.[90]

In 1979, the play *Tres Marías y una Rosa* (Three Marys and a Rose) opened in Santiago at Teatro Ángel, and briefly moved the troubles of poor women center stage.[91] It featured four women, three named Mary and a fourth, Rose, who was much younger and still a novice in the "real" world of marriage and survival. At home in a *población,* the women struggle with the everyday challenges of poverty. They experience a small ray of hope when they gain a church commission to earn money by producing one enormous quilt. As the Marys and the innocent Rose join together to sew the quilt, they are afforded ample time to talk about life. The older women speak of their struggles with husbands and of what they had to do to survive, given their lack of control over their own lives.

This play articulated *women's* views on gendered traditions of family life. It attracted record audiences during its extended run, despite (or perhaps because of) its uncensored critiques of marriage and patriarchy that were angry, combative, and liberating alike.[92] From opening night until November 1980, more than sixty thousand people attended the play.[93] The centrality of the female voice—and the attentiveness of the audience—was a sign of a welcome transgression. Even if the women in the play did not revolutionize the gender systems they exposed, *Three Marys and a Rose* presented the survival of communities as dependent on the organization of women. It also reflected new realities in a country that began to be transformed, when "real" women of different spheres of life mobilized against the regime.

Militant Motherhood and Women's Rights

The regime's praising the family as a pillar of social stability notwithstanding, many families could hardly function in a country subjected to strict curfews and arbitrary military raids and arrests. Glorified as mothers and wives protecting the moral values of family and nation, women also witnessed, paradoxically, the regime's violating these sacred roles. When they saw their families destroyed by arrests and disappearances, many reacted to the contradictions of gender-based doctrines that sought to prevent them from taking on economic and political responsibilities even when male breadwinners could no longer fulfill their traditional patriarchal roles. Women started to mobilize and, in the process of finding new voices as mothers, began to redefine the traditional connection between mother and home, the private space. As a consequence of the arrests and disappearances of family members, women not only linked the military state to domestic violence, but also recognized that the authoritarian and patriarchal practices used by the regime to control the public sphere resembled those employed by men to control women in the private sphere.[94] A political configuration of mothers' roles in the public sphere, once reserved for men, emerged as a result.[95] Women thus created their own forms of protest in the coup's immediate aftermath.

Initially, women's organizations emerged in response to political repression and economic need. After the coup, women rallied "in defense of life" to confront the rising culture of death and to protect and save family members and relatives.[96] The Agrupación de Mujeres Democráticas (Association of Democratic Women), for example, worked to locate missing family members in Santiago's National Stadium, which had been transformed into a concentration camp, or to give support to detainees who were released from prison. One woman recalled, "You never knew when someone was going to be released. Sometimes they would let someone out by 7 p.m. . . . with no money and no way to get home. If they didn't get home before the 8 p.m. curfew, the police would arrest them again. . . . So we organized the people with cars to be ready to pick up people at a moment's notice."[97] Solidarity groups and self-help organizations included consumer cooperatives, which consisted of more than three hundred groups in Santiago alone.[98] Women in poor neighborhoods networked in communal kitchens, housing organizations, and cottage industries to overcome both material poverty and feelings of fear and hopelessness.

Women's resistance expanded under the protective umbrella of the Church and with the support of the Vicaria de Solidaridad (Vicariate of Solidarity).[99] The newly founded vicariate documented human rights abuses and offered practical help.[100] Vicaria initiatives included workshops to teach women to make quilts (arpilleras), with scraps of recycled cloth. Chilean women's arpilleras, covered in images depicting life under the dictatorship, were sold all over the world. They raised awareness of the abuses endured under a dictatorship and contributed to the income of poor people trying to survive.[101] In 1975, founder Raúl Cardinal Silva Henríquez added an academic branch, the Academia de Humanismo Cristiano (Academy of Christian Humanism), which provided safe meeting spaces for human rights groups and study circles.

The Círculo de Estudios de La Mujer (Women's Studies Circle) was one of the first women's organizations that counted on the vicariate's support. It also helped transform the very nature of women's quest for rights.[102] In 1979, a small group of Santiago feminists, all members of the Círculo, sponsored a gathering "to discuss the situation of women in Chile." The response they received exceeded all expectation: more than three hundred women answered the call.[103] They came from different neighborhoods and brought with them a wide range of educational and personal experiences. Ema, one of the participants, commented on the meeting and the shared feelings of solidarity and collectivity that united the women in spite of their diversity: "When I left I had the worst argument with my husband; so when I came to the meeting I felt very bad, guilty, that I had caused trouble again, that my marriage would end. And the best thing was that the meeting started with everybody talking about how difficult it had been to get there, everybody had encountered similar problems: those who were married, with children, were feeling terribly guilty, felt that they had put the family second place. And, at the same time, their fears were connected to the coup and the dictatorship; well, for many people it meant that they had to shut the doors of the house, stay inside, and the family was the most important, trying to carry on in spite of the dangers outside."[104] Ema poignantly described the feelings of guilt familiar to many wives and mothers who had begun to challenge women's dependent roles. Her voice offers insights into the nature of change inspired by Círculo meetings and by many women at the time.

The twenty or so professional women who sponsored the first official call of the Círculo were already connected to a feminist tradition or to left-of-center politics. In 1979, they formed the organization to further the "struggle against all forms of discrimination and oppression against women."[105] As they set out to research and discuss the condition of women, they also envisioned their agenda as far beyond mere academics.[106] For them, their mission was "political, since it proposes to eliminate a form of domination that is strongly embedded in the social, economic and cultural spheres. The feminist commitment entails revolutionary changes because the elimination of sexual oppression compromises all forms of social relations. And it is necessarily democratic because only in conditions of equality between the sexes is it possible to create a social project that is just and libertarian."[107] They declared that the resistance to dictatorship and to gender-based discrimination in domestic settings went hand in hand.

Feminists Rosa Bravo, María Isabel Cruzat, Elena Serrano, and Rosalba Todaro—all among the founders of the Círculo—emphasized that "one is not born a woman, one learns to be a woman." They set out to share this insight with fellow Chileans, prepared to defend their rights.[108] The first meeting closed with an appeal for women to organize. In subsequent meetings, women not only presented their individual analyses of gender oppression, but they also agreed to work collectively as they rejected violations of *women's* rights.[109] Círculo meetings encouraged ongoing collective reflections on the condition of women in Chile, and participants like Ema were invited to draw conclusions about their roles in family, community, and nation.[110] Consciousness-raising (*concientización*) became one of the steps toward a new feminist praxis of human rights. Discussion topics ranged from institutional discrimination in the legal system to women's personal internalization of repressive roles.[111] Meeting participants challenged the military dictatorship and articulated the urgent need for action; they asked, "Where are the women who have disappeared?"[112] They articulated what was already familiar to some Chileans—namely, that men and women had become victims of state oppression. The disappearances, arrests, and brutal victimization of women were hardly compatible with the military's ideological exaltation of femininity and its quintessential incarnation, motherhood. A new reality demanded a new type of action: women insisted that "we believe that it is our, and only our, responsibility to demand that women receive their rights. If we don't fight for ourselves, no one will fight for us."[113]

In this environment, Círculo women were compelled not only to question motherhood as a generic and naturalized identity, but also to address *women*, not *mothers*, first. A document, especially prepared for the Círculo's initial outreach gathering, presented a reassessment of the meanings of motherhood. The document stated: "We have learned that motherhood is the fundamental reason for our existence. . . . We have learned to love our children, not as independent and autonomous people but as extensions of ourselves, as if we existed, for the world, only to the extent that they exist. . . . We have learned to use motherhood as a justification for what we do and what we don't do. . . . Some of us have learned to emancipate ourselves. . . . We work, we read, we are up-to-date with work issues, we can have conversations, analyze, intellectualize. . . . Nevertheless, we are between waves of guilt as a result of having abandoned the house and the children."[114] The text introduced women, and mothers, to a critique of the exploitation of women's reproductive labor and the contradictions of a capitalist, patriarchal society that domesticated women for the sake of the family yet refused to assign value to their labor. Motherhood, in this discourse, remained central to womanhood and remained the signifier of a collective identity in which nonmotherhood represented a void. The striking novelty in Círculo initiatives lay in its challenging motherhood as a fixed, essentialized identity and its connecting this to a new political praxis.[115]

Voluntary motherhood stood out as one of the themes that embodied the connection women made between old traditions and new rights. In September 1980, the Círculo arranged a gathering on "Population Policies and Birth Control." In a set of formal presentations, economists, physicians, a priest, and selected Círculo women addressed such issues as overpopulation and birth control, family-planning methodologies, and the Church's position on responsible parenthood. Next, presenters invited questions and comments from the audience, eager to hear the opinions of other women. Audience participants agreed on the need to defend women's liberation from prescribed motherhood, thereby declaring a new element of choice, which, they deemed, should be every woman's right. They also identified several obstacles to voluntary motherhood: limited access to information about family planning and to contraceptive devices; cultural prejudice and the weight of traditional norms that left little space for women's sexuality; and prejudices that wrongly condemned women who used birth control as sexual libertines. Participants concluded that a recognition of women's rights to equal citizenship with men required that their choices regarding birth control be legally and culturally respected.[116]

These women's propositions did not mark a radical departure from a "motherist" agenda to a new brand of "radical feminism." Instead, they endorsed a gradual process in which women would find novel responses to experiences of gender-based violence and combine those with the adoption of new obligations under the extreme conditions of military rule.[117] Chilean feminists documented that "since the foundation of the Círculo in 1979, the nongovernmental organizations that addressed [the role of] women in research and social activism multiplied: in 1987, there were eighty-seven institutions."[118] Groups from diverse class backgrounds contributed to promoting new forms of women's political participation and militant motherhood.

Pobladoras, women of poor neighborhoods, were as active as middle-class feminists and mobilized to address gender- and class-based exploitation.[119] Even though many poor women participated in mobilization for women's rights, they had a history of political mobilization quite different from that of such activists as the founders of the Círculo. One *pobladora* recalled: "We have always been organized; just like that. We had to, with our problems . . . we formed a committee to address unemployment. And we asked the Church for help."[120] Another *pobladora* activist made clear that many *pobladoras* agreed with the need to address the lack of gender equity proposed by middle-class or professional feminists, but confronted different challenges when trying to mobilize: "We could never count on the support of maids . . . we had to organize ourselves. Some women go to meetings with [all of] their children, I take just the younger ones."[121] Consciousness-raising, self-help strategies through collective organizing, and the critique of the double oppression through dictatorship and patriarchy also shaped the mobilization of poor women.

In 1980, the Committee for the Defense of Women's Rights (Comité de Defensa de los Derechos de la Mujer, CODEM) became one of the most important organizations founded by *pobladoras*. In their first campaign, CODEM activists demanded access to health care and birth control. In 1981, they launched their own journal and documented the implications of the changes in the health-care system for women's health, including high maternal mortality rates. The committee also presented analyses of teenage pregnancy, the lack of sexual education, and gender-specific demands that coincided with other feminist critiques of Chilean society.[122] In May 1982, CODEM, in collaboration with middle-class feminist organizers, held its first national meeting. Participants joined discussion groups that addressed such themes as "women and identity" and "women and sexuality."

They also planned for the future. In a plenary session, participants concluded that "women had to be integrated into the struggle for health, housing, work, [and] social and legal change." They had to organize as women "to confront repression."[123] Women presented a platform of demands and strategies to overcome the lack of gender equity in Chilean society and to ensure women's participation in the recreation of democratic rule.[124] The second national meeting, in November 1983, encouraged women to "politicize the private sphere" and to use their leadership skills to challenge traditional, patriarchal structures. One member noted that "we women discovered that we were ready to fight, and that we were prepared to demand the end of double-oppression. . . . Without significant social change, the liberation of women will not be possible [and] social change without the massive participation of women is neither possible, nor real."[125]

Other initiatives aimed at strengthening the ties between the many organizations formed by women in poor neighborhoods. In May 1982, *pobladora* leaders brought together more than twelve smaller organizations under one central leadership, now called the Movement of Shantytown Women (Movimiento de Mujeres Pobladoras, MOMUPO). One of the organizers, Clotilde Silva, showed that poor women, like professional feminists, had expanded the meanings of motherhood and the tasks they set for themselves. She explained that women's political participation was inspired by the failure of male political leadership and that "it is terrible to see how children grow up without hope for the future [under dictatorship]."[126] Although MOMUPO members acknowledged the double exploitation of women, which justified the need for an autonomous women's organization, they prioritized their working-class identity: "MOMUPO sees [itself] as part of the working class and understands that our class as a whole [including men] needs to confront . . . oppression."[127]

Women, then, would select the particular responsibilities most suited to them; they were not followers, but active agents whose choice shaped this process. Marina Valdés, leader of MOMUPO, demonstrated how women, while pursuing their goals, could and did seize interpretive power and transform some symbols of resistance. In their struggle against dictatorship, for example, they resorted to the banging of pots and pans, first introduced by the conservative women who had protested the Allende government. In a new representation of militant motherhood, aptly described by Valdés, "[b]anging on empty pots was a symbol of empty pots. It was to demonstrate your opposition to the [military] government." They banged the pots "because there was massive unemployment, because your family didn't have food to eat."[128]

In the 1980s, Las Protestas (the Protests), an intense period of women's resistance and public demonstrations, helped pave the way toward redemocratization. In December 1983, more than ten thousand women of different political and class backgrounds came together at the Caupolicán Theatre in Santiago to participate in what was the largest gathering since the military coup. Linked together under the motto of unity, they proclaimed that "freedom has a woman's name."[129] In subsequent public marches, protesters called for "democracia en el país y en la casa" (democracy in the country and at home).[130] Women also met, marched, and mobilized in support of Pinochet's 1988 plebiscite. More than 1.9 million women, or 51 percent, supported the "No" campaign, as did 58 percent of male voters.[131] From that moment, women's demands for rights appeared in a new light, connected to the right of equal citizenship under an elected government.

Other campaigns augmented the power of women's ongoing mobilization for *women's* rights. In late 1988 and the early months of 1989, a massive campaign guided by the motto "soy mujer, tengo derechos" (I am a woman, I have rights) demonstrated the significance of women's rights mobilization.[132] Women, as political actors with their own specific demands and particular agendas, had come to stay. Over the course of five, intensely active months of mobilization, forty-eight organized gatherings afforded women from all walks of life the opportunity to listen to presentations, read documents, and discuss what they saw as major challenges to women's rights. Campaigns reached far beyond the larger Santiago area and could count on the attendance of about seventeen hundred women from rural and urban backgrounds.[133] For many women who joined the campaign, the construction of a women's rights discourse and the formulation of demands were no longer marginal quests. "Soy mujer, tengo derechos" was set in motion by a new coordinating body, the Coordinator of Women's Social Organizations (La Coordinación de Organizaciones Sociales de Mujeres), formed by representatives of the largest women's groups in the nation.[134] Objectives included giving women spaces for individual expression, addressing problems that affected all women due to their roles in society, and identifying the problems and violations of women's rights that needed the most urgent attention.[135]

Diverse groups of women now discussed their experiences—no longer confined to motherhood—and enumerated specific demands that addressed shortcomings in women's rights. In general, women demanded equal rights with men in the realms of work and fair wages, health care, dignified housing, social security, and education. In particular, they proposed gender equity in all spheres, addressing politics, economics, and culture.[136] "Outreach" initiatives formed part of the larger campaign and exemplified the tone and the content of their demands. For example, when four hundred women participated in a protest

march in the center of Santiago on November 21, 1989, they carried signs point-
ing to the problem of violence against women: "Violence against women is a
crime, in the streets and at any time."[137] They illustrated the power of culture
and education and critically evoked their own role in the continuation of the
gender system they rejected: "First we raise machos, and next we get scared
of them."[138] Finally, they argued that a true democracy would take shape only
with the inclusion of female citizens with equal rights: "If women are involved,
then democracy evolves."[139] In the subsequent process of redemocratization,
other organized efforts by groups like National Coalition of Women for Democracy (Concertación Nacional de Mujeres por la Democracia) demonstrated
that women demanded a radical transformation of society and politics, away
from misguided democratic traditions that left intact gender-based hierarchies
and inequalities.[140] The transition toward the new democracy posed new challenges to gender equity.

In 1983, feminist Julieta Kirkwood issued a wise word of warning about
the power of patriarchy and remarked that the defeat of a dictatorship could
not be equated with the defeat of unrelenting authoritarian and patriarchal relations. She maintained that "authoritarianism [and inequality] can be found
throughout society . . . even among workers and peasants."[141] Feminism could
pose a challenge to "the hierarchical structure of society and the values underlying it," but the more it challenged the patriarchal power inherent in gender
or sex-role differentiation, the more resistance it would meet.[142] After all, too
many institutions and individuals profited from the institutionalized inequality
of women and men. The history of Chile's return to democracy offers ample
evidence of old and new obstacles that prevented the construction of a society
of equals, one consisting of women and men with equal rights. The Chilean
Civil Code well exemplified the traditional legal subordination of women, stating that "the husband has the right to oblige his wife to live with him and follow
him wherever he moves" and that "the husband is the chief of the conjugal society, and as such may freely administer his property and that of his wife."[143]
Legal changes adopted on the eve of democratic transition in 1989 eradicated
the husband's legal power to control and administer his wife's moves but left
intact the property rights that gave him sole control over all resources. The
regime also made another last-minute change that affected women's lives: it
criminalized abortion under all circumstances. Jaime Guzmán, lawyer and
influential ideologue of the military dictatorship, had helped secure the legal

backing of the position that "[t]he mother must give birth to her child, even if it will be born abnormal, if she did not plan it, if it was conceived as a result of a rape, and even if giving birth will kill her."[144]

Balancing the Strength of Resistance and the Burden of Military Legacies

Under military rule, patriotic values and family values went hand in hand, but were indeed subject to transgressions in multiple settings. Neither traditional values of family life and sexual behavior, nor meanings of motherhood were fixed categories solely controlled by representatives of the regime. Groups of doctors, educators, and women of different classes effectively disobeyed some of the rigid rules of military domination. Their initiatives provide abundant evidence of how, and to what extent, the regime's value system and politics were challenged and eventually weakened.

APROFA cleverly breached official military doctrine by keeping alive family-planning programs and by expanding sex education programs. Doctors justified the programs that undermined the military's pro-natalist stance by claiming to strengthen Chile on the path to development. Responsible parenthood and family planning would, after all, help control maternal and infant mortality and thereby boost the country's international reputation. In the same spirit, the health and education ministries contributed to national development by expanding programs to teach adolescents about "proper" understandings of sexuality. These programs were expected to help control teenage pregnancies and the spread of STDs. Other educators and physicians, acting independently of the ministries, encouraged workshops and open dialogues about sexuality, providing unprecedented spaces to question the boundaries of old gender roles and sexual norms.

Women's groups' subversion of the "master discourse" on "proper" motherhood was equally powerful. To navigate repressive daily conditions, women expanded their own understanding of mothers' roles. Women of different classes and diverse ties to feminism built new foundations for the mobilization of "mothers' rights"—rights that, until then, had been chained to traditional gender roles and patterns of family life. While male breadwinners were absent or silenced by the military, women took it upon themselves to lay the foundation for new paradigms of responsibilities: they connected "mothers' rights" to women's rights and to women's individual claims to civil liberties. Motherhood no longer functioned as the exclusive base to justify women's claims for human rights. Under siege, women's engagement for the survival of family members converted into politicized motherhood and reached unprecedented dimensions. Middle-class feminists promoted collective learning and cross-class activist strategies. Women from poor neighborhoods created survival strategies in defense of life. All made effective contributions to the struggle for democracy. But under redemocratization, those who mobilized in defense of women's rights noticed just how influential the legacies of dictatorship would be.

|| 6 ||

INTERNATIONAL ENCOUNTERS
AND WOMEN'S EMPOWERMENT
UNDER DICTATORSHIP
AND REDEMOCRATIZATION

[W]e feminists have found that traditional political practice, however women are involved, is segregationist and subordinating in all
sociopolitical sectors, whether the women are shantytown dwellers,
peasants, employees, or professionals.

Julieta Kirkwood, Chilean feminist, 1983

IN OCTOBER 1974, Joan Jara, widow of singer-songwriter Victor Jara, who
had been tortured and killed by the military, toured the United States with her
young children and the folk band Inti-Illimani. All had been exiled from Chile.
Now they used music to tell of the political violence that continued to shatter
their home country. Inti-Illimani summed up its message for a New York audience with the song "Zamba de los humildes" (Song of the poor): "If we must
wait for hope, we will wait for it singing."[1] In the same year, Joan Jara spoke
at American University in Washington, D.C., and granted interviews to newspapers to remind U.S. citizens that "my children and I represent many voices—
the voices of widows and orphans in Chile who are silenced by the military
junta. In their name, I demand that torture in Chile shall cease . . . that the political prisoners shall be freed . . . and that this military junta, murderers of their
own countrymen, shall be isolated and overthrown, so that democracy and
fundamental human rights may be restored in Chile."[2] These prominent exiles,
along with at least two hundred thousand other Chileans, were forced to leave
their homeland after the coup. This tragedy produced unexpected consequences;

it introduced many exiles to international solidarity campaigns in defense of human rights as well as to dynamic feminist movements. These feminist movements specifically confronted gender-based human rights violations.

Feminist historian Alicia Frohmann was actively involved in Chilean women's mobilization. Her work stresses the important role women's international connections played during the dictatorship. She points out that "the women's movement of the 1970s and 1980s was an international movement, and whatever happened concerning women, both in the industrialized and the developing countries, influenced debates and initiatives elsewhere."[3] Women's initiatives and concerns worldwide found increased legitimacy through the United Nations Decade for Women (1975–1985). Quests for women's rights and gender equity also gained strength through new networks women built in the Americas and in Europe. Thus Chilean women participated in two parallel, yet independent, sets of international meetings that strengthened their ties to feminism. The first were meetings held under the auspices of the United Nations. The second were regional Encuentros Feministas (Feminist Encounters), dedicated specifically to uniting women throughout Latin America and the Caribbean. Frohmann remembered the 1980s as the most "heroic" period of the women's movement, marked by women's contribution to the end of dictatorship in Chile.[4] But a new political climate under redemocratization, combined with a changed dynamic of women's movements, also posed new obstacles to gender equity in the 1990s.[5]

The history of feminist mobilization in Chile is linked to international human rights and feminist movements, and different women used those ties to buttress their demands for rights in the aftermath of the UN International Women's Year in 1975. Exiles and international travelers became active agents in the construction of a human rights agenda and demanded gender equity at home. Neither the processes of "translating" their concerns abroad, nor their attempts to "import" foreign feminist insights upon their return were free of tensions. Nonetheless, the specific consequences that Chilean women's international contacts produced can be traced. A fresh global paradigm of women's rights allowed feminists worldwide to increase their political weight at the nation-state level. It also framed the trajectory of women's mobilization in Chile. Initially, Chilean women built collective solidarity through consciousness-raising groups that identified and analyzed patterns of gender-based discrimination. Next, women's groups used these findings to prioritize political agendas and collaborate with international agencies, including the United Nations, to employ international standards of women's rights at home.[6] As some women concentrated on specific issues, such as gender-based violence and women's rights to reproductive health, the government implemented programs and legislation to rectify some gender-based rights violations. Simultaneously, international feminist gatherings encouraged Chilean women's groups to find their own feminist paths based on their specific historical trajectories.

The trajectory of women's mobilization from dictatorship to redemocratization illustrates the changing dynamic of women's mobilization. Clearly, women's feminist consciousness and their new language of rights proved easier to attain than mobilizing strategies that would unite middle-class and professional feminists, on the one hand, with poor women and grassroots-level feminists, on the other. Class differences, political disagreements about proper feminist strategy, and what some scholars have called the "NGO-ization" of women's mobilization posed new threats to their quest for gender equity.[7] In addition, Chilean women were faced with legacies of military rule that complicated their quest for rights. Just before the dictatorship returned power to civilians, military leaders dismantled the public health system to replace it with a private one and terminated the legal availability of therapeutic abortion. Women were now obliged to give birth under any circumstances, even if a pregnancy would result in the woman's certain death. To follow Chilean feminist Julieta Kirkwood's thoughts: "traditional political practice" in Chile continued to "subordinate" women. This placed another set of obstacles on women's path to citizenship rights equal to those of men

New Global Paradigms of Women's Rights and Redemocratization

In 1975, more than five thousand people from all over the world came to Mexico City to partake in the first United Nation's International Women's Year Conference or in the Non-Governmental Organizations (NGOs) Tribunal that convened simultaneously.[8] The 1970s marked the beginning of unprecedented global networking initiatives and mobilization for women's rights, a development closely intertwined with the initiatives of the UN. In Mexico, conference participants drafted a *World Plan of Action* that set the agenda for eliminating discrimination against women. It also extended International Women's Year to a Decade of Women (1975–1985). Affirming that equality had to begin in the family, the plan demanded a more equitable division of labor between men and women, or fathers and mothers, in household settings.[9] It also encouraged women to form NGOs and to mobilize in support of the plan. In the course of the Decade of Women, the number of global advocacy networks among women exploded, providing women with new opportunities to assume leadership roles in their struggle for gender equity.[13] In a parallel explosion of research, women documented, exchanged, and applied information regarding the conditions of women's lives. Pioneering research, enhanced visibility, and growing political clout helped women pressure governments to enhance gender equality.

At the conference in Mexico as well as at other UN meetings, activists elaborated a novel vision of women's rights that prompted even institutions of a neo-Malthusian bent, like the U.S. Population Council, to "rethink its position on women and on research into women's roles and status."[11] The Population Council consultant Anna Quandt, for example, reported on the Mexico conference and its meaning for the Population Council. Her detailed account recommended that council leaders consider women's individual needs and demands, women's rights to education and employment, and women's freedom from the legal and social discrimination that had limited their personal development, productive capacities, and reproductive choices.[12]

Unmatched international legal norms for women's rights set by the 1979 Convention on the Elimination of All Forms of Discrimination against Women (CEDAW) further pressured governments to commit to codifying gender equity. Concerned national leaders could choose to ratify CEDAW or to sign a modified version. In 1980, at the second World Conference in the UN Decade for Women held in Copenhagen, sixty-four states signed the convention and two ratified the document. In 1981, CEDAW was enacted after twenty nations ratified it.[13] These developments also led to more outspoken affirmations of women's rights. The Declaration and Program of Action of the 1993 World Conference on Human Rights, held in Vienna, officially acknowledged that "women's rights are human rights." Women's human rights "should form an integral part of the United Nations human rights activities."[14] In 1994, the UN World Conference on Population and Development, held in Cairo, defined and recognized the "reproductive rights" of both men and women, specifying that "reproductive health . . . implies that people are able to have a satisfying sex life and that they have the capability to reproduce and the freedom to decide if, when, and how often to do so."[15] In short, by the 1995 fourth UN World Conference on Women, held in Beijing, women's rights had become a central part of the official international human rights language and agenda.[16]

Chileans, meanwhile, participated in a remarkable transition to democracy after citizens rejected military rule in the 1988 military-sponsored plebiscite. In December 1989, for the first time in almost two decades, citizens elected members of Congress and a new president through a democratic electoral process.[17] Christian Democrat Patricio Aylwin won the election with a majority vote of 55 percent and was inaugurated in March 1990, bringing to power the new Coalition for Democracy Party (the Concertación de los partidos por la democracia or Concertación). Two months after taking office, he set up the Truth and Reconciliation Committee to investigate and report the human rights violations that had taken place under Pinochet's dictatorship. In subsequent years, the young democracy struggled to overcome the political legacy of dictatorship, most prominently present in the 1980 right-wing constitution written and ratified under Pinochet's regime. Opponents from the political center and the left moderated or silenced their critiques for the sake of peace in the process of transition. As a result, Pinochet prolonged his power and used it not only to protect the military but also to place the wife of the commander of the armed forces (rather than the president's wife) as the head of CEMA, the organization of Mothers' Centers.[18]

Negotiating Politics and Setting Priorities

Initially, women's groups were united by their common goal of defeating dictatorship, but partisan, financial, and class competitions contributed to a growing disunity among women's groups in the changed political climate.[19] Peruvian feminist Virginia Vargas, intimately familiar with Chilean women's mobilization, made clear that the decline of military rule required new strategies of feminist positioning: "the certainties of the 1980s about what the 'women in [the] movement' sought to change in reference to gender-based oppression . . . gave way to a period of major uncertainty, of a more reflective position, more removed from the big utopia, and instead anchored in more realistic visions, more open to connect its struggles and propositions to the transformative perspectives . . . of democratic civil societies."[20] When Chilean women formulated more "realistic visions," they often excluded feminists who proposed radical change. They also alienated poor, less educated women.

Indeed, class and political divisions among women's groups cultivated resentment, which created fissures. Many poor women felt that their views and concerns hardly even influenced policy propositions. *Pobladora* activist Coti Silva, for example, summed up her understanding of the changes that took place, reevaluated her own participation in the Movement of Shantytown Women (MOMUPO), and concluded that unity was a sentiment of the past: "I believe that it was very nice to mutually discover each other during [the dictatorship], but I feel that it ended after we returned to democracy, [when] each one went back to her place. I believe that necessity was what made us get together more, the truth is that we needed each other; the professional women, the intellectuals needed us, and we needed them. . . . I believe the chance for solidarity emerged; it was a necessary alliance. I know that it continues to be necessary and there are still some that do it that way, but it has been hard to reestablish; interests are different, other interests have emerged, but the women of the proletariat were again left alone."[21]

Indeed, as moderate middle-class feminists entered negotiations with the political representatives of the new democracy, they generally left their proletarian sisters behind and focused their attention on formal institutional reforms. In July 1988, twenty-two women's organizations drafted the "Demandas de las Mujeres a la Democracia" (Women's demands for democracy).[22] The demands addressed three major areas: women's citizenship and civil rights, women's rights as mothers, and the rights of female workers. The document further insisted that women be valued "not only as mothers, wives, or in the household," but also as full citizens with access to political rights equal to those of men.[23] Specifically, 30 percent of decision-making positions in government should be reserved for women—and an official institution at the ministerial level should manage the true democratization of public policies. Frohmann recalled that the initiative did not elicit an enthusiastic response among male politicians who preferred to ignore the call for quota regulations.[24] But women's demands for state-led feminist politics, for an institution specifically in charge of women's rights, met less resistance.

In December 1988, women from political parties, feminist groups, and other women's organizations founded the Concertación Nacional de Mujeres por la Democracia (National Coalition of Women for Democracy), an autonomous political coalition aimed at shaping the political direction of the Coalition of Parties for Democracy, the Concertación. They prepared a government program with a focus on gender: eleven commissions of women drafted recommendations for specific areas, such as health, work, family, and education. In the process, coalition members set political priorities not shared by all women's groups. Negotiating moderate propositions, they excluded "radical" demands for, for example, changes in abortion and divorce legislation.[25] The coalition alienated those feminists who had insisted on the importance of such legislative change. But it won the approval of a politically conservative opposition that had initially rejected their demands. In 1991, the goal to promote women's rights became an official part of government policy through the National Office for Women's Affairs (Servicio Nacional de la Mujer, SERNAM).[26]

The potential gains of SERNAM's state-led feminism remained the subject of ongoing debate and contributed to the lasting split among women's groups. Some groups insisted on the need of an autonomous feminist movement, independent from the state. Critics of SERNAM claimed that the agency isolated women's demands from mainstream politics and lamented that gender-specific legislation received varying degrees of attention depending on the changing interests of the state.[27] These critics also feared that politics had, once again, relied on the fixed dynamics of an *acuerdo de caballeros* (a gentlemen's agreement) that merely tolerated women's presence as an empty symbol of change.[28] Others strongly believed in integration, not autonomy, and supported SERNAM as a moderate yet viable approach to feminist demands. They argued that "the state is a key actor for women" that also had the power to channel resources toward women.[29] Supporters of state-led feminism applauded SERNAM's commitment to fulfilling the international norms of women's rights defined by CEDAW, as well as its efforts to implement legal changes and secure gender equity in work and family lives and citizenship rights.

SERNAM mediated the demands of different women's movements and gave women some power by promoting selected contribution to policy designs for particular government programs.[30] Women of the Concertación had gained the most access to shaping the feminist agenda of the new democracy, but their involvement did not end the tradition of male-based political structures and patriarchal party politics.[31] In addition, they did not overcome class divisions. *Pobladora* feminists and women from poor sectors of society testified to their ongoing exclusion from the making of the new democracy. Even female activists in NGOs from various class backgrounds pointed to the difficult relationships between SERNAM officials and Chilean women in civil society.

In its effort to build ties to women's groups, SERNAM prioritized NGOs over grassroots-level women's groups. The former often had a history of foreign or domestic funding and a more established organizational continuity. But even SERNAM's "favored" contacts, NGO activists, critiqued the nature of their relationship with state-led feminism. Rosana Ceorino, for example, from an

NGO working with *pobladoras*, complained that SERNAM "wanted to convert NGOs into intermediaries between the *pobladoras* of civil society and the State, and it was very manipulative. SERNAM would send a fax saying 'come here women,' and in the end we were getting fed up with that type of intermediation which was ultimately a manipulation or utilization on the part of the State to get the people it wanted for its events."[32] Another NGO member, Francisca Rodríguez, rejected the degree of control and cooptation SERNAM seemingly took for granted in its relation with women's groups. She said "[w]e are not going to run behind this merry-go-round of being summoned for projects, because that is the characteristic of the subsidiary state, which is every day summoning [organizations] for different projects and the whole world chases after these projects because of a lack of resources and ends up applying the policies of the State and abandoning the political proposals and plans of their own organizations."[33]

In SERNAM's relations with women of civil society, divisions along class- and political lines became as pronounced as divisions among degrees of "feminist expertise." The members of the women's collective Raíces (Roots), for example, noticed that SERNAM preferred to cooperate with middle-class feminists even when poor women had experiences to share and propositions to offer. Raíces women had plenty of both. Their collective, founded in 1991 as a Santiago-based feminist social work project, brought together *pobladoras* and popular educators, dedicated to education, consciousness-raising, and collective action.[34] Educators promoted mutual learning and incorporated the personal experiences of all participants. Workshops and educational handbooks produced by Raíces members found enthusiastic response, and youth-directed initiatives even inspired a younger generation of women to form an independent group, Nuevas Raíces (New Roots).[35] Nonetheless, Raíces members witnessed firsthand the top-down approach of professional feminists that dismissed community-based knowledge and prioritized professional expertise. They described the reaction of SERNAM staff to their ideas as outright disrespectful and felt that their formal proposals did not receive adequate attention. One Raíces member remarked that "our work isn't respected. We're seen as rebels. We don't have professional staff. We don't use language that community residents don't understand."[36] Indeed, the "languages" of women who mobilized for gender equity could not always be "translated" to everyone across class and political lines. This challenge was all too familiar to feminists who worked not just at the national level but who also participated in international feminist gatherings.

Global Feminisms: Discussing Diversity
and Setting Priorities

The 1975 UN International Women's Year conference held in Mexico underscored that economic and political differences between countries translated
into differential access to interpretive power. Women of "third world" countries
severely critiqued the dominant position "first world" women occupied at
meetings that were supposedly dedicated to the rights of all.[37] In her powerful
testimonial account, Domitila Barrios de Chungara, a woman of the Bolivian
mines, offered astute insights into the burdensome legacy of feminist difference
that became evident at the 1975 gathering. Barrios de Chungara had gained fame
in Bolivia for her persistent defense of the rights of mine workers and women and
traveled to Mexico in the capacity of a spokeswoman for her community.
It was her first experience abroad, and her first connection to international
feminism. She recorded her impressions upon entering the first overcrowded
meeting of the tribunal, the meeting of nongovernmental organizations that
paralleled the UN gathering:

> I imagined I'd hear things that would make me get ahead in life, in the
> struggle, in my work [for the community]. Well, at that moment a *gringa*
> went over to the microphone with her blond hair and . . . her hands in her
> pockets, and she said to the assembly: "I've asked for the microphone so I
> can tell you about my experience. Men should give us a thousand and one
> medals because we, the prostitutes, have the courage to go to bed with so
> many men." . . . Well, my friend and I left because there were hundreds of
> prostitutes in there talking about their problems. And we went into another
> room. There were the lesbians. And there, also, their discussion was about
> how "they feel happy and proud to love another woman . . . that they should
> fight for their rights . . . " . . . Those weren't my interests. And for me it was
> incomprehensible that so much money should be spent to discuss those things
> in the Tribunal. Because I'd left my *compañero* with the seven kids and him
> having to work in the mine every day. I'd left my country to let people know
> what my homeland's like, how it suffers, how in Bolivia the charter of the
> United Nations isn't upheld.[38]

Barrios de Chungara's assessment was echoed by the disappointed, disillusioned
reactions of other "third world" women. Many Latin American feminists came to
agree "on the basic irrelevance of the North American feminist model for Latin

American women's problems." It became clear that building international ties between "first" and "third" world feminists required new types of compromises.[39]

Some scholars have categorized the disagreements by distinguishing between "first world" feminists who prioritized "women's issues" and "third world" feminists who sought to address "political issues."[40] This division also became apparent at the 1980 UN Decade for Women World Conference in Copenhagen. A participant from the United States documented activities that reflected initiatives of the "political" camp: Bolivian women and those who supported their cause marched in protest of a coup that had taken place in Bolivia the day before. The Danish police intervened, and a few people got hurt. At another demonstration, women marched in solidarity with the women of Northern Ireland. Women from Ukraine held a hunger strike to protest conditions of abuse at home. At yet another event, refugee women from Palestine made a case for what they considered Zionist abuses. Some used the meeting to emphasize the importance of addressing the Arab-Israeli struggle from women's points of view.[41] On the other side were those who complained that the Copenhagen conference gave too much emphasis to "'Zionism', 'Racism', and 'Western Imperialism,' thereby ignoring the much needed struggle for women's rights and their legally subordinate status in over 75 of the 118 countries attending."[42]

Despite the fundamental disagreements over women's priorities, many participants engaged in fruitful dialogues. Miren Busto and Eugenia Hola, both at the theoretical and activist core of the Círculo back in Chile, used the 1980 meeting in Copenhagen to present insights into the severity of human rights abuses and the multiple settings of violence against women in Latin America. They insisted that international network building could become a concrete reality of global women's mobilization only after national and regional diversity was acknowledged and after the demands of "third world" women were seriously considered an integral part of international advocacy.[43] And many women, like a U.S. feminist who published a favorable review of Barrios de Chungara's testimony in 1982, acknowledged that embracing difference was an essential element of an international feminist discourse. The review recognized that "as a third world woman, [Domitila Barrios de Chungara] must face a double oppression: as a woman, and as a Bolivian oppressed by a government backed by imperialist dollars. . . . Her insights can offer us ways to remove the blinders we often wear as we study what the women's liberation movement is to us. If we are to make social change, we must not be exclusionary of any women, but rather work on understanding our differences and finding strength in our diversity."[44]

When the 1985 Nairobi conference closed the Decade for Women, differences persisted, but participants were no longer skeptical about the actual usefulness of future gatherings. Overall attendance had increased significantly, especially at the forum that accompanied the official meeting. It brought together about thirteen thousand delegates representing 157 NGOs, in a gathering lauded for its "recognition . . . that women have diverse perspectives, issues, and priorities."[45] Although Maureen Reagan, the leader of the U.S. delegation, characterized the conference as an "orgy of [political and ideological] hypocrisy" in light of persistent disagreements, many continued to build ties of "global sisterhood."[46] Official delegates at the conference proposed a fifteen-year plan to improve gender equity in health, education, and economic development. They also stipulated that the UN must have at least one more world conference with a focus on women before the new millennium. Women in Latin America and the Caribbean, meanwhile, set up parallel women's meetings to enhance the dialogue among feminists in the region, particularly regarding violations of human rights and women's rights under dictatorial rule. Chilean women gained recognition for the campaign of *democracia en el pais y en la casa*: their slogan for their attempt to "extend the concept of [political] democracy to the concept of democracy within the home."[47]

Global Encounters, Regional Feminisms, and Women's Empowerment

In Latin America, and in Chile, international feminist encounters set the stage for dialogue, for solidarity among different groups of women, and for networking that enhanced collective mobilization strategies for gender equity.[48] Chilean women met with foreign feminists and discussed feminist strategies as different women lent their experiences to the dialogue.[49] Chilean feminist Chela Borquez, for example, remembered that "[i]t helped me a lot to be out of the country so I could talk to women. While we were fighting the dictatorship the world was experiencing the [UN] Decade for Women. Women elsewhere were making advances more than we were. The visits to other countries and the conversations with other women allowed us to see what was happening."[50] Borquez and others exchanged information, shared problems, and discussed strategies for change. International conferences brought together women from different regions in the Americas and helped build knowledge and solidarity, even if women did not always agree about the priorities their feminist activism should set.

Individual women's feminist encounters abroad strengthened Chilean feminist positioning. Some women learned of feminist struggles when they spent time in Europe or the United States. Isabel Gannon, a founding member of the Círculo (the Women's Studies Circle), recalled: "I first became aware of feminism in the United States, where I was living, in California, from 1967 to 1970. My experience with women's lib changed my life and was a most gratifying discovery. Once conscious of the issue, as you well know, there is no turning back, and I was more than willing to join the Círculo from its very beginning, always with the idea on my mind that creating a movement needed consciousness raising groups—which I proceeded to form as soon as it was possible."[51] Gannon drew on what she experienced living abroad and shared it with other women upon returning home. She valued collective consciousness-raising as a tool not only for individual growth, but also for the unity and strength of women's mobilization. Chilean women's international travels and experiences provided one opportunity for women's empowerment through exchange and learning. Organized international feminist encounters specifically directed toward women of the Americas provided yet another.

Parallel to the ongoing official global meetings under UN auspices, feminists in Latin America and the Caribbean established sites for the exchange of knowledge regarding specific regional challenges to women's rights. Beginning in 1981, and roughly every two to three years thereafter, Latin American feminists met together at international Encuentros Feministas (Feminist Encounters), hosted by women's groups of different Latin American and Caribbean countries. The initiators—mostly middle-class, professional, and educated feminists—attempted to create regular forums where women in the region could exchange experiences, ideas, and strategies for change. The Encuentros over the years served as markers of shifting feminist priorities, affording Latin American and Caribbean feminists space to discuss their similarities and differences. In the words of some participants, they were "springboards for the development of a common Latin American feminist political language."[52]

The first Encuentro, set in Bogotá in 1981, was remembered by many women who had lived under dictatorships as a space free of censorship and fear, a stark contrast to context of human rights violations at home. Participants began to question patriarchal institutions and identified violations of women's rights, including their reproductive rights. They exposed both state-led violence and family violence as tools that perpetuated male dominance.[53] In a collective effort to diminish gender-based violence, they declared November 25 as the International Day of Nonviolence against Women.[54] For some, like prominent Chilean feminist Julieta Kirkwood, Bogotá symbolized the restoration of power by and for women. In her writings, she describes the meeting as a "(re-)conquest of space": women gained access to an international realm that was, until then, patrimony of patriarchal culture.[55] Other Chilean participants learned to connect the domestic violence against women in patriarchal societies to the political violence against women exhibited by military regimes. They translated this understanding into specific demands for "democracy in the nation and democracy at home" and, subsequently, into the motto that guided their mobilization against dictatorship.

At the 1983 Encuentro held in Lima, songs and workshops demonstrated the newfound solidarity, personal friendships, and collective theorizing among participants. Women started the meeting by singing feminist versions of popular songs, like the Colombian verse "There goes the Caiman . . . it goes to Barranquila," which became "There goes Patriarchy, . . . it goes down the drain."[56] Some participants recalled joyful feelings of solidarity and belonging, as they greeted other women they had met at the first Encuentro two years earlier. The organizers, a coalition of feminist groups from Peru, struggled to cope with the number of participants, which surpassed all expectations: more than six hundred women signed up for the event, including sixty from Chile.[57]

In addition to workshops, film screenings enhanced discussions of transnational feminist concerns, such as the commercial exploitation of women's bodies. A Peruvian group presented a groundbreaking documentary, *Miss Universo*, critiquing the Miss Universe contest held in Lima in 1982 and addressing the diversity of women's needs in Peru.[58] The filmmakers provided a critique of the cultural imperialism that constructed blond, slender women as the epitome of feminine beauty; they also exposed the contradictions between Peru's economic problems and real-life poverty and the money that had been invested in the pageant. The camera moved back and forth between the contestants' glamorous environment on stage and poor Peruvian women on an urban sidewalk, watching the spectacle on a television screen in a shop window. The construction of women's images through the media, as well as class and ethnic diversity among women's groups in the region, became important themes of analysis and activism in the growing movement.

At subsequent Encuentros in Brazil (1985), México (1987), Argentina (1990), El Salvador (1993), Chile (1996), the Dominican Republic (1999), Costa Rica (2002), and again in Brazil (2005), women negotiated both agreements and disagreements about the priorities of feminist organizing. The gatherings continued to promote consciousness-raising, solidarity, and collective learning. But the meetings also highlighted conflicts among participants with different experiences and expectations. At the 1985 Encuentro in Brazil, for example, academics, labor leaders, union organizers, and political activists lamented a "lack of resolutions, strategies and theories" and left dissatisfied. Others felt that the presentation of theories and resolutions "would handicap the dynamic thought process which is the very nature of an Encuentro."[59] The disagreements showed that all participants needed to learn to negotiate diversity—of class backgrounds, levels of education, ethnic identities, rural-urban divides, and generational differences.

Chilean feminists found their international counterparts to be as ideologically divided as they were themselves. Eliana Ortega, exiled from Chile, and Nancy Saporta Sternbach, a U.S. feminist with a long history of participation in feminist gatherings in the Americas, identified at least three competing feminist priorities when they participated in the 1985 Encuentro. One group believed "that the feminist struggle precedes all others, that the class and race struggles are products of patriarchal thinking and that with a feminist revolution, the others will follow." A second group of feminists preferred to address women's struggles in the context of race and class, seeking "liberation for all, transcending gender." Ortega and Saporta Sternbach identified a third group "whose major preoccupation was with survival and whose major affiliation was with a political party. Their goals are to attain basic human rights (an end to kidnapping, disappearances, torture, militarism, malnutrition, illiteracy and inflation, as well as freedom for political prisoners), and to insure that they are not violated." Although these positions were not mutually exclusive, they still showed that there was not simply one Latin American feminism, but instead many that coexisted and addressed multiple realities.[60]

Chilean women had long tried to settle disagreements between the *politicas,* women who prioritized their active engagement in party politics, and *feministas,* feminists who were primarily dedicated to feminism, including socialist feminism.[61] Both *politicas* and *feministas* agreed on the need to promote gender equity but often disagreed about the most appropriate path to implement change. Questions of feminist strategy became even more complex after redemocratization, as Chilean women negotiated the split between *institucionales,* feminists committed to working with traditional political institutions like parties and governments, and *autónomas,* women who believed that feminist goals would be compromised through such cooperation and could thrive only in an independent, autonomous form of mobilization.[62] In the 1990s, autonomous feminists became a significant symbolic force, also affecting women's mobilization and feminist political strategies. Even if, in quantity, the *autónomas* were not a large group, they maintained a pronounced public presence challenging the incomplete nature of democracy. When a few *autónomas* were taken into police custody after staging a demonstration in downtown Santiago, autonomous-feminist Margarita Pisano complained that "[a]utonomous movements are not permitted. You have to be linked to a political party. That's why this democracy is a disgrace."[63] *Autónomas* also had a significant impact on the organization of the seventh Encuentro held in Chile, where these deep divisions, and the diversity of Chilean and Latin American feminisms, moved to the forefront of debates.[64]

As a participant in the opening of the 1996 seventh Encuentro in Chile, I witnessed firsthand the rising tensions, hostility, and disagreements about the nature of feminist mobilization that had emerged with the decline of dictatorships and the redemocratization in the region.[65] When the Encuentro brought women from the Americas to the small Chilean coastal city of Cartagena, *autónomas* angrily rejected any collaboration between women's movements and traditional political institutions, like parties and states, and they made a plea for complete independence from such institutions. Complete autonomy of a feminist movement would surely protect the ideological purity of its goals but would also rob it of financial backing and supportive political alliances. Prominent Peruvian feminist Virginia Vargas, who was present at the meeting, reminded attendees that the political changes in the region required a careful rethinking of feminist strategies, less confrontation, and more negotiation: She said: "The feminist movement of the 90s . . . has begun to shift its emphasis. One of the significant changes has been the modification of its anti-government stance, towards a critical-negotiation position in relation to the state—and the formal international spaces. This has also meant the transformation of a defensive autonomy . . . from a logic of confrontation . . . towards a logic of negotiation, but from a strong, propositional, and therefore communicative, autonomy."[66]

Indeed, activist-scholars like Marysa Navarro, Sonia Alvarez, and others reiterated a number of its specific themes, which would be debated among feminists even long after the Encuentro had adjourned. In Navarro's words, feminists had to resolve "the autonomy of the feminist movement in its relation to the U.N., state-leaderships, political parties, nongovernmental organizations, and international networks."[67] In Alvarez's view, the negative side effects of feminist mobilization in NGOs needed to be articulated and resolved.[68] She acknowledged that Latin American NGOs had a history of successful feminist advocacy and had often helped advance progressive policies. But Alvarez warned that governments too often addressed NGO feminists as experts, intermediaries, or surrogates for civil society, rather than citizens who mobilized on behalf of women's rights. States' practice of subcontracting NGOs could isolate activists from civil societies. When NGO feminists received funding, they could, unjustly, increase their political weight in the midst of other women's groups, thereby diminishing the influence of women with more limited resources and further contributing to the split among women's groups.

As feminists continued to negotiate the effectiveness of specific feminist strategies, the Encuentros did make a difference: they helped set global standards of women's rights. Women initiated advocacy networks that developed long-term strategies to combat violence, to strengthen women's citizenship rights, and to defend reproductive rights. At the 1981 Encuentro in Colombia, they had successfully raised awareness of gender-based discrimination and human rights violations by implementing the Day of No More Violence Against Women on November 25. At the 1990 meeting in Argentina, they had initiated the Day of Decriminalization of Abortion in Latin America and the Caribbean, raising awareness of the high maternal mortality rate due to women's self-induced abortions, which still characterized a brutal reality for women in the region. Most important, the Encuentros stimulated ongoing dialogues among women from different countries who address questions of human rights and women's rights with a new vocabulary and specific demands. Women who lived in exile further contributed to this dialogue.

Exile and International Experiences in the Making of Chilean Feminisms

Like Chilean women at international conferences, women in exile carried the message of human rights abuses abroad and inspired a sense of solidarity and global sisterhood. They found widespread support in many Latin American countries, as well as in Canada and in the United States (figures 6.1 and 6.2). In Eu-

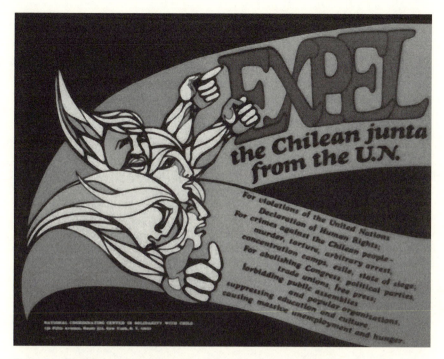

Figure 6.1. "Expel the Chilean junta from the United Nations for violations of the UN declaration of human rights." Yanker poster collection, National Coordinating Center in Solidarity with Chile, sponsor/advertiser. *Library of Congress, Prints and Photographs Division (POS 6–U.S., no. 365).*

rope, vibrant exile communities in European cities like Berlin, London, Madrid, and Rome contributed to ongoing awareness-raising and information campaigns intended to stop the abuses under dictatorship.[69] Spanish officials, for example, received 350 foreign delegations at a World Conference of Solidarity with Chile.[70] German activists brought together feminists and women of leftist political parties for awareness-raising and fundraising workshops in multiple German cities. Women in London collected donations side by side with exiled Chilean women to support "their sisters in Chile."[71] Italians and exiles in Rome launched the serial publication *Chile-América* that published a wide array of political commentary, academic research, and activist agendas.[72] And countless solidarity groups all over Europe and the United States called for a boycott of Chilean products like fruit and wine to increase economic pressure on the military government. In short, informal solidarity networks helped increase the interna-

Figure 6.2. "Whose side are you on? Since the military coup in September 1973: Boycott Chilean goods!" Yanker poster collection, Committee for the Defense of Human Rights in Chile, sponsor/advertiser, Brown, D., artist. *Library of Congress, Prints and Photographs Division (POS 6—Canada, no. 19).*

tional pressure on the Pinochet regime, and more formal networks followed. International women's groups would move from the "logic of solidarity" to organized "advocacy networks" that pressured individual governments, including Chile, to protect women's rights.[73]

The memories and personal experiences of exiles varied enormously. In some cases, the sense of having been condemned vied with feelings of betraying those left behind. For some, exile was akin to death, while others found it introduced them to new worlds.[74] Claudia, for example, a young, educated woman from Santiago, was overjoyed to return home in 1987 after thirteen years of exile in West Berlin. She recalled her perpetual longing for home during her long years abroad and remembered that she missed the playful *machismo* of Chilean society that did not exist in Germany. Claudia recalled her five years of life with a German man, a supportive partner who believed in sharing domestic duties, equal partnership, and joint parenting. She recalled how he dressed the kids in the morning, took care of the shopping, and often cooked and cleaned. "I think his whole energy was spent in his effort not to be a macho," Claudia lamented. She recalled that he conveyed a sense of sharing equality in partnership even in bed.[75] She, nonetheless, wanted to feel like a woman, to be seduced, perhaps conquered a little every day. Her experience as a woman was strikingly different from the experiences of most other women feminists, who brought home opposite messages from abroad. In short, although Claudia emphasized how she missed the "games," the seductive glances, and the tensions of Chilean *machismo* on the streets, other women critically reexamined how they could change gender relations in Chile. Many exiles who returned home recalled how their understanding of what it meant to be a woman had changed significantly.

Recalling the years of dictatorship, some Chilean feminists suggested that "exile constituted the most important link between national and international expressions of the feminist movement—and a vehicle for the diffusion of new ideas and forms of organization in the country."[76] Indeed, many women who left the familiar environment of home found that life in a foreign country triggered a reexamining of relationships and gender systems. Unfamiliar customs, a new language, and new relationships could inspire profound introspection. One woman from Santiago, long active in party politics back in Chile, experienced her first encounter with feminism while exiled in Germany. She described herself as "a typical example of a woman who begins to think about her domestic work and about motherhood." Initially isolated at home during the day, her only company was her three-month-old child. Lonely and impatient, she spent the day awaiting her husband's return from work. Driven by the need for human contact, she soon helped organize meetings with other exiles from Latin America and with German feminists, who all began to share experiences and insights. She recalled "that was when I began to notice the division of roles. . . . I had never asked myself about it before, and had accepted it." In the process, she began to define herself as a feminist.[77]

Some solidarity groups specifically focused on working with women, arguing that women often took the brunt of human rights abuses and military violence. A Chilean women's group in Hamburg, for example, suggested that women not only felt more pressure than men as they tried to protect their families, but that women were also "subjected to the most brutal sexual tortures."[78] Organizations of the German left published translations of Chilean underground journals and pamphlets like "Women's Voice" and exhibited photographs and drawings by women who had been imprisoned in military concentration camps. Prominent exile and MIR leader Carmen Castillo supported awareness-raising campaigns as she spent time with women's groups in Hamburg and Berlin. In numerous interviews, Castillo also addressed specific gendered concerns and shared her views on the role of women in revolutionary struggles. Audiences showed their eagerness to learn from Chilean experiences.[79] Chilean exiles collaborated with women of the German left as they explored women's roles in left-wing politics and discussed the obstacles to gender equity posed by traditional male-led political parties.[80] Yet despite these common interests, women from different worlds did not always understand one another right away.

In meetings set up by Chilean exiles and Berlin feminists, participants engaged in processes of self-reflection that also revealed cultural misunderstandings and barriers difficult to overcome. Seminars and workshops often addressed topics like partnership and sexuality, themes that, in the words of one Chilean participant, should be discussed with friends in private settings, not with people who merely joined the same solidarity committee, even if it was one geared toward women's needs.[81] Even as all participants made the effort to work "with women for women," German women reported that "behind the difficulties in their interaction lay different experiences in the process of socialization and understandings of the meaning of being a woman."[82] As German women listened to testimonial accounts of former political prisoners like Nieves, who came "from the concentration camp to exile in Berlin," or of Cecila, who shared experiences of women who were tortured, they also discovered the limits of mutual empowerment through solidarity.[83] Many women, after all, remained in Chile and still lived under the threat of arrest, torture, disappearance, or death. In the early stages of these cross-cultural encounters, many women found it easier to agree on class-based critiques of capitalist societies and temporarily set aside discussion of gender-based hierarchies and women's oppression.

Yet another group of exiles took feminist activism to a different level, using publications to reach a wide audience while abroad and eventually upon their return home. They contributed to collective awareness-raising and challenged the patriarchal master discourse through research, magazines, literature, and hands-on work with communities of women. Adriana Santa Cruz and Viviana Erazo, exiled in Mexico, began to work with local feminists. In the process, they identified themes of gender discrimination that affected women through-out Latin America and published *Compropolitan,* a small book with a big message that became a transformative tool of feminist consciousness-raising in the early 1980s.[84] Its title was derived from the Spanish verb *comprar* (to buy) and the title of the well-known glamour magazine *Cosmopolitan. Compropolitan* exposed media-marketing strategies of publishers who earned dirty money by (ab)using women. The authors provided a feminist critique of the media and decon-structed the transnational model of femininity that reduced women to consumers and sex objects. They revealed that advertisers manipulated Latin American women, teasing them into buying products for their supposed "mission" to con-quer men. Products like perfumes, stockings, and undergarments were high on the list of tools that allowed women to "take charge," the feminine way.[85]

Many former exiles continued to work for women's rights across the bor-ders of nation-states even after they returned home to Chile. In 1981, while in exile in Mexico, Santa Cruz and Erazo had started the journal *Mujer/fempress,* a constructive alternative to mainstream magazines tailored to women that would become a powerful international information network.[86] Santa Cruz came back from exile and led the editorial direction of the feminist magazine *Mujer/fempress* in Santiago. Published monthly, the journal offered news and background in-formation to a feminist community and dedicated special issues to particular themes; it provided feminist analyses of such topics as motherhood, the media, and the meanings of race, and discussed the characteristics of different femi-nisms.[87] Santa Cruz and others followed the mandate of the UN Decade for Women to document information about women and make it widely available. Historian Francesca Miller has noted that "between 1980 and 1988, 153 women's periodicals with a feminist or women's liberationist perspective came into publication in Latin America."[88] Indeed, these publications effectively translated solidarity networks into tools for gender equity.

Transnational advocacy groups in Latin America and in Chile also gained from the knowledge feminist activists produced in the United States. Dr. Marisa Matamala has spoken about international influences that inspired a women's health movement in Chile, recalling, "yes, there was a group in Boston, the Boston Women's Health Collective, that we all knew about."[89] Founded by participants of a 1969 women's liberation conference, the Boston Women's Health Book Collective (BWHBC) grew from grassroots initiatives into an organization known all over the Americas. Its initial publication, *Women and Their Bodies,* became an "underground success" due to its open exploration of women's health, women's life cycle, and women's sexuality. In 1973, BWHBC published *Our Bodies, Ourselves,* a landmark book and tool for women's empowerment. It fostered understanding of women's bodies, health, and sexuality to give women increased control over their own lives. In 1979, the book was translated into Spanish. *Nuestros cuerpos, nuestras vidas* inspired transnational advocacy networks among women who spoke similar "languages" of women's rights and health.[90] Matamala's engagement as a physician and feminist activist in general, and her interests in gender equity and women's health in particular, explained her early ties to the BWHBC. But the collective also provided others with the raw data for awareness-building campaigns and for transnational activism aimed at protecting women's health.[91] Chilean activists were among those who built ties to an international women's health movement that was, in the words of one participant, "bursting into worldwide bloom."[92]

In 1977, the BWHBC published the first edition of an *International Women and Health Resource Guide* in collaboration with Isis International, a new Rome-based advocacy network for women's health.[93] Isis, named in reference to the goddess of knowledge and creation, was founded by an international group of feminists in 1974.[94] In 1979, a small group of Chilean women exiled in Rome joined Isis and helped develop a Spanish edition of Isis's bulletin, *Women in Action / Mujeres en Acción.*[95] Ximena Charnes, one of the Chilean coordinators, recalled that "Isis has been a space for many women of diverse origins, nationalities and experiences, where we have been able to work and contribute to the women's movement. [It is] a space where we have learned to respect the varied opinions within our organization and within the movement in general. [Here, we feel] that all women share a point of view, information, a new sensibility, and that we all are enriching our selves in the process."[96] The cooperation among the members of Isis, female contributors, and readers of Isis publications furthered international advocacy among "women in movement."

In 1984, two of the Chilean women in Rome helped set up Isis headquarters in Santiago.[97] Between 1984 and 1995, Isis coordinated the Latin American and Caribbean Women's Health Network (LACWHN). Member, activist, and leader Amparo Claro supported LACWHN's primary missions: the "defense of women's human rights (social, economic, political, cultural, reproductive and sexual) throughout our region and, specifically, the defense of women's right to health throughout the life cycle [and the] affirmation of women's historic struggle for reproductive freedom and control over their own bodies, as a philosophical-political principle that inspires our action."[98] In her work, Claro has emphasized the importance of campaigns to reduce maternal mortality, to create proper statistics on the condition of women's health, and to build doctor-patient relationships that overcome the "masculine concept of women's health." She also highlights the importance of women's transnational advocacy to encourage legal changes at the national level: "We strongly believe that although a woman's reality in an industrialized country is not that of a woman in the Third World, our condition as a woman in a society that discriminates against us in so many different ways requires that we continue developing and consolidating the bonds of solidarity, sisterhood, creativity and love through communication, actions, and joint work."[99] Such efforts were especially needed given the dictatorship's legacy—namely, the military regime's new criminalization of therapeutic abortion.

The (Re-)Criminalization of Abortion

The "'Midwife of Death' Arrested," announced the daily La segunda on October 25, 1986. The article sensationalized the work of a "Madame Roxanna," a midwife supposedly widely known for her willingness to perform illegal abortions in her own home. She had been caught in the act and arrested in Arica, a city in northern Chile. She could be locked away in prison for between three to five years for performing illegal abortions.[100] La segunda's article reported merely one among many of the attacks on abortion brought before the public eye under dictatorship. In the words of First Lady Lucía Hiriart de Pinochet, abortion was "the most serious crime that can be committed."[101] Many shared her view. Carmen Grez—a public figure, female role model, and leader of the national

Women's Secretariat—compounded sexism with racism. Asked if she would not reconsider her position on abortion if her (fictitious?) fifteen-year-old daughter was raped, Grez responded definitively: "No. Not even if she was raped by a Black man. I could never justify an abortion."[102] All public condemnation of abortion contributed to the military mission to move abortion from the realm of the medical world back to criminal persecution.

The military made motherhood a patriotic duty as it instigated a population policy aimed at suppressing any conduct that could limit population growth, including birth control and induced abortion.[103] Therapeutic abortion, which had been legal when performed to save a mother's life, became a subject of debate in 1974, when Pinochet appointed a legal commission to prepare for the drafting of the new constitution in 1980. Jaime Guzmán, lawyer and influential ideologue under the regime, remained adamant about the need to outlaw abortions and to prosecute those who violated the law.[104] Although it was the role of Parliament to draft a new abortion law, Guzmán succeeded in adding a right-to-life clause to the constitution. Reinforcing his clause was yet another legal change that preceded the beginning of democracy and added longevity to enforced motherhood. In March 1989, just after the military was voted out of office, junta member Admiral José Toribio Merino proposed to increase the penalty for induced abortions to five years without parole, even if the mother would have died as a result of giving birth.[105] In August 1989, as one of its last legal acts, the military replaced Article 119 of the Chile Health Code with Act No. 18.826, stating that "no action may be executed that has as its goal the inducement of abortion."[106]

The number of women prosecuted for abortions skyrocketed in the 1980s. In her foundational research, Chilean attorney Lidia Casas has documented court cases that involved different "parties," including women who obtained abortions as well as providers and accomplices.[107] In the 1980s, approximately a thousand court cases involving abortion were reported annually; in 1983, criminal proceedings were brought against a thousand of more than forty-two thousand women who sought medical care for complications following spontaneous or induced abortions. Most trials concerned a single woman, but Casas reported that "up to six individuals have been tried in a single case."[108]

The new criminalization of abortion was accompanied by blatant misuse of medical records and violations of medical confidentiality, which provided the information that instigated arrests. In some cases, open memos on patients were passed among hospital personnel. Individual staff members also reported incidents, evident in, for example, a policeman's statement in court records in 1984: "He was doing the second round of his shift at the Children's Emergency Room in the Félix Bulnes Hospital, when around 0:30 the Midwife told him that [the woman] had induced her own abortion, and that I should take the necessary measures. I immediately sent notice to the Walker-Martínez Sub-station and kept the suspect, S.V.B.V., under arrest. During the interrogation she kept silent, and refused to say if there was a third party involved."[109] One public hospital in Santiago even "went so far as to give the legal department of the Ministry of Health a monthly list of all women who had received treatment for a suspected induced abortion."[110] Poverty and discrimination against the poor were a "common thread" in all cases. Public hospitals treated mostly low-income groups and were often unconcerned about violating the doctor-patient privilege of poor women, who were less likely to seek legal support and protest the violation of their rights.[111]

Poverty, lack of education, and limited information on birth control continued to present challenges that many women were unable to overcome. Anthropologist Monica Weisner, who worked with abortion patients in the 1980s, reported how misunderstandings about "contraceptives" often led to unwanted pregnancies.[112] Indeed, media advertising could contribute to women's confusions regarding birth control. A paracetamol commercial, popular on television, advertised the use of painkillers by showing a seductively dressed woman and playing romantic music, accompanied by the slogan "so that the night will be perfect." Misunderstanding the commercial, some viewers purchased the medication as birth control and often learned too late of their mistake. Weisner's interviews of women treated for septic abortions in hospital wards revealed that poverty was linked to limited education and erroneous ideas about reproductive anatomy and physiology. Some women believed they could conceive a child only around the time of menstruation. Others continued to rely on unscientific contraceptive techniques passed on through oral tradition.

Doctors sometimes failed to provide information to patients and removed birth control devices, such as IUDs, without offering alternative methods of protection. The case of Irma exemplifies the pain and dilemmas involved, made even worse by the criminalization of abortion. At the age of thirty-six, Irma, mother of four, had to have her IUD removed for medical reasons. Her doctor warned her that getting pregnant could be life-threatening due to her medical condition, but he did not give her information about alternative birth control. A few months later she was pregnant again. Fearing for her life, she sought a backstreet abortion and suffered toxic shock as a result. Her condition required a hysterectomy and the amputation of her left arm. Life got worse for Irma. She spent more than two months in the hospital, under police detention, and was sent to prison upon her discharge. In 1992, she was found guilty and given a three-year suspended sentence even as the country had moved toward redemocratization.[113]

Under redemocratization, women pointed to the contradictions between two final acts of the Pinochet dictatorship: the abolition of therapeutic abortion and the signing of CEDAW.[114] Not only did induced abortion pose a continuing threat to many lives, but legal specialists and transnational feminist activists also concurred that the termination of therapeutic abortion in Chile violated the principle that "safe and dignified healthcare is a major human right."[115] In light of this violation of women's citizenship rights, Chilean women reminded fellow citizens on March 8, 2003, International Women's Day, that "maternity should not be a product of fear imposed by law."[116] They also brought to the forefront another violation of women's health and rights: the (re)maternalization of women in Chile's health system.

Obstacles on the Path to Women's Right to Health

In the 1990s, some Chilean scholars and feminist activists demonstrated and protested that most government health programs intended for women reduced the health needs of women to their functions of biological and social reproduction.[117] This "maternalization of primary health services" addressed women not as autonomous individuals with rights to proper care, but as mothers and mediators of the health of their children.[118] Based on a survey of nine hundred women in three Santiago communities, sociologist Patricia Provoste found that outpatient clinics of the public health service attended predominantly women with small children. Neither adolescents nor women whose infants had grown up were among the patients.[119] A number of dangerous gaps in patient coverage were evident. The focus on women's reproductive health "left men out of the equation, [disconnected] from responsibilities in the realms of biological and social reproduction."[120] Next, health problems unrelated to maternity—such as mental health, aging, teenage health, domestic violence, and sexual abuse—received little attention in outpatient clinics. Finally, women who were not in the process of raising small children did not receive much needed preventive care, such as Pap tests and other procedures to screen for cancer of the cervix or uterus.

Neoliberal economic reforms set in motion under dictatorship also contributed to the deterioration of health care for women. Vast cuts in public expenditure on health increased the workload, eroded the salaries, and negatively affected the working conditions of medical and auxiliary staff, close to 70 percent of whom were women.[121] The lack of concern and respect for women health workers made clear that concerns over women's health were not a government priority.[122] Neoliberal health reforms also relied on women as "shock absorbers" who took on the role of permanent "volunteers" providing the health-care and day-care services family members were unable to afford.[123]

Women paid yet another price for biological difference. The neoliberal health reforms instigated by the military allowed private health insurance providers to offer women a reduced-price "no uterus policy" and to charge extra premiums for insurance that covered pregnancy-related services. Under dictatorship, Chilean health systems had opened the door to a system of health provider institutions (*instituciones de salud previsional*, ISAPRES), which attracted private sector investments and operated on a for-profit basis. ISAPRES reflected a strong bias in favor of well-employed male breadwinners and catered to high earners. Women were increasingly pushed to obtain insurance from the impoverished public health system instead. Since they were already disadvantaged by gender-based wage discrimination that paid them lower wages for equal work, they made considerably less appealing customers for ISAPRES.[124] The women who did find their way into private health coverage paid a disproportionate amount.[125]

As ISAPRES calculated the "risks" of insuring women of fertile age, the "threat" of childbirth became the primary reason to demand high contributions.[126] Ewig and others documented that in the early 2000s, women at the peak of childbearing age paid 3.2 times more than men for the same health coverage. ISAPRES charged high premiums even as women proved infertile or declared that they had no plans to bear children.[127] In the brutal logic of privatization, some ISAPRES responded to women's complaints by offering alternative coverage with benefits for women who had a hysterectomy, commonly referred to as *planes sin útero*, or "no-uterus plans." As poor young women were also targeted as customers for the more affordable plans, they often found themselves pregnant, yet without the means to pay for medical care.[128] Poor women often paid the price for the economic development strategies of a modernizing nation in the twenty-first century.

Under redemocratization in the 1990s and into the new millennium, Chilean women continuously felt the consequences of the ideological and economic legacies of military rule. They shouldered the burdens of unwanted (as well as wanted) motherhood, even after the military ceded its direct control over state policies. As it drafted the 1980 constitution, the military included a new right-to-life clause that could be removed only through the difficult process of amending the constitution. As one of its last acts, the dictatorship also changed the civil code to ban even therapeutic abortion. Many women were tried, and some went to prison, accused of having induced an abortion. Poor women bore the brunt, since they also paid the consequences of their childbearing capacity in the redesigned private health system, where they got more affordable insurance only if they "volunteered" to pay the price for childbearing out of their own pockets. The public health system faced challenges of its own; public health clinics gave preferential treatment to patients as mothers and neglected preventative care and the ailments of female patients that were unrelated to pregnancy and births. The issue of maternal health had been central to the broader discourse on modernity, citizenship, and the nation a century before. In early-twentieth-century debates, physicians had taken a stand in Chilean politics and had endorsed the rise of a welfare state and the establishment of the National Health Service (NHS) in 1952. Questions of maternal health remained at the forefront of political negotiations.

Strikingly, some life experiences of Chilean women in the twenty-first century seem all too similar to those of Chilean women in the early decades of the twentieth century. The criminalization of abortion by the dictatorship in 1989 is a throwback to the pre–World War II era, before the advent of preventative medicine and physicians' campaigns to diminish maternal mortality. The rematernalization of women in the health-care system is reminiscent of the medical discourse and doctors' practice in the earliest decades of the twentieth century, when the mother-child unit and doctors' efforts to manage "unfit mothers" marked the beginning of official public health initiatives. Yet health care in the neoliberal era is driven by the requirements of a competitive market place, which measures modernization by cost-benefit evaluations and the financial advantages to private investors. Not surprisingly, the quest to end violations of women's right to health care and reproductive choice have taken a central place in women's ongoing mobilization for gender equity.

In the past decades, an international movement for gender equity and women's empowerment has evolved. An unprecedented rights-based consensus combined human rights interests with women's rights.[129] As women mobilized for rights to health and reproductive freedom in Chile, they relied on the new global politics of women's rights that accepted feminist organizations as vehicles of social change.[130] Against the background of a new global paradigm of women's rights, and supported by the recommendations of CEDAW, Chilean women successfully claimed a more powerful voice as citizens with equal rights to men. Moderate feminists convinced the government to make a public and official commitment to gender equity, manifest in the creation of the National Women's Service, SERNAM.

In the 1990s and into the new millennium, international feminist gatherings, like the regional Encuentros, have continued to foster key feminist discussions in accordance with changing developments and women's concerns. Among those are the gender-specific impacts of globalization, the particular violations of the rights of lesbian women, concerns over teenage pregnancies, and, most prominently, violations of women's reproductive rights and the high death rates due to botched backstreet abortions.[131] Women at the forefront of international advocacy for women's health have documented the growing successes their lobbying has had on government health policies. Women in the Americas witnessed some improvements in women-centered care and increased attention given to women's concerns, but the case of Chile serves as a reminder that the improvements were accompanied by some setbacks in women's rights to health.

Chilean women have continued to rely on transnational and national feminist networks for collective empowerment as well as for consciousness-raising and political lobbying at home. Under the motto "Here we construct feminist power," the 2005 National Feminist gathering brought together more than 350 women from all over Chile in the city of Olmué. Participants made great efforts to come to terms with the many divisions among women's groups that shaped redemocratization. An older generation of feminists acknowledged difficulties of the past and negotiations that lay ahead. All agreed that those who stood out the most at the meeting were young women, who brought both the energy and the enthusiasm to tackle ongoing obstacles to women's rights. In the words of Katerin Barrales, coordinator of the Young Feminists, "a new generation that mobilizes on their own has power, but that does not mean that isolation is the best way [to mobilize]; we have to recognize the work of older generations. Our idea is to generate intergenerational dialogue."[132] Participants practiced what they preached and dedicated the opening ceremony to the thoughts and political propositions of feminist Julieta Kirkwood, who had died in 1985. In the three days that followed, they connected historical trajectories of women's mobilization to the analysis of the political strategies women should adopt in the democratizing nation of the future.

POSTSCRIPT

Democracy came and, hot on its heels, arrived the glorious and
majestic 21st century. We had waited for both with illusions, fears,
ideas, and dragons. The world did not end and the earth still rotates
around the sun. I like that. We have new opportunities to shine
bright on this planet.

The world that we inherited from the dictatorship has not yet
died a certain death. I do not like that. The mark it left is a tattoo
on the national soul; it makes me cry when I see its image, when I
watch how we built an intangible country, when I listen to words in
the wind, when I meet people with whom I shared the hard years,
and when we remember who we were back then.

Malucha Pinto Solari, actor and writer, 2007

MARGARITA CALDERÓN, *pobladora* organizer from La Victoria, remembered her invitation to Santiago's National Stadium to celebrate the return of
democracy and to listen to Patricio Aylwin a few months after he was elected
president of Chile in December 1989. She recalled how she put on her best
clothes to go to the stadium. This had also been the place where "her Nestor
had been, . . . where they had left him injured," injured to the point of no return. The National Stadium, used as a concentration camp by the dictatorship,
was not a place she had ever visited after her experience of violence and loss.
Once inside—invited to greet the returning democracy alongside artists, renowned politicians, and fellow Chileans—she could not help but look around
and imagine where Nestor might have been. She pictured him, where he might

have sat, somewhere in the rows, locked up. She felt the weight of their recent history. Her stomach turned when she heard Aylwin's calm voice, which stood in stark contrast to the terror of her own memories. When Aylwin began to speak of the military in his address, people in the stadium booed. Their jeering drowned Aylwin's words in sounds of protest, until he used his authority to silence them and insisted that he would be the president of all Chileans. Margarita Calderón felt that, although the leaders of this new democracy had invited her to participate in its unfolding, in reality, they never did.[1]

The importance of the memory of the recent past for creating a democracy in the present has formed an important part of a nascent scholarship on Chilean history.[2] Political leaders and activists within civil society have addressed questions of memory as they negotiated contemporary change and the future of democracy. But just as redemocratization has not yet included all Chileans as citizens with equal rights, not all Chileans share equal access to interpretive power. The memories of some are privileged over those of others. Margarita Calderón's reflections reveal that some Chileans carry the burden of the violence they experienced in the past. Other Chilean women have claimed that their memories, especially those that include the gendered aspects of human rights violations, including sexual violence and torture and the denial of women's reproductive rights, have not yet been given the attention they deserve. The histories and memories of women's struggles, thus, have to become part of the construction of a collective memory in contemporary Chile.[3]

New understandings of women's rights in Chile have developed in the midst of a long historical process of national and transnational negotiations involving motherhood, sexuality, political competitions, and terror. Feminist mobilization and women's access to citizenship rights were neither the inevitable outcome of economic modernization and political democracy nor the consequence of a linear progression that gradually improved the state of gender equity in the nation. Instead, they resulted from negotiations, still ongoing, that were shaped by both improvements and setbacks in the recognition of women as full and equal citizens. The struggles for rights by diverse groups of women have offered important clues to the variety of achievements or successes women could claim. Middle-class feminists and professional women often found it easier than poor women did to work with state institutions like SERNAM to assure that their concerns were addressed. And yet the poor, the *pobladoras,* articulated their own concerns about rights violations in their own context of class- and gender-based oppression and, as a result, developed different strategies for change. Even if *pobladoras'* views did not always conform to middle-class feminist terminologies, the former hardly had to be "taught" to recognize gender-based oppression and violence. Instead, *pobladora* feminists produced their own knowledge and held to specific means of resistance independent from middle-class feminists, even if they, as *pobladora* Coti Silva, put it, "went back to their places" in the aftermath of their brief mutual discovery and alliance during the dictatorship.[4]

In the 1990s and the new millennium, feminism has taken on a growing heterogeneity.[5] Once a *pobladora* organizer under the dictatorship, Aída Moreno has remained an advocate for women's rights: she founded a community center for women in Santiago's Huamachuco shantytown and has continued to work with other women who promote gender equity in their community and at home.[6] Other women, like María Chavez, have also applied past experiences to the present: Chavez helped found Mujeres Creando Futuro (Women Building the Future), at the beginning of redemocratization. She has reproduced the consciousness-raising activities first initiated under dictatorship and has joined others who want "to get to know ourselves, to see what it is to be a woman."[7] With redemocratization, personal development groups and self-help initiatives among women have represented one level of the lasting commitment to gender-based changes in society. Another level of commitment to gender equity was represented by advocacy groups and women's campaigns for legal changes.

In Chile, the women who prepared the 2005 National Feminist Meeting in Olmué were one among many women's groups who set new priorities for feminist activism in a democratic society. They aimed at uniting a Chilean women's movement and bringing it "up-to-date" with the realities of the new millennium. Their initiative was dedicated to merging the different expressions of feminism articulated across class and regional lines. In the words of participant-organizer Fanny Berlagoscky, women sought to locate a feminist space free from exclusions, overcoming the fragmentation that had weakened activist initiatives in the prior decade.[8] The Olmué organizers identified the lack of agreement concerning the most effective strategies for change as one of the major obstacles of feminist activism, an echo of the earlier critique voiced in the aftermath of the 1996 Latin American and Caribbean Feminist Enuentro in Cartagena. In 2005, feminists continued to express dissatisfaction with the nature of Chilean democracy and its failure to give equal attention to the needs of all citizens. But in spite of their criticisms of state policies, most agreed that feminist initiatives had to work within male-dominated political structures to effect change.

The patterns of Chilean women's mobilization for rights in Chile resembled other such movements across Latin America. Feminist scholar and activist Sonia Alvarez has asserted that all feminists had to adjust their strategies in light of changing political developments in postdictatorship societies.[9] Latin American feminists across the Southern Cone, specifically, had to revisit the practices that they adopted to confront the hostile conditions under the authoritarian regimes of the 1970s and 1980s. The terror of dictatorships had narrowed the range of feminist political strategies, and many women recalled that it was hardly easier, yet much simpler "back then" to be "united in our goals."[10] Nonetheless, as they were united as opposition, they were not necessarily united in feminist outlook and had to work through their differences under democratic governments. In most countries of the region, women have tried to settle the diversity of feminisms in civil society and have also chosen to interact directly with the state.

Chilean women also confront challenges that set them apart from other regional experiences. On the verge of the new millennium, Chile became the only nation in the world to prohibit the use of the word "gender" in Parliament. In 1995, some Senate members voiced fears that the term might "introduce the notion that there are not only two distinct sexes, but various, of diffuse and uncertain boundaries."[11] This antigender front brought temporary unity even among senators from opposite sides of the political spectrum. All were alarmed by the thought that the concept of gender could move Chile into dangerous deviations from the traditional, heterosexual, nuclear family that they saw as the essence of national tradition. Debates over women's rights on the nation-state level paralleled diverse feminist initiatives beyond the Chilean border. In the same year as senate members voiced their rejection of new terminologies, Chilean women rallied to strengthen global recognition of women's rights. As participants of the Fourth World Conference on Women held in Beijing, Chileans helped push an initiative for a Women's Citizenship Day. The Latin American and Caribbean women's movement had begun this project to call on governments to support women's full and equal citizenship. Women in Chile also joined a regional initiative to monitor the state of gender equity in Latin America through the Latin American Index of Fulfilled Commitment (IFC). As part of the IFC social watch, they have gathered statistics on women's political participation and access to power, on economic autonomy and poverty, and on women's health and reproductive rights.[12]

The different sites of debates on gender, one among politicians and legislators of the nation-state and the other among women-activists with ties to global feminism, elucidate the need to examine changes in both global paradigms of human rights and women's rights, as well as changing patterns of local women's mobilization, to understand the dynamic of women's struggles to gain and consolidate full and equal citizenship rights. Redemocratization, thus, is continuously shaped by the new dynamic of national and transnational advocacy networks for the twenty-first century. On the national level, women have lobbied for educational campaigns and legal measures against domestic violence and have sought health care and awareness-raising initiatives to address the lasting problem of teenage pregnancies. In 2006, 17 percent of the all pregnancies occurred among women between fifteen and nineteen years of age.[13] An advocacy network against violence reported that fifty-two women were killed by husbands or boyfriends in the first ten months of 2006 alone and criticized that reports of domestic violence often were not given adequate attention by authorities.[14]

Feminists linked the problem of teenage pregnancy to women's right to health and reproductive freedom, an important theme on their list of goals due to the lasting and painful evidence of the violation of such rights. Chilean health activists successfully lobbied for the legalization of "emergency contraception," a pill that women could use if other birth control measures had failed. Today, women above the age of fourteen can get emergency contraception free of charge in public health centers, without parental consent.[15] The new policy will significantly reduce the risk of unwanted pregnancy, and access to emergency contraception free of charge will protect all women, regardless of resources. Women can also use emergency contraception to avoid unwanted pregnancies and abortion. The availability of the new emergency contraception pill demonstrates a marked step forward, but unwanted pregnancy persists. In 1995, the Chilean CEDAW representative reported "that although abortion was illegal in Chile, in 1990 one out of every three pregnancies had ended in abortion."[16] Five years later, doctors documented that abortion remained one of the main causes of maternal mortality in the nation.[17]

Postscript

Women are still prosecuted for induced abortions, even as arrests slowly declined in the years that followed, from eighteen women prosecuted in 2003, to six in 2004, and four in 2005.[18] Heedless of its legality, women still seek abortion, even if they must risk the unsafe and illegal procedures that are far more likely to result in complications and death. This issue spans Latin America, where the regional estimate reached twenty-six unsafe abortions for every thousand women of reproductive age in 2006.[19]

In light of the peculiarities of its legislation, some scholars have called contemporary Chile a "puzzling combination of economic modernization and social conservatism."[20] Chile has had the highest rates of economic growth in the region and has been closely examined for its model economic reforms, drawing both praise and criticism.[21] It was also, however, one of the last countries in the world to legalize divorce, which occurred only in 2004. The bill took ten long years to work its way through Congress. The social conservatism that persisted in banning divorce and that continues to prevent the reinstatement of therapeutic abortion appears less puzzling when examined in the context of the political power of a newly conservative Catholic Church.

The Church's recent return to earlier doctrines—and an overt campaign against artificial birth control in the 1990s—has contributed to making women's access to reproductive rights difficult.[22] At the 1997 Conference of Responsible Parenthood at the Catholic University in Santiago, for example, Church officials promoted a position vigorously opposed to "forbidden methods" of family planning. A booklet on the "Regulation of Fertility," made available to each conference participant, aimed to justify the Church's views.[23] The text portrays procreation as the central mission of marriage and as the natural product of married love. Couples are reminded of the "illicit routes" that they must carefully avoid: abortion, sterilization, and all artificial means to separate the "conjugal act" from procreation. The rhythm method, relying on a woman's natural infertile periods, is presented as the only acceptable method of family planning. The booklet concludes with a reminder that all couples should embrace the message of the 1968 encyclical *Humanae vitae*, the Pope's official rejection of artificial birth control, as a passionate defense of life.[24]

The rigid message about the duty of motherhood was combined with the ambition to show a woman her proper place in society. Participants were also invited to read *Woman, What Is Your Mission*, which instructs wives to act as their husbands' collaborators.[25] It explains that a woman-wife is a mother by nature and a mother of humankind in the widest sense. Women are maternal beings who are naturally oriented toward caring for life and for others. To give life, to give birth, is the logical and required component of this existence. Couples who told their life stories and shared their views on life, procreation, and contraception with the audience at the conference added to the tone set by its organizers. They spoke candidly of momentary distress when household resources were scarce and raising many children was difficult. Yet every couple succeeded in overcoming each and every struggle by willingly accepting the Christian responsibility of procreation and submitting to one main message: it is a married couple's duty to accept all the children sent by God. This logic rejects motherhood as a choice. It also denies the material circumstances in the lives of many women who cannot afford to raise many children and who are, unlike the showcase couples at the conference, unable to overcome difficulties on their own.

Although recent statistics have shown that poor women continue to resort to induced abortions to terminate unwanted pregnancies, it is unclear what impact the morally conservative Church and the historical legacy of social conservatism has had on the views and behaviors of all Chileans. In 1991, a survey reported that only 22.4 percent of the population supported the legalization of induced abortions. A later survey that focused on the larger Santiago area showed that public opinion on abortion was divided almost equally: 51 percent rejected the legalization of therapeutic abortion altogether, while 49 percent believed it needed to be legalized. Only 23 percent of those in favor of legalization felt strongly or very strongly about the need for legal changes, suggesting a degree of ambivalence among proponents of decriminalization.[26]

Other indicators of change show less ambivalence: Chile's social conservatism has not prevented an increase of women's political participation—and of women in politics. Women's presence in politics has undergone significant changes in the past century. In the 1993 documentary *In Women's Hands*, left-of-center politician María Antonieta Saa recalled that "when I was a child, I had a lot of fantasies. . . . I wanted to be president." She also remembers that when she was born, women did not even have the right to vote.[27] Her personal engagement in a wide variety of political initiatives led to her deep commitment to women's education and her active involvement in the Women's Studies Circle under dictatorship, and the formulation of women's demands under redemocratization. In 1990, Saa became mayor of Conchalí, a suburb of Santiago, and a member of Parliament in 1994.[28] As an MP today, she stands at the forefront of ongoing campaigns against domestic violence and sexual abuse in particular and in defense of women's rights in general.

Some women in Chile have become decision makers at the highest level and have made real what was once a fantasy. In 2006, Michelle Bachelet made history by becoming Chile's first female president. She ran as a Socialist Party candidate, promised "change with continuity," and remained outspoken about her goals of addressing the needs of women and the poor.[29] Some of her political weight stemmed from real and symbolic connections to military rule, from her personal experience of prison, torture, and exile, and from her personal loss of family. The dictatorship, for example, killed her father. Today, President Bachelet can claim credit for an increase in women's access to political positions that has risen from a slow start to a remarkable high in some sectors of government.

Changes in formal political inclusion stand in sharp relief to earlier eras. During the early phases of redemocratization, women's access to the executive and legislative branches of government remained low: between 1990 and 1994, only 6.5 percent of senators were women and 5.8 percent of deputies. Some political parties boasted that 40 percent to 50 percent of their members were women, but even if some addressed the topic of political discrimination against women, few women held positions at important decision-making levels.[30] In 2006, Bachelet elevated the presence of women in Parliament to 15 percent (slightly below the Latin American average) and female senators to 50 percent (the highest percentage in Latin America).[31] Bachelet's election also shows that women have claimed access to political power without mobilizing the category of motherhood. Indeed, she is a mother and a woman in politics who has not used references to traditional maternal obligations in her successful bid to gain political power. Although we cannot conclude that the politics of motherhood can no longer limit women's access to equal rights, we can assert that women have reconfigured the meanings of motherhood and given it multiple dimensions that reach far beyond traditional essentialized characterizations of the mother as morally superior, domestic, and dependent on men. In the reconfigured space from mothers' rights to women's rights, women can claim citizenship rights equal to those of men.

The state of women's rights in Chile is not shaped by legislative change alone, and democracy does not lead to automatic improvements of women's rights. Feminists have struggled to find effective strategies to empower women in all sectors of society—and have also used the advantages of feminist networks in a global world. But despite successful alliances among different women's groups, on national and international levels, the movement is fragmenting; there is a diminished sense of urgency regarding a struggle for rights under democracy. Gender- and class-based hierarchies have found new expressions; new questions must be asked about the multiple factors that inhibit the rights of different groups of women. A rising religious-moral conservatism that denies motherhood as a choice is part of the new reality feminists currently address. Another set of obstacles has arisen from economic changes, especially from the neoliberal "economic miracle" that has restricted social services and access to public health.[32] Poor Chileans, and women, have paid the price.

In the twenty-first century, changed expressions of (gender-based) inequalities inspire new questions and innovative forms of activism. What strategies for women's empowerment are effective in this century, and how can international ties secure women's empowerment on the local level? How can activists build cross-national strategies and solidarity without compromising the national and local priorities of different groups of women? The female activists who have appeared in this book have helped provide some answers to these quests. As feminist activists at the national level, they have negotiated ways to help reshape policies in support of equal rights. As transnational advocates, they have fought for reproductive rights and the prevention of gender-based violence—and they have lobbied for changes relevant to the lives of all women. Their advocacy expertise has even compelled state officials to seek their advice as they negotiated policy changes and new legislation in Chile. Nonetheless, many female activists still represent a voice from outside the state and still must alert their fellow Chileans to the urgency of unmet requests for full citizenship rights.

NOTES

Introduction

1. Barros Borgoño, "La esclavitud de la mujer," as referenced in Lavrin, *Women, Feminism, and Social Change,* 368n3.

2. Díaz Arrieta honors her by including her in his profile of selected Chilean writers. See Díaz Arrieta, *Memorialistas chilenos, crónicas literarias,* 115.

3. She lamented that "society presents marriage as a woman's destiny, declaring her unable to be anything but a wife and a mother, all in the name of differences established by the nature of a woman and that of a man." Barros Borgoño, "La esclavitud de la mujer," *Revista de Santiago* 2 (1872–1873), 116.

4. For Mill's specific words, see Mill, *Subjection of Women,* 26.

5. Barros Borgoño, "La esclavitud de la mujer," 120.

6. According to Barros Borgoño, "As a result, only the one who felt she had the abilities required by this elevated mission would be a mother . . . [and] . . . all wives would be good [wives] because only those who had the proper natural faculties to be wives would be wives" (ibid., 120).

7. Iris Stolz evokes the meaning of this insult in her *Adiós General—Adiós Macho?,* 50.

8. Barbara Potthast titled her epic story of Latin American women *Of Mothers and Machos;* although this dichotomy and the juxtaposition of these binary opposing categories were central to the construction of power in Latin America, the Chilean case complicates the understanding of mothers' roles. It contributes specific evidence of the many meanings of motherhood and offers a more complex understanding of womanhood. See Potthast, *Von Müttern und Machos.* For an interesting collection of articles that offers great insights into complicated gender-based practices of inclusion and exclusion in different time periods and national/regional settings, see Potthast and Scarzanella, *Mujeres y naciones en América Latina.*

9. On *marianismo,* see Stevens, "Marianismo," 3–17. For a critical assessment of the concept, see Navarro, "Against Marianismo," 257–272.

10. Lavrin, *Women, Feminism, and Social Change,* 38.

11. For a detailed account of early elite and middle-class women's mobilization, see Verba, *Catholic Feminism and the Social Question,* and "Círculo de Lectura de Señoras."

12. For this process, but also for tensions within the MEMCh and feminists' changing tools, see Rosemblatt, *Gendered Compromises,* especially her discussion of feminists, socialists, and citizenship, 95–122. For the most extensive study of the MEMCh, see Antezana-Pernet, "Mobilizing Women in the Popular Front Era."

13. Joan Scott has long made the case for gender as a fundamental category in the construction of political hierarchies and as a primary way of signifying relationships of power; see Scott, *Gender and the Politics of History.*

14. See Nari, *Políticas de maternidad y maternalismo político,* and "Las prácticas anticonceptivas."

15. Of particular interest for this analysis is the work of Rebecca Cook, who connects human rights norms to reproductive and sexual rights. Her work exposes legislation and population policies that have often ignored women's own perceptions of their needs. See, for example, Cook, "Human Rights and Reproductive Self-Determination." For a definition of reproductive and sexual rights, and the core notion of "bodily integrity" or "control over one's body," see Correa and Petchesky, "Reproductive and Sexual Rights." Like the history of women's rights, motherhood has had growing significance in studies of women and gender roles in Latin America. One of the classic approaches is Chaney, *Supermadre*. Also see her own more recent assessment, Chaney, "Supermadre Revisited." For an interesting study of alternative constructions of motherhood, see Fiol-Matta, *Queer Mother for the Nation*.

16. Homero Manzi's tango "El Sur" originated, of course, in Buenos Aires—but tangos, when available, were popular in Chile. For reference to the complex sentiments connected to change and modernization, see, for example, Wilson, *Buenos Aires,* 210. The daily *El Mercurio* considered alcoholism "the source of all the ills of which our people complain." This was perhaps overstated but nonetheless showed the widespread sense of crisis in the 1920s. See Walter, *Politics and Urban Growth in Santiago,* 84–85.

17. "Conservemos a los niños y cuidemos a las madres," *El Mercurio*, April 2, 1908, as cited in Hutchison, *Labors Appropriate to Their Sex,* 208.

18. See especially Rosemblatt, *Gendered Compromises,* and Hutchison, *Labors Appropriate to Their Sex*. Rosemblatt's distinctive characterization of the Popular Front coalitions exposes the gendered dimensions of the compromise state in this period: in return for making working-class citizens respectable and for giving (limited) rights to women and men, state agencies and political leaders secured the male-led nuclear family as the foundation of social order. Hutchison's *Labors Appropriate to Their Sex* focuses on women's urban work and on the debates that challenged and (re-)constructed the roles of women workers. She effectively shows that gender affects and is affected by the dramatic changes of urbanization and industrialization. For the centrality of motherhood, see especially "The Making of Model Mothers," in Rosemblatt's *Gendered Compromises,* 167–174; and Hutchison's, "Women, Work, and Motherhood," in *Labors Appropriate to Their Sex,* 198–232. For a detailed study of negotiations over gender roles in mining communities, see Klubock, *Contested Communities*.

19. For the first full-scale Chilean Constitution, see Chile, *Constitución política del estado de Chile*.

20. Klimpel, *La mujer chilena,* 153.

21. Ibid., 158.

22. The exclusion of women from higher education and from specific professions is likely motivated by a complex set of reasons. Chile's first female engineer, Rosario Jacques, recalled that she signed up for a degree in engineering in 1923 because her parents feared she would "see naked people" if she signed up for medicine, her own favored career choice. Jacques, in the end, became an acclaimed engineer and came to like the field. Rosario Jacques, interview with the author, November 1997.

23. Caffarena quoted in *La Nación,* January 25, 1942, as cited in Rosemblatt, *Gendered Compromises,* 114.

24. Ginsburg and Rapp, "Politics of Reproduction" and *Conceiving the New World Order*.

25. This work has greatly profited from research that has begun to reevaluate those studies that have framed U.S.–Latin American interactions only as relations of domination and resistance or of exploitation and victimization. New scholarship has contributed fresh

understandings of global encounters. See, for example, Joseph, LeGrand, and Salvatore, *Close Encounters of Empire*. I acknowledge that some models of political, economic, and cultural imperialism can provide useful models for understanding specific chapters in U.S.–Latin American relations.

26. For early feminist ties, see especially Francesca Miller, "International Relations of Women of the Americas," and Francesca Miller, "Latin American Feminism and the Transnational Area," in *Women, Culture, and Politics in Latin America*, ed. Emilie Bergmann et al. (Berkeley: University of California Press, 1990), 10–26. Anne-Emmanuelle Birn and Donna Guy have documented Latin American women's creative involvement in multiple international gatherings. Birn demonstrates that local and national priorities of Latin American countries reshaped the agenda and global outlook at early Pan-American gatherings, not vice versa— an interpretation that Guy confirms. Guy also uncovers the important contributions and political leadership of Latin American women on such issues as child welfare at meetings held between 1916 and 1927. See Birn, "No More Surprising Than a Broken Pitcher?"; and Guy, "Pan American Child Congresses." Chileans were among the participants of the early Pan-American Child Congresses.

27. Htun, *Sex and the State*.

28. See Besse, *Restructuring Patriarchy*. Another valuable framework to analyze the nature of a reorganization of patriarchal relations is Florencia Mallon's concept of "democratic patriarchy" located in indigenous societies in Mexico. Mallon explores its application by older men who claim interpretive, judicial, and political power over women based on the notion of their responsibility as "good patriarchs." Both men and women participate in the construction and reproduction of this concept. Mallon, *Peasant and Nation*, 76. See also Mallon, "Exploring the Origins of Democratic Patriarchy in Mexico."

29. Zulawski, *Unequal Cures*, 119.

30. This "pro-life" reference stands as my term, not to be connected to its common use in the United States as "pro-life" versus "pro-choice."

31. I use this expression to characterize doctors' and politicians' efforts to employ women as part of the project of modernizing the nation. Doctors and politicians themselves did not use this expression.

32. McGee Deutsch, "Gender and Sociopolitical Change in Twentieth-Century Latin America," 293.

33. Ríos Tobar, "Chilean Feminism(s) in the 1990s: Paradox of an Unfinished Transition"; and Ríos Tobar, Godoy, and Guerrero, *Un nuevo silencio feminista?*.

Chapter 1. Public Health, Managed Motherhood, and Patriarchy in a Modernizing Nation

Epigraph: Sicard de Plauzoles, as evoked by social worker Luisa Fierro Carrera in 1929. See Fierro Carrera, *El servicio social en la maternidad*, 22.

1. Barr-Melej, *Reforming Chile*, 2. Barr-Melej states that the term *mesocracia* was used in Chile for much of the twentieth century, confirming the new importance of the middle sectors.

2. Mead, "Beneficent Maternalism," 120.

3. For studies on negotiations over patriarchy, see Besse, *Restructuring Patriarchy*; Mallon, *Peasant and Nation*; and Mallon, "Exploring the Origins of Democratic Patriarchy in Mexico."

For a good discussion of the roots and characteristics of Chilean patriarchy, and some unexpected places women made for themselves in mostly otherwise male-controlled settings, see Daitsman, "Unpacking the First Person Singular."

4. De Ramón, *Santiago de Chile*, 185.

5. On the number of female workers, see chapter 2 in Hutchison, *Labors Appropriate to Their Sex*. Hutchison exposed the ambiguities of census data on women's labor in this period: figures could show a dramatic decline in women's work only after changing definitions of employment and failed to reflect the spread of industrial sweatshops and domestic service.

6. Law 1838 of February 1906 defined the cleanliness of houses and simultaneously revealed the seriousness of the unhealthy conditions. The law gave tax exemption to working-class houses that met basic standards of health and hygiene. See "Casas higiénicas exentas de impuestos," *Boletín de la Oficina Sanitaria Panamericana (BOSP)* 6, no. 6 (June 1927): 496.

7. Collier and Sater, *History of Chile*, 177.

8. According to newspaper reports, women did not drink. See *El Mercurio* (Valparaiso), December 18, 1906, and June 15 and July 13, 1909, as cited in Collier and Sater, *History of Chile*, 176–177. For a discussion of prostitution and the (limitations of) government efforts to regulate prostitutes, see Góngora Escobedo, *La prostitución en Santiago*.

9. Guy, *White Slavery and Mothers Alive and Dead*, 30–31. For efforts to regulate prostitution in Santiago, see Walter, *Politics and Urban Growth in Santiago*, 34.

10. See Hutchison, *Labors Appropriate to Their Sex*, 48, 50.

11. A surprising number of women were independent singles with shifting relationships who worked for themselves or headed families. For women's choices and the implications of such arrangements, see Milanich, "Children of Fate." For a long view on changing family patterns in Chile, see Valenzuela, Tironi Barrios, and Scully, *El eslabón perdido*.

12. For the context of the economic and social changes, see Barr-Melej, *Refining Chile*. For a concise historical overview of church-state relations in Chile, see Lies and Malone, "Chilean Church: Declining Hegemony?" On the changing political landscapes and class conflict in urban Chile, see Scully, *Rethinking the Center*, 62–105.

13. Allende Gossens, *La realidad médico-social chilena*.

14. Eduardo Cruz Coke L., "The Chilean Preventive Medicine Act," *International Labour Review* 38, no. 2 (August 1938): 161–189. Another pioneering country was Uruguay, as discussed in Ehrick, *Shield of the Weak*.

15. María Angélica Illanes has argued that elites and middle-class professionals with access to state power sought a new social pact with popular classes: they contained popular agency by offering protection through state assistance. See Illanes, *Cuerpo y sangre de la política*. For a detailed study of social security, see Mesa-Lago, *Social Security in Latin America*.

16. For mortality rates as the "new barbarism," see Illanes, "Maternalismo popular e hibridación cultural."

17. For earlier welfare programs and the roots of health initiatives, see Horwitz Campos, et al., *Salud y estado en Chile*; and Illanes, *En el nombre del pueblo*. For mutual aid societies as the first collective response of workers to the "social question," see Gerald Michael Greenfield and Sheldon L. Maram, *Latin American Labor Organizations* (New York: Greenwood Press, 1987), 130.

18. Correa Cavada, Monckeberg, and Rivas Lombarda, *Estadísticas de Chile en el siglo XX*, 30. See also "Demografía: Chile," *BOSP* 8, no. 7 (July 1929): 714. High infant mortality also inspired regulations for inspections in the 1925 Health Code, drafted with the support of U.S.

physician John Long. See "La Mortalidad en Chile," *BOSP* 6, no. 10 (October 1927): 728. For the centrality of concern over children to policymaking, see also Black, "Taking Care of Baby."

19. Carlos Mönckeberg, Edwin Espic, and Manuel Guzmán Montt, "Maternidades y Hospitales," *Revista de beneficencia pública* 1, no. 3 (November 1917): 248–258.

20. Víctor Körner, "Protección de las madres durante el embarazo, el parto y el puerperio, y su influencia sobre la mortalidad infantil," in *Trabajos y actas del Primer Congreso Nacional de Protección á la Infancia: Celebrado en Santiago de Chile del 21 al 26 de septiembre de 1912*, ed. Manuel Camilo Vial (Santiago de Chile: Impr., Litografía y Encuadernación "Barcelona," 1912), 137.

21. Luis Calvo Mackenna, "Lo que deben saber las madres para criar bien a sus hijos: Cartilla de Puericultura al alcance del pueblo," in *Trabajos y actas del Primer Congreso Nacional*, 7.

22. Simon, "Reducción de la mortalidad infantil del primer año," 221; and ibid., 222.

23. Romero Aguirre, "El cuidado del embarazo."

24. Simon, "Reducción de la mortalidad infantil del primer año," 223.

25. Calvo Mackenna, "Lo que deben saber las madres para criar bien a sus hijos," 6–7.

26. Arturo Baeza Goñi, "Mortalidad Infantil: La falta de cultura de la madre chilena como causa predominante," *Revista de beneficencia pública* 8, no. 1 (March 1924): 58.

27. Ibid., 59.

28. Calvo Mackenna, "Lo que deben saber las madres para criar bien a sus hijos," 6–7.

29. For reference to breastfeeding at the 1912 Conference, see Congreso Nacional de Protección á la Infancia, and Vial, *Trabajos y actas del Primer Congreso Nacional de Protección á la Infancia*, 295–304. For wet-nursing as a crime, see Armando Zagal Anabalón, *Lactancia y nodrizas asalariadas (ley Roussel)* (Santiago, extended paper to apply for M.D. degree, Clínica de Enfermedades de Niños. Reader professor Luis Fuenzalida Bravo, Imprenta El Progreso, 1918), 3–8 and 13, as cited in Flores, "Rights of the Child in Chile" (online).

30. Rojas Flores, "Los derechos del niño en Chile." See also the English translation, Flores, "Rights of the Child in Chile" (online).

31. "Cartilla de Puericultura de la Sociedad Chilena de Pediatría," in *Revista Chilena de pediatría* 4 (April 1930): 213–216, as cited in Rojas Flores, "Los derechos del niño en Chile."

32. See Article 44, Sanitary Code enacted by DFL (Decreto con fuerza de ley) 226, May 15, 1931, *Diario Oficial*, May 29, 1931, as cited in Rojas Flores, "Los derechos del niño." See also Flores, "Rights of the Child in Chile" (online). For a study of the treatment of children and their "ritual integration" in the nation, see Rojas Flores, *Moral y prácticas cívicas en los niños chilenos*.

33. Father Rafael Edwards, in *Trabajos y actas del Primer Congreso Nacional*, 413–433. For a discussion of Father Edwards's concerns for the working mother, see also Hutchison, *Labors Appropriate to Their Sex*, 210.

34. Father Edwards as cited in Barr-Melej, *Reforming Chile*, 41.

35. The critique of the so-called unfit mother and its threat to Chilean progress was, at times, tied to moral arguments in yet another way: it included a critique of illegitimate birth as illegitimacy rates were, in the words of Nara Milanich, ranked on an imagined scale of civilization. See Milanich, "Historical Perspectives on Illegitimacy and Illegitimates in Latin America," 33. In specific situations, good motherhood could "wash away the dishonor of sex outside marriage" (see Rosemblatt, *Gendered Compromises*, 177).

36. On Social Christian views and practices, the roots of Christian democratic principles, and Rafael Edwards, see Samuel Valenzuela and Erika Maza Valenzuela, "The Politics

of Religion in a Catholic Country: Republican Democracy, *Cristianismo Social,* and the Conservative Party in Chile, 1850–1925," in *The Politics of Religion in an Age of Revival: Studies in Nineteenth-Century Europe and Latin America,* ed. Austen Ivereigh (London: Institute of Latin American Studies, 2000), 188–233.

37. For details on the consolidation of this relationship, see also Illanes, *En el nombre del pueblo.* For accounts of the origins of this approach in the nineteenth century, see Zárate, "Proteger a las madres," and *Dar a luz en Chile.* For the "mother-child dyad" in the history of feminism and health policies, also see Lavrin, *Women, Feminism, and Social Change,* 7, 111, 124.

38. See Croizet, *Lucha social contra la mortalidad infantil,* 28, as cited in Hutchison, *Labors Appropriate to Their Sex,* 209–210.

39. Dr. Lucas Sierra as quoted in "Conferencia Panamericana de Directores Nacionales de Sanidad Pública," *BOSP* 6, no. 3 (March 1927): 225.

40. For an analysis of the nature of the political alliances forged at the time, see Silva, "Forging Military-technocratic alliances," and Domínguez, "Carlos Ibáñez del Campo."

41. See "La Sanidad y Beneficencia en Chile," *BOSP* 8, no. 7 (July 1929): 647–651. The first Chilean Health Code had been ratified in 1918, stating that only physicians and certified midwives could attend women in birth and postpartum care; see "El consejo de gobierno local y la atención de los partos," *Revista de la Beneficencia Pública* 4, no. 3 (September 1920): 270–271.

42. Victoria García Carpanetti, "Algunas consideraciones sobre medicina social en la mujer obrera chilena," *Boletín médico social de la caja del seguro obligatorio* 4, no. 44–45 (1938): 15–25.

43. Hutchison effectively draws this conclusion based on parliamentary projects of the time. See Hutchison, *Labors Appropriate to Their Sex,* 198–232.

44. *Código del trabajo de Chile, promulgado por decreto ley No. 178, del 13-V-1931,* Libro I, Título IV y Libro III, Título IV, as cited in García Carpanetti, "Algunas consideraciones sobre medicina social," 17–18; also see Gallo Chinchilla, "Protección a la maternidad obrera," for details on regulations and the multiple institutions that began to address working mothers.

45. For a discussion of the multiple challenges to working women, see García Carpanetti, "Algunas consideraciones sobre medicina social," 18–20. García Carpanetti demanded an increase of restrictions on women's work in light of the realities she described.

46. "La semana del niño en Chile," *BOSP* 7, no. 8 (August 1928): 1004. For the 1929 celebration, see "Semana del niño en Chile," *BOSP* 8, no. 9 (September 1929): 975. For ongoing coverage of this tradition, see "Semana del recien nacido," *Revista chilena de pediatría* 3 (1932): 302–308. Jorge Rojas Flores has claimed that the ritual of the Children's Week originated at the Rotary Club in Chicago, and that the members of Chile's first Rotary Clubs, formed in Valparaíso in 1923 and in Santiago in 1924, introduced it to Chile. Pediatrician Luis Calvo Mackenna was a Rotarian. See Rojas Flores's section on "La semana del niño," in his *Moral y prácticas cívicas en los niños chilenos.*

47. "Semana de la madre en Chile," *BOSP* 8, no. 12 (December 1929): 1402–1403; also announced in *El Mercurio,* August 22, 1929. See also "Sesión del jueves 14 de noviembre de 1929: En homenaje a la semana de la madre," *Revista chilena de pediatría* 1 (1930): 142.

48. Alberto Bahamonde, "Centros de educación familiar," *Revista chilena de higiene y medicina preventiva* 1, no. 2–3 (January–March 1937): 142–149.

49. In 1925, some Chilean health officials endorsed sex education in primary and secondary schools as part of a campaign to control the spread of venereal disease, but parents'

disapproval prevented the implementation of such measures. See Lavrin, *Women, Feminism, and Social Change,* 139.

Some doctors and educators saw sex education as indispensable to improvements of public health. Between 1923 and 1925, Cora Mayer and Ernestina Pérez lectured on the subject and called for compulsory sex education for all children. Mayer promoted sex education as a component of preventive health care with a eugenic component. See Mayer, *La mujer, defensora de la raza* (Santiago: Impr. Santiago, 1925). For the influence of different strains of eugenics in Latin America, see Stepan, *Hour of Eugenics.* On Pérez and Mayer, also see Lavrin, *Women, Feminism, and Social Change,* 112, 139, and 396n51. In 1959, dramatist María Asunción Requena even published a play titled *El camino mas largo* (The longest road) about Chile's female doctor Ernestina Pérez. See Boyle, *Chilean Theater,* 28.

50. See Javier Rodríguez Barros, "Hacia la despoblación," *Revista médica de Chile* 51, no. 11–12 (November–December 1923): 788–805; and Mamerto Cádiz, "Consideraciones sobre la Higiene," *Revista médica de Chile* 49, no. 4 (April 1929): 265–282, for references to the dangers of population decline. As cited in Andrea del Campo Peirano, "La nación en peligro: El debate médico sobre el aborto en Chile en la década de 1930," in *Por la salud del cuerpo: Historia y políticas sanitarias en Chile,* edited by María Soledad Zárate Campos (Santiago: Ediciones Universidad Alberto Hurtado, 2008), 131–188.

51. See del Campo Peirano, "La nación en peligro," 139.

52. For evidence and testimonial accounts on Church views on women's sexuality, see Drogus and Stewart-Gambino, *Activist Faith.* Maria, a Chilean women interviewed in the 1990s, found that "very few people [in the church] are willing to let us discuss sexuality, reproductive rights, and health" (ibid., 171).

53. "La sanidad y asistencia social en Chile," *BOSP* 18, no. 1 (January 1939): 1–8. Excerpt from "mensaje del presidente de Chile al Congreso Nacional en mayo de 1938," 3.

54. Oswaldo Cifuentes, "Etapas del proceso sanitario chileno," *Revista chilena de higiene y medicina preventiva* 15, no. 1–2 (June 1953): 25–37, statistics on p. 25.

55. Cruz Coke L., "Chilean Preventive Medicine Act," 161–189.

56. Allende Gossens, *La realidad médico-social chilena.* See "El Dr. Allende nos expone la acción desarrollada desde el Ministerio de Salubridad," *Acción Social* 12, no. 100 (May 1941): 28–31, for some responses to Allende's text.

57. "Binomio Madre y Niño," in Allende Gossens, *La realidad médico-social chilena,* 77–86.

58. Ibid., passim.

59. Multiple scholars have commented on this image in Allende's book; see, for example, Illanes, *La batalla de la memoria,* 123; and Rosemblatt, *Gendered Compromises,* 160–161.

60. Allende Gossens, *La realidad médico-social chilena,* 87. "El Dr. Allende nos expone la acción desarrollada desde el Ministerio de Salubridad," *Acción social* 12, no. 100 (May 1941): 28–31.

61. *Caja del seguro obrero obligatorio.*

62. Physicians were not only closely connected to the political process of nation building in Chile, but they were also deeply involved in fundamental questions of policy-making. The medical profession reflected the political polarization, especially in the early decades of the twentieth century, when popular sectors demanded change. For insights, see Molina, *La cuestión social y la opinión de la elite médica,* and "Sujetos sociales en el desarrollo de las instituciones sanitarias en Chile." See also Valdivia Ortiz de Zárate, *La milicia republicana.*

63. For women's problems with male workers' politics, see especially Hutchison, *Labors Appropriate to Their Sex,* 59–96. For the gendered nature of women's integration in anarchist initiatives, see Hutchison, "'La Mujer Esclava' to 'la Mujer Limon.'"

64. McGee Deutsch, *Las derechas,* 24. Catholic women's organizations established worker cooperatives and Catholic unions to prevent leftist mobilization. See Hutchison, *Labors Appropriate to Their Sex,* 12.

65. See McGeeDeutsch, *Las derechas,* for the "era of the ligas" in Chile (pp. 59–77) and for the context of fascism (pp. 143–192); and ibid., 76.

66. Verba, *Catholic Feminism and the Social Question.* See also Elizabeth Q. Hutchison, "Señoras y Señoritas: Catholic Women Defend the *Hijas de Familia,*" in Hutchison, *Labors Appropriate to Their Sex,* 171–197.

67. See Verba, "Círculo de Lectura de Señoras," 6–33; and Verba, *Catholic Feminism and the Social Question.*

68. Franceschet, *Women and Politics in Chile,* 35.

69. Chaney, *Supermadre.*

70. Lavrin, *Women, Feminism, and Social Change,* 211–216.

71. Lavrin makes this point about Southern Cone feminists in ibid., 48.

72. Tripp, "Evolution of Transnational Feminisms," 57–58.

73. For the nature of their engagement and quests for married women's rights, also see United States, *World Court, Hearings . . . Relative to Executive A (71st Congress), Protocols Concerning Adherence of the United States to the Court of International Justice* (Washington, D.C.: U.S. Government Printing Office, 1932), 29–58.

74. Miller, "International Relations of Women of the Americas," 171–172.

75. See Birn, "No More Surprising Than a Broken Pitcher," 17–46; and Guy, "Pan American Child Congresses," 272–292. Chileans were among the participants of the early Pan-American Child Congresses.

76. See interview with Elena Caffarena in María Angelica Meza, *La otra mitad de Chile* (Santiago: CESOC, 1986), 49, as cited in Corinne Antezana-Pernet, "Peace in the World and Democracy at Home: The Chilean Women's Movement in the 1940s," in *Latin America in the 1940s: War and Postwar Transitions,* ed. David Rock (Berkeley: University of California Press, 1994), 171.

77. See Vergara, *Memorias de una mujer irreverente,* 174. Vergara also proposed voluntary motherhood.

78. As cited in Vidal, *La emancipación de la mujer,* 47.

79. For a first-rate overview of the political negotiations, see Antezana-Pernet, "Peace in the World."

80. "La mujer obrera es doblemente explotada" and "Proyecciones del movimiento emancipacionista femenino," *La mujer nueva* 1 (November 1935): 1–2.

81. "Los niños proletarios tienen hambre," *La mujer nueva* 1 (November 1935): 2.

82. *La mujer nueva* 22 (December 1938): 4 and 5.

83. For more detail on how MEMCh drew on traditional images of wives and mothers in charge of their families, see Antezana-Pernet, "Mobilizing Women in the Popular Front Era," 176–185.

84. See ibid., especially chapter 3, "Pragmatic Feminism: The MEMCh Campaigns," 133–202; and Antezana-Pernet, "Peace in the World," 171.

85. See image and caption in *La mujer nueva* 18 (November 1937): 1.

86. Ibid., 1.

87. Dr. Lucas Sierra as quoted in "Conferencia Panamericana de Directores Nacionales de Sanidad Pública," *BOSP* 6, no. 3 (March 1927): 179.

88. See *maternología* under *crónicas,* first in *BOSP* 9, no. 11 (November 1930): 1340–1352. In reference to Chile, the chronicle quotes excerpts of Luisa Fierro Carrera's contribution to the Chilean journal *Beneficencia* 2 (May 1930): 1113. Fierro Carrera lamented that institutional protection of motherhood was still limited in Santiago.

89. Allende as quoted in "Pan American Health Day," *BOSP* 19, no. 12 (December 1940): 1209.

90. Former Virchow student Max Westenhöfer taught social medicine at the University of Chile; Salvador Allende was one of his students. See Manríquez, "Professor Max Westenhöfer."

91. See, for example, Cueto, *Missionaries of Science.*

92. AJW (Andrew J. Warren) diary excerpt, July 1, 1946; Folder: University of Chile, School of Public Health, 1944–1948; RF, Record Group 1.1, Series 309, Box 1; Rockefeller Foundation Archives, Rockefeller Archive Center (hereafter cited as RFA, RAC).

93. "Informe Presentado por el Doctor J.D. Long al Gobierno de Chile a la terminación de sus funciones como Asesor Técnico del Servicio Nacional de Salubridad de ese país," *BOSP* 6, no. 5 (May 1927): 409–414. For details on Oswald Stein and the debates of legal reform in Chile, including question-and-answer sessions, see *Acción social* 12, no. 99 (April 1941): 1–9.

94. Lewis Hackett, "Orientaciones Modernas en la Salubridad," *Revista chilena de higiene y medicina preventiva* 4, no. 3 (December 1941): 241–252.

95. Cruz-Coke Madrid, "Cincuentenario de la gran reforma."

96. See correspondence by Rockefeller Foundation field officer J. H. Janney to Sawyer, June 7, 1943; Folder: University of Chile, School of Public Health, 1942–1943; RF, Record Group 1.1; Series 309; RFA, RAC.

97. J. H. Janney, Annual Report 1947, International Health Division, Chile, February 25, 1948; Folder: 1339; Rockefeller Foundation, Record Group 5, Series 3, Box 104; RFA, RAC, 123.

98. Ibid., 124.

99. Ibid.

100. For specific agreements with Rockefeller Foundation, see Neghme, *Reflexiones sobre la medicina.* Hernán Romero, "Formación universitaria del médico en relación con la Medicina Social," *Boletín médico social* 14, no. 151–153 (April–June 1947): 161–163. For Chilean understandings of the revolutionary character of social medicine, see also Hernán Romero, "Formación universitaria del médico en relación con la Medicina Social," *Boletín médico social,* 13, no. 144–145 (September–October 1946): 628–632.

101. For medical education at the time, see Neghme, "Reseña histórica de la educación médica en Chile."

102. For a discussion of the origin and application of this system in other Latin American regions, see Birn, "Revolution in Rural Health" and "Las unidades sanitarias."

103. Octavio Cabello González, "Influencia de la Unidad Sanitaria de Quinta Normal en la reducción de la mortalidad infantil de la comuna," *Revista chilena de higiene y medicina preventiva* 8, no. 1–2 (March–June 1946): 15–27. Carlos Salomón Rex, "Organización y funcionamiento de una unidad sanitaria," *Revista chilena de higiene y medicina preventiva* 8, no. 3 (September 1946): 137–198.

104. J. H. Janney, Annual Report 1947, International Health Division, Chile. February 25, 1948; Folder: 1339; Rockefeller Foundation, Record Group 5, Series 3, Box 104; RFA, RAC, 87. J. H. Janney, Annual Report 1944, International Health Division, Chile; Folder: 1332; Rockefeller Foundation, Record Group 5.3, Series 300, Box 103; RFA, RAC, 92.

105. J. H. Janney, Annual Report 1947, International Health Division, Chile. February 25, 1948; Folder: 1339; Rockefeller Foundation, Record Group 5, Series 3, Box 104; RFA, RAC, 84.

106. See the discussion under "Los Guerreros Blancos y su Ejército de Damas," in Illanes, *La batalla de la memoria*, 88–99 (chapter 2). Illanes presents the role of *visitadoras* and the efficiency of a "game" of social mediation under the control of male physicians. She emphasizes the category of class. See also "La visitación de la miseria: Enfermeras versus visitadoras," in Illanes, *En el nombre del pueblo*, 337–345.

107. For a discussion of medicine and social control from a gendered perspective, see Lupton, "Feminisms and Medicine."

108. For insights into the multiple functions of *visitadoras,* see Illanes, *La batalla de la memoria,* 88–122.

109. See Donzelot, *Policing of Families.* Donzelot's study of French society offers powerful evidence of a system of state intervention in family affairs. Behind the facade of social justice that officially motivated state intervention lay the realities of a "tutelary complex," a policing of those families not easily allowed to be part of the family of the nation.

110. Hackett, "Orientaciones modernas en la salubridad," 252.

111. Rosemblatt has analyzed the contradiction of the tasks of social workers in her *Gendered Compromises,* 123–148.

112. For a revealing discussion of the power relations at play when *visitadoras* entered the most intimate spheres in the lives of the poor, see María Angélica Illanes, "Las Escribas: Disciplinamiento sexual popular en tiempos de una modernidad contradictoria, Chile, 1935–1948," paper prepared for the Latin American Studies Association (LASA) Conference, Dallas, Texas, March 27–29, 2003.

113. See Salustio Barros Ortúzar's inaugural address, *Primer Congreso de Gotas de Leche* (Santiago, 1919), 82, as cited in Illanes, *La batalla de la memoria,* 93.

114. "Chile: Escuela de Enfermeras Sanitarias," *BOSP* 6, no. 7 (July 1927): 554; "Chile: Escuela Nacional de Enfermeras Sanitarias," *BOSP* 7, no. 4 (April 1928): 482; "Conferencia Panamericana de Directores Nacionales de Sanidad Pública," *BOSP* 6, no. 3 (March 1927): 171–193; and "Reorganización de la Escuela de Enfermeras de Chile," *BOSP* 8, no. 8 (August 1929): 844.

115. "Higiene materno-infantil: Chile," *BOSP* 8, no. 7 (July 1929): 670–671.

116. See reference to an army of women in "Los Guerreros Blancos y su Ejército de Damas," in Illanes, *La batalla de la memoria,* 88–99 (chapter 2).

117. See Hackett, "Orientaciones modernas en la salubridad," 245, for discourse on the new role of nurses, clearly distinguished from social workers.

118. Ibid.

119. Ibid., 246.

120. Rosemblatt, *Gendered Compromises,* 131.

121. Ibid., 126–148.

122. Developments in Chile fit the Gramscian pattern in the construction of hegemony. Gramsci sees the state as the instrument for conforming civil society to the economic

structure—in this case, to the rising needs of an industrializing, urban, capitalist society. As a prerequisite to fulfill this role, the state needed to be controlled by those who represent the change that has taken place in the economic structure. Gramsci, *Prison Notebooks.*

123. Jorge Mardones Restat, "Origen del Servicio Nacional de Salud," *Revista médica de Chile* 105, no. 10 (1977): 654–658; and Hernán Urzua, "Estructura inicial del Servicio Nacional de Salud," *Revista médica de Chile* 105, no. 10 (1977): 659–662.

124. *Madre universal, un relato de los honores recibidos por la Sra. Rosa Markmann de González Videla de Chile, durante se visita a los Estados Unidos de America, 6 de Mayo al 18 de Mayo, 1952* (New York: IBM World Trade Corporation, 1952).

Chapter 2. Local Agency, Changed Global Paradigms, and the Burden of Motherhood

Epigraph: Víctor Manuel Matus, "El problema del aborto," *Boletín de la Sociedad Chilena de Obstetricia y Ginecología* 3, no. 3 (April 1938): 193, as cited in del Campo Peirano, "La nación en peligro," 133. Dr. Gildo Zambra, interview with the author, November 1997; also see "Dr. Gildo Zambra: Los juicios de McNamara nos quitaron el sueño," *Asociación Chilena de Protección de la Familia: 21 Años* (1987): 13–14.

1. Gall, *Births, Abortions, and the Progress of Chile,* 7.

2. Matus, "El problema del aborto," cited in del Campo Peirano, "La nación en peligro," 1.

3. Zambra interview; and "Dr. Gildo Zambra," 13–14.

4. For insightful examples of the bumpy road toward gender equity and reproductive rights, see Shepard, *Running the Obstacle Course.*

5. For an overview of the history of fertility regulation in Chile, see Jiles Moreno and Rojas Mira, *De la miel a los implantes.*

6. The history of first experiments with the Pill, often conducted without the informed consent of participating women, well exemplified tensions between the progress of medicine, the goals of population control, the need for family planning, and the rights of local women that also shaped the history of family planning in Chile. See Marks, *Sexual Chemistry.* For the first clinical trials of the Pill in the United States and Puerto Rico and the difficulties of finding testing grounds and for scientists longing for a "a cage of ovulating females," see Gijswijt-Hofstra, van Heteren, and Tansey, *Biographies of Remedies,* 127. For a history of interests in fertility regulation that conflicted with women's needs in Puerto Rico, see Briggs, *Reproducing Empire,* and Ramirez de Arellano, *Colonialism, Catholicism, and Contraception.*

7. I concur with Linda Gordon's assertion that conflicts over reproductive rights are political in nature and must be seen in the changing political contexts in which they take shape. See Gordon, *Woman's Body, Woman's Right,* and *Moral Property of Women.*

8. On the need to adopt a global lens, see also Ginsburg and Rapp, "Politics of Reproduction," 311–343; and Ginsburg and Rapp, *Conceiving the New World Order.*

9. On Ibáñez see, for example, Fernández, "Beyond Partisan Politics in Chile"; and Valdivia Ortiz de Zárate, *Nacionalismo e Ibañismo.* Also see Rosa Marcela Miranda Cabezas, "Carlos Ibañez del Campo: La configuración del hombre político," master's thesis, Pontificia Universidad Católica de Chile, 1994.

10. On Alessandri see, for example, Arancibia Clavel, Góngora Escobedo, and Vial Correa, *Jorge Alessandri.*

11. Collier and Sater, *History of Chile,* 288–289.

12. Ibid.

13. De Ramón, *Santiago de Chile*.

14. Ivonne Szasz, "Women in the Labor Force and Migration: The Female Labor Market between 1950 and 1990 and Female Migration to Santiago, Chile," *Notas de población* 22, no. 59 (June 1994): 30.

15. Ibid., 9–50.

16. Participants of the 1936 Medical Congress in Valparaiso addressed the issue and concluded that only limited, therapeutic abortion would decrease the numbers of women who died or suffered health consequences of illegal abortions. MEMch's journal reported on the Congress and on the problem of abortion. See *La mujer nueva* 4 (February 1936): 1; and "A los enemigos del aborto pedimos protección para la madre obrera," *La mujer nueva* 6 (May 1936): 1.

17. García Carpanetti, "Algunas consideraciones sobre medicina social," 15–25, see 23.

18. *BOSP* 13, no. 8 (August 1934): 771; quotes from *El boletín de la Clínica Obstétrica (1931–1932)*; 1931: 1,566 live births, 663 abortions attended in the public health service at the University of Chile; 2,135 total live births (including home birth); 1932: 1,481 live births, 591 abortions, total live births 1,947 (p. 771). It is unclear what percentage of these statistics documented self-induced abortion, unwanted abortions, or still births.

19. Andrea del Campo Peirano has shown that between 1914 and 1918, some doctors tried to denounce the illegal practice of abortion and addressed what they suspected to be clandestine practices of doctors and midwives. See del Campo Peirano, "La nación en peligro."

20. Statistics at the time also did not differentiate between spontaneous and induced abortions. For early quests to improve documentation of the problem of abortion, see, for example, Moisés Amaral, *Los anticoncepcionales y el aborto criminal: Conferencia dada en la Sociedad Científica de Chile, en sesión de 28 de agosto de 1917* (Santiago: Imprenta Franco-Chilena, G. Gregorie, 1917); and Torres, *Mortinatalidad de Santiago*. Torres claimed that only two maternity wards in Santiago, in the San Borja and Salvador hospitals, collected data on abortions after 1915. As cited in del Campo Peirano, "La nación en peligro," 135.

21. "Aborto en Chile," *BOSP* 15, no. 11 (November 1936): 1,087.

22. Hernán Romero and José M. Ugarte, "Mortalidad Materna," *Revista chilena de higiene y medicina preventiva* 11, no. 2 (June 1949): 91–113. Quotes on pp. 98–99.

23. Shepard, "'Double Discourse' on Sexual and Reproductive Rights."

24. Ernst carried on her initiatives in the J. J. Aguirre Hospital in the 1930s, while Avendaño was active at Quinta Normal in the 1940s. See "Planificación de la familia," *Boletín San Juan de Dios* 13, no. 6 (November–December 1966): 417–418; Vargas Catalán, *Historia de la pediatría chilena*, 494–495.

25. See, for example, "Circular del Arzobispado," in *El Mercurio* and compiled in *BMCh* 12, no. 397 (January 25, 1936): 1, 3, and 6, as cited in del Campo Peirano, "La nación en peligro," 167.

26. See the section on "El aborto en la legislación chilena," in Klimpel, *La mujer, el delito y la sociedad,* 232.

27. Physicians could provide abortions without criminal penalties to save the woman's life, to prevent the birth of an infant with birth defects, and if pregnancies had been the outcome of rape or incest. Therapeutic abortion remained legal in Chile between 1931 and 1989.

28. "Detenida Doctora," *Clarin*, March 11, 1962, 6. For vilifications of midwives who induced abortions and for constructed associations of women with the devil in debates on female delinquency, see Ruggiero, "Devil and Modernity in Late Nineteenth-Century Buenos Aires."

29. Allende, *Paula,* 100.

30. Ibid., 102.

31. Hernán Romero, E. Medina, and J. Vildósola, "Aportes al conocimiento de la procreación," *Revista chilena de higiene y medicina preventiva* 15, no. 3–4 (July–December 1953): 73–90. For women's explanations of why they had abortions, see p. 77.

32. Norma's recollection is in Gall, *Births, Abortions, and the Progress of Chile,* 6–7.

33. See "Tegualda, la pionera," Nota de BBCMundo.com, available online at http://news.bbc.co.uk/go/pr/fr/-/hi/spanish/specials/2006/historias_de_mujeres2/newsid_4771000/4771186.stm.

34. Monreal as quoted in *Ercilla,* no. 1453 (March 27, 1963): 17.

35. Armijo and Monreal, "Epidemiology of Provoked Abortion in Santiago, Chile," and "Factores Asociados a las complicaciones del Aborto Provocado."

36. On Requena and Viel's projects, see JZM (John Maier) Trip Diary, Santiago, Chile, (March 16–19, 1965): 11–14, RF A76 309A Folder: University of Chile Family Planning 1965; unprocessed, RFA, RAC. The Harvard School of Public Health and the Rockefeller Foundation provided money and support for the projects.

37. See Foucault, *Discipline & Punish,* for insights into the ritual power of examination. Foucault encouraged critical analysis of processes of ritual examination to understand the construction and reconstruction of power. Foucault's work inspired a search for the option to document women's agency. Although it is difficult to document to what extent women could appropriate the discourse of examiners, the consequences of interviews hold valuable insights. Importantly, the impact of their testimony showed women's ability to rewrite the meaning of the examination, the ritual questioning on their practice of abortion—because women changed the nature of attention given to abortion in Chilean society.

38. Ministerio de Salud, República de Chile, as cited in Requena, *Aborto inducido en Chile,* 26.

39. Rolando Armijo referred to up to thirty-five abortions at the IPPF Conference in Santiago. See IPPF and Hankinson, *Proceedings of the Eighth International Conference of the International Planned Parenthood Federation,* 143. For more data provided by the first influential epidemiological studies on abortion, see Armijo and Monreal, "Epidemiology of Provoked Abortion," 143–159; and Mariano Requena, "Condiciones determinantes del aborto inducido," *Revista médica de Chile* 94 (November 1966): 714–722.

40. See, for example, Mariano Requena's presentations of the results of his study at a Milbank Symposium in New York, "Studies of Family Planning."

41. See Requena, "Aborto inducido en Chile," in Requena, *Aborto Inducido en Chile,* 20.

42. JZM (John Maier) Trip Diary, Santiago, Chile (March 16–19, 1965): 13, RF A76 309A Folder: University of Chile Family Planning 1965. Unprocessed, RFA, RAC.

43. Paxman et al., "Clandestine Epidemic," 209.

44. Romero and Vildósola, "Economía de vidas," especially 207–208; Armijo, Monreal et al., "Problem of Induced Abortion in Chile"; and Weisner, *Aborto Inducido,* and "Aborto Provocado."

45. S. Plaza and H. Briones, "El aborto como problema asistencial," *Revista Médica de Chile* 91, no. 4 (1963): 294–297.

46. IPPF, *Family Planning in Chile,* 3.

47. See Faúndes's account of his experiences as an intern in Faúndes and Barzelatto, *El drama del aborto,* 15.

48. Romero, "Chile," 241.

49. Faúndes and Barzelatto, *El drama del aborto*, 15.

50. Raymond L. Belsky contacted Mr. Leon Borzutzky-Friedman, representative of Johnson & Johnson International in Santiago, to follow up on data and sample plastic condoms sent the year before. See Belsky to Borzutzky-Friedman, October 1968, Population Council, Accession II, Box 6, Folder Correspondence/Reports/Studies, FC-O Chile 67–68, RFA, RAC.

51. Jaime Zipper, taped interview with the author, Santiago, October 1997.

52. Thiery, "Pioneers of the Intrauterine Device."

53. For details on other medical experiments, see George, "In Search of Closure for Quinacrine." George documents the trials with Quinacrine and Zipper's experiments with it as a sterilizing agent on Chilean women during the 1960s and 1970s (page 138). For additional evidence, see examples of Zipper's extensive publications on the subject: Zipper et al., "Quinacrine Hydrochloride Pellets"; Zipper, Stachetti, and Medel, "Human Fertility Control by Transvaginal Application"; and Zipper, Stachetti, and Medel, "Transvaginal Chemical Sterilization."

54. Faúndes and Hardy, "Contraception and Abortion Services," 284–297.

55. For Zipper's reading inspiration, see Oppenheimer, "Prevention of Pregnancy by the Gräfenberg Ring Method."

56. This and previous quote, Zipper interview, October 1997.

57. Ibid.

58. Zipper, Garcia, and Pastene, "Intra-Uterine Contraception with the Use of a Flexible Nylon Ring," 88.

59. Ibid., 120.

60. It is unclear how much detail the women knew about the metals they were testing. For evidence of ongoing research, see Zipper et al., "Metallic Copper as an Intrauterine Contraceptive Adjunct to the 'T' device"; and Zipper et al., "Contraception Through the Use of Intrauterine Metals. I. Copper as an Adjunct to the 'T' device."

61. Zipper, Garcia, and Pastene, "Intra-Uterine Contraception with the Use of a Flexible Nylon Ring," 93.

62. Miró to Kirk, June 25, 1963, Folder: FC-O Chile 1959–1963 CELADE, Collection: Population Council, Box 6, Accession II. Unprocessed material, RFA, RAC.

63. Ibid.

64. For details on the wide range of other Zañartu research experiments, see Folders 111 and 112, Population Council, Accession I, IV 3b4.2, Box 9; RFA, RAC.

65. Anna L. Southam, Ford Foundation, Notes on Chile, "University of Chile, March 28–April 4, 1966," Southam, 4/8/66, Folder: FC-O Chile 1964–66, Chile, University of Chile, Collection: Population Council, Box 6, Accession II. Unprocessed material: 4–5, RFA, RAC.

66. Ibid. Published research results provide ample evidence for ongoing studies in Chile and go beyond the scope of this book. For one set of Zipper's experiments that is still the subject of criticism by women's health activists, see Quinacrine experiments, first under the direction of Jaime Zipper. See also note 55, above.

67. See Faúndes and Hardy, "Contraception and Abortion Services," 284–297.

68. Tegualda Monreal, cited in "Lucha a muerte por la vida," *Ercilla*, no. 1656 (March 1, 1967): 11.

69. For studies on men and family planning in Chile, see Hall, "Male Use of Contraception and Attitudes Toward Abortion"; "Male Attitudes to Family Planning Education in Santiago, Chile," *Journal of Biosocial Science*; "Male Sexual Behavior and Use of Contraceptives"; "Male Attitudes to Family Planning Education in Santiago, Chile," *Family Planning Résumé*; and "Family Planning in Santiago, Chile."

70. Mariano Requena, "El problema del aborto inducido en una población obrera de Santiago. Uso y actitudes frente al empleo de anticonceptivos," Santiago: Celade, Serie A, no. 63, internal report; Requena, "Studies of Family Planning," 69–99; and Faúndes and Hardy, "Contraception and Abortion Services," 284–297.

71. See, for example, Benjamín Viel and Sonia Lucero, "*Contraceptive Services in Chile between 1964–1972*," *Revista médica de Chile* 101 no.9 (1973): 730–735; correspondence between Nagel to Maier (IPPF affiliated staff), July 5, 1973, Folder: International Planned Parenthood Federation, Family Planning, 1973–74, 75. RF, 100 A, A76, RFA, RAC.

72. Clinics in the northern health area, led by Dr. Puga, were much less popular in the medical community. They operated at a slower rate, perhaps because he chose to work with more expensive oral contraceptives. See Anna L. Southam, Ford Foundation, Notes on Chile, "University of Chile, March 28–April 4, 1966," Southam, 4/8/66, Folder: FC-O Chile 1964–66, Chile, University of, Collection: Population Council, Box 6, Accession II. Unprocessed material: 8–10, RFA, RAC.

73. Viel, "Results of a Contraceptive Program," 106.

74. Zambra led the Chilean Association for the Protection of the Family (APROFA). For APROFA's history, see later in this chapter. Zambra interview; also see "Dr. Gildo Zambra," 13–14.

75. Soledad Díaz, interview with the author, July 1998.

76. Monreal and Armijo's assertion is in *Ercilla*, no. 1453 (March 27, 1963): 17.

77. "Lucha a muerte por la vida," *Ercilla*, no. 1656 (March 1, 1967): 11.

78. Agrupación Médica Feminina. On the committee and reference to Mendoza's visit, see "Planificacion de la familia," *Boletín San Juan de Dios* 13, no. 6 (November–December 1966): 417–418.

79. "La Planificacion familiar en los dibujos animados," *Boletín* APROFA 4, no. 8 (August 1968): 1.

80. According to documentation by the Rockefeller Foundation, these family-planning projects included the "Viel-Requena show in the Western Health Region, a Faúndes operation in the Southern Region, the Avendaño-Zipper group at the Barros Luco, two units at the Hospital Aguirre under the obstetrician, Professor Puga and the gynecologist, Professor Wood; and two further units in the Central Region, one under Professor García, and one at the School of Public Health under Dr. Plaza and Professor Adriasola." See JZM (John Maier) Trip Diary, March 16–19, 1965; RF A76 309A Folder: University of Chile Family Planning 1965 (excerpt, no page number). Unprocessed, RFA, RAC. The Rockefeller and Ford foundations, as well as the Population Council, provided significant technical and financial support for these initiatives.

81. Romero, "Chile"; and Berelson, *Family Planning*, 237.

82. "Comité Chileno se entrevista con Director General de Salud," *Boletín del Comité Chileno de Protección de la Família* 1, no. 3 (August 1965): 1.

83. Viel, *La explosion demográfica*. Viel's book was first published in English in 1976, *Demographic Explosion*, 190–191.

84. Viel and others who feared the consequences of rapid population growth adopted a neo-Malthusian position, an updated interpretation of Reverend Thomas Malthus's influential publications in late-eighteenth-century England. Malthus, *Essay on the Principle of Population.* Unsettled by the impact of industrialization, population growth, and poverty that shaped his world, Malthus responded with dire warnings that pointed to an ever-widening gap between food production and population size.

85. See ads sponsored by the Campaign to Check the Population Explosion: "Hungry Nations Imperil the Peace of the World," *New York Times*, February 23, 1969, sec. IV, 5; and "The Population Bomb Threatens the Peace of the World," *New York Times*, February 9, 1969, sec. IV, 5.

86. Ibid. These ads had different titles and images, but the same text, signed by the same people, such as Eugene Black, former head of the World Bank; General William Draper Jr., former ambassador to NATO; Philip Hauser, University of Chicago; and Hugh Moore, founder of Dixie Cup Company. See also *New York Times*, December 14, 1969, 56.

87. The open letter to the president is in *New York Times*, December 13, 1964, sec. IV, 5, sponsored by the Hugh Moore Fund.

88. John D. Rockefeller III, "Introductory Remarks," in *Intra-Uterine Contraception, Proceedings of the Second International Conference, October 2–3, 1964, New York City.* Sponsored by the Population Council. International congress series, no. 86, edited by International Conference on Intra-Uterine Contraception and Sheldon J. Segal. Amsterdam: Excerpta Medica Foundation, 1965, 1.

89. Adriasola and Avendaño, "Population Program in Chile," 219.

90. Romero, "Chile"; and Berelson, *Family Planning*, 246.

91. For Viel, the *main* health problem in Chile remained accelerated population growth. See Viel to Weir, December 20, 1966, Folder: International Planned Parenthood Federation, 1971, Family Planning; RF, 100A, RFA, RAC. See also Viel, *La explosion demografica,* and "Family Planning in Chile"; Romero, *El control de la natalidad,* and *Población, desarrollo y control*; and Poblete Troncoso, *La explosión demográfica en América Latina.*

92. Thiery, "Pioneers of the Intrauterine Device," 15–23.

93. For the context and content of Rock's lectures, see John Charles Rock, Personal and Professional Papers, 1918–1983; Box 20, folder 32, Post-Graduate Course, Reproductive Physiology and Human Fertility Control, University of Chile, Santiago, November 15–30, 1965, and Oversized-box 25, folder 28; and Post-Graduate Course, Reproductive Physiology and Human Fertility Control, University of Chile, Santiago, November 15–30, 1965, Harvard Medical Library. For his reception in Chile, see "Curso para Graduados," *Boletín del Comité Chileno de Protección de la Familia* 1, no. 7 (December 1965): 1.

94. See statement by John Rock, Catholic physician and co-developer of the contraceptive pill, as cited in *New York Times*, December 9, 1964, 53.

95. Philip Hauser, professor of sociology at the University of Chicago, addressing a symposium at the Albert Einstein College of Medicine, Yeshiva University, New York, May 1963. See *New York Times*, May 28, 1963, 18. For reference to education, see Frank Wilder of the Ford Foundation, addressing an international conference of the Planned Parenthood Federation in Bandung, Indonesia, June 1969. He also cited more than seventy-five possible outlets for such messages, and suggested that they would be presented through the use of techniques used by American advertising companies to sell everything from cigarettes to cars. As reported in "New Ideas Cited on Birth Control: Bandung Conference Hears Call for Radical Changes," *New York Times*, June 8, 1969, 8.

96. Osborn, *Our Crowded Planet,* as reviewed in the *New York Times,* August 26, 1962, section VII, 6.

97. Gen. William H. Draper Jr., addressing a dinner sponsored by the 1963 Planned Parenthood Federation of America–World Population Emergency Campaign, as cited in the *New York Times,* May 8, 1963, 11.

98. President Lyndon B. Johnson, Speech to the United Nations, June 25, 1965.

99. For a history of the changing approaches to population control by the U.S. government, see Donaldson, "On the Origins of the United States Government's International Population Policy"; and John Sharpless, "World Population Growth, Family Planning, and American Foreign Policy."

100. Zipper, Garcia, and Pastene, "Intra-Uterine Contraception with the Use of a Flexible Nylon Ring," 90–91.

101. Ibid.

102. APROFA became a "full member" of the IPPF/WHR in and was granted *persona juridica* by the government by Decree No. 2194, on September 5, 1966. See Avendaño, *Desarrollo histórico de la planificación,* 13–14.

103. The NHS provided support without managing the family-planning programs. See Jorge Rosselot, "Regulación de la natalidad en el Servicio Nacional de Salud de Chile," *Cuadernos médico-sociales* 7, no. 2 (June 1966): 16–22.

104. Bernard Berelson, "Application of Intra-Uterine Contraception in Family Planning Programs," in *Intra-Uterine Contraception, Proceedings of the Second International Conference, October 2–3, 1964, New York City,* edited by International Conference on Intra-Uterine Contraception and Sheldon J. Segal. Sponsored by the Population Council. International congress series, no. 86 (Amsterdam: Excerpta Medica Foundation, 1965), 13.

Chapter 3. Planning Motherhood under Christian Democracy

Epigraph: "The Population Council: The Disney Film on Family Planning," *Studies in Family Planning* 1, no. 26 (January 1968), n.p. The U.S. Population Council sponsored the production of the film, and its president, Bernard Berelson, advertised it at the IPPF Santiago Conference. See Berelson to Romero, February 23, 1967, Folder FC Chile 66–67, IPPF Family Planning Conference, Santiago, Chile, Box 7; Population Council, Accession II, unprocessed material; RFA, RAC. W. Parker Mauldin, "Bernard Berelson: 2 June 1912–25 September 1979," *Studies in Family Planning* 10, no. 10 (October 1979): 259–262.

1. Levin to Romero, April 4, 1968, Folder: Chile, University of, Dr. Hernán Romero, FC-O Chile 67–68; Population Council, Box 6, Accession II, unprocessed material, RFA, RAC. For ongoing exchange on family planning between Population Council representatives and Chilean officials, also see Berelson to Romero, May 3, 1967; Romero to Berelson, April 25, 1967; and Berelson to Romero, March 23, 1967, Folder: Chile, University of, Dr. Hernán Romero, FC-O Chile 67–68; Population Council, Box 6, Accession II, unprocessed material, RFA, RAC.

2. APROFA showed this and other educational films. For more detail on the education campaigns put into practice by APROFA, see *Boletín APROFA* 13, no. 8 (1973): 6–7.

3. Tinsman explores gender and the sexual politics of the Chilean agrarian reform between 1950 and 1973, and gives particular attention to the consequences of the Christian Democrats' rural policies that promoted family-centered goals and appealed to a new partnership between the husband and wife. Policies encouraged couples to follow the ideal of

"gender mutualism," the harmonious cooperation between husband and wife, aimed at improving the quality of rural life. In this process, educational programs as well as new access to family planning increased rural women's decision-making power in personal relationships and in the home. But women's newfound power was accompanied by novel forms of male privilege that undermined gender equity. See Tinsman, *Partners in Conflict*.

The nature of change in the countryside helps explain some of the striking differences in family-planning practices between the rural Aconcagua Valley and Santiago. Christian Democratic policies of land reform *did* improve rural women's lives through the promotion of gender mutualism. Nonetheless, the agrarian reform "steered clear of measures that directly threatened the principle of men's authority over women" (see Tinsman, *Reviving Feminist Materialism,* 162). It seemed that the fear of uprooting this principle also guided rural family-planning programs: the programs focused on married couples, and a wife often needed her husband's consent to get contraceptives. In the Aconcagua Valley, this arrangement dominated even with a fresh focus on equality under the Unidad Popular government (1970–1973). Tinsman, *Partners in Conflict,* 163, 222.

In Santiago, women were often at the center of family-planning initiatives, and doctors such as Benjamín Viel, Mariano Requena, and Tegualda Monreal viewed the enhancement of *women's* decision-making power regarding contraception as part of the solution to the problem of maternal mortality and induced abortions. Some, most readily Viel, were adamant about their efforts to improve all women's access to contraception and insisted that it should not be contingent on a husband's consent. Viel believed that the resolution of two dilemmas, overpopulation and the abortion epidemic, depended on such measures. See Benjamín Viel, interview with the author, December 1996; Tegualda Monreal, interview with the author, September 1997; Mariano Requena, interview with the author, June 1997. Viel's approach was unusual, provocative, and very influential at the time. As the head of APROFA, he set the direction of programs and greatly enhanced women's access to contraception. Nonetheless, Viel did not challenge the principle of men's control over women and the patriarchal arrangements at the center of Chilean society.

4. John F. Kennedy, in John W. Gardner, *To Turn the Tide: A Selection from President Kennedy's Public Statements from His Election Through the 1961 Adjournment of Congress, Setting Forth the Goals of His First Legislative Year* (New York: Harper, 1962), 167.

5. Frei Montalva, "Alliance That Lost Its Way."

6. Frei Montalva, *Aims of Christian Democracy* (1964); and D'Antonio and Pike, *Religion, Revolution, and Reform*. See also Gazmuri, Clavel, and Escobedo, *Eduardo Frei Montalva (1911–1982)*.

7. Radical quests for change could stem from a wide variety of political and religious stands, ranging from *fidelismo* in Cuba, to liberation theology, to small islands of counterculture of the 1960s. On Chilean and Latin American experiences of Christian Democracy, see Mainwaring and Scully, *Christian Democracy in Latin America*. For the Chilean context, see Smith, *Church and Politics in Chile*. For other manifestations of quests for change—that is, the emergence of counterculture in the late 1960s—see Barr-Melej, "Siloismo and the Self in Allende's Chile."

8. "Metas para 3 de los 6 años de Frei: Su Programa y sus Hombres," *Ercilla*, no. 1537 (November 4, 1964): 21.

9. In the same campaign, Christian Democrats also promoted what Margaret Power has appropriately called a "scare campaign," trying to convince female voters to reject the

dangerous communism represented by Allende, in favor of Frei's moderate proposals. See especially the section on "The 1964 Scare Campaign," in her *Right-Wing Women in Chile,* 79–98 (chapter 3).

10. For references to the expansion of the electorate, like the secret ballot in 1958 and the 1964 mandatory voting, see Scully, *Rethinking the Center,* 107. For reference to the percentage of women registered to vote, see Borón, *La evolución del regimen electoral;* also cited in Oxman, *La participación de la mujer campesina en organizaciones,* 32.

11. Kyle and Francis, "Chile," 109.

12. Rubio, *La vuelta al pago en ochenta y dos años,* 116, as cited in Collier and Sater, *History of Chile,* 290.

13. Castañeda, *Contexto socioeconómico y causas del descenso,* 7 and 14.

14. Herrick, *Urban Migration and Economic Development in Chile.*

15. González Arraigada, *Surviving in the City,* 219.

16. Chile, *Ley No. 16.880.*

17. Chile, *Ley de Juntas de Vecinos.*

18. See "Anexo, Estatuto Tipo Para Centros de Madres," in Chile, CEMA, *Como Participar,* 110.

19. Ibid., 113.

20. Ibid., 111.

21. Oxman, *La participación de la mujer campesina.*

22. Covarrubias, "El Movimiento Feminista Chileno," 639, as cited in Valdés et al., *Centros de madres 1973–1989,* 9.

23. Gaviola Artígas et al., *"Queremos votar en las próximas elecciones."*

24. Kyle and Francis, "Chile," 109.

25. See, for example, Lechner and Levy, *Notas sobre la vida cotidiana III,* for a critical evaluation of the role of Mothers' Centers.

26. Weinstein, *Estado, mujeres de sectores populares y ciudadanía;* and Serrano, "Estado, Mujer y Política Social en Chile."

27. Valdés and Weinstein use this reference to sewing machines in *Mujeres que sueñan,* also cited in Power, *Right-Wing Women,* 111n38. See Power's insightful discussion of the "Debate on the Impact of Mothers' Centers," in her *Right-Wing Women in Chile,* 113–118.

28. See interviews with women conducted by Power, cited in her *Right-Wing Women,* 111.

29. See, for example, Gaviola Artígas, Lopresti, and Rojas, "Chile Centro de Madres."

30. "Anexo, Estatuto Tipo Para Centros de Madres," in Chile, CEMA, *Como Participar,* 113.

31. "John D. Rockefeller 3rd visita Chile," *Boletín APROFA* 2, no. 12 (December 1966): 3; see also "Conceptos Fundamentales de John D. Rockefeller 3rd," *Boletín APROFA* 2, no. 12 (December 1966): 1–2.

32. John D. Rockefeller III, Diary Excerpt, October 28–November 2, 1966; Folder 79, Box 11; John D. Rockefeller III Papers; RG 5; Series 3; Diaries, Personal Papers, 103–105 (quote on page 104), RFA, RAC.

33. For a full copy of the statement, see "Statement on Population from World Leaders (1966)" available online at http://www.popcouncil.org/mediacenter/popstatement.html.

34. See copy of the *United Nations World Leaders' Statement on Population,* John D. Rockefeller III Papers, Sub-series 4, Population Interests, 1965-(1970–1978), Folder 513, RFA, RAC.

35. Global Committee of Parliamentarians on Population and Development, "Statement on Population Stabilization by World Leaders," 787–788.

36. CELADE continued to attract international researchers from the Americas; three-quarters of the demographic studies were led by international organizations present in Chile. See Errázuriz, *El tratamiento del problema de población*.

37. For a detailed list on Chilean institutions and references to funding, see Lubin to Lamontagne, Background submitted to John D. Rockefeller III, October 5, 1966; Folder 821, IPPF Communication; John D. Rockefeller 3rd Papers, RG5, Series 3, Box 100, RFA, RAC.

38. As cited in J. Stycos, "Opposition to Family Planning in Latin America," 851.

39. Elizaga to Remiche, "Report on CELADE Activities," August 9, 1968. Folder: FC-Chile 67–68 CELADE; Population Council, Accession II, unprocessed material, Box 6, RFA, RAC.

40. See "Chapter IV, Frank Notestein," in Coale, *Ansley J. Coale*, 14–20.

41. Vekemans's persona was a challenge by itself. He was an outspoken anticommunist and self-declared leader against the "Red Menace." See Lernoux, *Cry of the People*, 25–27. Vekemans left Chile prior to President Allende's inauguration.

42. See Vekemans's own writing, for example on "overpopulation": Roger Vekemans, "La sobrepoblación y sus problemas," *Mensaje* 10, no. 97 (March–April 1961): 84–95. See also "Economic Development, Social Change, and Cultural Mutation," in D'Antonio and Pike, *Religion, Revolution, and Reform*; Vekemans, *Teología de la liberación y cristianos por el socialismo*; and Vekemans and Silva Fuenzalida, *Marginalidad, promoción popular y neo-marxismo*.

43. See, for example, DESAL and CELAP, *Fecundidad y anticoncepción en poblaciones marginales*.

44. For contradictions and for paternalistic elements under Chile's Revolution in Liberty, see also de Kadt, "Paternalism and Populism."

45. Centro Latinoamericano de Población y Familia, *Iglesia, población y familia*. Others shared this approach: Armand Mattelart, French intellectual and long-term resident of Chile, addressed the "spiritual challenge of the demographic explosion" and insisted that solutions had to be sought in connection to larger structural changes and proper ethics of development and economic redistribution. See "Las soluciones," in Mattelart, *El reto espiritual de la explosión demográfica*, 73–83.

46. For example, Seminario de Desarrollo, Población y Familia, *Ponencias del Seminario de Desarrollo, Población y Familia*.

47. For an insightful assessment of CELAP's role, see Sanders, *Family Planning in Chile*.

48. An editorial in the *New York Times* reflects this viewpoint: it argued that the major impediments to controlling the problem of increasing population growth in Latin America are "the religious prohibitions that bind Roman Catholics, poverty, and ignorance." See [editorial] *New York Times*, April 11, 1967. For views on Church influences see Sanders, "Population Planning and Belief Systems"; Stycos, *Catholicism and Birth Control in the Western Hemisphere*; and Hernández, *Catholic Church and Population Growth in Latin America*.

49. Losada de Masjuan, *Comportamientos anticonceptivos en la familia marginal*, 42.

50. Miró, "Some Misconceptions Disproved."

51. For larger insights into the "modernization" of the Catholic Church and its role in Chile, see Fleet and Smith, *Catholic Church and Democracy in Chile and Peru*. Also see Cleary and Stewart-Gambino, *Conflict and Competition,* especially "Redefining the Changes and Politics in Chile," 21–44 (chapter 2).

52. See José Aldunate Lyon, S. J., "El matrimonio y los hijos," *Mensaje* 1, no. 3 (December 1951): 129. Some of those critics also offered specific plans to accelerate Chilean agricultural production to avoid "population problems." See J. Antonio Errázuriz Hunneus, "La agricultura Chilena y al aumento de la población," *Mensaje* 1, no. 9 (June 1952): 328–331.

53. Between 1963 and 1968, the Pope did not take a definite public stand on population issues and contraception.

54. *Humanae vitae* (1968) addressed conjugal love and responsible parenthood as important dimensions in relationships between married couples and between parents and children. It presented a departure from Pope Pius XI's encyclical *Casti connubii* (1931), the definitive statement on sex and marriage before the Second Vatican Council. Traditional moral theologians often drew from St. Paul and St. Augustine, and saw marriage as an instrument for procreation and a remedy for sexual sins. Pope Paul VI spoke of contraception in very traditional modes; this seemed to contradict his affirmation of the centrality of conjugal love and responsible parenthood and caused debates among bishops, priests, and laity. For debates about *Humanae vitae* see, for example, Smith, *Humanae Vitae.*

55. As cited in Gross, *Last, Best Hope,* 169. In various Santiago neighborhoods, priests had encouraged birth control in response to the problem of abortion and maternal mortality. See Dr. Benjamín Viel, interview with the author, December 1996.

56. "Para Católicos: Un problema de conciencia," *Ercilla,* no. 1662 (April 12, 1967): 8.

57. "La Píldora Católica," *Ercilla,* no. 1537 (November 4, 1964): 37.

58. Jones and Nortman, "Roman Catholic Fertility and Family Planning," 1.

59. Francis X. Murphy and Joseph F. Erhart, "Catholic Perspectives on Population Issues," *Population Bulletin* 30, no. 6 (1975): 18–19. See also Hernández, *Catholic Church and Population Growth in Latin America.*

60. Some initiatives started before the 1960s. See, for example, Father William J. Gibbon's grant request submitted to the U.S. Population Council in 1953. He asked for a grant "to Loyola University for the purpose of underwriting a research project to create a definitive statement on the position of the Roman Catholic Church with regard to birth control." Frederick Osborn to Yorke Allen Jr., November 23, 1953, Collection: Population Council, Folder 76, Box 7, RGIV 3b4.2, RFA, RAC.

61. Hernández, *Catholic Church and Population Growth in Latin America,* 10–11.

62. "Pope Asks Ruling on Birth Control," *New York Times,* March 30, 1965, pp. 1, 6.

63. John D. Rockefeller 3rd to His Holiness Pope Paul VI, July 16, 1965, John D. Rockefeller 3rd Papers, Folder 511, Box 74, RG 5, Series 3, RFA, RAC.

64. John D. Rockefeller 3rd to His Holiness Pope Paul VI, October 8, 1965, John D. Rockefeller 3rd Papers, Folder 511, Box 74, Record Group 5, Series 3, Rockefeller Foundation Archives, RFA, RAC.

65. For Christians for Socialism, see, for example, Smith, *Church and Politics in Chile*; and Fernández Fernández, "Oral History of the Chilean Movement 'Christians for Socialism.'" While liberation theology and Social Catholics influenced a considerable group of clergy in Chile, other tendencies of the Church were present as well. In 1967 the "Sociedad chilena de defensa de la tradición, familia, y propiedad" suggested that Chile had become the ground of a Catholic progressivism. They rejected the postconciliation Church and presented a philosophy to counter the progressive Catholicism. Like another recent movement that published in the *Revista fiducia,* a journal with a strong anticommunist bent, it defended the anticommunist writings of Plinio Corrêa de Oliveira. Neither one of the groups had a large fol-

lowing but remained a persistent voice of opposition. See "Porque conducen la bolchevización de Chile: Nace sociedad para combatir los cambios," *Ercilla*, no. 1666 (May 10, 1967): 4–5.

66. See, for example, da Silveira, *Frei, el Kerensky chileno*. The book, first published in Portuguese, came with a preface by the same Plinio Corrêa de Oliveira who had shaped the dogmatic views promoted in the Chilean *Revista fiducia*.

67. The range of positions taken by Chilean clergy ranged from very conservative stands to innovative, even revolutionary ambitions. See, for example, "Sacerdotes chilenos en el Camino de Camilo Torres," *Punto final* 1, no. 2 (June 1967): 14–15.

68. Although the concrete impact of the pastorals cannot be documented, they helped spread progressive approaches to Chile's political and social conflicts of the time. On the Chilean episcopate see, for example, Thomas Sanders, "Chilean Episcopate," in Sanders, *Chilean Episcopate*, 1–30.

69. Ibid., 7.

70. "Chile Voluntad de Ser: La comunidad nacional y la iglesia católica de Chile," *Revista Católica*, no. 1009 (January–June 1968): 5340–5352. The document confirms the position of the Chilean Church in the 1960s as one which clearly reflected the influences of the Second Vatican Council (1962–1965), where a conservative tradition of centuries began to be transformed into a progressive one. For a discussion of these changes, also see Sanders, "Chilean Episcopate," 6–7.

71. "Declaración del Episcopado Chileno sobre la Planificación de la Familia," *Mensaje* 16, no. 159 (June 1967): 256–262.

72. Previous studies concerned with excessive population growth encouraged the Church to address the population problem. See, for example, Leñero Otero, *Población iglesia y cultura*.

73. Cardinal Raúl Silva Henríquez, "La Iglesia y la Regulación de la Natalidad: Palabras del Exmo. Sr. Cardenal Raúl Silva H. en la Academia de San Lucas de Santiago, Junio de 1967," *Mensaje* 16, no. 161 (August 1967): 362.

74. Bernard Häring, "La Crisis de La Encíclica: Oponerse puede y debe ser un servicio de amor hacia el Papa," *Mensaje* 17, no. 173 (October 1968): 476–484. For references to the international reactions that were published in Chile, see "Declaraciones de los episcopados nacionales acerca de 'Humanae Vitae,'" *Mensaje* 17, no. 175 (December 1968): 651–658; and Alting von Geusau, "International Reaction to the *Encyclical Humana Vitae*."

75. See "'Humanae Vitae': Ecos en la Prensa Mundial," *Mensaje* 17, no. 172 (September 1968): 425.

76. They pointed out that the encyclical was not infallible; the majority of bishops thought that the Pope's position was 'reformable'—because the matter required further study. The minority of bishops believed that the force of the encyclical and its consistency with tradition made it essentially infallible. Their letter closes with a paragraph asserting that Catholics might "adhere, after serious study and consultation, to one or the other of the theological opinions mentioned." See "Profesores de Teología de la U.C. de Santiago se refieren a 'Humanae Vitae'," *Mensaje* 17, no. 172 (September 1968): 426–428.

77. "Actitud de la mujer empleada o esposa de empleado frente al Control de Natalidad," *Boletín APROFA* 3, no. 9 (September 1967): 6.

78. See Sanders, "Chilean Episcopate," 16.

79. See Sanders, "Population Planning and Belief Systems."

80. "La Encíclica 'Humanae Vitae' (de la Vida Humana): Medios Anticonceptivos," *Revista Católica,* no. 1009 (January–June 1968): 5,367.

81. de la Jara, "Control de la natalidad," 24.

82. The Chilean experience confirms that the encyclical was at least as much about power as it was about sexuality. Some scholars and activists point out that the decentralization of authority inspired by the Second Vatican Council fueled tension on the Vatican level that supported a "purity" of the doctrine and a new insistence on traditional sexual ethics. See Keely, "Limits to Papal Power."

83. See IPPF, "U.S. Scientists to Attend World Birth Control Talks," January 23, 1967. Folder: FC Chile 66–67 IPPF Family Planning Conference, Santiago, Chile; Box 7; Population Council, Accession II, unprocessed material, RFA, RAC.

84. See IPPF, "U.S. Government Supports World Birth Control Talks," March 1967; Folder: FC Chile 66–67 IPPF Family Planning Conference, Santiago, Chile; Box 7; Population Council, Accession II, unprocessed material, RFA, RAC.

85. Valdivieso as quoted in IPPF and Hankinson, *Proceedings of the Eighth International Conference of the IPPF,* 2.

86. Ibid., 4.

87. Sanders, *Family Planning in Chile,* 13.

88. "Circular A.2.1. No. 3: Resumen de Normas Básicas sobre Regulación de la Natalidad en el Servicio Nacional de Salud," *Boletín APROFA* 5, no. 1 (January 1969): 1–5.

89. Frei as quoted in IPPF and Hankinson, *Proceedings of the Eighth International Conference of the IPPF,* 17.

90. Mardones as quoted in ibid., 518.

91. Héctor Suárez, "Los días prohibidas," *Punto final* 1, no. 7 (December 1965): 5–21.

92. Ibid., 5–6.

93. See "Juventud habló de sexo a nivel internacional," *La tercera* (April 13, 1967): 4.

94. "Juventud Chilena reclama libertad frente al sexo," *La tercera* (April 14, 1967): 6; and *La tercera* (April 18, 1967).

95. Romero quoted in *La tercera* (April 14, 1967): 6.

96. Adriasola to Pease, March 10, 1969, and Pease to Adriasola, April 1, 1969. Population Council, Accession II, unprocessed material, Box 6, Folder FC-O-Chile 1969, RFA, RAC.

97. Roger Vekemans, "Planificación Familiar: Reflexiones con ocasión de un Congreso," *Mensaje* 16, no. 158 (May 1967), apartado, 7 pages.

98. For references to Vekemans's accusations and Romero's response, see *Boletín APROFA* 3, no. 7 (July 1967): 3–6.

99. Benjamín Viel's rejection of Christian Democratic policies and his suspicion of Catholic influences that could "censor" his family-planning agenda were well known in Chile and among population planners in the United States. In a letter to the Population Council, Viel even joked about moving his operations to India, because he "would be delighted to go any place where there are not Christian Democrats." See Viel to Pease, December 9, 1968, folder FC-O Chile 67–68, box 6, Population Council, Accession II, unprocessed material, RFA, RAC.

100. "Circular A.2.1. No. 3: Resumen de Normas Básicas sobre Regulación de la Natalidad en el Servicio Nacional de Salud," *de la Asociación Chilena de Protección de la Familia* 5, no. 1 (January 1969): 3.

101. Adriasola as quoted in "Temas de actualidad: Planificación Familiar," *Boletín APROFA* 2, no. 4 (April 1966): 3–4.

102. "Servicio Nacional de Salud, Chile, y Asociación Chilena de Protección de la Familia acuerdan Plan de Acción a través de un Convenio," *Boletín APROFA* 5, no. 2 (February 1969): 3; APROFA's official membership of the IPPF was formalized in 1966. See *Boletín APROFA* 2, no. 2 (February 1966): 1–2.

103. "Control de la natalidad: Tema del día," *Boletín APROFA* 2, no. 3 (March 1966): 1.

104. IPPF and Hankinson, *Proceedings of the Eighth International of the IPPF*, 181.

105. "Chile: Chilean Association for Family Welfare" Folder: International Planned Parenthood Federation, Family Planning 1969–70, RF, A76, 100A, 8–9, RFA, RAC.

106. Romero, "Chile: The Abortion Epidemic," 136.

107. For the complexity of the logic applied, see also Hernán Romero, "Justificación de la Enseñanza de Demografía," *Cuadernos médico-sociales* 9, no. 3 (September 1968): 36–42; Hernán Romero, "El crecimiento de la población y el control de la natalidad," *Cuadernos médico-sociales* 10, no. 1 (March 1969): 5–21; and Hernán Romero, "El control de la natalidad y sus presuntos daños," *Vida médica* 20, no. 7 (July 1968): 8–10.

108. "Temas de actualidad," 3–4.

109. The importance of preserving the family had appeared in debates prior to the elections, where divorce, illegal in Chile since the "Ley de Matrimonio Civil" of 1884, was discussed in public; although some defended the legalization of divorce in light of Chilean realities (where annulment had become a common practice to allow for the separation of couples), the majority of officials argued that the legalization of divorce would threaten the stability of the family. See *Ercilla*, no. 1525 (August 12, 1964): 10–11.

110. See Romero, "Chile: The Abortion Epidemic," 144.

111. For an evaluation of the San Gregorio project, see also Requena B., Monreal, and Bogue, "Evaluation of Induced Abortion Control," 191–222.

112. See, for example, Viel's reports and statistics in *Project of Family Planning and Control of Induced Abortion in the Western Area of Santiago,* Folder 1201, IV 3B4.3a, Box 67, Population Council Grant Files, RFA, RAC.

113. Third Progress Report, San Gregorio Project, Director of the Project: Prof. Onofre Avendaño; Research Team: Aníbal Faúndes, Germán Rodríguez, Jaime Zipper; see Folder 1072; Box 62; Collection: Population Council; RG: IV 3B4.3a, RFA, RAC.

114. Gerald I. Zatuchni, "Site Visit—Postpartum Program, San Juan de Dios Hospital, Santiago de Chile, April 6–8, 1967"; Folder 1204; Population Council, Accession I, Narrative Reports, IV 3B4.3a, Box 67. RFA, RAC.; and ibid., 1.

115. Ibid., 2.

116. Ibid.; the IUDs were imported from the United States. See Viel to Zatuchni, April 1, 1968, Folder 1207, Population Council, Box 61, IV 3B4.3a, RFA, RAC.

117. "Hambre o carrera especial," *Ercilla,* no. 1666 (October 5, 1967): 7.

118. Laura's and Hilda's experiences are in Taller de Acción Cultural (Santiago), *La organización fue como nacer.*

119. Ibid., 49.

120. Ibid., 53.

121. Ibid., 71.

122. Allende tells this story with more detail in her book *Paula*, 140–143; she also refers to it in Allende, *My Invented Country.*

123. Guillermo Adriasola, "Salud y Natalidad," *Boletín APROFA* 6, no. 9 (September 1970): 1.

Chapter 4. Gendered Citizenship Rights
on the Peaceful Road to Socialism

Epigraph: Allende Gossens, *La historia que estamos escribiendo,* 204, quoted in Chaney, "Mobilization of Women in Allende's Chile," 7.

1. Henfrey and Sorj, *Chilean Voices,* 130–148.

2. See Pastrana and Threlfall, *Pan, techo y poder el movimiento de pobladores en Chile,* 71, 72. This *campamento* even gained a mythical reputation in Europe and the United States. See, for example, Cohen and Pearce, *Campamento* (film). For a history of the movement of *pobladores,* see also Garcés, *Tomando su sitio.*

3. The MIR did not form part of the Unidad Popular government, also because of its more radical political outlook. See Pastrana and Threlfall, *Pan, techo y poder,* 68–74.

4. Ibid., 69–74.

5. Henfrey and Sorj, *Chilean Voices,* 139.

6. Anthropologist Ton Salman found that military rule affected the political mobilization of men and women *pobladores* differently. Men, as a collective, "tended to withdraw into apathy and passivity," as they felt unable to act in conditions in which the state no longer responded to their pressures and demands. Men missed "the world where action could do some good" and moved from collective to individual survival strategies. Women, however, shifted their sense of collective responsibility toward their fellow women. See Salman, "Diffident Movement."

7. Henfrey and Sorj, *Chilean Voices,* 134.

8. Ibid., 137. For another testimonial account of women's participation (in the health front) in New Havana under the UP government, see Taller de Acción Cultural (Santiago, Chile), *La organización fúe como nacer,* 79–85.

9. Allende Gossens, *La historia que estamos escribiendo,* 204. Also see the convincing claims of Sandra McGee Deutsch, who has maintained that the Unidad Popular was guided by "[a] simplistic faith in socialism as the automatic solution to Chilean problems, including that of discrimination against women" (McGee Deutsch, "Gender and Sociopolitical Change in Twentieth-Century Latin America," 293).

10. For the position on birth control promoted by what I call the traditional left, see, for example, Arreola, *Programas de control natal.*

11. Alvarez, *Engendering Democracy in Brazil.*

12. Margaret Power has asserted that "the women who had the greatest impact on politics during this period were those who most *resisted* the changes proposed by the UP government." See Power, *Right-Wing Women in Chile,* 126.

13. For evidence of the different stages of CIA involvement in Chile, see United States Senate, *Covert Action in Chile;* and ibid., 7.

14. Kinzer, *Overthrow,* 198.

15. Kissinger as quoted in ibid., 198.

16. Kyle and Francis, "Chile," 107–109.

17. For details on the uses of family in the campaign, see Thomas, "Ties That Break and Bind," 35–88.

18. *El siglo*, August 4, 1970, 1.

19. *El siglo*, August 15, 1970. For debates on the legitimacy of family planning and population control, see also an article in which the Health Ministry's Dr. Fernando Rodriguez accuses Chilean "population planners" in *El mercurio*, July 5, 1970, 1, and a lengthy response by Dr. Benjamín Viel in *El mercurio*, July 18, 1970. For a slightly more balanced overview, see *Ercilla,* no. 1833 (August 5, 1970): 57–61.

20. Consuegra Higgins, "'Birth Control as the Weapon of Imperialism,'" 163–181 (chapter 9); Arreola, *Programas de control natal*; and Consuegra Higgins, *El control de la natalidad como arma del imperialismo.*

21. Viel believed that Allende could hold on to his position in spite of the opposition to family planning among sectors of the left. In his correspondence with the Population Council, he emphasized the new opportunities, enhanced by a victory over the Christian Democrats. "Due to the personal assurance of President Allende and without Catholics in power [it] seems to me it would be a pity to stop all the [family planning] work in this country." In Viel to Pease, November 2, 1970. Population Council, Accession II, unprocessed material, Box 6, Folder FC-O Chile 70. RFA, RAC.

22. Viel to Maier, October 30, 1970. Population Council, Accession II, unprocessed material, Box 6, Folder FC-O Chile 70. RFA, RAC.

23. Lininger to Berelson, July 8, 1971. Population Council, Accession II, unprocessed material, Box PC-AD 15, Folder Berelson- Countries- Chile, RFA, RAC.

24. International Planned Parenthood Federation, November 24, 1970; RFA, RAC.

25. See Pease to Files, June 11, 197. Population Council, Accession II, unprocessed material, Box 6, Folder FC-Chile. RFA, RAC. Nonetheless, Viel's postpartum programs came to an end. When he traveled to the San Juan de Dios Hospital in 1973, no initiatives had been taken to continue his postpartum program. Viel to Russel, February 13, 1973. Population Council, Grant Files, IV 3B4.3a, Box 67, Folder 1204. RFA, RAC.

26. Anti-Allende women helped shape the campaign. See their booklet Accion Mujeres de Chile, *"Mujer chilena . . . !tú deciderás,"* (Chile, n.d.).

27. *Clarín,* August 15, 1970, 6.

28. For the history of the Peaceful Road to Socialism and primary sources, see Cockcroft, *Salvador Allende Reader*; González Pino and Fontaine Talavera, *Los mil dias de Allende.* For the role of urban labor, see Winn, *Weavers of Revolution.* For revolutionary politics in the rural central valley, see Tinsman, *Partners in Conflict.* For a review on some of the extensive literature on the Peaceful Road to Socialism, see Hecht Oppenheim, "Chilean Road to Socialism Revisited."

29. Salvador Allende Gossens, "Primer Mensaje al Congreso Pleno de 21 de Mayo de 1971," in Quiroga Zamora, ed., *Obras escogidas*, 77–102.

30. See, for example, these three works by Harnecker and Uribe: *Explotadores y explotados*, *Explotación capitalista,* and *Lucha de clases.* Harnecker's manuals don't address the specific mechanisms of *women's* exploitation, however.

31. Allende had criticized Alliance for Progress policies long before the election campaign and the beginning of his presidential term. See Allende Gossens, *Punta del Este.*

32. Allende Gossens, "Discurso pronunciado en el Estadio Nacional de Santiago el 4 de noviembre de 1971," in Quiroga Zamora, ed., *Obras escogidas,* 156.

33. Allende Gossens, *La historia que estamos escribiendo,* 204, as cited in Chaney, "Mobilization of Women in Allende's Chile," 7.

34. For insightful evidence on the Unidad Popular's failure to address gender inequalities, see McGee Deutsch, "Gender and Sociopolitical Change in Twentieth-Century Latin America," 292–304.

35. Bambirra, "La mujer chilena en la transición al socialismo"; Bambirra referred to Benston, "Political Economy of Women's Liberation." In the United States, socialist feminists considered Benston's article one of the most important intellectual contributions to their struggle. For larger questions and developments of socialist feminisms, see Holmstrom, *Socialist Feminist Project*.

36. Bambirra, "La mujer chilena en la transición al socialismo," 4. See excerpts and translation also in Bambirra, "Chilean Woman," 34.

37. Bambirra, "La mujer chilena en la transición al socialismo," 4. See excerpts and translation also in Bambirra, "Chilean Woman," 34–36.

38. "La mujer cria hijos machistas," in Puz, *La mujer chilena*, 46.

39. Ibid., 46.

40. Ibid., 49.

41. Vidal, *La emancipación de la mujer*.

42. Ibid., 43.

43. Ibid., 89.

44. Ibid., 91.

45. Witker Velásquez, *Salvador Allende, 1908–1973*, 255, as cited in McGee Deutsch, "Gender and Sociopolitical Change in Twentieth-Century Latin America," 292.

46. Also see discussion of the process in McGee Deutsch, "Gender and Sociopolitical Change in Twentieth-Century Latin America," 292–293.

47. "Creación del Ministerio de la Familia," *Boletín APROFA* 7, no. 6 (June 1971): 1; and Allende Gossens, "Encuentro con las mujeres de Concepción," 9–10.

48. Oficina de informaciones y radiodifusión de la presidencia de la república, *Palabras del presidente de la república, Compañero Salvador Allende Gossens, pronunciadas en al inauguración de los cursos auxiliares de párvulos, edificio Gabriela Mistral, 8 enero de 1973* (Santiago: N.p., 1973), 3.

49. Ibid., 3.

50. See Oficina de informaciones y radiodifusión de la presidencia de la república, *Palabras del presidente de la república, Compañero Salvador Allende Gossens, al hacer entrega de la Torre Ex-UNCTAD a la Secretaria de la Mujer, Santiago, 18 de Octubre, 1972* (Santiago: N.p., 1972), 9.

51. Richards, *Pobladoras, Indígenas, and the State*, 34.

52. The nature of support envisioned by the government involved the political support of women as well as the full potential of female workers. For a study on women's work see María Ducci, Gili, and Illanes, *El trabajo*.

53. See Oficina de informaciones y radiodifusión de la presidencia de la república, *Palabras del presidente de la república, Compañero Salvador Allende Gossens, en el seminario "La mujer de hoy de América Latina," efectuado en el edificio Gabriela Mistral Santiago, 27 de Octubre de 1972* (Santiago: N.p., 1972), 5.

54. Ibid., 13.

55. Gaviola Artígas, Lopresti Martínez, and Rojas Mira, *Nuestra historia de mujeres*, 41.

56. Baltra as cited in Bambirra, "La mujer chilena en la transición al socialismo," 2.

57. Vidal, *La emancipación de la mujer*, 56.

58. *Como participar* (1970), 24.

59. Ibid., 24.

60. Vidal, *La emancipación de la mujer,* 79.

61. Ibid., 80.

62. "su papel ya no esta solo en el hogar y que su inteligencia y su talento pueden ser beneficio fuera de los cuatro paredes de su casa." From "Una evaluación: Los Centros de Madres," *Paula* 142 (June 1973): 83.

63. Ibid.

64. Mattelart, *Mass Media, Ideologies, and the Revolutionary Movement.*

65. For reference to the "new man," see *Programa básico de gobierno de la Unidad Popular* (Santiago: N.p., 1969), 31.

66. Butler Flora, "Roasting Donald Duck."

67. Dorfman and Mattelart, *Para leer al pato Donald,* and *How to Read Donald Duck.* For Kunzle's reflections on translating *How to Read Donald Duck,* see Kunzle, "Parts That Got Left out of the Donald Duck Book."

68. Dorfman and Mattelart also addressed gender and sexuality. Their critique made clear that Donald—or others—did not have sex and did not engage in relations deemed "inappropriate" to readers. See Dorfman and Mattelart, *How to Read Donald Duck,* 39.

69. In Flora, "Roasting Donald Duck," 168.

70. See especially Korowin, "*Luchar para cantar, cantar para no olvidar.*" The movement was named in 1969, by Ricardo Garcia, radio personality and later founder of *Alerce* (1976). Also see the videorecording of Jara's music and documentary of his life, *The Right to Live in Peace* (1999).

71. For insights into the movement, also see Torres, *Perfil de la creación musical*; Rodríguez Musso, *La nueva canción chilena*; and Barraza, *La nueva canción chilena.*

72. See, for example, the lyrics of Quilapayun's "Vamos Mujer."

73. Inti-Illimani, *Canto al programa* (1970). For the lyrics, see also "Canto al Programa," in Rodríguez Musso, *La nueva canción chilena,* 219–230.

74. Kunzle, "Chile's La Firme versus Itt."

75. Ibid., 124.

76. Chaney, "Mobilization of Women in Allende's Chile," 11. The same journal also delivered different, more innovative messages and opened up public debates on counterculture and sexuality. See, for example, Mario Gómez López, "Exclusivo," *Ramona* 1, no. 1 (October 29, 1971): 49, an interview with guru "Silo," who openly addressed sexuality. Also cited in Barr-Melej, "Siloísmo and the Self in Allende's Chile," 748.

77. Andreas, *Nothing Is As It Should Be.*

78. Ibid., 41–43.

79. *Que pasa* 50 (March 30, 1972): 47.

80. See *La tercera,* March 29, 1972, 6; *La nacion,* March 28, 1972, 6; *El mercurio,* March 29, 1972, 4; *Revista vea* 1710 (April 6, 1972): 10–11; and *Novedades* 73 (March 31, 1972).

81. *Revista vea* 1710 (April 6, 1972): 10.

82. Juan de Onis, "Chile's Leading Marxist: Salvador Allende," *New York Times,* September 7, 1970, 9.

83. See *Vida médica* 22, no. 12 (December 1970): 10.

84. "El gobierno de Allende y los medicos," *Vida médica* 22, no. 11 (November 1970): 12–14.

85. *Vida médica* 22, no. 12 (December 1970): 22.

86. Chile, Contradoría General de la República, *Decreto Supremo No. 54.*

87. Hernán Romero, "Desarrollo de la Medicina y la Salubridad en Chile," *Revista médica de Chile* 100 (1972): 853–876.

88. For some experiences on local health-care approaches, see Infante, "Primary Health Care in a Local Community."

89. The role of the councils was defined in Decree No. 602, National Health Service, Chile, August 30, 1971. The decree specified consumer majority in each council, an arrangement which was not accepted uncritically. Many physicians felt that their decision-making authority began to be undermined when substantial functions were given to nonprofessionals and consumers. In 1972, many physicians joined the wave of strikes to protest UP policies. See Arturo Jiron, "Open Letter to the President," *El mercurio* (August 30, 1973); see also Belmar and Sidel, "International Perspective on Strikes and Strike Threats by Physicians."

90. *Vida médica* 22, no. 12 (December 1970): 21–24.

91. *Revista Paula* 54 (January 1970): 10–11; *Revista Paula* 132 (1972): 10–12; and *Revista Paula* 140 (March 1972): 87–89 and 108–113.

92. Chile, Allende Gossens, *Primer mensaje del presidente de Chile al país en la inauguración del periodo ordinario de Sesiones del Congreso Nacional* (1971), as cited in Faúndes and Hardy, "Contraception and Abortion Services," 291.

93. Tegualda Monreal, interview with the author, September 1997.

94. Faúndes and Hardy, "Contraception and Abortion Services," 284–297.

95. Monreal interview.

96. Faúndes and Hardy, "Contraception and Abortion Services," 295.

97. Ibid., 295.

98. See Jiménez, "Salud y Población," as cited in Larraín, *La sociedad médica de Santiago,* 285.

99. *Boletín APROFA* 9, no. 8 (1973): 1. For a copy of the agreement signed between the NHS and APROFA, see pp. 4 and 6. For a summary of the "Programa de Atención Integral de la Mujer," see p. 5.

100. *Boletín APROFA* (December 1970): 3–4.

101. Viel and Lucero, "Experiencia con un plan anticonceptivo en Chile."

102. Dr. Gildo Zambra, interview with the author, November 1997.

103. Zambra interview.

104. Capetanopulos and Cabrera, "Entrenamiento para un programa de informacion y educacion"; *Boletín APROFA* 9, no. 8 (1973): 1; and Hardy and Capetanopulos, *Informe anual.*

105. Videla de Plankey, "Las mujeres pobladores de Chile y el proceso revolucionario."

106. Unlike any other government in Chile, the Unidad Popular increased its electoral support midway through a six-year administration—winning 43.39 percent of the vote—against 56.61 percent of CODE.

107. Mattelart and Cheang, *Michéle Mattelart reading* The Chilean Press Avant-coup.

108. Müller-Plantenberg, *Frauen und Familie im gesellschaftlichen Befreiungsprozess,* 133–134.

109. See a translated version of Vuskovic's speech in Johnson, *Chilean Road to Socialism,* as cited in Townsend, "Refusing to Travel La Vía Chilena," 61.

110. Chile, Oficina de informaciones, *Palabras del presidente de la república, Compañero Salvador Allende Gossens, pronunciadas en al inauguración de los cursos auxiliares de párvulos,* 4.

111. Ibid., 5.

112. Ibid., 6, 7.

113. Ibid., 7.

114. Baldez, "Nonpartisanship as a Political Strategy," 279–280.

115. Ibid., 277–278.

116. Camilla Townsend first showed that middle- and upper-class women were joined by working-class women who came on their own terms, with a political agenda of their own. See Townsend, "Refusing to Travel La Vía Chilena," 43–63.

117. On right-wing women in Chile, see especially Power, *Right-Wing Women in Chile*; see also Crummett, "El Poder Feminino"; and Garrett-Schesch, "Mobilization of Women During the Popular Unity Government."

118. Quilapayun, see lyrics of "Las Ollitas."

119. Power, *Right-Wing Women in Chile,* 156. Also see Power's insightful discussion of the multiple reactions to and implications of the March, on pp. 156–168.

120. Camilla Townsend refers to these reactions. See Townsend, "Refusing to Travel La Vía Chilena," 43.

121. Ibid.

122. Ana Maria as quoted in White, *Chile's Days of Terror,* 80–81.

123. *La prensa,* December 5, 1971, as cited in Power, *Right-Wing Women in Chile,* 164.

124. Power reminds us that "conservative women were neither static nor inflexible" and "did not hail exclusively from the upper classes." As organizers of one of the first women's protest marches to make history, and as an ongoing presence in Chilean politics, "they cannot be . . . dismissed summarily as *viejas momias* (old mummies)," since they were of different ages and varied class backgrounds. See Power, "Defending Dictatorship," 300. Power also comments on the origins of the term. Supporters of the Chilean left referred to the opposition as mummies "to convey the idea that they were members of the dead bourgeois class" (p. 300).

125. Andreas, "Chilean Woman," 121–125; and Mattelart, "Chile," 279–301.

126. For the role of Poder Feminino and the Anti-Allende movement, see Power, *Right-Wing Women in Chile*, especially 169–247; also see Baldez, *Why Women Protest,* 98–122.

127. Particio Guzmán's documentary *La batalla de Chile* shows the women of the opposition in angry outburst even against the military; women of Poder Feminino heckled and insulted military personnel for what they considered a lack of action against the Unidad Popular. See Guzmán, *Battle of Chile.*

128. Mattelart, "Chile," 283. See also Power, *Right-Wing Women in Chile,* 229.

129. Power, *Right-Wing Women in Chile,* 229.

130. Andreas, *Nothing Is As It Should Be,* 21.

131. "Combativa manifestación femenina de apoyo al gobierno popular," *Las noticias de ultima hora* (September 6, 1973):1.

132. As cited in Crummett, "El Poder Feminino," 103.

133. David Belnap, "Women Played Big Role in Allende Fall: Pressure Both Subtle and Obvious Forced Military's Hand," *The Capitol Times,* February 4, 1974, as quoted in Garrett-Schesch, "Mobilization of Women During the Popular Unity Government," 101.

134. Harnecker, *La lucha de un pueblo sin armas.*

135. Valdés as quoted in Shayne, *Revolution Question, 77.* For reference to the number of elected women in the Senate and Parliament, see Aylwin, Correa, and Piñera E., *Percepción del rol político de la mujer una aproximación histórica,* 85.

136. Valdés in Shayne, *Revolution Question,* 77.

Chapter 5. From Mothers' Rights to Women's Rights in a Nation under Siege

Epigraph: Kirkwood, *Ser política en Chile los nudos de la sabiduría feminista,* 10–11, as cited in Agosín, "Visions and Transgressions," 208. Julia Kirkwood, renowned Chilean feminist writer, theorist, and activist, had a profound impact on the development of feminisms in Chile and Latin America. She was known not only for her critical writings, but also for her participation in pioneering feminist groups that defended women's rights under dictatorship, such as the Círculo de Estudios de la Mujer and the Casa de la Mujer La Morada. Kirkwood died of cancer in 1985.

1. As cited in Pastrana and Threlfall, *Pan, techo y poder,* 86.

2. Hilda's recollection is in Taller de Acción Cultural (Santiago, Chile), *La organización fue como nacer,* 87.

3. As quoted in Maloof, *Voices of Resistance,* 122.

4. Lucía Hiriart de Pinochet, as quoted in *Cema Chile* (Santiago: CEMA-Chile, n.d.).

5. Kirkwood, *Ser política en Chile los nudos de la sabiduría feminista,* 10–11, as cited in Agosín, "Visions and Transgressions," 208.

6. As Marjorie Agosín has put it, "in the view of the state, women became subversive mothers." See Agosín, *Ashes of Revolt,* 140.

7. There are many excellent studies on the nature of women's engagement under dictatorship. Patricia Chuchryk has documented the rise of a feminist movement that emerged when women mobilized to challenge the regime. See Chuchryk, "Protest, Politics, and Personal Life"; see also Chuchryk, "From Dictatorship to Democracy." Lisa Baldez, in *Why Women Protest,* has examined the particular circumstances in which women's movements could make a difference in Chile's political history. For insights into the variety of women's groups and different forms of resistance, see also Adams, *"Art in Social Movements"*; Palestro, *Mujeres en movimiento, 1973–1989*; and Valdés and Weinstein, *Mujeres que sueñan las organizaciones de pobladoras.* The Círculo de Estudios de la Mujer was also referred to as Círculo de Estudios de la Condición de la Mujer. Here I use the more frequent reference, Círculo de Estudios de la Mujer, and refer to it as "Círculo" hereafter.

8. Htun, *Sex and the State.*

9. In 1974, the regime ordered an expert commission to examine family planning—uniting military and civilian experts, including APROFA's family planners. The commission confirmed that beneath its rigid rhetoric and its subsequent pro-natalist policies, the military considered alternative positions on the subject. See "Comisión Nacional de Planificación Familiar y Paternidad Responsable," *Asociación Chilena de Protección de la Familia* 10, no. 5–6 (May–June 1974): 3.

10. As cited in Spooner, *Soldiers in a Narrow Land,* 49.

11. The regime justified its immediate, massive, violent campaigns against Allende's supporters and those suspect of leftist political affiliation also through propaganda published in the *White Book of the Change* (first published in Spanish, then translated into English), which claimed to document an undercover plot, leftists' access to Cuban arms, and the "true" danger posed by "subversives" prior to the coup. See Chile, *Libro blanco del cambio de gobierno en Chile;* and Chile, *White Book of the Change of Government in Chile.*

12. Some scholars have addressed the military coup as continuity of military professionalism, also present in a wider Latin American context. See Nunn, "Military Professionalism

and Professional Militarism in Brazil," and "New Thoughts on Military Intervention in Latin American Politics." For traditions of military intervention in the region, also see Loveman and Davies, *Politics of Antipolitics.*

13. See, for example, Drake and Jaksic, *Struggle for Democracy in Chile*; Ensalaco, *Chile Under Pinochet*; Hecht Oppenheim, *Politics in Chile*; and Spooner, *Soldiers in a Narrow Land.*

14. Valenzuela, "El fundamento de la dominación patriarcial en Chile," as cited in Ríos Tobar, "'Feminism Is Socialism, Liberty, and Much More.'"

15. Lucía Hiriart de Pinochet quoted in Chile, *Valores patrios y valores familiares,* 11.

16. Ibid., 21.

17. Pinochet Ugarte, *Mensaje a la mujer chilena,* 7. For references to the philosophical underpinnings of the regime's gender politics, also see Miller, *Latin American Women and the Search for Social Justice,* 183–184.

18. Chile, *Valores patrios y valores familiares,* 24.

19. For evidence of this construction of women's roles, see also Munizaga, *El discurso público de Pinochet.*

20. Valdés and Weinstein, *Mujeres que sueñan: Las organizaciones de pobladoras*, 76–77.

21. For references to volunteers and to divisions within CEMA, see Chile, CEMA, *Fundación CEMA Chile* (1984). See also Bunster, "Watch out for the Little Nazi Man That All of Us Have Inside," 487. See also Margaret Power, "Right-Wing Women, Sexuality, and Politics in Chile during the Pinochet Dictatorship, 1973–1990," in *Right-Wing Women,* ed. Bacchetta and Power. Power points to a continuity in right-wing women's motivation: they helped defeat Allende and supported the dictatorship to uphold their conservative understanding of motherhood and sexuality.

22. *Memoria CEMA-Chile, 1980–1981,* 6, as cited in Valdés and Weinstein, *Mujeres que sueñan las organizaciones de pobladoras,* 76.

23. "Opiniones," Fundación CEMA-Chile, Revista aniversario CEMA-Chile, October 1982–October 1983 (Santiago: La Fundación, 1983), 130.

24. Julio Canessa Robert as quoted in ibid., 130.

25. Valdés et al., *Centros de madres 1973–1989,* 32–33.

26. For an example of the First Lady's control of women's "double-militancy" in community groups, see Valdés and Weinstein, *Mujeres que sueñan: Las organizaciones de pobladoras,* 77.

27. As cited in Valdés et al., *Centros de Madres, 1973–1989,* 38.

28. Teresa Valdés, "Los Centros de Madres," *La época,* November 16, 1989.

29. Stolz, *Adiós General—Adiós Macho?* 97.

30. See Lechner and Levy, *Notas sobre la vida cotidiana III,* as cited in Comando por el NO, "*Quietas y controladas,*" 6.

31. Chile, *Siete años de voluntariado aniversario 1980, discursos,* 5, 14. See also Chile, *Diez años de voluntariado 1973–1983*; and Chile, *Memoria.*

32. For a discussion of the similarities between women and soldiers, and a reminder that both the model-mother and the model-soldier are constructions of a patriarchal regime that expects their sacrifice, see Valenzuela, *La mujer en el Chile military,* 102–104.

33. Iris Stolz has reported that the volunteers also helped display public support for the regime after the failed plot to kill Pinochet in 1986. See Stolz, *Adiós General—Adiós Macho?* 94.

34. "Entrevista a la madre del año: Doña Doralisa, a Fertile Woman," in Chile, CEMA, *Fundación CEMA-Chile, Revista aniversario CEMA-Chile, octubre 1982–octubre 1983,* 41–42.

35. Rajevic, *El libro abierto del amor y el sexo en Chile,* 23. Rajevic tells Leontina Huetel's story in her book. Even if the number of unauthorized removals could not be documented,

many women canceled visits to local health-care centers out of fear of the "care" they might receive. Soledad Díaz, interview with author, Santiago, April 1997.

36. Kommunistischer Bund and Chile-Frauengruppe Hamburg, *Frauen in Chile,* 33. Cited in *Chile-Nachrichten* 31. The author also drew comparisons to fascism and its pro-natalist policies.

37. Spoerer as cited in Scarpaci, "HMO Promotion and Privatization in Chile," 553.

38. For changes in the Chilean health-care system, see Reichard, "Ideology Drives Health Care Reforms in Chile"; Jiménez de la Jara and Bossert, "Chile's Health Sector Reform"; Navarro, "What Does Chile Mean"; and Heyermann, *Municipio, descentralización y salud.* For more detail and the steps taken by the military, see Scarpaci, *Primary Medical Care in Chile.*

39. Sagaris, "Health Care in Chile," 177.

40. Kubal, "Contradictions and Constraints in Chile's Health Care and Education Decentralization," 115–116.

41. Scarpaci, *Primary Medical Care in Chile,* 24.

42. Dr. Maria Isabel Matamala, interview with the author, Santiago, April 1997.

43. "Chileans, in Change, Oppose Birth Curbs," *New York Times,* May 7, 1979, 11.

44. Ricardo Cruz-Coke, *Revista médica de Chile* 109, no. 1 (January 1981): 68–72. For connections drawn between population size and nacional security, also see Seminario para comunicadores especializados, *Cuántos debemos ser los chilenos y por que?.*

45. Chile, Oficina de Planificación Nacional ODEPLAN, *Política poblacional aprobada por su excelencia el presidente de la república,* 7. Family-planning leader Benjamín Viel, now back in Chile, challenged the incumbent health minister on the matter and defended the health measures of previous governments—but to no avail. See Benjamín Viel, *Revista médica de Chile* 108, no. 1 (January 1981): 255–268.

46. National Security as a justification of changing policies was closely related to border conflicts with neighboring countries that escalated in the same year. Ultimately, the Pope helped prevent the outbreak of war between Chile and Argentina, but the tension inspired a focus on national defense that significantly shaped public policies. Fear of population decline was pronounced in scholarly analysis as well. See Valenzuela Arellano, "Tendencias de la natalidad y fecundidad en Chile," 87–91. The author comments on recent fertility trends in Chile and argues that a decline of birth rates should cause concern.

47. Chile, Oficina de Planificación Nacional ODEPLAN, *Política poblacional aprobada por su excelencia el presidente de la república,* 7; and Instituto de la Mujer, Área de Salud, *Las políticas de planificación familiar,* 4.

48. See also Jiles Moreno and Rojas Mira, "El régimen militar."

49. Chile, *Circular Number 3G/188, Actualización de la Actividad Paternidad Responsable.* In some instances the pro-natalist stance survived: at the Mexico City World Population Conference, the Chilean delegates suggested that "given that the human element is the primordial factor in development, Chile finds an increase in its population to be necessary. Huge sections of the country are still underpopulated." United Nations, *International Conference on Population. Report of the International Conference on Population, 1984.* For pro-natalism and the lingering pro-natalist stance, also see Valenzuela, *La mujer en el Chile militar,* 81–84.

50. Dr. Augusto Schuster Cortes as quoted in Chile, *Circular Number 3G/188, Actualización de la Actividad Paternidad Responsable,* 1; and ibid.

51. See "Chilenos opinan sobre aborto, la Píldora, y libertad sexual," *Asociación Chilena de Protección de la Familia* 12, no. 6 (June 1976): 4–5.

52. Capetanópulos et al., *Informe Anual Programa Monitores de Paternidad Responsable*, 11.

53. Ibid., 12.

54. Ibid., 7, 6.

55. Asociación Chilena de Protección de la Familia, *Memoria 1974, Departamento "Información y Educación"* (Santiago: APROFA, 1974), 9. For activities in CEMAs, the Women's Secretariat, Ministries of Education and Health, and in universities, see also Asociación Chilena de Protección de la Familia, *Departamento "Información y Educación"* (Santiago: APROFA 1976), 8–9.

56. Asociación Chilena de Protección de la Familia, *Memoria 1974, Departamento "Información y Educación"* (Santiago: APROFA, 1974), 11.

57. The meeting was run by Dr. Patricia Schiller of the American Association of Sex Educators (AASEC) and was the outcome of joint efforts by APROFA and the Pan-American Health Organization, *Memoria 1975, Departamento "Información y Educación"* (Santiago: APROFA, 1975), 1.

58. "Distribución comunitaria de anticonceptivos en América Latina," *Asociación Chilena de Protección de la Familia* 13, no. 3–4 (March–April 1977): 3.

59. For a critique on the treatment of sexuality in education and an overview of early approaches, see also Silva Dreyer, *Las políticas de planificación familiar.*

60. Asociación Chilena de Protección de la Familia, Departamento "Información y Educación," *Boletín Técnico: Número Especial, V Seminario Nacional de Perfeccionamiento para el Personal del Departamento de Información y Educación de "APROFA"* (Santiago: APROFA, 1977), 16.

61. *Asociación Chilena de Protección de la Familia* 15, no. 1–2 (January–February 1979): 6–7.

62. Asociación Chilena para la Protección de la Familia, *APROFA 1980* (Santiago: Asociación Chilena de Protección de la Familia), 15.

63. Ibid., 14.

64. Wulf, "Teenage Pregnancy and Childbearing in Latin America and the Caribbean," 19–20.

65. Asociación Chilena de Protección de la Familia, *Síntesis de la Memoria APROFA 1977* (Santiago: APROFA 1978), 3.

66. "Opiniones sobre planificación familiar," *Asociación Chilena de Protección de la Familia* 15, no. 3–4 (March–April 1979): 4.

67. Ibid., 5.

68. *Asociación Chilena de Protección de la Familia* 16, no. 9–12 (September–December 1980): 2.

69. Benjamín Viel, "La Planificación Familiar en Chile y su Efecto Sobre los Índices de Salud," *Boletín APROFA* 24, no. 7–12 (July–December 1988): 3–15.

70. See Pena O. et al., "Perfil de la adolescente embarazada controlada en consultorio del S.S.M.," 162–165; and *Congreso Nacional de Investigadores Sociales y Medico-Sociales sobre la Juventud Chilena* (Santiago) 1 (June 1986).

71. Hamel, "Sexualidad y embarazo en la adolescencia," 30–43.

72. Viel, "La planificación familiar," 9.

73. Ibid., 9.

74. Gomensoro, *Embarazo de adolescentes*; and Viel, "La planificación familiar," 9.

75. "Maternidad precoz, problema nacional," *Punto final* 8, no. 197 (October 1989): 22.

76. For examples of some of the purges in other fields, see Oteiza, "Purged Professors, Screened Students, Burned Books," 52–56.

77. Silva Dreyer, *Las políticas de planificación familiar,* 6.

78. For reference to these modificatory decrees and to sex education, see Feringa, "Reproductive Rights under the Chilean Military Dictatorship," 37–40.

79. For reference to Decree 362, see Feringa, "Reproductive Rights under the Chilean Military Dictatorship," 40. For details on the changes, see "Legislación al dia: Enfermedades de transmisión sexual," *Asociación Chilena de Protección de la Familia: 21 Años* (1987): 22–23.

80. "Legislación al dia: Enfermedades de transmisión sexual," *Asociación Chilena de Protección de la Familia: 21 Años* (1987): 22–23.

81. Valenzuela, "Evolving Roles of Women Under Military Rule," 164.

82. Ibid., 163–164.

83. Stolz, *Adiós General—Adiós Macho?* 48–49.

84. Ibid., 30–31.

85. Ibid., 121.

86. Heliette Saint Jean, Edith Asriel, Ximena Fuentes, Hanna Bitran, and Maria Elena Zalazar, "Grupo de orientacion para mujeres con disfunciones sexuales," *Boletín de la Oficina Sanitaria Panamericana* 102, no. 3 (1987): 257–262.

87. Stolz, *Adiós General—Adiós Macho?* 72, 74; also see Milena Vodanovic, "La vida sexual de las chilenas," *Apsi,* August 22, 1988.

88. Valdés, *Venid, benditas de mi Padre las pobladoras, sus rutinas y sus sueños,* 227–251.

89. Stolz, *Adiós General—Adiós Macho?,* 68–70.

90. Ibid., 53.

91. The play was cowritten by David Benavente and the *Taller de Investigación Teatral* (TIT).

92. Fanny Berlagoscky, personal communication with author, January 2007.

93. See "Las Tres Marías Haces Las Maletas (La Rosa, También)" [The Three Marías Pack Their Bags (and Rosa, Too)], *Las últimas noticias,* November 3, 1980, as cited in Nelson, *Political Bodies,* 88n23, 250–251.

94. Kirkwood, *Ser política en Chile: Los nudos de la sabiduría feminista,* 180.

95. Richard, "Género, valores y diferencia(s)," 201, as discussed in Green, "Diamela Eltit."

96. Valdés, *El movimiento social de mujeres.* Valdés divides the history of the women's movement between 1973 and 1989 in four phases: women in defense of life (1973–1976); feminist approaches by professional women (1977–1981); active mobilization against dictatorship based on specific demands (1982–1986); and, finally, women's participation in the prospects of democratization (1987–1989). See especially pages 30–47. CODEM and MUDECHI had ties to the MIR (Movimiento de Izquierda Revolucionario) and the Communist Party, respectively; see Valdés, *El movimiento social de mujeres,* 36–37.

97. As cited in Baldez, *Why Women Protest,* 129.

98. Razeto, *Las organizaciones económicas populares.*

99. For the role of the Church and moral resistance, see Lowden, *Moral Opposition to Authoritarian Rule in Chile.*

100. On the Vicariate of Solidarity, also see Fruhling, "Resistance to Fear in Chile," 121–141.

101. Moya-Raggio, "'Arpilleras'"; and Baldez, *Why Women Protest,* 130.

102. Women formalized their institutional affiliation in 1979 but had to overcome certain prejudices against women's mobilization. Reminiscent of traditional gender systems, they were deemed trustworthy only after they submitted personal data on their families. Academy representatives requested a list of names and occupations from Círculo members,

and it was not until women identified themselves through their husbands that they were seen as acceptable affiliates. See Chuchryk, "Protest, Politics, and Personal Life," 360–361nn28, 29. Ford Foundation grants, already supporting a number of South American progressive women's groups, significantly eased the negotiations between the Academy and Círculo women. See Cornelia Butler Flora, personal correspondence with the author, January 2007.

103. Bravo et al., "Y así va creciendo," 26.

104. As cited in Gaviola Artígas, Largo, and Palestro, "'Si la mujer no está, la democracia no va,'" 81.

105. Círculo de Estudios de la Mujer, "Reflexiones sobre la práctica feminista," as cited in Ríos Tobar, "'Feminism Is Socialism, Liberty, and Much More.'"

106. Bravo et al., "Y así va creciendo," 26.

107. Círculo de Estudios de la Mujer, "Reflexiones sobre la práctica feminista," 129–134.

108. See Bravo et al., "Y así va creciendo," 26.

109. Crispi, *Tejiendo Rebeldías*.

110. Adriasola et al., *Algunas ideas respecto a la condición de la mujer*, 280.

111. See Ipsen, "Women's Movement in Chile," 96–97; and Bravo et al., "Y así va creciendo," 26.

112. Adriasola et al., *Algunas ideas respecto a la condición de la mujer*, 14.

113. Ibid., 14.

114. Ibid., 4–6.

115. For more detail on working groups set up by Círculo women, see Butler Flora, "Socialist Feminism in Latin America," 21.

116. For transcripts of the presentations and questions by the audience recorded at the meeting, see Círculo de Estudios de la Condición de la Mujer, *Políticas de población y control de la natalidad* (Santiago: Academia de Humanismo Cristiano, 1980).

117. Chilean women who mobilized under dictatorship shared characteristics with motherist groups whose action was "predicated upon overcoming the private/public divide" and made mothers central to the public stage. See Radcliffe and Westwood, "*ViVa*," 18.

118. Valdés and Weinstein, *Mujeres que sueñan las organizaciones de pobladoras*, 195.

119. Ton Salman has argued that women, more than men, engaged in *collective* resistance under dictatorship; he also proposed that the lasting political involvement of shantytown social movements under redemocratization was compromised by the top-down incentives that inspired their mobilization. Salman, "Diffident Movement," 8–31; and Salman, *Diffident Movement*.

120. López-Stewart and Gumberger, *Ich bringe das Salz: Chilenische Frauen berichten*, 108.

121. Cleary, *Frauen in der Politik Chiles*, 225.

122. See, for example, *Vamos mujer* 3 (1989): 7–8, 10.

123. Cleary, *Frauen in der Politik Chiles*, 214.

124. For references to CODEM and MOMUPO, also see Schöttes, *Lebensbedingungen, Widerstand und Verfolgung von Frauen in Chile*, 47–48; and Cleary, *Frauen in der Politik Chiles*, 206–233.

125. Cleary, *Frauen in der Politik Chiles*, 219–220.

126. "Mujeres, volverémos a casa?" in Silva and Movimiento de Mujeres Pobladoras, Chile, *No estas muerto*, 34.

127. Cleary, *Frauen in der Politik Chiles*, 221. Patricia Richards has argued that class-based concerns remained central to *pobladora* activism; see Richards, *Pobladoras, Indígenas, and the State*, 84.

128. As cited in Baldez, *Why Women Protest*, 148.

129. Valdés, *Las mujeres y la dictadura militar en Chile*, 35.

130. See Frohmann and Valdés, "Democracy in the Country and in the 'Home': The Women's Movement in Chile," *Serie estudios sociales*, No. 55, for insights into women's reconceptualization of democracy.

131. *La epoca*, October 7, 1988, 9. Margaret Power's work on right-wing women offers a number of insights into the historical reasoning of conservative women and argues that many Chilean women sought to affirm their conservative notions of womanhood, motherhood, and sexuality, as they supported the dictatorship. See Power, "Right-Wing Women, Sexuality, and Politics in Chile during the Pinochet Dictatorship, 1973–1990," in her *Right-Wing Women*, 273–286 (chapter 19).

132. Coordinación de Organizaciones Sociales de Mujeres, "*Soy Mujer...Tengo Derechos.*"

133. Ibid., 1–6.

134. La Coordinación de Organizaciones Sociales de Mujeres was founded in 1988 by some of Santiago's major feminist organizations. Initially, its main objective was to coordinate the annual preparations for International Women's Day. See ibid., 1.

135. See ibid., 5.

136. These demands were published in the final document produced by participants of the campaign and appeared in connection to problems women identified. The document offers remarkable insights into the complexity of obstacles to women's rights and participants approaches to finding solutions. See "Cuadro General," in ibid., 47–49.

137. "La violencia contra la mujer es un delito, en la calle y en cualquier sitio." See Anexo No. 6, "Consignas Utilizadas en el Acto del Paseo Ahumada (21/11/1989)," in ibid., 47–49.

138. "Machistas los criamos, y después nos espantamos." See Anexo No. 6, "Consignas Utilizadas en el Acto del Paseo Ahumada (21/11/1989)," in ibid., 47–49.

139. "La democracia va si la mujer está." See Anexo No. 6, "Consignas Utilizadas en el Acto del Paseo Ahumada (21/11/1989)," in ibid., 47–49.

140. Montecino Aguirre and Rossetti, *Tramas para un nuevo destino.*

141. Kirkwood, *La política del feminismo en Chile*, 5.

142. Kirkwood, "Women and Politics in Chile," 625.

143. Htun, *Sex and the State*, 73.

144. Actas Oficiales de la Comisión Constituyente, Sesión 87, November 14, 1974. As cited in Lagos Lira, *Aborto en Chile: El deber de parir*, 11.

Chapter 6. International Encounters and Women's Empowerment under Dictatorship and Redemocratization

Epigraph: Kirkwood, *Ser política en Chile*, 43, as cited in Agosín, "Visions and Transgressions," 212.

1. "Anger Yields Hope in Stirring Songs of Chilean Group," *New York Times*, October 17, 1974, 55.

2. Dawson, "Joan Jara and Chile," 7.

3. Alicia Frohmann, informal interview with the author, November 1996. For the quotation, see Frohmann and Valdés, "Democracy in the Country and in the Home: The Women's Movement in Chile," in *Challenge of Local Feminisms Women's Movements in Global Perspective*, ed. Basu and McGrory, 283.

4. Frohmann and Valdés, "Democracy in the Country and in the Home," in *Challenge of Local Feminisms,* 283.

5. Marcela Ríos Tobar has shown the difficulties of Chilean feminists to secure spaces for gender-based concerns and access to political participation. Ríos Tobar, "Chilean Feminism(s) in the 1990s"; see also Ríos Tobar, Godoy, and Guerrero, *Un nuevo silencio feminista?*.

6. In her compelling study of the 1979 CEDAW, Susanne Zwingel has shown that Chilean women's groups, as well as the newly founded government office the National Office for Women's Affairs (Servicio Nacional de la Mujer, SERNAM), evoked CEDAW to strengthen their negotiating power in their quest for women's rights. See Zwingel, "How Do International Women's Rights Norms Become Effective in Domestic Contexts?" especially 244–278.

7. On the new dynamic, or the "NGO-ization" of women's movements, see Alvarez, "Advocating Feminism."

8. Zinsser, "United Nations Decade for Women."

9. United Nations, *World Plan of Action for the Implementation of the Objectives of the International Women's Year*; see also Fraser, "Becoming Human," 906.

10. Keck and Sikkink, *Activists Beyond Borders Advocacy Networks in International Politics,* 168–169.

11. See Anna Quandt, *A Report on International Women's Year Conference and Its Meaning for the Population Council* (July 17, 1975), 1, 3, RBF, unprocessed material, Box 408, Folder: Pop. Council, Inc. 4, January 1975–December 1975.

12. Ibid.

13. "Short History of CEDAW Convention," available online at http://www.un.org/womenwatch/daw/cedaw/history.htm. Also see Zwingel, "From Intergovernmental Negotiations to (Sub)National Change."

14. Vienna Declaration and Programme of Action, U.N. GAOR, World Conference on Human Rights, 48th Sess., 22d plen. mtg., U.N. Doc. A/CONF.157/24 (1993), reprinted in 32 I.L.M. 1661 (1993), paragraph 18, as cited in Fraser, "Becoming Human," 903.

15. As cited in Center for Reproductive Law and Policy and Foro Abierto de Salud y Derechos Reproductivos, *Women Behind Bars Chile's Abortion Laws,* 25.

16. *Fourth World Conference on Women: Action for Equality, Development, and Peace, Beijing Declaration and Platform for Action,* adopted September 15, 1995, U.N. GAOR, ch. III, paragraphs 41–44, U.N. Doc. A/CONF.177/20 (1995), reprinted in *Report of the Fourth World Conference on Women* (1995) (recommended to the UN General Assembly by the Committee on the Status of Women on October 7, 1995), as cited in Fraser, "Becoming Human," 904.

17. Angell and Pollack, "Chilean Elections of 1989."

18. Waylen, *Engendering Transitions,* 74–75.

19. See reference in Schuurman and Heer, *Social Movements and NGOs in Latin America,* 97.

20. Vargas Valente, *Ciudadanía,* as cited in Molina, "De la denuncia a la contrucción de la igualdad," 189.

21. Interview with Coti Silva by Julie D. Shayne, in Shayne, *Revolution Question.*

22. "Demandas de las mujeres a la democracia," *La epoca,* July 1, 1988, 9.

23. Alicia Frohmann, "Las demandas de las mujeres a la democracia," *Mensaje* 371 (August 1988): 342.

24. Frohmann, "Las demandas de las mujeres a la democracia," 341–342; Frohmann and Valdés, "Democracy in the Country and in the Home," in *Challenge of Local Feminisms,* 286; and Frohmann interview.

25. Montecino Aguirre and Rossetti, *Tramas para un nuevo destino*.

26. Waylen, "Women's Movements, the State, and Democratization in Chile."

27. For a critical assessment of the role of SERNAM, see Blofield and Haas, "Defining a Democracy"; Franceschet, *Women and Politics in Chile*, 111–114; and Baldez, "La política partidista y los límites del feminismo de estado en Chile." For a study of SERNAM that addresses the impact political parties have on women's political representation and on state gender policies, see Macaulay, "Gender Politics in Brazil and Chile."

28. Frohmann and Valdés, "Democracy in the Country and in the Home," in *Challenge of Local Feminisms*, 290.

29. Weinstein, *Estado, mujeres de sectores populares y ciudadanía*, 19.

30. Franceschet, *Women and Politics in Chile*, 114–115.

31. Strongholds of male-dominated political tradition, parties resisted gender quotas or other novel systems that could help increase the number of women running for office. Political parties' monopolization of the realm of formal politics provided often insurmountable barriers to women's participation. See Franceschet, *Women and Politics in Chile*, 85–86.

32. See the complete interview with Rosana Ceorino in Franceschet, "'State Feminism' and Women's Movements," 25.

33. Francisca Rodríguez as quoted in ibid., 25.

34. Finn, "Raíces," 450.

35. Ibid., 448–470.

36. Ibid., 463.

37. I share the concern of many scholars who have criticized the use of terms like *third world* and *first world*; here, I use the terms as a reflection of the dividing categories and of the nature of conflict of the time period I discuss. Chandra Talpade Mohanty, for example, has commented on the misleading characteristics of the terms, which not only reinforce existing economic, political, and cultural hierarchies, but also oversimplify similarities among countries labeled in such manner. See Talpade Mohanty, "Under Western Eyes," 183n1.

38. Barrios de Chungara and Viezzer, *Let Me Speak!*, 198.

39. Butler Flora, "Socialist Feminism in Latin America," 7.

40. Rosemarie Putnam Tong had made the distinction between "women's" and "political" issues, which, of course, included many nuances and manifestations. See Putnam Tong, *Feminist Thought*, 228–229.

41. See West, "U.N. Mid-decade for Women," 2.

42. See Putnam Tong, *Feminist Thought*, 229.

43. Busto and Hola, "Contacto en Copenhague."

44. This author also added further insights on her personal reaction: "As a white lesbian feminist academic, I am always angry about the oppression I face each day as a woman, a lesbian, and as a member of the working class. However, I am also aware of the privilege I have as a white woman in this country in relation to women of color in this society and third world women around the world." See Albrecht, "Let Me Speak!" 14.

45. Putnam Tong, *Feminist Thought*, 229. Çağatay, Grown, and Santiago, "Nairobi Women's Conference," 402.

46. Reagan as quoted in Putnam Tong, *Feminist Thought*, 229.

47. Çağatay, Grown, Santiago, "Nairobi Women's Conference," 406.

48. Patricia Chuchryk has suggested that it was the contact with feminism abroad that became the initial stimulus to identify the nature and context of women's problems in Chile,

which had been, until then, "a problem without a name." See Chuchryk, "Protest, Politics, and Personal Life," 379–380.

49. The connection between travel abroad and feminism in Chile has also been documented in Ríos Tobar et al. See Ríos Tobar, Godoy, and Guerrero, *Un nuevo silencio feminista?*, 193–194.

50. Interview with Chela Borquez by Julie D. Shayne, in Shayne, *Revolution Question*, 113.

51. Isabel Gannon, personal communication with the author, February 2007.

52. Saporta Sternbach et al., "Feminisms in Latin America," 396.

53. Due to activists' seemingly irreconcilable commitments to either party politics or feminism, disagreements persisted on the strategies of women's involvement in the future.

54. "Testimonio," *Boletín No. 6* (September–October 1981): 5

55. Kirkwood, *Ser Politica en Chile*, 233–249; and Navarro, "El primer encuentro feminista de Latinoamérica y el Caribe."

56. Disch, "Encuentro Feminista Latinoamericano y del Caribe," 1.

57. On the number of women who signed up for the event, see ibid., 1. See "Fiesta en Lima," in Crispi, *Tejiendo Rebeldias*, 63.

58. Grupo Chaski and Garabato, *Miss Universo en el Peru Lima, Julio 1982* (film); also Disch, "Encuentro Feminista Latinoamericano y del Caribe," 1.

59. Ortega and Saporta Sternbach, "Gracias a la Vida," 1.

60. Ortega and Saporta Sternbach, "Gracias a la Vida," 1; also see Küppers, *Feministamente Frauenbewegung in Lateinamerika,* 110–111. Küppers cites the personal insights of participants at the fifth Encuentro in Argentina (1990).

61. Ríos Tobar, "'Feminism Is Socialism," 129–134.

62. On autonomous feminism, see Lidid and Maldonado, *Movimiento feminista autónomo, 1993–1997*; and Zwingel, *Demokratie im Land und im Haus,* 104–108. On the trajectory of feminist development, see Gaviola Artígas, Largo, and Palestra, *Una historia necesaria mujeres en Chile, 1973–1990*; and Pisano, *Reflexiones feministas.* On the rise of divisions, also see Baldez, *Why Women Protest,* 184–191.

63. Margarita Pisano in a 1994 interview with Lisa Baldez, as cited in Baldez, *Why Women Protest,* 190.

64. On the seventh Encuentro, see Waylen, *Engendering Transitions,* 88; and Gobbi, "VII Encuentro Feminista Latinoamericano y del Caribe."

65. The opening meeting, for example, reflected division, not unity, and women of different "convictions" brought banners and pamphlets to emphasize their views as they sat in opposite sides of the meeting hall.

66. Vargas Valente, "Carta hacia el VII Encuentro Feminista Latinoamericano y del Caribe. Chile. 1996," 15.

67. See Marysa Navarro, "Algunas reflexiones sobre el VII Encuentro Feminista Latinoamericano y del Caribe," in *Encuentros, (des) encuentros y búsquedas el movimiento feminista en América Latina*, ed. Cecilia Olea Mauleón (Lima, Peru: Flora Tristan, 1998), 110.

68. See Alvarez, "Advocating Feminism"; and Sonia Alvarez, "The 'NGOization' of Latin American Feminism," in *Cultures of Politics / Politics of Cultures: Re-Visioning Latin American Social Movements*, ed. Sonia E. Alvarez, Evelina Dagnino, and Arturo Escobar (Boulder, Colo.: Westview Press, 1998), 306–324.

69. See, for example, Komitee Solidarität mit Chile, *Konterrevolution in Chile Analysen u. Dokumente z. Terror*; and Berger, *Solidarität mit Chile: Die österreichische Chile-Solidaritätsfront,*

1973–1990. There is a substantial body of literature on Chilean exile. For some selections that reflect the regional scope, see Marita Eastmond, *Dilemmas of Exile: Chilean Refugees in the U.S.A* (Göteborg, Sweden: Acta Universitatis Gothenburgensis, 1997); Kay, *Chileans in Exile*; Thomas Wright and Rody Oñate, *Flight from Chile: Voices of Exile*, trans. Irene Hodgson (Santiago: Documentas, 1987); Sznajder and Roniger, "Exile Communities and Their Differential Institutional Dynamics"; and Montupil, *Exilio, derechos humanos y democracia*.

For explicit references to gender or women's experiences of exile, see Martina Schöttes, *Lebensbedingungen, Widerstand und Verfolgung von Frauen in Chile* (Berlin: Berliner Institut für Vergleichende Sozialforschung, 1991); Martina Schöttes and Monika Schuckar, *Frauen auf der Flucht* (Berlin: Edition Parabolis, 1994); Gabriella Gutiérrez y Muhs, *Communal Feminisms: Chicanas, Chilenas, and Cultural Exile: Theorizing the Space of Exile, Class, and Identity* (Lanham, Md.: Lexington Books, 2007); Marjorie Agosín and Emma Sepulveda, *Amigas: Letters of Friendship and Exile* (Oxford: Isis, 2004); Escobar Mónica, "Exile and National Identity: Chilean Women in Canada," Ph.D. dissertation, University of Toronto, 2000; Julie Shayne, "Tears of Resistance: Gender, Culture, and Emotions in the Chilean Diaspora," paper presented at the Pacific Sociological Association, Portland, Oregon, 2008; Julie Shayne, *They Used to Call Us Witches: Feminism, Culture, and Resistance in the Chilean Diaspora* (Lanham, Md.: Lexington Books, forthcoming); and Marilú Mallet, Dominique Pinel, Michael Rubbo, Guy Borremans, Michel Descombes, Isabel Allende, Maria Luisa Segnoret, Pascale Laverrière, and Milicska Jalbert, *Journal inacheve* (New York: Women Make Movies, 1995).

70. Centro de Estudios y Documentación, "La Conferencia Mundial de Solidaridad con Chile."

71. Palma, *Women in Chile Yesterday and Today*, 1.

72. Centro de Estudios y Documentación, *Chile–América* (Rome: Centro de Estudios y Documentación, 1974), no. 1–88/89 (September 1974–July/October 1983); see also the supplement, Centro de Estudios y Documentación, *Chile–America Supplemento*.

73. Women moved from the "logic of mutual solidarity and identity" to the "logic of international advocacy." Shepard and Alvarez have asserted that a second stage began in the 1990s, now shaped by the "logic of transnational advocacy." See Alvarez, "Thoughts on Distinctive Logics of Transnational Feminist Activism," 42.

74. For an excellent discussion of the many dimensions of the exile experience, see Rebolledo, *Memorias del desarraigo*. See also del Pozo, *Exiliados, emigrados y retornados chilenos en América y Europa*.

75. Stolz, *Adiós General—Adiós Macho?*, 124–125 (quotation on 125).

76. Guzmán, Mauro, and Araujo K, *La violencia doméstica como problema público y objeto de políticas*, as cited in Ríos Tobar, Godoy, and Guerrero, *Un nuevo silencio feminista?*.

77. See her account in Ríos Tobar, Godoy, and Guerrero, *Un nuevo silencio feminista?*, 195–196.

78. Kommunistischer Bund and Chile-Frauengruppe Hamburg, *Frauen in Chile*, 7. Komitee Solidarität mit Chile, *Lateinamerika-Nachrichten Chile-Nachrichten*; *Chronik der laufenden Ereignisse in Chile*; Koordinationsgruppe der Chilesolidaritätsgruppen Westberlin und Lateinamerika-Nachrichten, *Chile der Mut zu überleben*; and Chile-Nachrichten, *Kirche in Lateinamerika*.

79. Komitee für die Freiheit der Politischen Gefangenen Frauen in Chile, *Frauensolidarität Möglichkeiten und Probleme emanzipatorischer Politik*, 3.

80. For the voice of some Chilean exiles on the subject matter, see Diaz, *Roles and Contradictions of Chilean Women*.

81. Komitee für die Freiheit der Politischen Gefangenen Frauen in Chile, *Frauensolidarität Möglichkeiten und Probleme emanzipatorischer Politik,* 79.

82. Ibid., passim and 79.

83. Ibid., 54–69 (Nieves), and ibid., 46–53 (Cecila).

84. Küppers, *Feministamente Frauenbewegung in Lateinamerika,* 232–233; Santa Cruz and Erazo, *Compropolitan.*

85. Santa Cruz and Erazo, *Compropolitan,* 100–101.

86. Adriana Santa Cruz, "Fempress: A Communication Strategy for Women," *Gender and Development* 3, no. 1 (February 1995): 51–55. Instituto Latinoamericano de Estudios Transnacionales, and Fempress, *Mujer/fempress.* See also Hiriart, "Mujer/fempress."

87. For a reference to *Mujer/fempress,* see Asunción Lavrin, *The Americas* 47, no. 2. (October 1990): 224. For an example of its publication on motherhood, see Adriana Santa Cruz, Graciela Torricelli, and Viviana Erazo, *La maternidad, Mujer/fempress especial* (Santiago, Chile: ILET, 1987); ILET, *La mujer y el humor;* ILET, *La mujer y el humor, no. 2;* Santa Cruz, Torricelli, and Erazo, *La pareja;* ILET, *Contraviolencia;* ILET, *La mujer indígena;* ILET, *Debate del aborto;* ILET, *Demandas de las mujeres;* Amado and Portugal, *Violencia en los medios;* and ILET, *Precursoras del feminismo en America Latina* (Santiago: ILET, 1991).

88. Miller, *Latin American Women,* 227.

89. María Isabel Matamala, interview with the author, August 1998.

90. Boston Women's Health Book Collective, *Mission Statement;* also see Norsigian et al., "Boston Women's Health Book Collective and Our Bodies, Ourselves." For its global and ongoing influences, see, for example, Farah, "Our Bodies, Ourselves: The Egyptian Women's Health Book Collective," 16–17, 25; and Yanco, "'Our Bodies, Ourselves' in Beijing." For its new edition, see Boston Women's Health Book Collective, *Our Bodies, Ourselves: A New Edition for a New Era.*

91. *Resource Centers and Information Program,* Objectives and Background, n.d.; see also Jaime Penney, informal interview with the author, (BWHBC), June 9, 2000.

92. Portugal and Matamala, "Women's Health Movement"; and Ana María Portugal et al., "Movimiento de salud de las mujeres: Una vision de la decada," in *Genero, mujer y salud en las Americas* (1993). For the quotation, see Boniol and Calma Santoalla, "Coming a Long Way Together," 44.

93. The *Resource Guide* presented information on international resources for women's health, including a list of nongovernmental organizations, books, and films. In addition, it provided background information on, for example, the "control of women by medical institutions" and "Self-Help," health and the environment, and reproductive issues. See *International Women and Health Resource Guide,* Preliminary Draft Edition, July 1980. On ISIS, see also *Network for Primary Health Care and Popular Education,* Newsletter #3, October 1986; ISIS International, Organization and Functioning of the ISIS International Resource Center, Santiago, Chile, November 1989.

94. Charnes, "Seventeen Years Later," 54.

95. Isis International, *Isis International Women's Journal;* Isis International, *Women's International Bulletin;* Isis International, *Women in Action;* and Isis International, *Mujeres en acción* (Rome: Isis International, 1984).

96. Ximena Charnes as cited in Portugal, "Moving Around with Our Feet Firmly on the Ground," 72.

97. Boniol and Calma Santoalla, "Coming a Long Way Together," 44.

98. "LACWHN Mission and Principles," available online at http://www.reddesalud .org/english/sitio/003.htm.

99. Claro, "Latin America," 2 and 21.

100. *La segunda,* October 25, 1986, as cited in Stolz, *Adiós General—Adiós Macho?,* 87.

101. See *La tercera de la hora,* November 6, 1991, as cited in Power, "Sex, Politics, and Right Wing Women in Chile," 8.

102. See *El mercurio,* April 19, 1981, also cited in Power, "Sex, Politics, and Right Wing Women in Chile," 8.

103. Chile, Oficina de Planificación Nacional ODEPLAN, *Política poblacional aprobada por su excelencia el presidente de la república.* Motherhood as a patriotic duty had other violent dimensions. While the military assumed that all women were mothers "naturally," mothers could take on "saintly" or "whorish" qualities according to their political engagement or willingness to cooperate with the regime. Feminist, activist, and victim of military violence Marisa Matamala emphasized that torture also had a gendered dimension that affected women as mothers. Motherhood, in this context, could "liberate" women from immediate mistreatment or death if the military chose to emphasize the moral superiority of women as mothers. "Bad mothers," sometimes women with a history of political engagement or mere affiliation with a "dissident," could be punished for their involvements outside the realm of motherhood. Punishment could include tormenting mothers by presenting proof that their children were tortured or with simply threatening their torture. See Adriana Gomez's interview with Maria Isabel Matamala, in Gomez, "Chile's Military Dictatorship Incorporated Traditional Gender Roles," 63–67. Matamala stresses the importance of examining torture from a gender perspective and comments on the way motherhood was addressed by the regime.

104. Casas Becerra, "Women Prosecuted and Imprisoned for Abortion in Chile," 29.

105. See *La nación,* March 25, 1989, 46.

106. *Annual Review of Population Law* 16 (1989): 28.

107. See Casas Becerra, "Women Prosecuted and Imprisoned for Abortion in Chile," 29–36. For more details of her study, see Center for Reproductive Law and Policy and Foro Abierto de Salud y Derechos Reproductivos, *Women Behind Bars Chile's Abortion Laws.* For an assessment of abortion policies, see also Oyarzún S., "Aborto en Chile."

108. Casas Becerra, "Women Prosecuted and Imprisoned for Abortion in Chile," 30.

109. Center for Reproductive Law and Policy and Foro Abierto de Salud y Derechos Reproductivos, *Women Behind Bars Chile's Abortion Laws,* 53.

110. As cited in Casas Becerra, "Women Prosecuted and Imprisoned for Abortion in Chile," 33.

111. For particular challenges and "reproductive decisions" related to urban poverty, see also Raczynski and Serrano, *Mujer y familia en un sector popular urbano.*

112. Monica Weisner, interview with the author, March 1997.

113. Casas Becerra, "Women Prosecuted and Imprisoned for Abortion in Chile," 31–32.

114. The end of therapeutic abortion violates a number of basic women's rights, including reproductive rights. See Barzelatto et al., *El aborto en Chile elementos para el debate.*

115. The abortion epidemic represents a lasting challenge to women's health in Chilean society. Multiple authors from a wide range of disciplines have connected the problem of in-

duced abortion to the shortcomings of education on sexuality and of ongoing obstacles to gender equity that especially affects young women. See Herrera Rodríguez, *El aborto inducido*; and Lagos Lira, *Aborto en Chile*. The persecution for abortion made the lives of poor women even more difficult. With the termination of therapeutic abortion, it is the poor who are persecuted for having had an abortion and serve prison terms as a result. See Casas-Becerra, *Women Behind Bars*. See also Shepard, "'Double Discourse' on Sexuality and Reproductive Rights," 247–270. Shepard reminds readers that poor women carry a double burden in contemporary Chile: they are most affected by unsafe induced abortion; it is mostly poor women who suffer the harsh consequences of the double discourse on legal persecution and imprisonment for abortion (p. 257).

Others have pointed to the difficulties of securing women's reproductive rights in contemporary Chile. See Fuentes and Dávila, *Promesas de cambio,* for evidence on the lack of attention and unwillingness to give priority to the topic of abortion also by the Chilean left (p. 181). Mala Htun has referred to the efforts of feminist leaders to promote the legal rights of citizens to sex education and contraception in a bill introduced to Congress in 2000 and of multiple efforts to decriminalize abortion. All efforts were made to no avail, given that most politicians are unwilling to touch the topic. See Htun, *Sex and the State*, 168. The final quotation in the paragraph is from Cook and Dickens, "Human Rights Dynamics of Abortion Law Reform," 2.

116. LACWHN, *Women's Health Journal,* 14.

117. Díaz and Hurtado, *Acciones y programas estatales en salud dirigidos a las mujeres,* 70.

118. Provoste Fernández, "Los servicios públicos y los derechos de las mujeres," 55–56. See also Provoste Fernández, *La construcción de las mujeres en la política social.*

119. Ibid.

120. Díaz and Hurtado, *Acciones y programas estatales en salud dirigidos a las mujeres,* 70–71.

121. Chant and Craske, *Gender in Latin America,* 125. See also Grau et al., *La salud de las mujeres.*

122. See Chant and Craske, *Gender in Latin America,* 126.

123. Ewig, "Reproduction, Re-reform, and the Reconfigured State."

124. Ibid.

125. In 2001, this was slightly more than a third of women with medical insurance. See ibid., 6.

126. Merino interview, as cited in ibid, 6.

127. See *Ramirez Caballero* (2001), 2, as cited in ibid., 7.

128. Other scholars have supported Ewig's critique and showed that these plans had negative consequences also for young fertile women: as ISAPRES marketed the "no-uterus-plans" to young women of fertile age, these women took the risk of getting pregnant without proper coverage. See Arteaga, "La lógica brutal de la privatización."

129. In this context, Aili Mari Tripp has pointed to the global dimensions of feminist mobilization. See Tripp, "Evolution of Transnational Feminisms."

130. Gómez de la Torre Vargas and Matus, *Instrumentos internacionales de derechos humanos de las mujeres.*

131. "Some History on Latin America and Caribbean Feminist Encounters," available online at http://www.10feminista.org.br/es/node/16.

132. See "Chilenas celebran Encuentro Feminista Nacional," available online at http://www.mujereshoy.com/secciones/3215.shtml.

Postscript

Epigraph: Pinto Solari, reflecting on the importance of history and memory, in *Cartas de la memoria*, 233.

1. See Margarita Calderón's letter in Pinto Solari, *Cartas de la memoria*, 234–235.

2. For oral histories of life under Pinochet, and for discussions of ways to conceptualize memory types, address competing memories, and assess the meanings of memories, see Steve J. Stern's multivolume study, *Memory Box of Pinochet's Chile*; his *Remembering Pinochet's Chile: On the Eve of London, 1998* (Durham, N.C.: Duke University Press, 2004); and his *Battling for Hearts and Minds: Memory Struggles in Pinochet's Chile, 1973–1988* (Durham, N.C.: Duke University Press, 2006). For the importance of memory to specific groups, often excluded from full participation in democracies, see Temma Kaplan, *Taking Back the Streets Women, Youth, and Direct Democracy* (Berkeley: University of California Press, 2004). For specific insights into one woman's efforts to reverse the burden of memory and seize interpretive power, see the history of Nieves Ayress in Temma Kaplan, "Reversing the Shame and Gendering the Memory," *Signs* 28, no. 1 (Autumn 2002): 179–199.

3. See Acuña Moenne, "Embodying Memory."

4. Silva as cited in Shayne, *Revolution Question*, 106.

5. Baldez and Kirk, "Gendered Opportunities," 133–150, especially 143. Also see Ríos Tobar, "Paradoxes of an Unfinished Transition."

6. For the context of Aída Moreno's life, see Richards, *Pobladoras, Indígenas, and the State*, 86–87.

7. Ibid., 87–88.

8. Fanny Berlagoscky, personal communication with the author, December 2007.

9. Alvarez, "Advocating Feminism," 181–209; and Alvarez, "Latin American Feminisms 'Go Global.'"

10. Sonia Alvarez gathered these comments in interviews with Latin American feminists. See Alvarez, "Advocating Feminism: The Latin American NGO 'Boom,'" available online at http://www.mtholyoke.edu/acad/latam/schomburgmoreno/alvarez.html.

11. See Oyarzún, "Engendering Democracy in the Chilean University," 24.

12. Valdés, Muñoz B., and Donoso O., *1995–2003: Have Women Progressed?*.

13. Stange, "Chile and Emergency Contraception."

14. Malinowski, "Thousands of Chileans to March Against Femicide."

15. Stange, "Chile and Emergency Contraception."

16. See UN, CEDAW, "Concluding Observations: Chile."

17. Szot and Moreno, "Mortalidad por aborto en Chile."

18. See Daniela Estrada, "Clamor de autonomía sexual y reproductiva," Ips (Inter Press Service), available online at http://www.ipsnoticias.org/nota.asp?idnews=42312.

19. See UN, CEDAW, "Concluding Observations: Chile."

20. Htun, *Sex and the State*, 3.

21. For a critical assessment on the meaning of Chile's economic development, see Winn, *Victims of the Chilean Miracle*.

22. Jean Franco has shown that the conservative role of the Church affects the wider Latin American region. Argentine Bishops, for example, rejected the use of the word "gender" in public education. Franco quotes the Auxiliary Bishop of Buenos Aires, Hector Aguer, and documents his critique of the word "gender." Bishop Aguer rejected its use, arguing it

"intended to provoke an ideological shift and to generate a new conception of the human person, of subjectivity, marriage, the family and society. In short what is proposed is a cultural revolution." In addition, he warned that the use of the word "as a purely cultural construct, detached from the biological, . . . makes us into fellow travelers of radical feminism." See Franco, "Gender Wars." For the Chilean context, see Lies, "Clash of Values." On the resurgence of conservative control, also see Stewart-Gambino et al., "Earthquake Versus Erosion."

23. Fernández Montero, *Regulación de la natalidad*.

24. Ibid., 33

25. Fernández Montero, *Mujer, cuál es tu misión*.

26. Lies, "Clash of Values"; the reference to opinion polls is on p. 73.

27. "In Women's Hands: The Changing Roles of Women," written, produced, and directed by Rachel Field and Juan Mandelbaum. The 1992 documentary depicts the activism of Chilean women under dictatorship and shows that women's political engagement was often motivated by women's responsibilities in families in communities. It is part of a series of documentaries that accompany Peter Winn's textbook, *Americas: The Changing Face of Latin America and the Caribbean*.

28. See Saa Díaz, "Ficha parlamentaria."

29. See Larry Rother, "A Leader Making Peace with Chile's Past," *New York Times,* January 16, 2006; and Larry Rother, "Chile Inaugurates First Woman to Serve as Its President," *New York Times,* March 12, 2006.

30. See UN CEDAW, "Concluding Observations: Chile."

31. In 2006, about 18 percent of the seats of national legislatures in Latin America and the Caribbean were held by women; see Paxton and Hughes, *Women, Politics, and Power,* 218 and 228–229.

32. See Winn, *Victims of the Chilean Miracle*.

BIBLIOGRAPHY

Archives

Asociación Chilena de Protección de la Familia (APROFA), Santiago, Chile
Economic Commission for Latin America and the Caribbean (CELADE), Santiago, Chile
Fundación Allende, Santiago, Chile
Fundación Frei, Santiago, Chile
Hospital San Juan de Dios, Santiago, Chile
International Planned Parenthood Federation (IPPF), New York, New York
Mensaje, Santiago, Chile
Princeton University Office of Population Research (OPR), Princeton, New Jersey
Rockefeller Foundation Archives, Tarrytown, New York
United Nations Population Fund (UNFPA), New York, New York

Newspapers

Capitol Times, 1974
Clarín, 1962–1970
El comercio, 1982
El mercurio, 1906–1972
El siglo, 1970
La época, 1988–1989
La nación, 1927–1972
La prensa, 1971
Las noticias de ultima hora, 1973
La tercera, 1967–1972
Las últimas noticias, 1980
New York Times, 1963–1979

Periodicals

Acción social, 1941
Apsi, 1988
Beneficencia, 1930
Boletín Asociación Chilena de Protección de la Familia, 1965–1987
Boletín de la Oficina Sanitaria Panamericana, 1927–1939
Boletín médico social, 1946
Boletín Médico Social de la Caja del Seguro Obligatorio, 1935–1938
Boletín San Juan de Dios, 1966
Chile-Nachrichten, 1974–1977
Cuadernos médico-sociales, 1966–1969
El boletín de la clínica obstétrica 1931–1932, 1931

International Labour Review, 1938

Jornada católica de estudios médicos, 1936

La mujer nueva, 1913–1935

MEMCh'83, 1985 (Movimiento Pro-Emancipación de la Mujer Chilena, Movement for the Emancipation of Chilean Women)

Mensaje, 1964–1970

Movimiento feminista, 1988

Novedades, 1972

Population Bulletin, 1946–1953

Punto final, 1965–1989

Que pasa, 1972

Revista católica, 1968

Revista chilena de higiene y medicina preventiva, 1937–1953

Revista chilena de pediatría, 1930–1932

Revista de asistencia social, 1933

Revista de beneficencia pública, 1917–1924

Revista médica de Chile, 1963–1981

Revista Paula, 1970–1973

Revista vea, 1972

Studies in Family Planning, 1968

Vamos mujer, 1989

Vida médica, 1968–1970

Films

Cambridge Documentary Films. *Killing Us Softly: Advertising's Image of Women.* Cambridge, Mass.: Cambridge Documentary Films, 1979.

Cohen, Tom, and Richard Pearce. *Campamento.* Maryknoll, N.Y.: Maryknoll World Productions, 1973.

Field, Rachel, and Juan Mandelbaum. "In Women's Hands: The Changing Roles of Women." In *Americas.* Annenberg/CPB collection. Produced by Judith Vecchione and Raul Julia. South Burlington, Vt.: Annenberg/CPB Project, distributor, 1993.

Fundación Víctor Jara, Carmen Luz Parot, and Mauricio Torres. *Víctor Jara: El derecho de vivir en paz—The Right to Live in Peace.* Santiago: Fundación Víctor Jara, 1999.

Grupo Chaski, and Garabato (Firm). *Miss Universo en el Peru Lima, Julio 1982.* Lima, Peru: Garabato, 1983.

Guzmán, Patricio. *The Battle of Chile: The Struggle of an Unarmed People / La batalla de Chile, la lucha de un pueblo sin armas.* New York: First Run/Icarus Films, 1990.

Mallet, Marilú, Dominique Pinel, Michael Rubbo, Guy Borremans, Michel Descombes, Isabel Allende, Maria Luisa Segnoret, Pascale Laverriére, and Milicska Jalbert. *Journal inachevé.* New York: Women Make Movies (distributor), 1995.

Government Publications

Chile. *Constitución política del estado de Chile. Promulgada el 23 de octubre de 1822.* Santiago: Imprenta del Estado, 1822. Available online at http://www.memoriachilena.cl/temas/documento_detalle.asp?id=MC0019509.

————. *Circular Number 3G/188, Actualización de la Actividad Paternidad Responsable*. Ministerio de Salud: Santiago, August 19, 1985.

————. *Código del Trabajo de Chile, promulgado por decreto ley no. 178, del 13-V-1931, Libro I, Título IV y Libro III, Título IV.* 1931.

————. *Código Sanitario* (National Health Code). 1931.

————. Consejería Nacional de Desarrollo Social. *Política general y objetivos de la Consejería Nacional de Desarrollo Social*. Santiago, 1971.

————. *Decreto No. 602*. National Health Service, Chile, August 30, 1971.

————. *Decreto No. 2194*. September 5, 1966.

————. *Diez años de voluntariado 1973–1983*. [Santiago]: La Secretaría, 1983.

————. *Ley 226*, May 15, 1931.

————. *Ley de Juntas de Vecinos*, August 7, 1968. Chile. Ley no. 16.880: Organizaciones comunitarias. Diario oficial no. 27.113. [Santiago: M. Barrientos C.], 1968.

————. *Ley No. 16.880*. Juntas vecinales, centros de madres, y otras organizaciones comunitarias. Reglamento de la Ley no. 16.880. "Estatuto tipo" para juntas de vecinos. [Santiago]: Ediciones Gutenberg, 1973.

————. *Libro blanco del cambio de gobierno en Chile, 11 de septiembre de 1973*. Santiago: Editorial Lord Cochrane, 1973.

————. *Memoria*. Santiago: La Secretaría, 1979.

————. *Siete años de voluntariado aniversario 1980, discursos; artículos de prensa*. Santiago: Secretaría Nacional de la Mujer, 1980.

————. *Valores patrios y valores familiares*. Cuadernos de Difusión 7. Santiago: Secretaria Nacional de la Mujer, 1982.

————. *White Book of the Change of Government in Chile, 11th of September*. Santiago: Empresa Editora Nacional Gabriela Mistral, 1974.

Chile. Allende Gossens, Salvador. *Primer mensaje del presidente de Chile al país en la inauguración del periodo ordinario de sesiones del Congreso Nacional*. 1971.

Chile. *Cema Chile*. Santiago: CEMA-Chile, n.d.

Chile. CEMA. *Como participar: Juntas de vecinos, centros de madres, clubes deportivos, centros culturales, etc*. Santiago: Editora Nacional Quimantú, 1970.

————. *Memoria CEMA-Chile, 1980–1981*.

————. *Fundación CEMA Chile*. [Chile]: Depto. de RR.PP. de Cema Chile, 1984.

————. *Fundación CEMA-Chile. Revista aniversario CEMA-Chile, octubre 1982–octubre 1983*. Santiago: La Fundación, 1983.

————. "Entrevista a la madre del año: Doña Doralisa, a fertile woman." *Fundación CEMA-Chile. Revista aniversario CEMA-Chile, octubre 1982–octubre 1983*. Santiago: La Fundación, 1983.

Chile. Contradoría General de la República. *Decreto Supremo No. 54*. Aprueba Reglamento para la Constitución y Funcionamiento de los Comités Paritarios de Higiene y Seguridad. March 11, 1969.

Chile. Oficina de informaciones y radiodifusión de la presidencia de la república. *Palabras del presidente de la república, Compañero Salvador Allende Gossens, al hacer entrega de la Torre Ex-UNCTAD a la secretaria de la mujer. Santiago, 18 octubre 1972*. Santiago: N.p., 1972.

————. *Palabras del presidente de la república, Compañero Salvador Allende Gossens, en el seminario "La mujer de hoy de América Latina. Edificio Gabriela Mistral. Santiago, 27 octubre 1972*. Santiago: N.p., 1972.

————. *Palabras del presidente de la república, Compañero Salvador Allende Gossens, pronunciadas en al inauguración de los cursos auxiliares de párvulos. Edificio Gabriela Mistral. Santiago, 8 de enero 1973.* Santiago: N.p., 1973.

Chile. Oficina de Planificación Nacional ODEPLAN. *Política poblacional aprobada por su excelencia el presidente de la república y publicada en el Plan Nacional Indicativo de Desarrollo (1978–1983) en noviembre 1978.* Santiago: N.p., 1979.

United Nations. Committee on the Elimination of Discrimination Against Women (CEDAW). "Concluding Observations: Chile." U.N. Doc. A/50/38 (1995). Available online at http://www1.umn.edu/humanrts/cedaw/cedaw-chile.htm.

————. *Definition of Reproductive Health.* New York: World Health Organization, Office at the United Nations, 1994.

————. Division for the Advancement of Women. "Short History of CEDAW Convention." Available online at http://www.un.org/womenwatch/daw/cedaw/history.htm.

————. International Conference on Population. *Report of the International Conference on Population, 1984, Mexico City, August 6–14, 1984.* New York: United Nations, 1984.

————. *World Plan of Action for the Implementation of the Objectives of the International Women's Year: A Summarized Version.* New York: United Nations Center for Economic and Social Information, 1976.

United States and Lyndon B. Johnson. *Public Papers of the Presidents of the United States Lyndon B. Johnson, Containing the Public Messages, Speeches, and Statements of the President, 1965.* Washington, D.C.: U.S. Government Printing Office, 1966.

United States Department of State. Assorted Documents of National Security Archives. Available at online at "The Case against Pinochet: Ex-Dictator Indicted for Condor Crimes," http://www.gwu.edu/~nsarchiv/NSAEBB/NSAEBB125/index2.htm.

————. "Memorandum for the Record," August 3, 1976. Available online at National Security Archives, http://www.gwu.edu/~nsarchiv/NSAEBB/NSAEBB125/condor04.pdf.

United States Senate. *Covert Action in Chile, 1963–1973.* Staff Report of the Select Committee to Study Governmental Operations with Respect to Intelligence Activities. United States Senate. Washington, D.C.: U.S. Government Printing Office, 1975.

Unpublished Manuscripts and Conference Proceedings

Adriasola, Guillermo, and Onofre Avendaño. "Population Program in Chile." In *Intra-Uterine Contraception, Proceedings of the Second International Conference, October 2–3, 1964, New York City.* Sponsored by the Population Council. International congress series, no. 86, edited by International Conference on Intra-Uterine Contraception and Sheldon J. Segal. Amsterdam: Excerpta Medica Foundation, 1965.

Alvarez, Sonia. "Thoughts on Distinctive Logics of Transnational Feminist Activism." University of California Santa Cruz. 1999.

Antezana-Pernet, Corinne. "Mobilizing Women in the Popular Front Era: Feminism, Class, and Politics in the Movimiento Pro-Emancipación de la Mujer Chilena (MEMCH), 1935–1950." Ph.D. dissertation, University of California at Irvine, 1996.

Black, Victoria Lynn. "Taking Care of Baby: Chilean State-Making, International Relations, and the Gendered Body Politic, 1912–1970." Ph.D. dissertation, University of Arizona, 2002.

Capetanopulos, Irini, and R. Cabrera. "Entrenamiento para un programa de informacion y educacion: Programa 'Monitores de paternidad responsible.'" In *Programas y estrategias de información y educación en planificación familiar en America Latina: Memorias del Segundo Seminario de Directores de Informacion y Educación, San Jose, Costa Rica, Septiembre 15–20, 1975,* edited by Rene Jaimes, 39–53. New York: IPPF, Western Hemisphere Region, 1976.

Chaney, Elsa. "The Mobilization of Women in Allende's Chile." Paper prepared for the Southern Political Science Association, Comparative Politics Panel, Atlanta, Georgia, November 3, 1972.

Chuchryk, Patricia. "Protest, Politics, and Personal Life: The Emergence of Feminism in a Military Dictatorship, Chile, 1973–1983." Ph.D. dissertation, York University, Toronto, 1984.

Círculo de Estudios de la Mujer. "Reflexiones sobre la práctica feminista." Paper presented at the Third Encounter for Popular Education, Santiago, June 1983.

Claro, Amparo. "Latin America: A Difficult Continent for Women and Women's Health." National Association of Women and the Law (Association nationale de la femme et du droit), Ottawa, 1989. Paper presented at "Women and Law, International Perspectives," Eighth Biennial Conference of the National Association of Women and the Law, February 1989, Montréal, Québec.

Congreso Nacional de Investigadores Sociales y Medico Sociales sobre la Juventud Chilena 1. "La medición de la inteligencia, el destino educativo de menores y adolescentes con bajo rendimiento escolar y la ética profesional: Un estudio exploratorio." *Versión de ponencias abreviadas Primer Congreso Nacional de Investigadores Sociales y Médico-Sociales sobre la Juventud Chilena.* Department of Sociology, University of Chile, Santiago, June 1986.

Congreso Nacional de Protección a la Infancia, and Manuel Camilo Vial. *Trabajos y actas del Primer Congreso Nacional de Protección a la Infancia: Celebrado en Santiago de Chile del 21 al 26 de septiembre de 1912: Tomo único.* Santiago: Impr., Litografía y Encuadernación "Barcelona," 1912.

Escobar, Mónica. *Exile and National Identity: Chilean Women in Canadá.* Ph.D. dissertation, University of Toronto, 2000.

Feringa, Barbara. "Reproductive Rights under the Chilean Military Dictatorship." Paper prepared for Steven Isaacs, Attorney at Law, Center for Population and Family Health, Columbia University, May 12, 1992.

Fernández Abara, Joaquín. "El Ibañismo (1937–1952): Un caso de populismo en la política chilena." Master's thesis, Pontificia Universidad Católica de Chile, 2003.

Fernández, M. Elisa. "Beyond Partisan Politics in Chile: The Carlos Ibáñez Period and the Politics of Ultranationalism between 1952–1958." Ph.D. dissertation, University of Miami, 1996.

International Planned Parenthood Federation (IPPF) and R. K. B. Hankinson, eds. *Proceedings of the Eighth International Conference of the International Planned Parenthood Federation, Santiago, Chile, 9–15 April, 1967.* London: IPPF, 1967.

Ipsen, Annabel. "The Women's Movement in Chile, from Grassroots to Nongovernmental Organization: A Case Study of La Casa de La Mujer, La Morada." Master's thesis, University of New Mexico at Albuquerque, July 2000.

Körner, Víctor. "Protección de las madres durante el embarazo, el parto y el puerperio, y su influencia sobre la mortalidad infantil." In *Trabajos y actas del Primer Congreso Nacional de Protección a la Infancia: Celebrado en Santiago de Chile del 21 al 26 de septiembre de 1912,* edited by Manuel Camilo Vial. Santiago: Impr., Litografía y Encuadernación "Barcelona," 1912.

Korowin, Erika. "*Luchar para cantar, cantar para no olvidar*: Memory, Resistance, and the Legacy of the *Nueva Canción* Movement in Chile, 1965–2005." Master's thesis, University of Arizona, 2006.

Kunzle, David. "The Parts That Got Left out of the Donald Duck Book, or, How Karl Marx Prevailed over Carl Barks." Paper presented at the Marxism and Art History session of the College Art Association Meeting in Chicago, February 1976.

Milanich, Nara B. "The Children of Fate: Families, Class, and the State in Chile, 1857–1930." Ph.D. dissertation, Yale University, 2002.

Miranda Cabezas, Rosa Marcela. "Carlos Ibañez del Campo: La configuración del hombre político." Master's thesis, Pontificia Universidad Católica de Chile, 1994.

Nuñez Carrasco, Lorena. "Living on the Margins: Illness and Healthcare among Peruvian Migrants in Chile." Ph.D. dissertation, Leiden University, Netherlands, 2008.

Power, Margaret. "Right-Wing Women and Chilean Politics, 1964–1973." Ph.D. dissertation, University of Illinois at Chicago, 1997.

———. "Sex, Politics, and Right Wing Women in Chile: Pro-(Heteronormative) Family and Pro-Pinochet." Paper prepared for the conference of the Latin American Studies Association (LASA), Dallas, Texas, March 27–29, 2003.

Proceedings of the Eighth International Conference of the International Planned Parenthood Federation, Santiago, Chile, April 9–15, 1967. London: IPPF, 1967.

Rockefeller, John D. III "Introductory Remarks." In *Intra-Uterine Contraception, Proceedings of the Second International Conference, October 2–3, 1964, New York City.* Sponsored by the Population Council. International Congress series, no. 86. Edited by International Conference on Intra-Uterine Contraception and Sheldon J. Segal. Amsterdam: Excerpta Medica Foundation, 1965, 1–4.

Roy, Francoise. "Female Migration and Labor in Latin America: The Case of Domestic Servants in Santiago De Chile." Master's thesis, University of Florida, 1983.

Seminario de Desarrollo, Población y Familia. "Ponencias del Seminario de Desarrollo, Población y Familia: Hotel Jaragua, Santo Domingo, 4, 5 y 6 de diciembre, 1968." [Santo Domingo]: El Arzobispado, 1968.

Shayne, Julie. "Tears of Resistance: Gender, Culture, and Emotions in the Chilean Diaspora." Paper presented at the Pacific Sociological Association, Portland, Oregon, 2008.

Silva, Patricio. *In the Name of Reason: Technocrats and Politics in Chile.* University Park: Pennsylvania State University Press, 2008.

Stuardo Tomasevic, Ricardo. "La interpelación al pueblo por Carlos Ibañez del Campo durante su campaña electoral de 1952: Todo pasó siempre en Septiembre: Nostalgia, pasión y muerte de un sueño prohibido." Master's thesis, Pontificia Universidad Católica de Chile, 1998.

Thomas, Gywnn. "Ties That Break and Bind: The Uses of Family in the Political Struggles of Chile, 1970–1990." Ph.D. dissertation, University of Wisconsin at Madison, 2005.

Valenzuela, Maria Elena. "El fundamento de la dominación patriarcial en Chile." Paper presented at the Second Chilean Sociology Congress, Santiago, Chile, August 1986.

Weisner, Monica. "Aborto Provocado: Estudio antropológico en mujeres jóvenes de sectores populares." Actas del Primer Congreso Chileno de Antropología. Santiago: Sociedad Chilena de Antropología, 1988.

Zipper, Jaime, M. L. Garcia, and L. L. Pastene. "Intra-Uterine Contraception with the Use of a Flexible Nylon Ring: Experience in Santiago de Chile." *Intra-Uterine Contraception: Proceedings of the Second International Conference, October 2–3, 1964, New York City.* Sponsored by the Population Council, International Congress Series no. 86. New York: Excerpta Medica Foundation, 1965.

Zwingel, Susanne. "How Do International Women's Rights Norms Become Effective in Domestic Contexts? An Analysis of the Convention on the Elimination of All Forms of Discrimination against Women (CEDAW)." Ph.D. dissertation, Ruhr-Universität Bochum, Germany, 2005. Also available online at http://deposit.d-nb.de/cgi-bin/dokserv?idn=97814287X.

Books and Articles

Abel, Christober. "External Philanthropy and Domestic Change in Colombian Health Care: The Role of the Rockefeller Foundation, ca. 1920–1950." *Hispanic American Historical Review* 75, no. 3 (1995): 339–376.

Acuña Moenne, María Elena. "Embodying Memory: Women and the Legacy of the Military Government in Chile." *Feminist Review* 79 (2005): 150–161.

Adams, Jacqueline. "Art in Social Movements: Shantytown Women's Protest in Pinochet's Chile." *Sociological Forum* 17, no. 1 (2002): 21–56.

Adriasola, Claudia, et al. *Algunas ideas respecto a la condición de la mujer.* Santiago: Academia de Humanismo Cristiano, 1979.

Agosín, Marjorie. *Ashes of Revolt.* Fredonia, N.Y.: White Pine Press, 1996.

————. "Visions and Transgressions: Some Notes on the Writing of Julieta Kirkwood." In *Reinterpreting the Spanish American Essay: Women Writers of the Nineteenth and Twentieth Centuries,* edited by Doris Meyer. Austin: University of Texas Press, 1995.

————, and Emma Sepulveda. *Amigas: Letters of Friendship and Exile.* Oxford: Isis, 2004.

Albrecht, Lisa. "Let Me Speak!" *Off Our Backs* 12, no. 3 (March 31, 1982): 14.

Alessandri, Jorge, Ana María Contador, et al., ed. *Continuismo y discontinuismo en Chile: Discurso de asunción al mando.* Santiago: Bravo y Allende Editores, 1989.

Alexander, Robert J. "Social Security in Chile." *Social Forces* 28, no. 1 (October 1949), 53–58.

Allende Gossens, Salvador. "Encuentro con las mujeres de Concepción: El Ministerio de la Familia." In *La mujer y el socialismo.* Concepción, Chile: University of Concepción, 1972.

————. *La historia que estamos escribiendo: El presidente Allende en Antofagasta.* Santiago: Consejería de Difusión de la Presidencia de la Repblica, 1972.

————. *La realidad médico-social chilena: Síntesis.* Santiago: Ministerio de Salubridad, Previsión y Asistencia Social, 1939.

————. *Obras escogidas (1970–1973).* Edited by Patricio Quiroga Zamora. Barcelona: Editorial Crítica, 1989.

————. *Punta del Este: La nueva estrategia del imperialismo.* Montevideo, Chile: Editorial Dialogo, 1967.

————. *Salvador Allende, 1908–1973: Prócer de la liberación nacional.* Edited by Alejandro Witker Velásquez. México: Universidad Nacional Autónoma de México, 1980.

Allende, Isabel. *My Invented Country: A Nostalgic Journey Through Chile.* Translated by Margaret Sayers Peden. New York: HarperCollins, 2003.

————. *Paula.* Translated by Margaret Sayers Peden. New York: HarperCollins, 1995.

Alting von Geusau, Leo. "International Reaction to the Encyclical *Humanae Vitae*." *Studies in Family Planning* 1, no. 50 (1970): 8–12.

Altman, Dennis. *Global Sex*. Chicago: University of Chicago Press, 2001.

Alvarez, Sonia E. "Advocating Feminism: The Latin American NGO 'Boom.'" *International Feminist Journal of Politics* 1, no. 2 (1999): 181–209.

———. *Advocating Feminism: The Latin American NGO "Boom."* Available online at http://www .mtholyoke.edu/acad/latam/schomburgmoreno/alvarez.html.

———. *Engendering Democracy in Brazil: Women's Movements in Transition Politics*. Princeton, N.J.: Princeton University Press, 1990.

———. "Latin American Feminisms 'Go Global': Trends of the 1990s and Challenges for the New Millennium." In *Cultures of Politics, Politics of Culture: Re-visioning Latin American Social Movements*, edited by Sonia E. Alvarez, Evelina Dagnino, and Arturo Escobar, 293–324. Boulder, Colo.: Westview Press, 1998.

———, et al. "Encountering Latin American and Caribbean Feminisms." *Signs* 28 (2003): 537–580.

Amado, Ana María, and Ana María Portugal. *Violencia en los medios*. Mujer/fempress especial. Santiago: Instituto Latinoamericano de Estudios Transnacionales (ILET), 1989.

Ambrosio Brieva, Valeria, et al. *Compromisos antes de tiempo: Adolescentes, sexualidad y embarazo*. Santiago: Corporación de Salud y Políticas Sociales (CORSAPS), 1991.

Anarchist Alliance of Aotearoa. *How to Read Donald Duck: From the Noble Savage to the Third World: Imperialist Ideology in the Disney Comix*. [Auckland] Aotearoa [New Zealand]: Anarchist Alliance of Aotearoa, 1980.

Andreas, Carol. "The Chilean Woman: Reform, Reaction, and Resistance." *Latin American Perspectives* 4, no. 4 (Autumn 1977): 121–125.

———. *Nothing Is As It Should Be: A North American Feminist Tells of Her Life in Chile Before and After the Golpe Militar*. Cambridge, Mass.: Schenkman Pub. Co., 1976.

Angell, A., and S. Castairs. "The Exile Question in Chilean Politics." *Third World Quarterly* 9, no. 1 (1987): 148–166.

Angell, Alan, and Benny Pollack. "The Chilean Elections of 1989 and the Politics of the Transition to Democracy." *Bulletin of Latin American Research* 9, no. 1 (1990): 1–23.

Antezana-Pernet, Corinne. "Chilean Feminists, the International Women's Movement, and Suffrage, 1915–1950." *Pacific Historical Review* 69, no. 4 (November 2000): 663–688.

———. "El MEMCH en provincia. Movilización femenina y sus obstáculos, 1935–1942." In *Disciplina y desacato: Construcción de identidad en Chile, siglo XIX y XX*, edited by Lorena Godoy et al. Santiago: Eds. CEDEM-SUR, 1995.

Arancibia Clavel, Patricia, Alvaro Góngora Escobedo, and Gonzalo Vial Correa. *Jorge Alessandri, 1896–1986: Una biografía. Memorias y biografías*. Santiago: Zig-Zag, 1996.

Araya Chiappa, Pedro. "Servicio madre y niño de la Caja de Seguro Obligatorio." *Boletín médico social* 13, no. 142 (July 1946): 378–387.

Armijo, Rolando, and Tegualda Monreal. "Epidemiology of Provoked Abortion in Santiago, Chile." *Journal of Sex Research* 1, no. 152 (July 1965): 143–159.

———. "Factores Asociados a las complicaciones del Aborto Provocado." *Revista chilena de obstetricia y ginecología* 29 (1964): 33–42.

Armijo, Rolando, Tegualda Monreal, R. Puffer, M. Requena B., and C. Tietze. "The Problem of Induced Abortion in Chile." *Milbank Memorial Fund Quarterly* 43, no. 4, part 2 (October 1965): 263–280.

Arnaiz, María del Carmen, and Michael Monteón. *Movimientos sociales en la Argentina, Brasil y Chile, 1880–1930*. Buenos Aires: Éditorial Biblos, 1995.

Arreola, Teresa. *Programas de control natal: Arma del imperialismo*. New York: Women's International Resource Exchange Service, 1976.

Arteaga, Ana Maria. "La lógica brutal de la privatización." *Control ciudadano*. Available online at http://rrojasdatabank.info/dbinfo2/chile2003_esp.pdf.

Avendaño, Onofre. *Desarrollo histórico de la Planificación de la Familia en Chile y en el Mundo*. Santiago: Association for the Protection of the Family (APROFA), 1975.

Aylwin, Mariana, Sofía Correa, and Magdalena Piñera E. *Percepción del rol político de la mujer una aproximación histórica*. Santiago: Instituto Chileno de Estudios Humanísticos, 1986.

Baldez, Lisa. "La Política Partidista y los Límites del Feminismo de Estado en Chile." In *El modelo Chileno: Democracia y desarrollo en los noventa*, edited by Paul Drake and Iván Jaksic, 407–433. Santiago: LOM Ediciones, 1999.

————. "Nonpartisanship as a Political Strategy: Women Left, Right, and Center in Chile." In *Radical Women in Latin America Left and Right*, edited by Victoria González and Karen Kampwirth. University Park: Pennsylvania State University Press, 2001.

————. *Why Women Protest: Women's Movements in Chile*. New York: Cambridge University Press, 2002.

————, and Celeste Montoya Kirk. "Gendered Opportunities: The Formation of Women's Movements in the United States and Chile." In *The U.S. Women's Movement in Global Perspective*, edited by Lee Ann Banaszak, 133–150. Lanham, Md.: Rowman & Littlefield Publishers, 2006.

Bambirra, Vania. "The Chilean Woman." *New Chile*. New York: North American Congress on Latin America (NACLA), 1972.

————. "La Mujer Chilena en la transición al socialismo." *Punto final* 133 (June 22, 1971): 3–4.

Barclay, William, Joseph Enright, and Reid T. Reynolds. "Population Control and the Third World." *NACLA Newsletter* 4, no. 8 (December 1970): 1–18.

Barraza, Fernando. *La nueva canción chilena*. Santiago: Editora Nacional Quimantú, 1972.

Barr-Melej, Patrick. *Reforming Chile: Cultural Politics, Nationalism, and the Rise of the Middle Class*. Chapel Hill: University of North Carolina Press, 2001.

————. "Siloismo and the Self in Allende's Chile: Youth, 'Total Revolution,' and the Roots of the Humanist Movement." *Hispanic American Historical Review* 86, no. 4 (2006): 747–784.

Barrios de Chungara, Domitila, and Moema Viezzer. *Let Me Speak! Testimony of Domitila, a Woman of the Bolivian Mines*. New York: Monthly Review Press, 1978.

Barros Borgoño, Martina. "La esclavitud de la mujer." *Revista de Santiago* 2 (1872–1873).

Barzelatto, José, et al. *El aborto en Chile elementos para el debate*. Santiago: CORSAPS, 1996.

Bell, Susan G., and Karen M. Offen. *Women, the Family, and Freedom: The Debate in Documents*. Stanford, Calif.: Stanford University Press, 1983.

Belmar, R., and V. W. Sidel. "An International Perspective on Strikes and Strike Threats by Physicians: The Case of Chile." *International Journal of Health Services* 5, no. 1 (1975): 53–64.

Belmar, Roberto. "Evaluation of Chile's Health Care System, 1973–1976: A Communiqué from Health Workers in Chile." *International Journal of Health Services* 7, no. 3 (1977): 531–540.

Benavente, David, and Taller de Investigación Teatral (TIT). *Tres Marías y una Rosa*. Chile: N.p., 1979.

Benston, Margaret. "The Political Economy of Women's Liberation." *Monthly Review* 21 (September 1969): 13–27.

Berger, Herbert. *Solidarität mit Chile: Die österreichische Chile-Solidaritätsfront, 1973–1990*. Vienna: Edition Volkshochschule, 2003.

Besse, Susan K. *Restructuring Patriarchy: The Modernization of Gender Inequality in Brazil, 1914–1940*. Chapel Hill: University of North Carolina Press, 1996.

Birn, Anne-Emanuelle. "No More Surprising Than a Broken Pitcher? Maternal and Child Health in the Early Years of the Pan American Sanitary Bureau." *Canadian Bulletin of Medical History* 19, no. 1 (2002): 17–46.

———. "Las Unidades Sanitarias: La Fundación Rockefeller *versus* el Modelo Cárdenas en México," in *Salud, cultura y sociedad en América Latina*, edited by Marcos Cueto, 203–233. Washington, D.C., and Lima: Pan-American Health Organization and Instituto de Estudios Peruanos, 1996.

———. "A Revolution in Rural Health?: The Struggle over Local Health Units in Mexico, 1928–1940." *Journal of the History of Medicine and Allied Sciences*, 53, no.1 (1998): 43–76.

Blofield, Merike H., and Liesl Haas. "Defining a Democracy: Reforming the Laws on Women's Rights in Chile, 1990–2002." *Latin American Politics and Society* 47, no. 3 (2005): 35–68.

Blum, Ann. "Breaking and Making Families: Adoption and Public Welfare, Mexico City, 1938–1942." In *Sex in Revolution: Gender, Politics, and Power in Modern Mexico*, edited by Jocelyn Olcott, Mary K. Vaughan, and Gabriela Cano, 127–144. Durham, N.C.: Duke University Press, 2006.

Bock, Gisela, and Pat Thane, eds. *Maternity and Gender Politics: Women and the Rise of European Welfare States, 1880–1950s*. London: Routledge, 1991.

Boniol, Leti, and Annie Calma Santoalla. "Coming a Long Way Together: Isis and Marilee Karl." *Women in Action* (December 31, 1999): 44–56.

Borón, Atilio. *La evolución del regimen electoral y sus efectos en la representación de los intereses populares: El caso de Chile*. Escuela Latinoamericana de Ciencia Política y Administración Pública. Estudios, no. 24. Variation: Est. ELACP, no. 24., 1971.

Boston Women's Health Book Collective. *Mission Statement*. N.p., n.d.

———. *Our Bodies, Ourselves: A New Edition for a New Era*. New York: Simon & Schuster, 2005.

Boyle, Catherine M. *Chilean Theater, 1973–1985: Marginality, Power, Selfhood*. Rutherford, N.J.: Fairleigh Dickinson University Press, 1992.

Bracht, Neil F. "Social Work in Health Care: A Guide to Professional Practice." *Human Rights Quarterly* 3, no. 2 (May 1981): 53–60.

Bravo, Rosa, María Isabel Cruzat, Elena Serrano, and Rosalba Todazo. "Y así va creciendo . . . el feminismo en Chile." In *Movimiento feminista en América Latina y el Caribe: Balance y perspectivas*. Santiago: Ediciones Isis Internacional de las Mujeres, 1986.

Briggs, Laura. *Reproducing Empire: Race, Sex, Science, and U.S. Imperialism in Puerto Rico*. Berkeley: University of California Press, 2002.

Bunster, Ximena. "Watch out for the Little Nazi Man That All of Us Have Inside: The Mobilization and Demobilization of Women in Militarized Chile." *Women's Studies International Forum* 11, no. 5 (1988): 485–491.

Busto, M. A., and E. Hola. "Contacto en Copenhague." *Boletín* no. 3 (September–October 1980): 2–5.

Butler Flora, Cornelia. "Roasting Donald Duck: Alternative Comics and Photonovels in Latin America." *Journal of Popular Culture* 18, no. 1 (Summer 1984): 163–183.

———. "Socialist Feminism in Latin America." *Women in International Development*. Working Paper No. 14. Office of Women in International Development. East Lansing: Michigan State University, 1982.

Çağatay, Nilüfer, Caren Grown, and Aida Santiago. "The Nairobi Women's Conference: Toward a Global Feminism?" *Feminist Studies* 12, no. 2 (Summer 1986): 402.

Capetanopulos, Irini, and Rene Cabrera. "Entrenamiento para un programa de información y educación: Programa Monitores de Paternidad Responsable." In *Programas y estrategias de información y educación en planificación familiar en América Latina: Memorias del seminario*, edited by Rene Jaimes. New York: IPPF, 1976.

Capetanópulos, Irini, et al. *Informe Anual Programa 'Monitores de Paternidad Responsable.'* Santiago: APROFA, 1974.

Casas Becerra, Lidia. *Women Behind Bars*. New York: Center for Reproductive Law and Policy, 1998.

———. "Women Prosecuted and Imprisoned for Abortion in Chile." *Reproductive Health Matters* 5, no. 9 (May 1997): 29–36.

Castañeda, Tarsicio. *Contexto socioeconómico y causas del descenso de la mortalidad infantil en Chile. Documento de Trabajo no. 28*. Santiago: Centro de Estudios Públicos, 1984.

Center for Reproductive Law and Policy. *Reproductive Rights 2000: Moving Forward*. New York: Center for Reproductive Law and Policy, 2000.

———, and Foro Abierto de Salud y Derechos Reproductivos. *Women Behind Bars: Chile's Abortion Laws: A Human Rights Analysis*. New York: Center for Reproductive Law and Policy, 1998.

Centro de Estudios y Documentación. *Chile–América Supplemento*. Rome: Centro de Estudios y Documentacion, 1974.

———. "La Conferencia Mundial de Solidaridad con Chile." *Chile–América* (Rome) 48–48 (November–December 1978): 20–22.

Centro Latinoamericano de Población y Familia. *Iglesia, población y familia*. Santiago: Ed. Universitaria, 1967.

Centros de Información de los Derechos de la Mujer (Chile). *Trabajadora de casa particular: Conoce y defiende tus derechos*. Santiago: SERNAM, 1992.

Chaney, Elsa. *Supermadre: Women in Politics in Latin America*. Austin: University of Texas Press, 1979.

———. "Supermadre revisited." In *Women's Participation in Mexican Political Life*, edited by Victoria Elizabeth Rodríguez, chapter 5. Boulder, Colo.: Westview Press, 1998.

Chant, Sylvia, and Nikki Craske. *Gender in Latin America*. New Brunswick, N.J.: Rutgers University Press, 2003.

Charnes, Ximena. "Seventeen Years Later" ('Diecisiete años despues'). *Women in Action (Mujeres en Acción)* (January 1991): 54.

Chile-Nachrichten. *Kirche in Lateinamerika*. Berlin: Chile-Nachrichten, 1977.

Chronik der laufenden Ereignisse in Chile (Ausz. aus d. Chile-Nachrichten). Berlin 45, Lorenzstr. 65: C. Müller-Plantenberg [Selbstverl.], 1975.

Chuchryk, Patricia M. "From Dictatorship to Democracy: The Women's Movement in Chile." In *The Women's Movement in Latin America: Feminism and the Transition to Democracy*, edited by Jane S. Jaquette, 65–107. Boston: Unwin Hyman, 1989.

Círculo de Estudios de la Condición de la Mujer. *Políticas de población y control de la natalidad*. Santiago: Academia de Humanismo Cristiano, 1980.

Cleary, Eda. *Frauen in der Politik Chiles zur Emanzipierung chilenischer Frauen während der Militärdiktatur Pinochets*. Aachen, Germany: Alano, 1988.

Cleary, Edward L., and Hannah W. Stewart-Gambino. *Conflict and Competition: The Latin American Church in a Changing Environment*. Boulder, Colo.: Lynne Rienner Publishers, 1992.

Coale, Ansley J. *Ansley J. Coale: An Autobiography*. Philadelphia: American Philosophical Society, 2000.

Cockcroft, J., ed. *Salvador Allende Reader: Chile's Voice of Democracy*. New York: Ocean Press, 2000.

Cohen, Miriam, and Michael Hanagan. "The Politics of Gender and the Making of the Welfare State, 1900–1940: A Comparative Perspective." *Journal of Social History* 24, no. 3 (1990): 469–484.

Collier, David, ed. *The New Authoritarianism in Latin America*. Princeton, N.J.: Princeton University Press, 1979.

Collier, Simon, and William F. Sater. *A History of Chile, 1808–2002*. New York: Cambridge University Press, 2004.

Comando por el NO. *"Quietas y Controladas": La acción del gobierno militar hacia las mujeres*. Santiago: Comando por el NO, 1988.

Congreso Nacional de Médicos Católicos de Chile. *Ponencias y conclusiones: Estudio médico-moral y social*. Santiago: Academia de Médicos San Lucas, 1947.

Constable, Pamela, and Arturo Valenzuela. *A Nation of Enemies: Chile under Pinochet*. New York: W.W. Norton, 1993.

Consuegra Higgins, José. "'Birth Control as the Weapon of Imperialism': A Marxian View of Foreign Assistance for Family Planning Programs." In *The Dynamics of Population Policy in Latin America*, edited by Terry L. McCoy, 163–181. Cambridge, Mass: Ballinger Pub. Co., 1974.

———. *El control de la natalidad como arma del imperialismo*. Buenos Aires: Editorial Galerna, 1969.

Cook, Rebecca J. "Human Rights and Reproductive Self-Determination." *American University Law Review* 44, no. 4 (1995): 975–1016.

———, and Bernard M. Dickens. "Human Rights Dynamics of Abortion Law Reform." *Human Rights Quarterly* 25, no. 1 (2003): 1–59.

Coordinación de Organizaciones Sociales de Mujeres. *"Soy Mujer . . . Tengo Derechos": Campaña de Discusión*. Santiago: FLACSO-SEPADE, 1991.

Correa Cavada, Mónica, María Olivia Monckeberg, and Hugo Rivas Lombarda. *Estadísticas de Chile en el siglo XX*. Santiago: INE, 1999.

Correa Prieto, Luis. *El presidente Ibáñez, la política y los políticos: Apuntes para la historia*. Santiago: Editorial Orbe, 1962.

Correa, Sônia, and Rosalind P. Petchesky. "Reproductive and Sexual Rights: A Feminist Perspective." In *Population Policies Reconsidered: Health, Empowerment, and Rights*, edited by Gita Sen, Adrienne Germain, and Lincoln C. Chen, 107–123. Boston: Harvard Center for Population and Development Studies, 1994.

Cotler, Julio, Richard R. Fagen, and Heraclio Bonilla. *Latin America and the United States: The Changing Political Realities*. Stanford, Calif.: Stanford University Press, 1974.

Covarrubias, Paz. "El Movimiento Feminista Chileno." In *Chile: Mujer y sociedad*, edited by Paz Covarrubias and Rolando Franco. Santiago: Fondo de las Naciones Unidas para la Infancia, 1978.

————. *El movimiento feminista chileno*. Santiago: Academia de Humanismo Cristiano, Círculo de la Condición de la Mujer, 1981.

Craske, Nikki. *Women and Politics in Latin America*. New Brunswick, N.J.: Rutgers University Press, 1999.

————, and Maxine Molyneux. *Gender and the Politics of Rights and Democracy in Latin America*. Houndmills, Basingstoke, Hampshire: Palgrave, 2002.

Cream, Julia. "Women on Trial: A Private Pillory?" In *Mapping the Subject: Geographies of Cultural Transformation*, edited by Steve Pile and Nigel Thrift, 158–169. London: Routledge, 1995.

Crispi, Patricia, ed. *Tejiendo Rebeldías: Escritos feministas de Julieta Kirkwood*. Santiago: CEM La Morada, 1987.

Critchlow, Donald T. "Birth Control, Population Control, and Family Planning: An Overview." *Journal of Health Policy* 7, no. 1 (1995): 1–21.

Croizet, E. *Lucha social contra la mortalidad infantil en el período de lactancia*. Santiago: Litografía i Encuadernación Barcelona, 1912.

Crummett, M. de los Angeles. "El Poder Feminino: The Mobilization of Women Against Socialism in Chile." *Latin American Perspectives* 4, no. 4 (Autumn 1977): 103–113.

Cruz-Coke Madrid, Ricardo. "Cincuentenario de la gran reforma de la educación médica chilena (1945)." *Revista médica de Chile* 123, no. 8 (1995): 1041–1044.

Cueto, Marcos. "Los ciclos de la erradicación: La Fundación Rockefeller y la salud pública latinoamericana, 1918–1940." In *Salud, cultura y sociedad en América Latina*, edited by Marcos Cueto, 179–201. Lima: IEP Eds. y OPS, 1996.

————, ed. *Missionaries of Science: The Rockefeller Foundation and Latin America*. Bloomington: Indiana University Press, 1994.

Daitsman, Andy. "Unpacking the First Person Singular: Marriage, Power, and Negotiation in Nineteenth-Century Chile." *Radical History Review* 70 (Winter 1998): 27–48.

Dairiam, Shanthi. "Applying the CEDAW Convention for the Recognition of Women's Health Rights (Convention on the Elimination of All Forms of Discrimination Against Women)." *Arrows for Change* (May 1, 2002). Available online at http://www.thefreelibrary.com/Applying%20the%20CEDAW%20Convention%20for%20the%20recognition%20of%20women%27s%20health...-a090988094.

D'Antonio, William V., and Frederick B. Pike, eds. *Religion, Revolution, and Reform: New Forces for Change in Latin America*. New York: Praeger Publishers, 1964.

da Silveira, Fabio Vidigal Xavier. *Frei, el Kerensky chileno*. Buenos Aires: Cruzada, 1967.

Dawson, Anne. "Joan Jara and Chile." *Off Our Backs* 4, no. 11 (November 30, 1974): 7.

de Kadt, Emanuel. "Paternalism and Populism: Catholicism in Latin America." *Journal of Contemporary History* 2, no. 4 (October 1967): 89–106.

de la Jara, María Eugenia. "Control de la natalidad: Una solución y un problema." *Amiga* 21 (April 5, 1967): 24.

del Campo Peirano, Andrea. "La nación en peligro: El debate médico sobre el aborto en Chile en la década de 1930." In *Por la salud del cuerpo: Historia y políticas sanitarias en Chile*, edited by María Soledad Zárate Campos, 131–188. (Santiago: Ediciones Universidad Alberto Hurtado, 2008).

del Pozo, José, ed. *Exiliados, emigrados y retornados chilenos en América y Europa, 1973–2004*. Santiago: RIL Editores, 2006.

De Ramón, Armando. *Santiago de Chile, 1541–1991: Historia de una sociedad urbana*. Santiago: Editorial Sudamericana, 2000.

DESAL (Centro para el Desarrollo Económico y Social de América Latina) and CELAP (Centro Latinoamericano de Población y Familia). *Fecundidad y anticoncepción en poblaciones marginales*. Santiago: DESAL, 1970.

Díaz Arrieta, Hernán. *Memorialistas chilenos, crónicas literarias*. Santiago: Zig-Zag, 1960.

Diaz, Gladys. *Roles and Contradictions of Chilean Women in the Resistance and in Exile: Collective Reflections of a Group of Militant Prisoners*. New York: Women's International Resource Exchange Service, 1979.

Díaz, Marcela, and Marcela Hurtado. *Acciones y programas estatales en salud dirigidos a las mujeres, 1990–1993*. Documento de trabajo 56. Santiago: FLACSO–Programa Chile, 1993.

Dinges, John. *The Condor Years: How Pinochet and His Allies Brought Terrorism to Three Continents*. New York: New Press, 2004.

Disch, Estelle. "Encuentro Feminista Latinoamericano y del Caribe: Latin American and Caribbean Feminists Meet." *Off Our Backs* 13, no. 10 (November 1983): 1.

Domínguez, Francisco. "Carlos Ibáñez del Campo: Failed Dictator and Unwitting Architect of Political Democracy in Chile, 1927–31." In *Authoritarianism in Latin America Since Independence,* edited by Will Fowler, 45–72. Westport, Conn: Greenwood Press, 1996.

Donaldson, P. J. "On the Origins of the United States Government's International Population Policy." *Population Studies* 44, no. 3 (1990): 385–399.

Donzelot, Jacques. *The Policing of Families*. New York: Random House, 1979

Dooner, Patricio. *Cambios sociales y conflicto político: El conflicto político nacional durante el gobierno de Eduardo Frei (1964–1970)*. Santiago: Corporación de Promoción Universitaria, 1984.

Dorfman, Ariel, and Armand Mattelart. *How to Read Donald Duck: Imperialist Ideology in the Disney Comic*. New York: International General, 1991.

———. *Para leer al pato Donald*. Valparaíso, Chile: Ediciones Universitarias de Valparaiso, 1971.

Drake, Paul W., and Ivan Jaksic, eds. *The Struggle for Democracy in Chile, 1982–1990*. Lincoln: University of Nebraska Press, 1991.

Dreier, John C. *The Alliance for Progress: Problems and Perspectives*. Baltimore, Md.: Johns Hopkins University Press, 1962.

Drogus, Carol Ann, and Hannah W. Stewart-Gambino. *Activist Faith: Grassroots Women in Democratic Brazil and Chile*. University Park: Pennsylvania State University Press, 2005.

Ducci, María Angélica, Margarita Gili, and Marta Illanes. *El trabajo: Un nuevo destino para la mujer chilena?* Santiago: Instituto Laboral y de Desarrollo Social, 1972.

Eastmond, Marita. *The Dilemmas of Exile: Chilean Refugees in the U.S.A.* Göteborg, Sweden: Acta Universitatis Gothenburgensis, 1997.

Edwards, Thomas L. *Economic Development and Reform in Chile: Progress under Frei, 1964–1970*. East Lansing: Latin American Studies Center, Michigan State University, 1972.

Ehrick, Christine. *The Shield of the Weak: Feminism and the State in Uruguay, 1903–1933*. Albuquerque: University of New Mexico Press, 2005.

Eltit, Diamela. *Crónica del sufragio femenino en Chile*. Santiago: SERNAM, 1994.

Ensalaco, Mark. *Chile Under Pinochet: Recovering the Truth*. Philadelphia: University of Pennsylvania Press, 1999.

Errázuriz, Margarita M. *El tratamiento del problema de población en la producción de los científicos sociales en Chile, 1958–1972.* Santiago: Centro Latinoamericano de Demografía, 1974.

Ewig, Christina. "Reproduction, Re-reform, and the Reconfigured State: Feminists and Neoliberal Health Reforms in Chile." In *Beyond States and Markets: The Challenges of Social Reproduction,* edited by Isabella Bakker and Rachel Silvey, 143–158. New York: Routledge Press, 2008.

Farah, Nadia. "Our Bodies, Ourselves: The Egyptian Women's Health Book Collective." *Middle East Report* 173 (November–December 1991): 16–17, 25.

Faúndes, Aníbal, Germán Rodríguez, and Onofre Avendaño. "Effects of a Family Planning Program on the Fertility of a Marginal Working-Class Community in Santiago." *Demography* 5, no. 1 (1968): 122–137.

Faúndes, Aníbal, and José Barzelatto. *El drama del aborto: En busca de un consenso.* Bogotá, Colombia: Tercer Mundo Editores, 2005.

Faúndes, Anibal, and Ellen Hardy. "Contraception and Abortion Services at Barros Luco Hospital, Santiago, Chile." In *Abortion in Psychosocial Perspective,* edited by Henry Philip David et al., 284–297. New York: Springer, 1978.

Fernández Fernández, David. "Oral History of the Chilean Movement 'Christians for Socialism,' 1971–73." *Journal of Contemporary History* 34, no. 2 (April 1999): 283–294.

Fernández Montero, P. Jaime. *Mujer, cuál es tu misión.* Santiago: N.p., 1995.

———. *Regulación de la natalidad: Doctrina católica y controversias.* Santiago: Departamento de Pastoral Familiar, n.d.

Fierro Carrera, Luisa. *El servicio social en la maternidad . . . memoria para optar al titulo de Visitadora social.* Santiago: La Ilustración, 1929.

Finn, Janet L. "Raíces: Gender-Conscious Community Building in Santiago, Chile." *Affilia* 17, no. 4 (Winter 2002): 448–470.

Fiol-Matta, Licia. *A Queer Mother for the Nation: The State and Gabriela Mistral.* Minneapolis: University of Minnesota Press, 2002.

Fisher, Jo. *Out of the Shadows: Women, Resistance, and Politics in South America.* New York: Monthly Review Press, 1993.

Fleet, Michael, and Brian H. Smith. *The Catholic Church and Democracy in Chile and Peru.* Notre Dame, Ind.: University of Notre Dame Press, 1997.

Flora, Cornelia Butler. "Roasting Donald Duck: Alternative Comics and Photonovels in Latin America." *Journal of Popular Culture* 18, no. 1 (Summer 1984): 163–183.

Flores, Jorge Rojas. *The Rights of the Child in Chile: An Historical View, 1910–1930.* Translated by Cristina Labarca Cortés. In *Historia (Santiago).* 2007, vol. 3, selected edition. Available online at http://socialsciences.scielo.org/scielo.php?script=sci_arttext&pid=S0717-71942007000100002&lng=en&nrm=iso>.

Fontaine Aldunate, Arturo. *Apuntes políticos.* Santiago: Universidad Santo Tomás, 2003.

Foucault, Michel. *Discipline and Punish: The Birth of the Prison.* New York: Vintage Books 1995.

Franceschet, Susan. "'State Feminism' and Women's Movements: The Impact of Chile's Servicio Nacional de la Mujer on Women's Activism." *Latin American Research Review* 38, no. 1 (2003): 25.

———. *Women and Politics in Chile.* Boulder, Colo.: Lynne Rienner Publishers 2005.

Franco, Jean. "The Gender Wars." *NACLA Report on the Americas* 29, no. 4 (January–February 1996). Available online at http://www.hartford-hwp.com/archives/42a/038.html.

Fraser, Arvonne S. "Becoming Human: The Origins and Development of Women's Human Rights." *Human Rights Quarterly* 21, no. 4 (1999): 853–906.

Freeman, Marsha. *Women's Rights and Reproduction: Capacity and Choice*. Minnesota, Minn.: Humphrey Institute of Public Affairs, 1991.

Frei Montalva, Eduardo. *The Aims of Christian Democracy*. New York: N.p., 1964.

————. "The Alliance That Lost Its Way." *Foreign Affairs* 45, no. 3 (April 1967): 437–448.

————. *The Mandate of History and Chile's Future*. Papers in International Studies: Latin America series, no. 1. Athens: Ohio University, Center for International Studies, Latin America Program, 1977.

Frei Montalva, Eduardo, and Javier Lagarrigue A. *Un mundo nuevo: Respuesta a una carta*. Santiago: Ediciones Nueva Universidad, Universidad Católica de Chile, 1973.

Frohmann, Alicia, and Teresa Valdés. "Democracy in the Country and in the 'Home': The Women's Movement in Chile." *Serie estudios sociales*, no. 55. Santiago: FLACSO, 1993.

————. "Democracy in the Country and in the Home: The Women's Movement in Chile." In *The Challenge of Local Feminisms: Women's Movements in Global Perspective*, edited by Amrita Basu and C. Elizabeth McGrory, 276–301. Boulder, Colo.: Westview Press, 1995.

Fruhling, Hugo. "Resistance to Fear in Chile: The Experience of the Vicaria de la Solidaridad." In *Fear at the Edge: State Terror and Resistance in Latin America*, edited by Juan E. Corradi, Patricia Weiss Fagen, and Manuel A. Garretón Merino, 121–141. Berkeley: University of California Press, 1992.

Fuentes, Claudio, and Mireya Dávila. *Promesas de cambio: Izquierda y derecha en el Chile contemporáneo*. Santiago: FLACSO–Chile/Editorial Universitaria, 2003.

Gall, Norman. *Births, Abortions, and the Progress of Chile: American Universities Field Staff Report*. West Coast South America series 19, no. 2. Hanover, N.H.: American Universities Field Staff, 1972.

Gallo Chinchilla, Margarita. "Protección a la maternidad obrera." In *La mujer ante la legislación chilena: Derechos político y social*. Colección Síntesis del Derecho Chileno, 120–141. Santiago: University of Chile, 1945.

Gálvez Pérez, Thelma, and Rosa Bravo Barja. "Siete décadas de registro del trabajo femenino, 1854–1920." *Revista estadística y economía* 5 (1992): 1–52.

Garcés, Mario. *Tomando su sitio: El movimiento de pobladores de Santiago, 1957–1970*. Santiago: LOM, 2002.

Gardner, John W. *To Turn the Tide: A Selection from President Kennedy's Public Statements from His Election Through the 1961 Adjournment of Congress, Setting Forth the Goals of His First Legislative Year*. New York: Harper, 1962.

Garrett-Schesch, P. "The Mobilization of Women During the Popular Unity Government." *Latin American Perspectives* 2, no. 1 (Spring 1975): 101–103.

Gaviola Artígas, Edda, Lorella Lopresti Martínez, and Claudia Rojas Mira. *Nuestra historia de mujeres*. Santiago: Ediciones La Morada, 1988.

Gaviola Artígas, Edda, Ximena Jiles Moreno, Lorella Lopresti, and Claudia Rojas. *"Queremos votar en las próximas elecciones": Historia del movimiento femenino Chileno, 1913–1952*. Santiago: Centro de Análisis y Difusión de la Condición de la Mujer, 1986.

Gaviola Artígas, Edda, Eliana Largo, and Sandra Palestra. "'Si la mujer no está, la democracia no va.'" *Proposiciones* 21 (1992): 79–85.

————. *Una historia necesaria mujeres en Chile, 1973–1990*. Santiago: N.p., 1994.

Gaviola Artígas, Edda, Lorella Lopresti, and Claudia Rojas. "Chile Centro de Madres: ¿La Mujer Popular en movimiento?" In *Nuestra memoria, nuestro futuro: Mujeres e historia:*

América Latina y el Caribe, edited by María del Carmen Feijóo. Ediciones de las mujeres, no. 10. Santiago: Isis Internacional, 1988.

Gazmuri R., Cristián, Patricia Arancibia Clavel, and Alvaro Góngora Escobedo. *Eduardo Frei Montalva (1911–1982)*. Sección de obras de historia. Santiago: Fondo de Cultura Económica, 1996.

George, Asha. "In Search of Closure for Quinacrine: Science and Politics in Contexts of Uncertainty and Inequality." In *Reproductive Agency, Medicine, and the State: Cultural Transformations in Childbearing*. Vol. 3, *Fertility, Reproduction, and Sexuality*, edited by Maya Unnithan-Kumar, 137–160. New York: Berghahn Books, 2004.

Giddens, Anthony. *The Transformation of Intimacy, Sexuality, Love, and Eroticism in Modern Societies*. Stanford, Calif.: Stanford University Press, 1992.

Gijswijt-Hofstra, Marijke, G. M. van Heteren, and E. M. Tansey, eds. *Biographies of Remedies: Drugs, Medicines, and Contraceptives in Dutch and Anglo-American Healing Cultures*. Amsterdam: Rodopi, 2002.

Ginsburg, Faye, and Rayna Rapp. *Conceiving the New World Order: The Global Politics of Reproduction*. Berkeley: University of California Press, 1995.

————. "The Politics of Reproduction." *Annual Review of Anthropology* 20 (1991): 311–343.

Global Committee of Parliamentarians on Population and Development. "A Statement on Population Stabilization by World Leaders." *Population and Development Review* 11, no. 4 (December 1985): 787–788.

Gobbi, Carina. "VII Encuentro Feminista Latinoamericano y del Caribe: El encuentro que no fue?" Seventh Latin American and Caribbean Feminist Encounter: The Encounter That Wasn't? *Mujer/fempress* 183 (1996): 8–9.

Gomensoro, Arnaldo. *Embarazo de adolescentes*. New York: Consejo Regional de la Región del Hemisferio Occidental de la IPPF, 1984.

Gómez, Adriana. "Chile's Military Dictatorship Incorporated Traditional Gender Roles in Its Efforts of Political Domination." *Women's Health Journal* (2005): 63–67.

Gómez de la Torre Vargas, Maricruz, and Verónica Matus. *Instrumentos internacionales de derechos humanos de las mujeres*. Santiago: Programa de Mujeres, Comisión Chilena de Derechos Humanos, 1994.

Góngora Escobedo, Alvaro. *La prostitución en Santiago, 1813–1931: Visión de las elites*. Santiago: Dirección de Bibliotecas Archivos y Museos, 1994.

González Arriagada, Alejandro. *Surviving in the City: The Urban Poor of Santiago de Chile, 1930–1970*. Uppsala, Sweden: Upsaliensis Academiae, 2000.

González, Carlos A. *Ley de violencia intrafamiliar*. Santiago: Ediciones Publiley, 1998.

González Pino, M., and A. Fontaine Talavera, eds. *Los mil dias de Allende*, 2 vols. Santiago: Centro de Estudios Públicos, 1997.

González, Victoria, and Karen Kampwirth. *Radical Women in Latin America Left and Right*. University Park: Pennsylvania State University Press, 2001.

Gordon, Lincoln. *A New Deal for Latin America: The Alliance for Progress*. Cambridge: Harvard University Press, 1963.

Gordon, Linda. *The Moral Property of Women: A History of Birth Control Politics in America*. Chicago: University of Illinois Press: 2002.

————. *Woman's Body, Woman's Right*. Revised edition. New York: Penguin: [1974] 1990.

————, ed. *Women, the State, and Welfare*. Madison: University of Wisconsin Press, 1990.

Gramsci, Antonio. *Prison Notebooks*. New York: International Publishers, 1971.

Grau, Olga, María Isabel Matamala, Ruth Meyer, and Adriana Vega. *La salud de las mujeres trabajadoras de salud*. Santiago: GICAMS, Area Salud de la Mujer, 1991.

Grayson Jr., George W. "Chile's Christian Democratic Party: Power, Factions, and Ideology." *Review of Politics* 31, no. 2. (April 1969): 147–171.

Green, Mary. "Diamela Eltit: A Gendered Politics of Writing." *Cardiff University New Readings* 6 (December 5, 2000). Available online at http://www.cardiff.ac.uk/euros/subsites/newreadings/volume6/greenm.html.

Gross, Leonard. *The Last, Best Hope: Eduardo Frei and Chilean Democracy*. New York: Random House, 1967.

Guy, Donna J. "The Pan American Child Congresses, 1916 to 1942: Pan Americanism, Child Reform, and the Welfare State in Latin America." *Journal of Family History* 23, no. 3 (July 1998): 272–292.

———. "The Politics of Pan-American Cooperation: Maternalist Feminism and the Child Rights Movement, 1913–1960." *Gender and History* 10, no. 3 (1998): 449–469.

———. *White Slavery and Mothers Alive and Dead: The Troubled Meeting of Sex, Gender, Public Health, and Progress in Latin America*. Lincoln: University of Nebraska Press: 2000.

Guzmán, Virginia, Amalia Mauro, and Kathya Araujo K. *La violencia doméstica como problema público y objeto de políticas*. Santiago: Centro de Estudios de la Mujer, 2000.

Gysling, Jacqueline. *Salud y derechos reproductivos: Conceptos en construcción*. Santiago: FLASCO-programa Chile, November 1993.

Gutiérrez y Muhs, Gabriella. *Communal Feminisms: Chicanas, Chilenas, and Cultural Exile: Theorizing the Space of Exile, Class, and Identity*. Lanham, Md.: Lexington Books, 2007.

Hall, M. F. "Family Planning in Santiago, Chile: The Male Viewpoint." *Studies in Family Planning* 2, no. 7 (July 1971): 143–147.

———. "Male Attitudes to Family Planning Education in Santiago, Chile." *Family Planning Résumé* 1, no. 1 (1977): 73–75.

———. "Male Attitudes to Family Planning Education in Santiago, Chile." *Journal of Biosocial Science* 3, no. 4 (October 1971): 403–416.

———. "Male Sexual Behavior and Use of Contraceptives in Santiago, Chile." *American Journal of Public Health* 62, no. 5 (May 1972): 700–709.

———. "Male Use of Contraception and Attitudes Toward Abortion, Santiago, Chile, 1968." *Milbank Memorial Fund Quarterly* 48, no. 2 (April 1970): 145–166.

Hamel, Patricia. "Sexualidad y embarazo en la adolescencia." *Digesto familiar* 28, no. 161 (January–February 1987): 30–43.

Hardon, Anita Petra. "The Needs of Women Versus the Interests of Family Planning Personnel, Policy-makers and Researchers: Conflicting Views on Safety and Acceptability of Contraceptives." *Social Science and Medicine* 35, no. 6 (September 1992): 753–766.

Hardy, Ellen, and Irini Capetanopulos. *Informe anual: Proyecto "Líderes de Paternidad Responsable."* Santiago: APROFA, 1972.

Harkavy, Oscar. *Curbing Population Growth: An Insider's Perspective on the Population Movement*. New York: Plenum Press, 1995.

Harnecker, Marta. *La lucha de un pueblo sin armas: Los tres años de gobierno popular*. Chile: N.p., 2003.

———, and Gabriela Uribe. *Explotación capitalista*. Cuadernos de educación popular, 2. Santiago: Quimantú, 1972.

————. *Explotadores y explotados*. Cuadernos de educación popular, 1. Santiago: Quimantú, 1972.

————. *Lucha de clases*. Cuadernos de educación popular, 4. Santiago: Quimantú, 1972.

Hecht Oppenheim, Lois. "The Chilean Road to Socialism Revisited." *Latin American Research Review* 24, no. 1 (1989): 155–183.

————. *Politics in Chile: Democracy, Authoritarianism, and the Search for Development*. Boulder, Colo.: Westview Press, 1993.

Henfrey, Colin, and Bernardo Sorj. *Chilean Voices: Activists Describe Their Experiences of the Popular Unity Period*. Hassocks, England: Harvester Press, 1977.

Hernández, Pedro F. *Catholic Church and Population Growth in Latin America: A Survey of the Bases of the Catholic Position on Population Problems*. Baton Rouge: Latin American Studies Institute, Louisiana State University, 1969.

Herrera Rodríguez, Susana. *El aborto inducido: Víctimas o víctimarias?* Santiago: Catalonia, 2004.

Herrick, Bruce. *Urban Migration and Economic Development in Chile*. MIT Monographs in Economics, no. 6. Cambridge: MIT Press, 1966.

Heyermann, Beatriz. *Municipio, descentralización y salud*. Seminario sobre "Municipalización de los Servicios Sociales." Santiago: Latin American and Caribbean Institute for Economic and Social Planning (ILPES) / Economic Commission for Latin America and the Caribbean (CEPAL), 1994.

Hiriart, Berta. "Mujer/fempress: Latin American Women's News Agency." In *Compañeras: Voices from the Latin American Women's Movement*, edited by Gabriele Küppers. London: Latin American Bureau, 1994.

Hodgson, Dennis, and Susan Cotts Watkins. "Feminists and Neo-Malthusians: Past and Present Alliances." *Population and Development Review* 23, no. 3 (September 1997): 469–523.

Holmstrom, Nancy. *The Socialist Feminist Project: A Contemporary Reader in Theory and Politics*. New York: Monthly Review Press, 2002.

Horwitz Campos, Nina, et al. *Salud y estado en Chile: Organización social de la salud publica, periodo del Servicio Nacional de Salud*. Santiago: OPS-Chile, 1995.

Htun, Mala. *Sex and the State: Abortion, Divorce, and the Family Under Latin American Dictatorships and Democracies*. Cambridge: Cambridge University Press, 2003.

Huneeus, Carlos, and María Paz Lanas. "Ciencia Política e Historia: Eduardo Cruz-Coke y el Estado de Bienestar en Chile, 1937–1938." *Historia* 35 (2002): 151–186.

Hutchison, Elizabeth Q. *Labors Appropriate to Their Sex: Gender, Labor, and Politics in Urban Chile, 1900–1930*. Durham, N.C.: Duke University Press, 2001.

————. "'La Mujer Esclava' to 'la Mujer Limon': Anarchism and the Politics of Sexuality in Early-Twentieth-Century Chile." *Hispanic American Historical Review* 81, no. 3–4 (2001): 519–553.

Icken Safa, Helen. "Women's Social Movements in Latin America." *Gender and Society* 4, no. 3, Special Issue: Women and Development in the Third World (1990): 354–369.

Illanes, María Angélica. *Cuerpo y sangre de la política: La construcción histórica de las visitadoras sociales, Chile, 1887–1940*. Santiago: LOM, 2005.

————. *En el nombre del pueblo, del estado y de la ciencia: Historia social de la salud pública, Chile 1880–1973*. Santiago: Colectivo de Atención Primaria, 1993.

————. *Historia del movimiento social y de la salud pública en Chile, 1885–1920: Solidaridad, ciencia y caridad*. Santiago: Colectivo de Atención Primaria, 1989.

————. *La batalla de la memoria. Ensayos históricos de nuestro siglo. Chile, 1900–2000*. Santiago: Planeta/Ariel, 2002.

————. "Maternalismo popular e hibridación cultural. Chile 1900–1920." *Nomadías* (June 1999): 185–211.

Infante, Antonio. "Primary Health Care in a Local Community." In *Social Policy from the Grassroots: Nongovernmental Organizations in Chile,* edited by Charles Downs et al., 19–65. Westview Special Studies in Social, Political, and Economic Development. Boulder, Colo.: Westview Press, 1989.

Instituto de la Mujer, Área de Salud. *Las políticas de planificación familiar y educación sexual en Chile: Resumen 1.* Santiago: 1989.

ILET. *Contraviolencia.* Mujer/fempress especial. Santiago: ILET, 1988.

————. *Debate del aborto.* Mujer/fempress especial. Santiago: ILET, 1989.

————. *Demandas de las mujeres.* Santiago: ILET, 1988.

————. *La mujer y el humor.* Santiago: ILET, 1988.

————. *La mujer y el humor, no. 2.* Mujer/fempress especial. Santiago: ILET, 1988.

————. *La mujer indígena.* Santiago: ILET, 1988.

————. *Precursoras del feminismo en America Latina.* Santiago: ILET, 1991.

Instituto Latinoamericano de Estudios Transnacionales (ILET), and Fempress. *Mujer/fempress.* Santiago: ILET, 1986.

Ipas. "Women's Groups in Latin America and the Caribbean Urge Decriminalization of Abortion." Available online at http://www.ipas.org/Library/News/News_Items/Womens_groups_in_Latin_America_the_Caribbean_urge_decriminalization_of_abortion.aspx.

IPPF. *Family Planning in Chile: A Profile of a Development of Policies and Programmes.* London: IPPF, 1979.

Isis International. *Women's International Bulletin.* Rome: Isis International, 1982.

————. *Isis International Women's Journal.* Rome: Isis International, 1984.

————. *Women in Action.* Rome: Isis International, 1984.

————. "Organization and Functioning of the Isis International Resource Center." Santiago, Chile: N.p., 1989.

Jalil, Roberto, et al. "El hijo de madre adolescente, Curacavi 1983." *Boletín del Hospital de San Juan de Dios* 33, no. 3 (May–June 1986): 202–207.

Jaquette, Jane S. *The Women's Movement in Latin America: Feminism and the Transition to Democracy.* Boston: Unwin Hyman, 1989.

Jiles Moreno, Ximena, and Claudia Rojas Mira. "El régimen militar, su política pronatalista y la jibarización de los programas de paternidad responsable." In *De la miel a los implantes: Historia de las políticas de regulación de la fecundidad en Chile,* 175–199. Santiago: CORSAPS, 1992.

Jiménez de la Jara, Jorge, and Thomas Bossert. "Chile's Health Sector Reform: Lessons from Four Reform Periods." *Health Policy* 32 (1995): 155–166.

Jiménez, Oscar. "Salud y Población." *Revista médica de Chile* 99 (1971): 442–443.

Johnson, D., ed. *The Chilean Road to Socialism.* New York: Anchor Books, 1973.

Jones, Gavin, and Dorothy Nortman. "Roman Catholic Fertility and Family Planning: A Comparative Review of the Research Literature." *Studies in Family Planning* 1, no. 34 (October 1968): 1–27.

Joseph, Gilbert M., Catherine LeGrand, and Ricardo Donato Salvatore, eds. *Close Encounters of Empire: Writing the Cultural History of U.S.–Latin American Relations.* Durham, N.C.: Duke University Press, 1998.

Kaplan, Temma. "Female Consciousness and Collective Action: The Case of Barcelona, 1910–1918." *Signs* 7, no. 3 (1982): 545–560.

————. *Women, Youth, and Direct Democracy: Taking Back the Streets.* Berkeley: University of California Press, 2004.

Kay, Diana. *Chileans in Exile: Private Struggles, Public Lives.* Wolfeboro, N.H.: Longwood Academic, 1987.

Keck, Margaret E., and Kathryn Sikkink. *Activists Beyond Borders: Advocacy Networks in International Politics.* Ithaca, N.Y.: Cornell University Press, 1998.

Keely, Charles B. "Limits to Papal Power: Vatican Inaction After *Humanae Vitae*." *Population and Development Review* 20. Supplement: *The New Politics of Population: Conflict and Consensus in Family Planning* (1994): 220–240.

Kinzer, Stephen. *Overthrow: America's Century of Regime Change from Hawaii to Iraq.* New York: Times Books, 2006.

Kirkwood, Julieta. *El feminismo como negación del autoritarismo.* Santiago: Programa FLACSO, 1983.

————. *Feministas y políticas.* Santiago: Programa FLACSO, 1984.

————. *La política del feminismo en Chile.* Santiago: Programa FLACSO, 1983.

————. *Seminarios.* Santiago: Ediciones Documentas, 1987.

————. *Ser política en Chile: Los nudos de la sabiduría feminista.* Santiago: Editorial Cuarto Propio, 1990.

————. "Women and Politics in Chile." *International Social Science Journal* 35 (1983): 625–637.

Klimpel, Felícitas. *La mujer chilena: El aporte femenino al progreso de Chile, 1910–1960.* Santiago: Editorial Andrés Bello, 1962.

————. *La mujer, el delito y la sociedad.* Buenos Aires: El Ateneo, 1946.

Klubock, Thomas Miller. *Contested Communities: Class, Gender, and Politics in Chile's El Teniente Copper Mine, 1904–1951.* Durham, N.C.: Duke University Press, 1998.

Komitee für die Freiheit der Politischen Gefangenen Frauen in Chile. *Frauensolidarität: Möglichkeiten und Probleme emanzipatorischer Politik: Erfahrungen am Beispiel Chile.* West Berlin: Selbstverlag Das Komitee, 1977.

Komitee Solidarität mit Chile. *Konterrevolution in Chile: Analysen u. Dokumente z. Terror.* Reinbek (bei Hamburg), Germany: Rowohlt, 1973.

————. *Lateinamerika-Nachrichten Chile-Nachrichten.* West Berlin: Lateinamerika-Nachrichten, 1977.

Kommunistischer Bund and Chile-Frauengruppe Hamburg. *Frauen in Chile.* Hamburg: Verlag Arbeiterkampf, 1976.

Koordinationsgruppe der Chilesolidaritätsgruppen Westberlin und Lateinamerika-Nachrichten. *Chile der Mut zu überleben: 5 Jahre Militärdiktatur: Ausstellung von Stoffbildern aus dem chilenischen Widerstand.* Berlin: Lateinamerika-Nachrichten, 1978.

Kopplin, Erika. "Aspectos psico sociales de la embarazada y madre adolescente." In *Compromisos antes de tiempo: Adolescentes, sexualidad y embarazo*, edited by Valeria Ambrosio, 49–65. Santiago: Corporación de Salud y Políticas Sociales, 1985.

Kornbluh, Peter. *The Pinochet File: A Declassified Dossier on Atrocity and Accountability*. New York: New Press, 2003.

Koven, Seth, and Sonya Michel. "Womanly Duties: Maternalist Politics and the Origins of Welfare States in France, Germany, Great Britain, and the United States, 1880–1920." *American Historical Review* 95, no. 4 (1990): 1076–1108.

———, eds. *Mothers of a New World: Maternalist Politics and the Origins of Welfare States*. New York: Routledge, 1993.

Kubal, Mary Rose. "Contradictions and Constraints in Chile's Health Care and Education Decentralization." *Latin American Politics and Society* 48, no. 4 (Winter 2006): 105–135.

Kunzle, David. "Chile's La Firme versus Itt." *Latin American Perspectives* 5, no. 1 (Winter 1978): 119–133.

Kyle, Patricia A., and Michael Francis. "Chile: The Power of Women at the Polls." In *Integrating the Neglected Majority: Government Responses to Demands for New Sex-Roles*, edited by Patricia A. Kyle. Brunswick, Ohio: King's Court Communications, 1976.

Küppers, Gabriele. *Feministamente: Frauenbewegung in Lateinamerika*. Wuppertal, Germany: P. Hammer, 1992.

Lagarde, Marcela. "Maternidad, Feminismo y Democracia." In *Repensar y politizar la maternidad: Un reto de fin de milenio*, edited by Cecilia Talamante Díaz et al., 19–36. Mexico City: Grupo de Educación Popular con Mujeres, 1994.

Lagos Lira, Claudia. *Aborto en Chile: El deber de parir*. Santiago: LOM Ediciones, 2001.

Larraín, Camilo. *La sociedad médica de Santiago y el desarrollo histórico de la medicina en Chile*. Santiago: Sociedad Medica de Chile, 2002.

Latin American and Caribbean Women's Health Network (LACWHN). "Mission and Principles." Available online at http://www.reddesalud.org/english/sitio/003.htm.

———. *Women's Health Journal*. Santiago: Isis International, 2003.

Lavrin, Asunción. "Suffrage in South America: Arguing a Difficult Case." In *Suffrage and Beyond: International Feminist Perspectives*, edited by Caroline Daley and Melanie Nolan, 184–209. Auckland: Auckland University Press-Pluto Press, 1994.

———. *Women, Feminism, and Social Change in Argentina, Chile, and Uruguay, 1890–1940*. Lincoln: University of Nebraska Press, 1998.

———, ed., *Sexuality and Marriage in Colonial Latin America*. Lincoln: University of Nebraska Press, 1989.

Lechner, Norbert, and Susana Levy. *Notas sobre la vida cotidiana III: El disciplinamiento de las mujeres*. Santiago: Facultad Latinoamericana de Ciencias Sociales, 1984.

Leibenstein, Harvey. "Pitfalls in Benefit-Cost Analysis of Birth Prevention." *Population Studies* 23 (1969): 161–170.

Leñero Otero, Luis. *Poblacíon, iglesia y cultura; sistemas en conflicto*. Mexico City: Instituto Mexicano de Estudios Sociales, 1970.

Lernoux, Penny. *Cry of the People: The Struggle for Human Rights in Latin America—the Catholic Church in Conflict with U.S. Policy*. New York: Penguin Books, 1982.

Levinson, Jerome I., and Juan De Onis. *The Alliance That Lost Its Way: A Critical Report on the Alliance for Progress*. Chicago: Quadrangle Books, 1970.

Lidid, Sandra, and Kira Maldonado. *Movimiento feminista autónomo (1993–1997)*. Santiago: Ediciones Tierra Mía, 1997.

Lies, William M. "A Clash of Values: Church-State Relations in Democratic Chile." In *After Pinochet: The Chilean Road to Democracy and the Market*, edited by Silvia Borzutzky and Lois Hecht Oppenheim, 64–90 (chapter 4). Gainesville: University Press of Florida, 2006.

Lies, William, and Mary Fran T. Malone. "The Chilean Church: Declining Hegemony?" In *The Catholic Church and the Nation-State: Comparative Perspectives*, edited by Paul Christopher Manuel, Lawrence C. Reardon, and Clyde Wilcox, 89–100. Washington, D.C.: Georgetown University Press, 2006.

López-Stewart, Patricia, and Elisabeth Gumberger. *Ich bringe das Salz: Chilenische Frauen berichten: Erfahrungen, Situationen, Positionen*. Bremen, Germany: Edition CON, 1985.

Losada de Masjuan, Josefina. *Comportamientos anticonceptivos en la familia marginal*. Santiago: DESAL and CELAP, 1968.

Loveman, Brian. *Chile: The Legacy of Hispanic Capitalism*. New York: Oxford University Press, 1979.

———. *For La Patria: Politics and the Armed Forces in Latin America*. Wilmington, Del.: SR Books, 1999.

———, and Thomas M. Davies, eds. *The Politics of Antipolitics: The Military in Latin America*. Wilmington, Del.: Scholarly Resources, 1997.

Lowden, Pamela. *Moral Opposition to Authoritarian Rule in Chile, 1973–90*. St. Antony's Series. New York: St. Martin's Press, 1996.

Lupton, Deborah. "Feminisms and Medicine." In *Medicine as Culture: Illness, Disease, and the Body in Western Societies*. London: Sage Publications, 2003.

Lycklama à Nijeholt, G., Virginia Vargas, and Saskia Wieringa. *Women's Movements and Public Policy in Europe, Latin America, and the Caribbean*. Vol. 2, *Gender, Culture, and Global Politics*. New York: Garland Publishing, 1998.

Macaulay, Fiona. *Gender Politics in Brazil and Chile: The Role of Parties in National and Local Policymaking*. Basingstoke, England: Palgrave Macmillan, 2006.

MacEóin, Gary. *Chile, Under Military Rule*. New York: International Documentation and North America (IDOC and NA), 1974.

Mainwaring, Scott, and Timothy Scully. *Christian Democracy in Latin America: Electoral Competition and Regime Conflicts*. Stanford, Calif.: Stanford University Press, 2003.

Malinowski, Matt. "Thousands of Chileans to March Against Femicide." *Women's eNews* (November 4, 2007). Available online at http://www.womensenews.org/article.cfm?aid=3372.

Mallon, Florencia. "Exploring the Origins of Democratic Patriarchy in Mexico: Gender and Popular Resistance in the Puebla Highlands, 1850–1876." In *Women of the Mexican Countryside, 1850–1990: Creating Spaces, Shaping Transitions*, edited by Heather Fowler-Salamini and Mary K. Vaughan, 3–26. Tucson: University of Arizona Press, 1994.

———. *Peasant and Nation: The Making of Postcolonial Mexico and Peru*. Berkeley: University of California Press, 1995

Maloof, Judy. *Voices of Resistance: Testimonies of Cuban and Chilean Women*. Lexington: University Press of Kentucky, 1999.

Malthus, Thomas Robert. *Essay on the Principle of Population, 1798*.

Manríquez, German. "Professor Max Westenhöfer (1871–1957) in Chile." *Revista médica de Chile* 123, no. 10 (October 1995): 1313–1317.

Marks, Lara V. *Sexual Chemistry: A History of the Contraceptive Pill*. New Haven, Conn.: Yale University Press, 2001.

Mass, Bonnie. "A Historical Sketch in the American Population Control Movement." *International Journal of the Health Services* 4 (1974): 651–676.

———. *The Political Economy of Population Control in Latin America*. Montreal, Quebec: Editions Latin America, 1972.

————. *Population Target: The Political Economy of Population Control in Latin America*. Toronto, Ontario: Latin American Working Group, 1976.

Mattelart, Armand. *El reto espiritual de la explosión demográfica*. Santiago: Editorial del Pacífico, 1965.

————. *Mass Media, Ideologies, and the Revolutionary Movement*. Marxist Theory and Contemporary Capitalism, no. 30. Brighton, Sussex: Harvester, 1980.

Mattelart, Michèle. "Chile: The Feminine Version of the Coup d' Etat." In *Sex and Class in Latin America*, edited by June C. Nash and Helen Icken Safa, 279–301. New York: Praeger, 1976.

————, and Shu Lea Cheang. *Michèle Mattelart Reading* The Chilean Press Avant-coup, or, *Everyday It Gets Harder to Be a Good Housewife*. New York: Paper Tiger Television, 1980.

Mauldin, W. Parker. "Bernard Berelson: 2 June 1912–25 September 1979." *Studies in Family Planning* 10, no. 10 (October 1979): 259–262.

Maza Valenzuela, Erika. "Catholicism, Anticlericism, and the Quest for Women's Suffrage in Chile." Helen Kellogg Institute for International Studies, University of Notre Dame, Working Paper 214 (1995): 184–209.

McGee Deutsch, Sandra. "Gender and Sociopolitical Change in Twentieth-Century Latin America." *Hispanic American Historical Review* 71, no. 2 (May 1991): 259–306.

————. *Las Derechas: The Extreme Right in Argentina, Brazil, and Chile, 1830–1939*. Stanford, Calif.: Stanford University Press, 1999.

Mead, Karen. "Beneficent Maternalism: Argentine Motherhood in Comparative Perspective, 1880–1920." *Journal of Women's History* 12, no. 3 (2000): 120–145.

Mesa-Lago, Carmelo. *Social Security in Latin America: Pressure Groups, Stratification, and Inequality*. Pittsburgh: University of Pittsburgh Press, 1978.

Miguens, Jose Enrique. "The New Latin American Military Coup." In *Militarism in Developing Countries*, edited by Kenneth Fidel, 99–123. New Brunswick, N.J.: Transaction Books, 1975.

Milanich, Nara. "The Casa de Huerfanos and Child Circulation in Late-Nineteenth-Century Chile." *Journal of Social History* 38, no. 2 (Winter 2004): 311–340.

————. "Historical Perspectives on Illegitimacy and Illegitimates in Latin America." In *Minor Omissions: Children in Latin American History and Society*, edited by Tobias Hecht, 72–101. Madison: University of Wisconsin Press, 2002.

Mill, John Stuart. *The Subjection of Women*, edited by Edward Alexander. 1869. Reprint, New Brunswick, N.J.: Transaction Publishers, 2001.

Miller, Francesca. "The International Relations of Women of the Americas, 1890–1928." *The Americas* 43, no. 2 (October 1986): 171–182.

————. *Latin American Women and the Search for Social Justice*. Hanover. N.H.: University Press of New England, 1991.

Miró, Carmen. "Some Misconceptions Disproved." In *Family Planning and Population Programs: A Review of World Developments*, edited by International Conference on Family Planning Programs and Bernard Berelson, 615–634. Chicago: University of Chicago Press, 1966.

Moenm, Elizabeth. "Women's Rights and Reproductive Freedom." *Human Rights Quarterly* 3, no. 2 (May 1981): 53–60.

Molina, Carlos. *La cuestión social y la opinión de la élite médica. Chile: 1880–1890*. Santiago: Departamento de Ciencias Históricas, University of Chile, 2000.

————. "Sujetos sociales en el desarrollo de las instituciones sanitarias en Chile: 1889–1938." *Polis* 3, no. 9 (University of Chile, 2004). Available online at http://redalyc .uaemex.mx/redalyc/pdf/305/30500919.pdf.

Molina, Natacha. "De la denuncia a la contrucción de la igualdad." In *Veredas por cruzar 10 años, Instituto de la Mujer*, edited by Guadalupe Santa Cruz, 181–204. Santiago: El Instituto de la Mujer, 1997.

Molyneux, Maxine. *Women's Movements in International Perspective: Latin America and Beyond.* New York: Palgrave, 2001.

Montecino Aguirre, Sonia, and Josefina Rossetti. *Tramas para un nuevo destino propuestas de la Concertación de Mujeres por la Democracia.* N.p., 1990.

Montupil, Fernando, ed. *Exilio, derechos humanos y democracia: El exilio chileno en Europa.* Santiago: Casa de América Latina and Servicios Gráficos Caupolicán, 1993.

Moulián, Luis, and Gloria Guerra. *Eduardo Frei M. (1911–1982): Biografía de un estadista utópico.* Santiago: Editorial Sudamericana, 2000.

Moulián, Tomás. *El gobierno de Ibáñez, 1952–1958. Material docente sobre historia de Chile, no. 2.* Santiago: Programa FLACSO, 1986.

————, and Isabel Torres Dujisin. *Las candidaturas presidenciales de la derecha: Ross e Ibáñez.* Santiago: Programa FLACSO, 1986.

Moya-Raggio, Eliana. "'Arpilleras': Chilean Culture of Resistance." *Feminist Studies* 10, no. 2 (1984): 277–290.

Müller-Plantenberg, Clarita. *Frauen und Familie im gesellschaftlichen Befreiungsprozess: Drei Analysen zur chilenischen Situation zwischen 1964 und 1982.* Frankfurt am Main, Germany: Verlag K.D. Vervuert, 1983.

Munizaga, Giselle. *El discurso público de Pinochet.* Buenos Aires: CESOC and CENECA, 1983.

Mutchler, David E. *The Church as a Political Factor in Latin America: With Particular Reference to Colombia and Chile.* Praeger Special Studies in International Politics and Public Affairs. New York: Praeger, 1971.

Nari, Marcela. "Las prácticas anticonceptivas, la disminución de la natalidad y el debate médico, 1890–1940." In *Política, médicos y enfermedades: Lecturas de la historia de la salud en la Argentina*, edited by Mirta Zaida Lobato and Adriana Alvarez, 151–189. Buenos Aires: Editorial Biblos, 1996.

————. *Políticas de maternidad y maternalismo político.* Buenos Aires: Editorial Biblos, 2004.

Navarro, Marysa. "Against Marianismo." In *Gender's Place: Feminist Anthropologies of Latin America*, edited by Rosario Montoya, Lessie Jo Frazier, and Janise Hurtig, 257–272. New York: Palgrave Macmillan, 2002.

————. "El primer encuentro feminista de Latinoamérica y el Caribe." In *Sociedad, subordinación y feminismo*, edited by Magdalena León, 261–267. Bogotá, Colombia: Asociación Colombiana para el estudio de la población, 1982.

Navarro, Vicente. "What Does Chile Mean: An Analysis of Events in the Health Sector Before, During, and After Allende's Administration." *Milbank Memorial Fund Quarterly.* Health and Society 52, no. 2 (Spring 1974): 93–130.

Neghme, Amador. *Reflexiones sobre la medicina y la salubridad en Chile.* Santiago: Impr. Universitaria, 1950.

————. "Reseña histórica de la educación médica en Chile: Desde 1933 a la fecha." *Anales de la Universidad de Chile* 5, no. 14 (1987): 49–60.

Nelson, Alice A. *Political Bodies: Gender, History, and the Struggle for Narrative Power in Recent Chilean Literature*. Lewisburg, Pa.: Bucknell University Press, 2002.

Norsigian, Judy, et al. "The Boston Women's Health Book Collective and Our Bodies, Ourselves: A Brief History and Reflection." *Women's Health Journal* 2 (2000): 72–77.

Nunn, Frederick M. *Chilean Politics, 1920-1931; The Honorable Mission of the Armed Forces*. Albuquerque: University of New Mexico Press, 1970.

———. *The Military in Chilean History: Essays on Civil-Military Relations, 1810–1973*. Albuquerque: University of New Mexico Press, 1976.

———. "Military Professionalism and Professional Militarism in Brazil, 1870–1970: Historical Perspectives and Political Implications." *Journal of Latin American Studies* 4, no. 1 (May 1972): 29–54.

———. "New Thoughts on Military Intervention in Latin American Politics: The Chilean Case, 1973." *Journal of Latin American Studies* 7, no. 2 (November 1975): 271–304.

———. *The Time of the Generals: Latin American Professional Militarism in World Perspective*. Lincoln: University of Nebraska Press, 1992.

Oppenheimer, W. "Prevention of Pregnancy by the Gräfenberg Ring Method." *American Journal of Obstetrics and Gynecology* 78 (August 1959): 446–454.

Ortega, Eliana, and Nancy Saporta Sternbach. "Gracias a la vida: Recounting the Third Latin American Feminist Meeting in Bertioga, Brazil, July 31–August 4, 1985." *Off Our Backs* 26, no. 1 (January 1986): 1.

Osborn, Fairfield, ed. *Our Crowded Planet: Essays on the Pressures of Population*. Conservation Foundation. Garden City, N.Y.: Doubleday, 1962.

Oteiza, Enrique "Purged Professors, Screened Students, Burned Books." In *Chile, Under Military Rule*, edited by Gary MacEóin. New York: IDOC/North America, 1974.

Oyarzún, Kemy. "Engendering Democracy in the Chilean University." *NACLA Report on the Americas* 33, no. 4 (2000): 24–29.

Oyarzún S., Lorena. "Aborto en Chile." In *Sin censura reportajes ganadores "Concuro Periodismo Joven,"* edited by Fabián Llanca. Colección Nuevo periodismo. Santiago: LOM Ediciones, 2000.

Oxman, Verónica. *La participación de la mujer campesina en organizaciones: Los centros de madres rurales*. Santiago: Grupo de Investigaciones Agrarias, Academia de Humanismo Cristiano, 1983.

———. *La violencia sexual en Chile*. Santiago: SERNAM, 1995.

Palestro, Sandra. *Mujeres en movimiento, 1973–1989*. Santiago: FLACSO, Serie Estudios Sociales no. 14, 1991.

Palma, Catalina. *Women in Chile: Yesterday and Today*. London: Chile Solidarity Campaign, 1984.

Palmer, Steven. "Central American Encounters with Rockefeller Public Health, 1914–1921." In *Close Encounters of Empire: Writing the Cultural History of U.S.–Latin American Relations*, edited by Gilbert M. Joseph, Catherine LeGrand, and Ricardo Donato Salvatore, 311–333. Durham, N.C.: Duke University Press, 1998.

Pappas-Deluca, Katina. "Transcending Gendered Boundaries: Migration for Domestic Labour in Chile." In *Gender, Migration, and Domestic Service*, edited by Janet Henshall Momsen, 95–110. London: Routledge, 1999.

Pastrana, Ernesto J., and Mónica Threlfall. *Pan, techo y poder el movimiento de pobladores en Chile, 1970–1973*. Buenos Aires: Ediciones Siap-Planteos, 1974.

Paxman, John M., et al. "The Clandestine Epidemic: The Practice of Unsafe Abortion in Latin America." *Studies in Family Planning* 24, no. 4 (July–August 1993): 205–226.

Paxton, Pamela Marie, and Melanie M. Hughes. *Women, Politics, and Power: A Global Perspective.* Los Angeles: Pine Forge Press, 2007.

Pena O., Edita, et al. "Perfil de la adolescente embarazada controlada en consultorio del S.S.M." In *Versión de ponencias abreviadas.* University of Chile, Faculty of Philosophy, Humanities, and Education. Department of Sociology. Santiago: Casa Central, 1986.

Pinochet Ugarte, Augusto. *Mensaje a la mujer chilena: Texto del discurso pronunciado por el Presidente de la Junta de Gobierno.* Santiago: Ed. Nacional Gabriela Mistral, 1974.

Pinto Lagarrigue, Fernando. *Alessandrismo versus Ibañismo.* Santiago: Editorial La Noria, 1995.

Pinto Solari, Malucha. *Cartas de la memoria: Patrimonio epistolar de una generación de mujeres Chilenas.* Santiago: Catalonia, 2007.

Pisano, Margarita. *Reflexiones feministas.* Santiago: Centro de Análisis y Difusión de la Condición de la Mujer, 1990.

Poblete Troncoso, Moisés. *La explosión demográfica en América Latina.* Buenos Aires: Editorial Schapire, 1967.

Pollack Petchesky, Rosalind. "Reproductive Freedom: Beyond 'A Woman's Right to Choose.'" *Signs* 5, no. 4 (Summer 1980): 661–685.

Pope John Paul. *Fruitful and Responsible Love.* New York: Seabury Press, 1979.

Pope Pius XI. *Encyclical Letter (Casti Connubii) of His Holiness Pius XI; By Divine Providence Pope, to Our Venerable Brethren Patriarchs, Primates, Archbishops, Bishops, and Other Local Ordinaries Enjoying Peace and Communion with the Apostolic See, on Christian Marriage, in View of the Present Conditions, Needs, Errors, and Vices That Affect the Family and Society.* London: Catholic Truth Society, 1931.

Population Council and John D. Rockefeller III. "Statement on Population from World Leaders." Available online at http://www.popcouncil.org/mediacenter/popstatement.html.

Portugal, Ana Maria. "Moving Around with Our Feet Firmly on the Ground." *Women in Action* (December 31, 1999): 72. Available online at http://www.isiswomen.org/wia/wia299/isis00004.html.

———, and María Isabel Matamala. "Women's Health Movement: A View of the Decade." In *Gender, Women, and Health in the Americas,* edited by Elsa Gómez, 269–280. Washington, D.C.: Pan American Health Organization, 1993.

———, and MujeresHoy. "Chilenas celebran Encuentro Feminista Nacional." July 13, 2005. Available online at http://www.mujereshoy.com/secciones/3215.shtml.

Potthast, Barbara. *Von Müttern und Machos: Eine Geschichte der Frauen Lateinamerikas.* Wuppertal, Germany: Hammer, 2003.

———, and Eugenia Scarzanella. *Mujeres y naciones en América Latina: Problemas de inclusión y exclusión.* Frankfurt, Germany: Vervuert, 2001.

Powell, Sandra. "Political Change in the Chilean Electorate 1952–1964." *Western Political Quarterly* 23, no. 2 (June 1970): 364–383.

Power, Margaret. "Defending Dictatorship: Conservative Women in Pinochet's Chile and the 1988 Plebiscite." In *Radical Women in Latin America: Left and Right,* edited by V. González and K. Kampwirth, 299–324. University Park: Pennsylvania State University Press, 2001.

———. *Right-Wing Women in Chile: Feminine Power and the Struggle against Allende, 1964–1973.* University Park: Pennsylvania State University Press, 2002.

———, and Paola Bacchetta, eds. *Right-Wing Women: From Conservatives to Extremists Around the World*. New York: Routledge, 2002.

Provoste Fernández, Patricia. *La construcción de las mujeres en la política social*. Santiago: Instituto de la Mujer, 1995.

———. "Los servicios públicos y los derechos de las mujeres." In *Veredas por cruzar 10 años, Instituto de la Mujer*, edited by Guadalupe Santa Cruz. Santiago: El Instituto, 1997.

Putnam Tong, Rosemarie. *Feminist Thought: A More Comprehensive Introduction*, 2nd ed. Boulder, Colo.: Westview Press, 1998.

Puz, Amanda. *La mujer chilena*. Santiago: Editora Nacional Quimantú, 1972.

Raczynski, Dagmar, and Claudia Serrano. *Mujer y familia en un sector popular urbano resultados de un estudio de casos*. Apuntes CIEPLAN, no. 47. Santiago: CIEPLAN, 1984.

Radcliffe, Sarah, and Sallie Westwood, eds. *'ViVa': Women and Popular Protest in Latin America*. London: Routledge, 1993.

Rajevic, Pía. *El libro abierto del amor y el sexo en Chile*. Santiago: Planeta, 2000.

Ramirez de Arellano, Annette B. *Colonialism, Catholicism, and Contraception: A History of Birth Control in Puerto Rico*. Chapel Hill: University of North Carolina Press, 1983.

Razeto, Luis. *Las organizaciones económicas populares: La experiencia de las nuevas organizaciones económicas populares en Chile, situación y perspectivas*. Santiago: Programa de Economía del Trabajo, Academia de Humanismo Cristiano, Arzobispado de Santiago, 1983.

Rebolledo, Loreto. *Memorias del desarraigo: Testimonios de exilio y retorno de hombres y mujeres de Chile*. Providencia, Santiago: Catalonia, 2006.

Recabarren, Luis Emilio, Ximena Cruzat, and Eduardo Devés V. *Recabarren, escritos de prensa*. Santiago: Terranova, 1985.

Reed, James. *The Birth Control Movement and American Society: From Private Vice to Public Virtue*. Princeton, N.J.: Princeton University Press, 1984.

Reichard, Stephen. "Ideology Drives Health Care Reforms in Chile." *Journal of Public Health Policy* 17, no. 1 (1996): 80–98.

Requena, Mariano. "Studies of Family Planning in the Quinta Normal District of Santiago: The Use of Contraceptives." *Milbank Memorial Fund Quarterly* 43, no. 4, part 2 (October 1965): 69–99.

———, ed. *Aborto inducido en Chile*. Santiago: Sociedad Chilena de Salud Publica, 1990.

———, Tegualda Monreal, and Donald J. Bogue. "Evaluation of Induced Abortion Control and Family Planning Programs in Chile." *Milbank Memorial Fund Quarterly* 46, no. 3, part 2: Current Research on Fertility and Family Planning in Latin America (July 1968): 191–222.

Richard, Nelly. "Género, valores y diferencia(s)." In *Residuos y metáforas: Ensayos de crítica cultural sobre el Chile de la transición*, 199–218. Santiago: Cuarto Propio, 1998.

Richards, Patricia. *Pobladoras, Indígenas, and the State: Conflicts over Women's Rights in Chile*. New Brunswick, N.J.: Rutgers University Press, 2004.

Ríos Tobar, Marcela. "Chilean Feminism(s) in the 1990s: Paradox of an Unfinished Transition." In *Gender and Civil Society: Transcending Boundaries*, edited by Jude Howell and Diane Mulligan, 139–162 (chapter 7). London: Routledge, 2005.

———. "Chilean feminism(s) in the 1990s." In *Gender and Civil Society Transcending Boundaries*, edited by Jude Howell and Diane Mulligan. London: Routledge, 2005.

———. "'Feminism Is Socialism, Liberty and Much More': Second-Wave Chilean Feminism and Its Contentious Relationship with Socialism." *Journal of Women's History* 1, no. 3 (2003): 129–134.

————. "Paradoxes of an Unfinished Transition: Chilean Feminism in the Nineties." *International Feminist Journal of Politics* 5, no. 2 (2003): 256–281.

————, Lorena Godoy, and Elizabeth Guerrero. *Un nuevo silencio feminista? La transformación de un movimiento social en el Chile posdictadura.* Santiago: Centro de Estudios de la Mujer, 2003.

Rodríguez Musso, Osvaldo. *La nueva canción chilena: Continuidad y reflejo.* Havana, Cuba: Casa de las Américas, 1988.

Rodríguez Villouta, Mili. *Ya nunca me verás como me vieras: Doce testimonios vivos del exilio.* Santiago: Ediciones del Ornitorrinco, 1990.

Rojas Flores, Jorge. "Los derechos del niño en Chile: Una aproximación histórica, 1910–1930." *Historia* no. 40 (2007): 129–164.

————. *Moral y prácticas cívicas en los niños chilenos, 1880–1950.* Santiago: Ariadna Ediciones, 2004.

Romaggi, Marisabel, and Patricia Henríquez. "Características socio demográficas de la población adolescente en Chile." In *Corporación de Salud y Políticas Sociales. Compromisos antes de tiempo: Adolescentes, sexualidad y embarazo,* edited by Valeria Ambrosio Brieva et al., 16–33. Santiago: CORSAPS, 1991.

Romero Aguirre, Fernando. "El cuidado del embarazo y la asistencia del parto como factores de protección a la infancia." In *Trabajos y actas del Primer Congreso Nacional de Protección á la Infancia: Celebrado en Santiago de Chile del 21 al 26 de septiembre de 1912,* edited by Manuel Camilo Vial, 210–218. Santiago: Impr., Litografía y Encuadernación "Barcelona," 1912.

Romero, Hernán. *El control de la natalidad: Prejuicios y controversias.* Santiago: Editorial Universitaria, 1964.

————. "Chile." In *Family Planning and Population Programs: A Review of World Developments,* edited by International Conference on Family Planning Programs and Bernard Berelson, 235–247. Chicago: University of Chicago Press, 1966.

————. "Chile: The Abortion Epidemic." In *Family Planning Programs: An International Survey,* edited by Bernard Berelson, 134–145 (chapter 13). New York: Basic Books, 1969.

————. *Población, desarrollo y control de natalidad en América Latina: Prejuicios y controversias.* Mexico City: Editorial Diana, 1969.

————, and Jerjes Vildósola. "Economía de vidas." *Revista chilena de higiene y medicina preventiva* 14, no. 4 (December 1952): 197–212.

Rosemblatt, Karin Alejandra. *Gendered Compromises: Political Cultures and the State in Chile, 1920–1950.* Chapel Hill: University of North Carolina Press, 2000.

Rubio, José Roberto. *La vuelta al pago en ochenta y dos años: Memorias del loco Pepe.* Santiago: Ediciones Ráfaga, 1967.

Ruggiero, Kristin. "The Devil and Modernity in Late Nineteenth-Century Buenos Aires." *The Americas* 59, no. 2 (October 2002): 221–233.

Saa Díaz, María Antonieta. *Ficha Parlamentaria.* Available online at http://www.camara.cl/dips/fichas/ficha_2.asp?vdip=892.

Sagaris, Lake. "Health Care in Chile: Doctors Take on a Declining System." *Canadian Medical Association Journal* 136, no. 2 (January 1987): 174–178.

Salman, Ton. *The Diffident Movement: Disintegration, Ingenuity, and Resistance of the Chilean Pobladores, 1973–1990.* Amsterdam: Thela, 1997.

————. "The Diffident Movement: Generation and Gender in the Vicissitudes of the Chilean Shantytown Organizations, 1973–1990." *Latin American Perspectives* 21, no. 3 (Summer 1994): 8–31.

Sanders, Thomas Griffin. *The Chilean Episcopate*. Fieldstaff reports, 15, no. 3. Hanover, N.H.: American Universities Field Staff, 1968.

———. *Family Planning in Chile*. Part 2, *The Catholic Position*. West Coast South America Series 14, no. 5. New York: American Universities Field Staff, 1967.

———. "Population Planning and Belief Systems: The Catholic Church in Latin America." In *Are Our Descendants Doomed?* edited by Harrison Brown and Edward Hutchings Jr., 306–329. New York: Viking Press, 1972.

Santa Cruz, Adriana. "Fempress: A Communication Strategy for Women." *Gender and Development* 3, no. 1 (February 1995): 51–55.

———, and Viviana Erazo. *Compropolitan, el orden transnacional y su modelo femenino un estudio de las revistas femeninas en América Latina*. Mexico City: Editorial Nueva Imagen, 1981.

Santa Cruz, Adriana, Graciela Torricelli, and Viviana Erazo. *La pareja*. Mujer/fempress especial. Santiago: ILET, 1986.

Saporta Sternbach, Nancy, et al. "Feminisms in Latin America: From Bogotá to San Bernardo." *Signs* 17, no. 2 (1992): 393–434.

Scarpaci, Joseph L. "Help-Seeking Behavior, Use, and Satisfaction Among Frequent Primary Care Users in Santiago de Chile." *Journal of Health and Social Behavior* 29, no. 3 (September 1988): 199–213.

———. "HMO Promotion and Privatization in Chile." *Journal of Health Politics, Policy, and Law* 12 (1987): 551–567.

———. "Primary-Care Decentralization in the Southern Cone: Shantytown Health Care as Urban Social Movement." *Annals of the Association of American Geographer* 81, no. 1 (March 1991): 103–126.

———. *Primary Medical Care in Chile: Accessibility Under Military Rule*. Pittsburgh: University of Pittsburgh Press, 1988.

Schneider, Cathy. *Shantytown Protest in Pinochet's Chile*. Philadelphia: Temple University Press, 1995.

Schöttes, Martina. *Lebensbedingungen, Widerstand und Verfolgung von Frauen in Chile*. Berlin: Berliner Institut für Vergleichende Sozialforschung, 1991.

———, and Monika Schuckar. *Frauen auf der Flucht*. Berlin: Edition Parabolis, 1994.

Schuurman, Frans J., and Ellen Heer. *Social Movements and NGOs in Latin America: A Case-Study of the Women's Movement in Chile*. Nijmegen Studies in Development and Cultural Change, vol. 11. Saarbrücken, Germany: Breitenbach, 1992.

Scott, Joan Wallach. *Gender and the Politics of History*. New York: Columbia University Press, 1988.

Scully, Timothy R. *Rethinking the Center: Party Politics in Nineteenth- and Twentieth-Century Chile*. Stanford, Calif.: Stanford University Press, 1992.

Seminario para comunicadores especializados. *¿Cuántos debemos ser los chilenos y por que?* Santiago: ACHIPA, 1981.

Serrano, Claudia. "Estado, mujer y política social en Chile." In *Políticas sociales, mujeres y gobierno local*, edited by Dagmar Raczynski and Claudia Serrano, 195–216. Santiago: CIEPLAN, 1992.

Sharpless, John. "World Population Growth, Family Planning, and American Foreign Policy." *Journal of Policy History* 7, no. 1 (1995): 72–102.

Shaw, Paul. *Land Tenure and the Rural Exodus in Chile, Colombia, Costa Rica, and Peru.* Gainesville: University Presses of Florida, 1975.

Shayne, Julie D. *The Revolution Question: Feminisms in El Salvador, Chile, and Cuba.* New Brunswick, N.J.: Rutgers University Press, 2004.

———. *They Used to Call Us Witches: Feminism, Culture, and Resistance in the Chilean Diaspora.* Lanham, Md.: Lexington Books, forthcoming.

Shepard, Bonnie. "The 'Double Discourse' on Sexuality and Reproductive Rights in Latin America: The Chasm between Public Policy and Private Actions." In *Perspectives on Health and Human Rights,* edited by Sofia Gruskin et al., 247–271 (chapter 12). New York: Routledge, 2005.

———. *Running the Obstacle Course to Sexual and Reproductive Health: Lessons from Latin America.* Westport, Conn.: Praeger Publishers, 2006.

Sigmund, Paul E. *Liberation Theology at the Crossroads: Democracy or Revolution?* New York: Oxford University Press, 1990.

Silva, Ana Maria, and Instituto de la Mujer. *Tendencias generales de la fecundidad en Chile 1960–1987.* Santiago: Instituto de la Mujer, 1990.

Silva Dreyer, Ana María. *Las políticas de planificación familiar y educación sexual en Chile.* Santiago: Instituto de la Mujer, Area de Salud, 1989.

Silva, Clotilde, and Movimiento de Mujeres Pobladoras. *Chile, no estas muerto: Compromisos y demandas desde la Iglesia de los pobres.* Santiago: Centro Ecuménico Diego de Medellín, n.d.

Silva, Patricio. "Forging Military-technocratic Alliances: The Ibáñez and Pinochet Regimes in Chile." In *The Soldier and the State in South America: Essays in Civil-Military Relations,* edited by Patricio Silva, 87–107. Houndmills, Basingstoke, England: Palgrave, 2001.

———. *In the Name of Reason: Technocrats and Politics in Chile.* University Park: Pennsylvania State University Press, 2008.

Silva, Uca, and Ximena Ahumada. *Sensibilización sobre violencia intrafamiliar a carabineros de Chile SERNAM, 1992–1993.* Santiago: Servicio Nacional de la Mujer, 1994.

Silva Di Liscia, María. "Dentro y Fuera del Hogar: Mujeres, Familia, y Medicalización en Argentina, 1870–1940." *Signos históricos* 13 (January–June 2005): 94–119. Available online at http://redalyc.uaemex.mx/redalyc/pdf/344/34401305.pdf.

Simon, Robert. "Reducción de la mortalidad infantil del primer año por la asistencia a las madres antes, durante y después del parto." In *Trabajos y actas del Primer Congreso Nacional de Protección á la Infancia: Celebrado en Santiago de Chile del 21 al 26 de septiembre de 1912,* edited by Manuel Camilo Vial. Santiago: Impr., Litografía y Encuadernación "Barcelona," 1912.

Skocpol, Theda. *Protecting Soldiers and Mothers: The Political Origins of Social Policy in the United States.* Cambridge: Belknap Press of Harvard University Press, 1995.

Smith, Brian H. *The Church and Politics in Chile: Challenges to Modern Catholicism.* Princeton, N.J.: Princeton University Press, 1982.

Smith, Janet E. *Humanae Vitae: A Generation Later.* Washington, D.C.: Catholic University of America Press, 1991.

Snow, Rachel C., and Gita Sen. *Power and Decision: The Social Control of Reproduction.* Boston: Harvard School of Public Health, 1994.

Spooner, Mary Helen. *Soldiers in a Narrow Land: The Pinochet Regime in Chile*. Berkeley: University of California Press, 1994.

Stange, Jen. "Chile and Emergency Contraception." Planned Parenthood, December 20, 2006. Available online at http://www.plannedparenthood.org/issues-action/birth-control/chile-ec-11184.htm.

Stepan, Nancy. *The Hour of Eugenics: Race, Gender, and Nation in Latin America*. Ithaca, N.Y.: Cornell University Press, 1991.

Stephen, Lynn. "Gender, Citizenship, and the Politics of Identity." *Latin American Perspectives* 28, no. 6 (November 2001): 54–69.

Stern, Steve J. *The Memory Box of Pinochet's Chile*. 3 vols. Durham, N.C.: Duke University Press, 2004.

Stevens, Evelyn. "Marianismo: The Other Face of Machismo in Latin America." In *Confronting Change, Challenging Tradition: Women in Latin American History*, edited by Getrude M. Yeager, 3–17. Wilmington, Del.: Scholarly Resources, 1994.

Stewart-Gambino, Hannah, et al. "Earthquake Versus Erosion: Church Retreat and Social Movement Decline." In *Activist Faith: Grassroots Women in Democratic Brazil and Chile*, edited by Carol Ann Drogus and Hannah W. Stewart-Gambino, 70–102 (chapter 4). University Park: Pennsylvania State University Press, 2005.

Stolz, Iris. *Adiós General—Adiós Macho? Frauen in Chile*. Cologne, Germany: Pahl-Rugenstein, 1989.

Stoner, Lynn K. *From the House to the Streets: The Cuban Woman's Movement for Legal Reform, 1898–1940*. Durham, N.C.: Duke University Press, 1991.

Stycos, Joseph Mayone. *Catholicism and Birth Control in the Western Hemisphere*. Notre Dame, Ind.: Congregation of Holy Cross, 1967.

———. "Opposition to Family Planning in Latin America: Conservative Nationalism." *Demography* 5, no. 2 (1968): 846–854.

Szasz, Ivonne. "La mujer en el trabajo y la migración: El mercado laboral femenino entre 1950 y 1990 y la inmigración de mujeres a la ciudad de Santiago de Chile." *Notas de población* 22, no. 5 (June 1994): 9–50.

Sznajder, Mario, and Luis Roniger. "Exile Communities and Their Differential Institutional Dynamics: A Comparative Analysis of the Chilean and Uruguayan Political Diasporas." *Revista de ciencia política* (Santiago) 27, no. 1 (2007): 43–66.

Szot, Jorge, and Cristina Moreno. "Mortalidad por aborto en Chile: Analisis epidemiologico, 1985–2000." *Revista chilena de obstetricia y ginecología* 68, no. 4 (2003): 309–314.

Taller de Acción Cultural (Santiago, Chile). *La organización fue como nacer de nuevo: Laura, Hilda, Mary, Graciela, Isabel*. Santiago: El Taller, 1986.

Talpade Mohanty, Chandra. "Under Western Eyes: Feminist Scholarship and Colonial Discourses." In *Comparative Political Culture in the Age of Globalization: An Introductory Anthology*, edited by Hwa Yol Jung, 159–190 (chapter 6). Lanham, Md.: Lexington Books, 2002.

10 Encontro Feminista. "History of Feminist Encounters." September 3, 2005. Available online at http://www.10feminista.org.br/es/node/16.

Tentler, Leslie Woodcock. *Catholics and Contraception: An American History*. Cushwa Center Studies of Catholicism in Twentieth-century America. Ithaca, N.Y.: Cornell University Press, 2004.

Thiery, M. "Pioneers of the Intrauterine Device." *European Journal of Contraception and Reproductive Health Care* 2, no. 1 (March 1997): 15–23.

Thomlinson, Ralph. "Prevented Births, Naturalness, and Roman Catholic Doctrine." *Journal of Sex Research* 8, no. 2 (1972): 73–100.

Tinsman, Heidi. *Partners in Conflict: The Politics of Gender, Sexuality, and Labor in the Chilean Agrarian Reform, 1950–1973*. Durham, N.C.: Duke University Press, 2002.

———. "Reviving Feminist Materialism: Gender and Neoliberalism in Pinochet's Chile." *Signs* 26, no. 1 (Autumn 2000): 145–188.

Torres, Isaura. *Mortinatalidad de Santiago (abortos i nacidos muertos)*. Santiago: Impr. El progreso, 1918.

Torres, Rodrigo. *Perfil de la creación musical en la nueva canción chilena desde sus orígenes hasta 1973*. Santiago: CENECA, 1980.

Townsend, Camilla. "Refusing to Travel La Vía Chilena: Working Class Women in Allende's Chile." *Journal of Women's History* 4, no. 3 (Winter 1993): 43–63.

Traba, Marta. *Conversación al sur*. Mexico City: Siglo Veintiuno Editores, 1981.

Tripp, Aili Mari, "The Evolution of Transnational Feminisms: Consensus, Conflict, and New Dynamics." In *Global Feminism: Transnational Women's Activism, Organizing, and Human Rights*, edited by Mayra Marx Ferree and Aili Mari Tripp, 51–75 (chapter 3). New York: New York University Press, 2006.

Unidad Popular. *Programa básico de gobierno de la Unidad Popular*. Santiago: n.d., 1969.

———. *Programa básico de gobierno de la Unidad Popular: Las primeras 40 medidas del Gobierno Popular: 20 puntos básicos de la reforma agraria del gobierno de la Unidad Popular*. Santiago: 1970.

Valdés, Teresa. *El movimiento social de mujeres y la producción de conocimientos sobre la condición de la mujer*. Serie Estudios Sociales no. 43. Santiago: FLACSO, 1993.

———. *Las mujeres y la dictadura militar en Chile*. Material de Discusión, no. 94. Anexo III. Santiago: FLACSO, 1987.

———. "Mujeres y derechos humanos: 'menos tu vientre.'" *Documento de trabajo, serie estudios sociales*, no. 8. Santiago: FLACSO, 1990.

———. *Venid, benditas de mi padre las pobladoras, sus rutinas y sus sueños*. Santiago: Facultad Latinoamericana de Ciencias Sociales, 1988.

———, and María Cristina Benavente. *El poder en la pareja, la sexualidad y la reproducción*. FLACSO-Chile, 1999.

———, and Miren Busto, eds. *Sexualidad y reproducción: Hacia la construcción de derechos*. Santiago: FLACSO/CORSAPS, 1994.

———, Jacqueline Gysling, and María Cristina Benavente. *Género y políticas de población en Chile*. Santiago: FLACSO, 1994.

———, Ana María Muñoz B., and Alina Donoso O. *1995–2003: Have Women Progressed? Latin American Index of Fulfilled Commitment*. Santiago: FLACSO, 2005.

———, and Marisa Weinstein. *Mujeres que sueñan las organizaciones de pobladoras: 1973–1989*. Santiago: Facultad Latinoamericana de Ciencias Sociales, 1993.

———, Marisa Weinstein, María Isabel Toledo, and Lilian Letelier. *Centros de madres 1973–1989: Solo disciplinamiento?* Santiago: Programa FLACSO-Chile, 1989.

Valdivia Ortiz de Zárate, Verónica. *La milicia republicana: Los civiles en armas*. Santiago: Dibam, 1992.

———. *Nacionalismo e Ibañismo*. Santiago: Universidad Católica Blas Cañas, 1995.

Valenzuela Arellano, Luis. "Tendencias de la natalidad y fecundidad en Chile." *Revista Geográfica de Valparaiso* 10 (January–December 1979): 87–91.

Valenzuela, Arturo. *The Breakdown of Democratic Regimes: Chile*. Baltimore, Md.: Johns Hopkins University Press, 1978.

———. "Eight Years of Military Rule in Chile." *Current History* 81, no. 472 (February 1982): 64–88.

———, and J. Samuel Valenzuela. *Chile: Politics and Society*. New Brunswick, N.J.: Transaction Books, 1976.

Valenzuela, Maria Elena. "The Evolving Roles of Women Under Military Rule." In *The Struggle for Democracy in Chile, 1982–1990,* edited by Paul W. Drake and Ivan Jaksic, 161–187. Latin American studies series. Lincoln: University of Nebraska Press, 1995.

———. *La mujer en el Chile militar: Todas íbamos a ser reinas*. Santiago: Ed. Chile y America, CESOC, 1987.

Valenzuela, Samuel J., Eugenio Tironi Barrios, and Timothy Scully, eds. *El eslabón perdido: Familia, modernización y bienestar en Chile*. Santiago: Taurus, 2006.

Vargas Catalán, Nelson A. *Historia de la pediatría Chilena: Crónica de una alegría*. Santiago: Editorial Universitaria, 2002.

Vargas Valente, Virginia. "Carta hacia el VII Encuentro Feminista Latinoamericano y del Caribe. Chile. 1996." In *Encuentros, (des) encuentros y búsquedas el movimiento feminista en América Latina*, edited by Cecilia Olea Mauleón, 13–33. Lima, Peru: Flora Tristan, 1998.

———. "Ciudadanía. Un debate feminista en curso." In *La ciudadanía a debate*, edited by Eugenia Hola and Ana Maria Portugal. Santiago: Isis International, 1997.

Vekemans, Roger. *Caesar and God: The Priesthood and Politics*. Maryknoll, N.Y.: Orbis Books, 1972.

———. *Teología de la liberación y cristianos por el socialismo*. Bogotá: CEDIAL, 1976.

———, and Ismael Silva Fuenzalida. *16 estudios de interpretación social latinoamericana de Roger Vekemans e Ismael Fuenzalida*. CIDOC cuadernos no. 34, 35. Cuernavaca, Mexico: Centro Intercultural de Documentación, 1969.

———, and Ismael Silva Fuenzalida. *Marginalidad, promoción popular y neo-marxismo: Críticas y contracríticas*. Bogotá: CEDIAL, 1976.

———, and Ramón Venegas. *Seminario de promoción popular*. Santiago: Centre para el Desarrollo Económico y Social de América Latina, 1966.

Verba, Ericka Kim. *Catholic Feminism and the Social Question in Chile, 1910–1917: The Liga De Damas Chilenas*. Lewiston, N.Y.: E. Mellen Press, 2003.

———. "The Círculo de Lectura de Señoras [Ladies' Reading Circle] and the Club de Señoras [Ladies' Club] of Santiago, Chile." *Journal of Women's History* 7, no. 3 (Fall 1995): 6–33.

Vergara, Marta. *Memorias de una mujer irreverente*. Santiago: Editora Nacional Gabriela Mistral, 1974.

Vidal, Virginia. *La emancipación de la mujer*. Santiago: Quimantú, 1972.

Videla de Plankey, Gabriela. "Las mujeres pobladores de Chile y el proceso revolucionario." In *Perspectivas femeninas en América Latina*, edited by María del Carmen Elu de Leñero, 194–209. México City: SEP, Dirección General de Divulgación, 1976.

Viel, Benjamín. *The Demographic Explosion: The Latin American Experience*. New York: Irvington Publishers, 1976.

———. "Family Planning in Chile." *Journal of Sex Research* 3, no. 4 (November 1967): 284–291.

————. *La explosión demográfica. ¿Cuantos son demasiados?* Santiago: Editions of the University of Chile, 1966.

————. *La medicina socializada: y su aplicación en Gran Bretaña, Unión Soviética y Chile.* Santiago de Chile: Ediciones de la Universidad de Chile, 1964.

————. "Results of a Contraceptive Program Based on IUD's in Chile." In *Proceedings of the Family Planning Research Conference: A Multidisciplinary Approach, Exeter, England, September 27–28, 1971.* International Congress Series, no. 260, edited by Family Planning Research Conference, Alfredo Goldsmith, and R. Snowden, 103–107. Amsterdam: Excerpta Medica, 1972.

————, and Sonia Lucero. "Experiencia con un plan anticonceptivo en Chile." *Revista médica de Chile* 101, no. 9 (September 1973): 730–735.

Vinovskis, Maris. *An "Epidemic" of Adolescent Pregnancy? Some Historical and Policy Considerations.* New York: Oxford University Press, 1988.

Vitale, Luis. *Chile: Tres claves para el siglo XX: Arturo Alessandri, Carlos Ibañez del Campo, república socialista.* Buenos Aires: Libros del retorno, 1988.

Waitzkin, Howard, et al. "Social Medicine Then and Now: Lessons from Latin America." *American Journal of Public Health* 91, no. 10 (October 2001): 1592–1601.

Walter, Richard J. *Politics and Urban Growth in Santiago, Chile, 1891–1941.* Stanford, Calif.: Stanford University Press, 2004.

Waylen, Georgina. *Engendering Transitions: Women's Mobilization, Institutions, and Gender Outcomes.* Oxford: Oxford University Press, 2007.

————. "Women's Movements, the State, and Democratization in Chile: The Establishment of SERNAM." In *Getting Institutions Right for Women in Development*, edited by Anne Marie Goetz, 90–103. New York: Zed Books, 1997.

Weinstein, Marisa. *Estado, mujeres de sectores populares y ciudadanía.* Santiago: FLACSO-Chile, 1996.

Weisner, Monica. *Aborto inducido, estudio antropológico en mujeres urbanas de Bajo Nivel socioeconómico.* Santiago: University of Chile, 1982.

West, Lois. "U.N. Mid-decade for Women." *Off Our Backs* 10, no. 9 (October 31, 1980): 2.

White, Judy. *Chile's Days of Terror: Eyewitness Accounts of the Military Coup.* New York: Pathfinder Press, 1974.

Wilson, Jason. *Buenos Aires: A Cultural and Literary History.* Oxford: Signal Books, 2007.

Winn, Peter. *Americas: The Changing Face of Latin America and the Caribbean.* 1992; reprint, Berkeley: University of California Press, 2006.

————. *Weavers of Revolution: The Yarur Workers and Chile's Road to Socialism.* New York: Oxford University Press, 1986.

————, ed. *Victims of the Chilean Miracle: Workers and Neoliberalism in the Pinochet Era, 1972–2002.* Durham, N.C.: Duke University Press, 2004.

Witker Velásquez, Alejandro. *Los trabajos y los días de Recabarren.* Havana: Casa de las Américas, 1977.

————. *Salvador Allende, 1908–1973: Prócer de la liberación nacional.* México City: Universidad Nacional Autónoma de México, 1980.

Woll, Allen L. "The Comic Book in a Socialist Society: Allende's Chile, 1970–1973." *Journal of Popular Culture* 9, no. 4 (Spring 1976): 1039–1045.

Wright, Thomas, and Rody Oñate. *Flight from Chile: Voices of Exile,* translated by Irene Hodgson. Santiago: Documentas, 1987.

Wulf, Deidre. "Teenage Pregnancy and Childbearing in Latin America and the Caribbean: A Landmark Conference." *International Family Planning Perspectives* 12, no. 1 (March 1986): 17–22.

Würth Rojas, Ernesto. *Ibáñez, caudillo enigmático*. Santiago: Editorial de Pacífico, 1958.

Yanco, Jennifer J. "'Our Bodies, Ourselves' in Beijing: Breaking the Silences." *Feminist Studies* 22, no. 3 (Fall 1996): 511–517.

Zárate, María Soledad. *Dar a luz en Chile, Siglo XIX. De la 'ciencia de hembra' a la ciencia obstétrica*. Santiago: Centro de Investigaciones Barros Arana and the University of Alberrto Hurtado, 2007.

———. "Proteger a las madres: Origen de un debate público, 1870–1920." *Nomadías* (June 1999): 163–182.

———, ed. *Por la salud del cuerpo: Historia y políticas sanitarias en Chile*. Santiago: Ediciones Universidad Alberto Hurtado, 2008.

Zatuchni, G. I., J. D. Shelton, A. Goldsmith, and J. J. Sciarra, eds. *Female Transcervical Sterilization*. Philadelphia: Harper and Row, 1983.

Zinsser, Judith P. "The United Nations Decade for Women: A Quiet Revolution." *The History Teacher* 24 (November 1990): 19–29.

Zipper, Jaime, et al. "Contraception Through the Use of Intrauterine Metals. I. Copper as an Adjunct to the 'T' Device. The Endo-uterine Copper 'T'." *American Journal of Obstetrics and Gynecology* 109, no. 5 (March 1, 1971): 771–774.

———. "Metallic Copper as an Intrauterine Contraceptive Adjunct to the 'T' Device." *American Journal of Obstetrics and Gynecology* 105, no. 8 (December 15, 1969): 1274–1278.

———. "Quinacrine Hydrochloride Pellets: Preliminary Data on a Nonsurgical Method of Female Sterilization." *International Journal of Gynaecology and Obstetrics* 18 (1980): 275–279.

Zipper, Jaime, E. Stachetti, and M. Medel. "Human Fertility Control by Transvaginal Application of Quinacrine on the Fallopian Tube." *Fertility and Sterility* 21, no. 8 (August 1970): 581–589.

———. "Transvaginal Chemical Sterilization: Clinical Use of Quinacrine Plus Potentiating Adjuvants." *Contraception* 12 (1975): 11–21.

Zulawski, Ann. *Unequal Cures: Public Health and Political Change in Bolivia, 1900–1950*. Durham, N.C.: Duke University Press, 2007.

Zwingel, Susanne. *Demokratie im Land und im Haus: Die Rolle von Frauenorganisationen im Demokratisierungsprozess Chiles*. Demokratie und Entwicklung, Bd. 26. Hamburg, Germany: Lit, 1997.

———. "From Intergovernmental Negotiations to (Sub)national Change: A Transnational Perspective on the Impact of CEDAW." *International Feminist Journal of Politics* 7, no. 3 (September 2005): 400–424. Published summary "CEDAW: The Women Formula." Available online at http://www.opendemocracy.net/author/Susanne_Zwingel.jsp.

INDEX

Note: Page numbers in italics refer to figures.

abortion: Catholic Church on, 52, 87–88;
criminalization of, 8, 143, 160–61,
165, 185–88, 245n115; demand for,
123; impact of double discourse
system on, 51; medicalization of, 47,
56, 62–63, 69–70; as ongoing issue,
197–98; public opinion on, 145, 199;
right-to-life clause of 1980 Constitution, 186, 190; Unidad Popular policy
on, 122–23
abortion, legalization of: contemporary
efforts toward, 245n115; debate on,
under Unidad Popular, 122–23; doctors' support for, 50; therapeutic
abortions, 52, 214n27
abortion, therapeutic: debate on, under
Unidad Popular, 122, 123; legalization
of, 52, 214n27; military regime's
recriminalization of, 143, 186, 188,
190, 245n115
The Abortion (film), 96–97
abortions, illegal: arrests and prosecutions
for, 52, 185–86, 190, 198; birth control as answer to, 45, 46–47, 50,
55–56, 62; criminal penalties, 52, 186;
dangers of, 44–45, 53, 55, 187–88;
decline in, after introduction of birth
control, 61, 70, 97; doctors' denuncia-
tion of, 214n19; health officials' concerns about, 45; higher risk for poor
women in, 54–55; as justification for
birth control experimentation, 58, 60;
and maternal mortality rates, 6, 45,
49, 50–51, 55, 69–70, 122, 137, 178,
197, 214n16; recognition of, as public
health problem, 54, 69–70, 94; research and documentation on, 50–51,
53–54, 63, 70; selected reasons for
epidemic of, 245n115; suppression of
debate on, 50–51; techniques, 55

Academia de Humanism Cristiano (Academy of Christian Humanism), 154
Act No. 18.826 (1989), 186
Adriasola, Guillermo, 66, 92, 93–94, 96,
100–101
agency of women: birth control debate and,
215n37; medical professionals' control
of family planning, 15, 56, 57–58, 62,
68, 69, 73–74, 98, 231n89; protest
against dictatorship and, 11, 135, 153,
158, 159; under Unidad Popular government, 104
Agrupación de Mujeres Democráticas (Association of Democratic Women), 153
Aguayo, Carmen Gloria, 78; and Christian
Democrats' efforts to mobilize female
electorate, 78
Aguer, Hector, and reference to fear of using
the term "gender," 247n22
Aguirre Cerda, Pedro, 18, 28
alcoholism: and domestic violence, 103; in
early twentieth century, 16
Alessandri Palma, Arturo, 18
Alessandri Rodríguez, Jorge, 48, 106
Allende, Hortensia Bussi de, 115
Allende, Isabel, 52–53, 100
Allende Gossens, Salvador: on abortion, 122;
on American partnership in health
care, 34–35; calls for social reform,
28–29; death of, 131; and election of
1958, 48; and election of 1970, 101,
106; and family planning programs,
107; and health care policies, 121–22;
as minister of health, 18; opposition's
undermining of, 109–10, 125–26; on
social and political liberty, 110; as traditional leftist, 104; on women's issues, 113–14; on women's role, 102,
104, 110, 113–14, 114–15, 127. *See
also* Unidad Popular government

Alliance for Progress, 74
Alvarez, Sonia, 104, 177–78, 196
Alywin, Patricio, 167
Amiga (periodical), 89
Ana (Mothers' Center participant), 116
Ana (*pobladora*), 152
Ana Maria (protester), 129–30
Andreas, Carol, 119–20
Angela (*pobladora*), 152
Antezana-Pernet, Corinne, 33
anti-Americanism: in Latin America, 47–48; in Unidad Popular regime, 124–25
Antonio Ríos, Juan, 18
Appleman, Philip, 67
APROFA. *See* Chilean Association for the Protection of the Family
Argentina: maternalization of women in, 4; women's rights in, 8, 136
Armijo, Rolando, 54, 63
art and culture under Unidad Popular government, 117–20
Asociación Chilena de Protección de la Familia. *See* Chilean Association for the Protection of the Family
Association of Democratic Women (Agrupación de Mujeres Democráticas), 153
authoritarian regimes, and women's rights, 136
Avendaño, Onofre, 36, 51, 66, 122
Aylwin, Patricio, 193–94

Bachelet, Michelle, 200
Baeza Goñi, Arturo, 22
Bahamonde, Alberto, 27
Baltra, Mireya, 115
Bambirra, Vania, 111
Barrales, Katerin, 191
Barrios de Chungara, Domitila, 171, 172
Barr-Melej, Patrick, 13
Barros Borgoño, Martina, 1–2, 293n6
Barros Luco Hospital, 57–58, 92, 97, 123
Batista, Fulgencio, 47
The Battle of Chile (Guzman), 132, 232n127
Belnap, David, 131
Belsky, Raymond L., 216n50
beneficent materialism, 14, 30–31
Benston, Margaret, 111
Berelson, Bernard, 69

Berlagoscky, Fanny, 195
Besse, Susan, 8
Beveridge, William, 35
biological differences. *See* "natural" qualities of women
birth control: Catholic Church on, 84–89, 93, 100, 198, 223n65, 224n76; decline in abortions after introduction of, 61, 70, 97; delay in addressing need for, 43; early advocates of, 45, 62; emergency contraception, legalization of, 197; poor women's concerns about, 61; public opinion on, 145; religious views and, 83–84, 88; traditional methods of, 51; women's desire for, 54; women's right to, 219n3. *See also* family planning
birth control, access to: in 1930s and 1940s, 51; groups asserting control of, 46–47; medical professionals' control of, 15, 56, 57–58, 62, 68, 69, 73–74, 98, 231n89; under Unidad Popular, 104
birth control, support for: as answer to illegal abortion crisis, 45, 46–47, 50, 55–56, 62; as basis for gender equity, 46; to control population, 46, 47; by doctors, 45, 47, 55–56, 148; women's reproductive rights not considered in, 45–46, 47, 62, 68, 70
birth control, as weapon of imperialism, 104, 106, 228n20; as weapon used against Chileans, 106
birth control experimentation, 56–62, 66–67, 70, 213n6; and abuse of women as "human material," 47, 56, 60; and informed consent, 57–58, 60; lack of concern for subjects of, 60; on men, 59–60
birth control information: MEMCh spreading of, 32; for men, 61; poor women's access to, 61; suppression of, 27–28, 52–53, 61, 143–44, 150, 156; women's confusion about, 187
Bogolawski, John, 121
Boletin APROFA (periodical), 95
Born to Starve (Tydings), 67
Borquez, Chela, 173
Borzutsky-Friedman, Leon, 216n50

Boston Women's Health Book Collective (BWHBC), 184
boycotts of Chilean goods under military rule, 179–81, *180*
Bravo, Rosa, 155
Brazil, women's rights in, 8, 136
breastfeeding, as obligation of mother, 22–23
Breeding Ourselves to Death (Lader), 67
Busto, Miren, 172
BWHBC. *See* Boston Women's Health Book Collective

Caffarena, Elena, 6, 32
Calderón, Margarita, 193–94
Calvo Mackenna, Luis, 22
campamentos: gender relations in, 103; military regime suppression of, 134–35; women's activism in, 102–3, 115, 134; women's daily struggles in, 103–4
Campos, Héctor, 122
Casas, Lidia, 186
Casti connubii (papal encyclical), 85, 223n54
Castillo, Carmen, 182
Castro, Fidel, 47, 128
Catholic Church: on abortion, 52, 87–88; on birth control, 84–89, 93, 100, 198, 223n65, 224n76; and defense of human rights, 157; rejection of feminist discourse, 247n22; resistance to social reform, 198–99; support for women's resistance to military regime, 154; on women's role, 198–99
Catholics: proselytizing of workers, 30; views on causes of poverty, 23. *See also* Social Catholics.
Caupolicán Theatre, 158–59
CEDAW. *See* Convention on the Elimination of All Forms of Discrimination against Women
CELADE. *See* Latin American Center for Demography
CELAP. *See* Latin American Center for Population
CEMA. *See* Central Organization for Mother's Centers
CEMA-Chile. See Fundación Graciela Letelier de Ibáñez, CEMA-Chile

censorship, under military regime, 137, 144
Central Intelligence Agency (CIA), 105
Central Organization for Mother's Centers (CEMA), 77
Central Unica de Trabajadores (the National Workers Syndicate; CUT), 112
Centro Latinoamericano de Demografía (Latin American Center for Demography; CELADE), 82
Centro Latinoamericano de Población y Familia (Latin American Center for Population; CELAP), 82
Centro para el Desarrollo Económico y Social de América Latina (Latin American Center for Social and Economic Development; DESAL), 82
Centros de Madres. *See* Mothers' Centers
Ceorino, Rosana, 169–70
Chaney, Elsa M., 31
Charnes, Ximena, 184
Chavez, María, 195
"Chile, Will to Be" (pastoral letter, 1968), 87
Chile-América (periodical), 179
Chilean Assembly of Communist Women, 111
Chilean Association for the Protection of the Family (Asociación Chilena de Protección de la Familia; APROFA): educational programs under Christian Democracy rule, 71; educational programs under military regime, 146–48, 161; family planning ambassadors, 93; family planning services, 94, 94–96, 95, 101; international support for, 124; and leadership by Benjamín Viel, 220n3; research activities, 82, 88, 89; Rockefeller and, 79; under Unidad Popular, 124, 125
Chilean Committee for the Protection of the Family (Comité Chileno de Protección de la Familia), 63–64
The Chilean Social-Medical Reality (Allende), 18, 38, 121
The Chilean Woman (Puz), 111–12
Chilean Women's Medical Association, 63
choice, and motherhood, 1, 9; and limited space for women's, 45–47, 51, 56, 61–62, 68, 70

Index

Christian Democratic government
(1964–1970): CELAP and, 82–83; and
election of 1964, 75; family planning
policies, 68, 73–74, 75, 93–98, 100;
land takeovers under, 99, 102; limited
success of, 101; program of, 74–75;
promoción popular (popular promotion)
program, 75, 76, 83; realities of urban
poverty and, 75–76; reinvention of
family unit under, 219n3; and rights of
women, 76; wooing of women's support, 78
Christian Democratic Party: and election of
1970, 106; and election of 1989, 167;
founding of, 74; opposition to Unidad
Popular government, 126, 128; support for, 48; U.S. support of, 105
Christians for Socialism, 87
Christina (victim of illegally induced abortion), 44–45
Chuchryk, Patricia, 241n48
CIA. *See* Central Intelligence Agency
Círculo de Estudios de La Mujer (Women's
Studies Circle), 136, 154–57, 199
Círculo de Lectura de Señoras (Ladies'
Reading Circle), 30
citizenship rights of women, Christian
Democrats and, 76
Civil Code of Chile, and legal authority of
males, 8, 31, 160
Claro, Amparo, 185
class and political divisions: Chilean efforts
to address, 28–29; in international
feminist networks, 171–73, 176–78; in
women's groups, under redemocratization, 167–70, 191, 194–95, 201
class struggle, subjugation of women's
movement to, 111–13
Claudia (Chilean exile), 181
Club de Señoras (Ladies' Club), 30
Coalition for Democracy Party (Concertación de los partidos por la
democracia): accommodation of feminist demands, 169–70; election of,
167; feminist demands for reform,
168; women's class and political divisions under, 167–70
Coalition of Parties for Democracy, 168

CODE. *See* Confederacion Democratica
CODEM. *See* Committee for the Defense of
Women's Rights
Cold War: Alliance for Progress and, 74; and
fear of population explosion, 65; im-
pact on Latin America, 47–48; and
U.S. intervention in Chile, 105
Combative Women, 131
Comité Chileno de Protección de la Familia
(the Chilean Committee tor the Pro-
tection of the Family), 63–64
Committee for the Defense of Women's
Rights (Comité de Defensa de los
Derechos de la Mujer; CODEM), 136,
157–58
Communist Party, 106
Compropolitan (Santa Cruz and Erazo), 183
Concertación de los partidos por la democ-
racia. *See* Coalition for Democracy
Party
Concertación Nacional de Mujeres por la
Democracia (National Coalition of
Women for Democracy), 160, 168
Confederacion Democratica (CODE), 126
Conference of Responsible Parenthood
(1997), 198–99
consciousness raising, 155, 164, 174, 195
conservative women: anti-Allende activism,
104–5, 127–31; defense of moral-
religious view of sexuality, 150–51;
demographic characteristics, 232n124;
and rise of women's political involvement, 133; support of military regime,
293n131
Constitution of 1822, 5
Constitution of 1925, 5, 18
Constitution of 1980, 167, 186, 190
contraception. *See* birth control
Convention on the Elimination of All Forms
of Discrimination against Women
(1979; CEDAW), 166, 169, 191, 240n6
Cook, Rebecca, 204n15
Coordinating Office of Mothers' Centers
(Coordinadora de Centros de Madres;
COCEMA), 115
Coordinator of Women's Social Organiza-
tions (La Coordinación de Organiza-
ciones Sociales de Mujeres), 159

Corrêa de Oliveira, Plinio, 223n65
Croizet, E., 24
Cruzat, María Isabel, 155
Cruz Coke, Eduardo, 28, 144
Cuadernos de educación popular (Notebooks for popular education; Harnecker), 110
Cuban revolution, 47–48
El cuerpo humano (the human body) exhibit, 120–21
culture and art under Unidad Popular government, 117–20
culture of silence, regarding sexuality and reproduction, 50–53, 91–92
CUT. *See* Central Unica de Trabajadores

Damas Chilenas. *See* Liga de Damas Chilenas
Day of Decriminalization of Abortion in Latin America and the Caribbean, 178
Day of No More Violence Against Women, 178
Decade for Women, 7, 164, 165–66, 183. *See also* United Nations
Decade for Women World Conference (Copenhagen, 1980), 172
Decade for Women World Conference (Nairobi, 1985), 173
"Declaration of the Chilean Episcopate about Family Planning" (1967), 87
Decree 300 (1981), 150
Decree 362 (1983), 150
Decree 4002 (1980), 150
del Rio, Alejandro, 25
"Demandas de las Mujeres a la Democracia" (Women's demands for democracy), 168
democracy: Chile's motion toward, 48; secret ballot system, 48; and women's rights, 8. *See also* redemocratization
Department for Female Labor Studies, 78
Department of Sanitary Education, 39
DESAL. *See* Latin American Center for Social and Economic Development
Díaz, Soledad, 62–63
dictatorship, and women's rights, 8
Disney, *Family Planning* film, 71–72, 72, 117
diversity, feminists' need to learn to negotiate, 172, 176

divorce: legalization of, 198; and stability of family unit, 226n109
doctors: control of family planning, 15, 56, 57–58, 62, 68, 69, 73–74, 98, 100–101, 231n89; efforts to control health management, 24; global alliance for population control, 7; international ties of, 34, 42; maternalization of women by, 4, 15; medicalization of problems related to modernization, 38; political activism of, as Chilean characteristic, 37; support for sex education, 92; support of family planning, 45, 47, 55–56, 63–64, 148
doctors' political power: and perpetuation of capitalism, 41–42; public health initiatives and, 14, 25, 37, 209n62
domestic violence: alcoholism and, 103; as ongoing issue, 197; poor women and, 149
Donald Duck, 71–72, 72, 117
Dorfman, Ariel, 117
double discourse system, on sexual morality, 51; as explanation of silence on abortion, 51
double standard in moral codes, 99–100; Allende on, 114; and teenage pregnancy, 149

economic modernization, 198
Education on Sexuality for Students campaign, 147–48
Edwards, Monseñor Rafael, 23. *See also* Social Catholics.
Ehrlich, Paul, 67
election of 1970: campaign, 105–8; competition for women's votes, 106, 108; results, 108–9; U.S. interventions in, 105
election of 1989, 138, 167
election of 2006, 200
elite class, conspiracy of silence about sexuality, 53
elite women/mothers: abortions by, 53; and beneficent materialism, 14, 30; as model for poor, 22, 38–39; opposition to Unidad Popular, 128
El Loco Pepe, 75

Ema (Women's Study Circle participant), 154, 155
employment for women: in early twentieth century, 16, 17; mid-twentieth century, 49, 76; modernization and, 42. *See also* working women
Encuentros Feministas (Feminist Encounters), 164, 174–78, 191, 195
Erazo, Viviana, 183
Ercilla (periodical), 63, 85
Ernst, Amalia, 51
Eva (periodical), 126
Ewig, Christina, 189
exiles from military regime: activism abroad, 178–81, *179, 180,* 182–83; and connection to international rights organizations, 163–64; as link to international feminist groups, 181–82; number of, 137; personal experiences of, 181; publications, 183–84

Family Ministry (Ministerio de la Familia), 113–14
family planning: doctors' support for, 45, 47, 55–56, 63–64, 148; as human right, 80, 149; modernization and, 64, 72–73; propaganda efforts for, 67, 71–72, *72,* 96–97, 218n95; Women's Studies Circle forum on, 156. *See also* birth control
Family Planning / Planificación Familiar (film), 71–72, *72,* 117, 147
family-planning clinics, women's use of, 97
family planning programs: under Christian Democrats, 68, 73–74, 75, 93–98, 100; institutionalization of, 63–64, 68, 70; international support for, 63–64, 67–69, 79–81, 82, 97, 124; left's characterization of as foreign plot, 106–7; under military regime, 142–45; and patriarchal structures, strengthening of, 73; under Unidad Popular, 104, 107, 112–13, 123–24
family unit: APROFA reinvention of, 96; and fertility regulation programs, 63; reinvention of under Christian Democrats, 219n3; stability of, divorce and, 226n109; types of, in early twentieth century, 17

Fatherland and Liberty (Patria y Libertad), 128
Faúndes, Aníbal, 55–56, 107, 122, 123
feminist discourse, Catholic Church's rejection of, 247n22
Feminist Encounters (Encuentros Feministas), 164, 174–78, 191, 195
feminist networks, international: benefits of, 173–75; Chilean women's participation in, 163–66; class and political division in, 171–73, 176–78; exiles as link to, 181–82; history of, 7–8; Latin American women's participation in, 31–32, 205n26; ongoing work of, 191; regional forums and initiatives, 174–78, 196–97
feminist networks, under military regime, 135
feminists, Latin American: contemporary adjustments in activist strategy, 196; disillusionment with North American feminist model, 171–72; embrace of motherhood, 3; publications, 183–85
feminists in Chile: activism under military regime, 154–55; contesting of motherhood ideal, 6, 31–32; demands for women's rights, 32; embrace of motherhood ideal, 31; fragmentation under redemocratization, 195–96, 201; history of, 7–8, 31, 237n96; *institucionales vs. autónomas,* 177; under military regime, 135–36; ongoing struggles of, 194–201; and *pobladoras,* 157–59; *politicas vs. feministas,* 176; reassessment of motherhood, in Pinochet-era, 155–57, 161–62; under redemocratization, class and political divisions, 167–70, 191; suffrage movement, 30; under Unidad Popular, 110–13. *See also* women's activism
fempress (Mujer; periodical), 183
Fierro Carrera, Luisa, 13
financial crisis of early 1980s, 137
La Firme (comic book), 117, 119
First National Congress for the Protection of Childhood (1912), 19–21, 22
Ford Foundation, 60, 63, 67, 82, 218n95
Foucault, Michel, 215n37

France, control and management of women by public health programs, 212n109
Franceschet, Susan, 31
Franco, Jean, 247n22
Frei Montalva, Eduardo: address to IPPC conference, 90–91; failure to deliver on promises, 101; family planning and, 79–81; government of, 74–75; meeting with Rockefeller, 79. *See also* Christian Democratic government
Frohmann, Alicia, 164, 168
Fuentealba, Luis, 60
Fundación Graciela Letelier de Ibañez, CEMA-Chile, 139–40, 141, 147

Gannon, Isabel, 174
García Carpanetti, Victoria, 50
Gaudium et Spes (1965), 86
Gazitua, Dr., 50
gender, Chilean Parliament's prohibition of term, 196
gender equity: commitment to, under redemocratization, 191; demands for, under Coalition for Democracy (Concertación) rule, 168; demands for, under military regime, 159–60; incomplete adoption of, under redemocratization, 194; rise of international movement for, 191; *World Plan of Action* (International Women's Year conference), 165–66
gender hierarchies: fear of uprooting, 219n3; Mothers' Centers' perpetuation of, 77, 78; unfit mother concept and, 15
gender mutualism, 219n3
gender relations, in New Havana, 103
gender system, Chilean: women challenging, 154, 156; history of challenges to, 15; under military regime, 138; motherhood as central concept in, 2; social workers' perpetuation of, 38–39; under Unidad Popular government, 117, 119, 131; women's shaping of, 3; women's use of against Unidad Popular government, 130
Ginsburg, Faye, 6–7
globalization, gender-specific impacts of, 191

global political climate, impact on women, 6–7
Gomez-Rogers, Carlos, 60
González Videla, Gabriel, 18
Good Neighbor Policy, 36
Gräfenberg, Ernst, 57
Gramsci, Antonio, 212n122
Grez, Carmen, 185–86
Guatemala, U.S. intervention in (1954), 47
Guevara, Ernesto "Che," 47
Guzmán, Jaime, 160–61, 186
Guzman, Patricio, 132, 232n127

Hackett, Lewis, 38, 40
Harnecker, Marta, 110, 132
health, violations of Chilean women's right to, 188
health care. *See* public health programs
health-care workers. *See* medical professionals
Health Code of 1931, 52
health insurance: introduction of, 28; under military regime, discrimination against women in, 189, 190; Workers' Compulsory Insurance Fund, 24–25
health officials. *See* medical professionals
health provider institutions (*instituciones de salud previsional*; ISAPRES), 189
higher education for women, history of, 5–6, 204n22
Hilda (New Havana resident), 135
Hola, Eugenia, 172
"How to Read Donald Duck" (Dorfman and Mattelart), 117
Htun, Mala, 8, 136, 245n115
Huetel, Leontina, 142, 148
Humanae vitae (On human life; papal encyclical), 84–85, 88, 89, 198, 223n54
Human Reproduction (film), 147
human rights abuses of military regime, 137–38, 153, 233n11, 245n103; documentation of, 154; Truth and Reconciliation Committee, 167
human rights movement, global: Chilean participation in, 164–65; integration with women's rights movement, 166, 191; and Pinochet's departure, 138
Huneus, Pablo, 148
husband's legal power, 8, 31, 160

IACW. *See* Inter-American Commission of Women

Ibáñez del Campo, Carlos, 18, 24–25, 43, 48

identity, women's, rise of political involvement and, 133

IFC. *See* Latin American Index of Fulfilled Commitment

Illanes, María Angelíca, 206n15

imperialism, as misleading concept, 7

industrialization: and employment for women, 17; urge to protect mothers from, 5

infant mortality rates: doctors' efforts to address, 19–22, 28, 42; early twentieth century, 19; high, persistence of, 48–49; and maternalization of health policies, 23–24; and unfit mother concept, 14

informed consent, birth control experimentation and, 57–58, 60

instituciones de salud previsional (health provider institutions; ISAPRES), 189

Institute of Small Infant Care, 21

Inter-American Commission of Women (IACW), 31, 32

International Day of Nonviolence against Women, 175

International Planned Parenthood Federation (IPPF): APROFA and, 68; programs in Chile, 63–64; Santiago conference (1967), 73, 89–93, 97, 99, 121; Viel employment at, 107

International Women and Health Resource Guide (BWHBC), 184, 244n93

International Women's Day, 112, 188

International Women's Year (1975), 164–65

International Women's Year conference (Mexico, 1975), 165–66, 171

Inti-Illimani (band), 118, 163

intrauterine devices (IUDs): doctors' control over, 62; military regime's removal of, 142, 187, 234n35; popularity of, 61, 98; promised impact of, 69; testing of, 57–59

In Women's Hands (film), 199

IPPF, International Planned Parenthood Federation

Irma (abortion patient), 187–88

ISAPRES. *See instituciones de salud previsional*

Isis International, 184–85

IUDs. *See* intrauterine devices

Jacques, Rosario, 204n22

Janney, J. H., 36

Jara, Joan, 163

Jara, Victor, 117, 163

Jiménez, Oscar, 121, 123–24

John Paul II (pope), 151

Johnson, Lyndon B.: Frei government and, 74–75; on population control, 67

Johnson & Johnson International, 56, 216n50

Kennedy, John F., 74

Kinzer, Stephen, 105

Kirk, Dudley, 59

Kirkwood, Julieta, 134, 135, 160, 163, 165, 175, 192

Kissinger, Henry, 105

Körner, Victor, 19

Kunzle, David, 119

Labor Code of Chile, 25

LACWHN. *See* Latin American and Caribbean Women's Health Network

Lader, Lawrence, 67

Ladies' Club (Club de Señoras), 30

Ladies' Reading Circle (Círculo de Lectura de Señoras), 30

land takeovers, under Christian Democrats, 99, 102

Latin America: anti-Americanism in, 47–48, 124–25; Cold War and, 47–48

Latin American and Caribbean Women's Health Network (LACWHN), 185

Latin American Center for Demography (Centro Latinoamericano de Demografia; CELADE), 82

Latin American Center for Population (Centro Latinoamericano de Población y Familia; CELAP), 82–83, 90

Latin American Center for Social and Economic Development (Centro para el Desarrollo Económico y Social de América Latina; DESAL), 82

Latin American feminists: contemporary adjustments in strategy, 196; disillusionment with North American feminist model, 171–72; embrace of motherhood, 3; publications, 183–85

Latin American Index of Fulfilled Commitment (IFC), 197

Laura (New Havana resident), 102–3

Lavrin, Asunción, 3

Law 4054, 29

Law of Neighborhood Organizations, 76

leftists: characterization of family planning as foreign plot, 106–7; women in cultural productions of, 119

leftist women, under Unidad Popular, 110–13

legal authority of husbands, 8, 31, 160

legal norms for women's rights, global, 166, 178, 191

Lessons for Life: Focusing on Young People project, 148

life expectancy, 48

Liga de Damas Chilenas, 30

Lippes loops, 98

El Loco Pepe, 75

Long, John, 35

Losada de Masjuan, Josefina, 83–84

machismo, women's views on, 181

Manuel Matus, Victor, 44, 45

March of Empty Pots and Pans, 127–30

Mardones, Francisco, 64

Mardones Restat, Francisco, 91

Mardones Restat, Jorge, 42

marginalization of women, history of, 5–6

Maria (*pobladora*), 152

marianismo, and limits of concept of, 2–3

Marimbo, Doralisa, 141–42

Marin, Gladys, 122

Maritain, Jacques, 74

Markmann de González Videla, Rosa 43, 77

married women: as consumers of abortion, 54; husband's legal power, 8, 31, 160; limits on, 31

Marxism, support for, 48

Matamala, Marisa, 184, 245n103

maternal body, threats to, and political reform, 28–29

maternalization of women: by Allende (Salvador), 102, 104, 110, 113–14, 114–15, 127; in Argentina, 4; by

Catholic Church, 198–99; by doctors, 4, 15; by military regime, 135, 138–39, 188–89, 190

maternal mortality rates: and Catholic tolerance of birth control, 87–88; illegal abortions and, 6, 45, 49, 50–51, 55, 69–70, 122, 137, 178, 197, 214n16; as justification for birth control experimentation, 60

maternity insurance, introduction of, 28

Mattelart, Armand, 117

Mattelart, Michele, 126

Mayer, Cora, 209n49

McGee Deutsch, Sandra, 30

Mead, Karen, 14

media: and birth control debate, 63, 66, 85, 104; CIA black propaganda and, 105; conservative control of, 126; construction of women's images through, 175; feminist critiques of, 183; on sex education, 92; and teenage pregnancy, 149

medical confidentiality, under military regime, 186–87

medical education, reform of (1945), 35–36

medical professionals: control of family planning, 15, 56, 57–58, 62, 68, 69, 73–74, 98, 100–101, 231n89; female, control and management of women by, 38–41; justifications for control over women's reproduction, 46–47; maternalization of women by, 4, 15. *See also* doctors

MEMch. *See* Movimiento Pro-Emancipación de la Mujer Chilena

Memchistas. *See* Movimiento Pro-Emancipación de la Mujer Chilena

men, birth control experimentation on, 59–60

Mendoza, Ofelia, 63

Mensaje (periodical), 93

El mercurio (newspaper), 5, 145–46

middle class, conspiracy of silence about sexuality, 53

middle class women/mothers: abortions by, 53; and beneficent materialism, 14, 30–31; as model for poor, 22, 38–39

migration, from rural to urban, 13, 48; and female migrants, 13, 49

Milbank Memorial Fund, 67
militant mothers, under Unidad Popular
    government, 104–5
military coup (1924), 24–25
military coup (1973), 110, 130–32
military regime: control of women under,
    138–42; criminalization of abortion, 8,
    143, 160–61, 165, 185–88, 245n115;
    discussion of sexuality under, 136,
    145–52, 161; economic policies,
    137–38; ending of, 138, 159; family
    planning programs under, 142–45;
    focus on national defense, 235n46; in-
    ternational boycotts of, 179–81, 180;
    legacies of, 167, 190, 193–94; neo-
    liberal economic reforms, 189, 190;
    privatization under, 143; pro-natalist
    policies, 142–45, 148, 186, 235n49;
    public health policies, 188–89, 190;
    suppression of campamentos, 134–35;
    terror tactics of, 137–38, 153, 233n11,
    245n103; Truth and Reconciliation
    Committee and, 167; women's activism
    under, 153–61, 161–62; women's
    movements under, 135–36; women's
    resistance to, 135, 238n119; wo-
    men's rights under, 8, 136; women's
    role under, 135, 138–39. See also exiles
    from military regime; human rights
    abuses of military regime
Mill, John Stuart, 1
Miller, Francesca, 31–32, 183
Ministerio de la Familia (Family Ministry),
    113–14
Ministry of Education, sex education pro-
    grams, 150
Ministry of Hygiene, Health Care, and So-
    cial Security, 24–25
Miró, Carmen, 59–60, 84; as director of
    Center for Demography in Santiago,
    59; as critic of doctors' unsupervised
    medical experiments, 59
Miss Universe (film), 175
model mothers, characteristics of, 22
modernization: anxiety about, 4–5; and
    changing means of limiting women,
    9; economic, 198; and employment
    for women, 42; and family planning,

64, 72–73; impact on women, 13–14,
    42; and meaning of motherhood,
    4–5; medicalization of problems
    related to, 38; and unfit mothers con-
    cept, 19–21
MOMUPO. See Movimiento de Mujeres
    Pobladoras
Monckeberg, Fernando, 148
Le monde (newspaper), 134
Monreal, Tegualda, 53–54, 63, 122, 123,
    219n3
moral codes, double standard in, 99–100
moral-religious paradigms: and birth con-
    trol, 83–84, 88; and conceptions of
    sexuality, 27–28; conservative women's
    defense of, 150–51; contemporary
    persistence of, 198–99, 201; and dou-
    ble discourse system, 51
Moreno, Aída, 195
mother-child unit, as basis of Chilean public
    health programs, 28–29, 42
motherhood: calls for population control
    and, 69; as central concept in Chilean
    gender system, 2; as patriotic duty
    under military regime, 186, 245n103;
    and political activism, 130; as political
    tool, under military regime, 135, 141;
    reassessment of, in Pinochet-era femi-
    nism, 155–57, 161–62; women's
    views on, 151
motherhood, constructions of, 2; contempo-
    rary reconfiguration of, 200; doctors
    and policymakers' efforts to control,
    7; feminist's contesting of, 6, 7–8; as
    indication of rights, 3–4; mothers as
    saviors of the nation, 10, 73, 91,
    96–98, 100–101
mothers, model, characteristics of, 22
Mothers' Centers: under Christian Democ-
    rats, 76–79; under Coalition for
    Democracy, 167; under military
    regime, 138, 139–40, 142, 147; under
    Unidad Popular government, 79,
    115–17
Movement for the Emancipation of
    Chilean Women. See Movimiento
    Pro-Emancipación de la Mujer
    Chilena

Movimiento de Izquierda Revolucionaria
(the Movement of the Revolutionary
Left; MIR), 102
Movimiento de Mujeres Pobladoras (Movement of Shantytown Women;
MOMUPO), 136, 158, 168
Movimiento Pro-Emancipación de la Mujer
Chilena (Movement for the Emancipation of Chilean Women; MEMch), 3;
founding of, 6, 32; issues addressed by,
6; program of, 32–33. *See also La mujer
nueva*
Mujer (fempress; periodical), 183
Mujeres Creando Futuro (Women Building
the Future), 195
Mujeres en Acción (Women in Action; periodical),
184
La mujer nueva (The new woman; periodical),
6, 32–33
music, under Unidad Popular, 117–18

Nari, Marcela, 4
National Association of Catholic Students,
74
National Coalition of Women for Democracy (Concertación Nacional de
Mujeres por la Democracia), 160
National Council for Protection of Childhood (Patronato Nacional de la Infancia), 39
National Falange, 74
National Feminist Meeting (Olmué, Chile,
2005), 191, 195
National Health Service (NHS): contract
with APROFA, 94; establishment of,
14, 42; and family planning programs,
63–64, 68; "Official Norms of Birth
Control," 90, 93; and population control research, 82; on religion and contraception, 88; sex education programs, 150; under Unidad Popular,
123–24
National Office for Women's Affairs (Servicio Nacional de la Mujer; SERNAM),
169–70, 191
National Party (Partido Nacional), 126,
128
National School of Sanitary Nurses, 39

National Women's Service (SERNAM). *See*
National Office for Women's Affairs
National Workers Syndicate (Central Unica
de Trabajadores; CUT), 112
"natural" qualities of women: Allende on,
114–15; as justification for oppression,
1; military regime's views on, 138–39
Navarro, Elcira, 116
Navarro, Marysa, 2–3, 177–78
neoliberal economic reforms, under military
regime, 189, 190
neo-Malthusian paradigm, 218n84; global
alliance for, 7; Viel and, 65
New Havana (Nueva La Havana): attraction
of intellectuals and artists to, 103;
founding of, 102; gender relations in,
103; political structures in, 102–3, 134
New Roots (Nuevas Raíces), 170
New Song movement, 118
New York Times (newspaper), 105, 121, 144
NGOs (nongovernmental organizations):
negative side-effects of, 178; SERNAM
prioritization of, 169–70; and UN
Decade for Women conferences, 173
NHS. *See* National Health Service
Nixon, Richard M., 74
nongovernmental organizations. *See* NGOs
Norma (abortion client), 53
Notestein, Frank, 82
Nuestros cuerpos, nuestras vidas (BWHBC), 184
nueva canción movement, 117–18
Nueva La Havana. *See* New Havana
Nuevas Raíces (New Roots), 170

ODEPLAN. *See* Office of Government
Planning
Office for Family Education (OFE), 27
Office of Government Planning (ODE-
PLAN), 144
Onetto, Enrique, 148
Onis, Juan de, 121
"On Social and Political Responsibility in
the Present Hour" (pastoral letter,
1962), 87
On the Subjection of Women (Mill), 1
Ortega, Eliana, 176
Osborn, Fairfield, 67
Our Bodies, Ourselves (BWHBC), 184

Palma, Irma, 149
Pan-American Child Congress, 32
Pan-American Health Organization, 34, 147
Pan-Americanism, women's movement and, 32
Pan-American Union, 31
Parliamentary Republic (1882–1920), ending of, 17–18
Partido Nacional (National Party), 126, 127–28
Patria y Libertad (Fatherland and Liberty), 128
Patronato Nacional de la Infancia (National Council for Protection of Childhood), 39
patriarchy, reference to Chilean characteristics of, 206n3; military regime as expression of, 138, lasting power of, 160
Paula (periodical), 100, 116, 122
Paul VI (pope), 85, 86
Peaceful Road to Socialism: and election of 1970, 108–9; opposition's undermining of, 109–10, 125–26; and women's agency, 104; women's role in, 110–11
Pease, Clifford, 93
La Pelusa, 99
Penal Code of Chile, on abortion, 52
People's Magazine, 147
Pérez, Ernestina, 209n49
physicians. See doctors
the Pill, experiments with, 213n6
Pincus, Gregory, 66, 67
Pinochet, Augusto: departure from power, 138; and plebiscite of 1988, 138, 159, 167; seizure of power, 133, 137; on women's nature, 139. See also military regime
Pinochet, Lucía Hiriart de, 135, 138, 139, 140, 185
Pinto Solari, Malucha, 193
Pisano, Margarita, 177
Pius XI (pope), 85, 223n54
Pius XII (pope), 85
Pizano, Maria, 31
Pizarro Ramirez, Zunilda, 146
Planificación Familiar (Family Planning; film), 71–72, 72
plebiscite of 1988, 138, 159, 167

pobladoras: activism of, 103, 157–59; exclusion from feminist groups under redemocratization, 167–70; feminist consciousness in, 103, 227n6; response to military rule, 227n6; struggles of, 152, 194–95; views on sexuality, 151; women's groups, 136
Poblete, Renato, 122
Poblete Troncoso, Moisés, 66
Poder Feminino (Feminine Power), 130, 131
political office, women in, and motherhood ideal, 31
political participation of women: and election of 1964, 75; and fall of Unidad Popular, 130–31; history of, 6, 31; increase in, under redemocratization, 199–200; mobilization of motherhood for, 3, 31, 33; political parties as barrier to, 241n31; in Unidad Popular regime, 127–30, 133
political parties, as barrier to women's political participation, 241n31
political systems, variance in women's rights in, 8
poor women: access to birth control information, 61; concerns about birth control, 61; employment, 76; failure of doctors to address poverty of, 98; and illegal abortions, risks of, 54–55; impact of unfit mother concept on, 14, 15; limited tools available to, 22; Mothers' Centers and, 78; unique struggles of, 194–95. see also pobladoras; poverty
Popular Front governments (1938–1952): Mothers' Centers and, 77; public health policies, 14, 28; and securing of male-led family, 204n18; social welfare policies, 18–19
The Population Bomb (Ehrlich), 67
population control: birth control supported as means of, 46, 47; calls for, 64–68, 69; global alliance for, 7; propaganda efforts, 67, 218n95
population explosion, fear of, 65–66
Population Policy of the Chilean Government, 144
pots and pans, banging of, 127–28, 158
Potthast, Barbara, 203n8

Index

poverty: failure to address structural causes of, 23; urban, Christian Democrats and, 75–76; views on causes of, 23; and women, attention drawn to, 33–34. *See also* poor women

Power, Margaret, 227n9

Prado, Rodrigo, 60

president of Chile, first female, 200

Preventive Medicine Act of 1938, 28

professional women: and double standard, 99–100; prejudice against, 6, 204n22

pro-life discourse, definition specific to Chile, 205n30; APROFA's use of, 93, 95

pro-life, specific to defense of birth control in Chile, 46–47, 63–64

promoción popular (popular promotion) program, 75, 76, 83

property rights, discrimination in, 8, 160

prostitution, in early twentieth century, 17

Las Protestas (the Protests), 158–59

Provoste, Patricia, 188

public health programs: control and management of women by, 21–23, 29, 36–43, 37, 212n109; and doctors' political power, 14, 25; establishment of, 19–22, 24–25; international influence on, 34–37, 42; maternalization of, 23–24; under military regime, 143–45, 188–89, 190; mother-child unit as basis of, 28–29; obligations imposed on mothers, 22–23; as ongoing issue, 197; in Popular Front governments, 14, 28; propaganda campaigns, 26–27; protections for working women, 25, 26, 34; under Unidad Popular, 120–25; women's lack of power to question, 60–61

Public Health System of Chile, founding of, 7

Pueblo, Peyuco, 118

Punto final (periodical), 91

Pupkin, Marcus, 60

Puz, Amanda, 111–12

Quandt, Anna, 166

Quilapayun (band), 118, 128

quilts, Vicaria de Solidaridad program, 154

Quimantú press, 111, 117

Quinta Normal, research in, 36–37, 54

Radio Cooperativa, family planning show, 148

Raíces (Roots), 170

Ramona (periodical), 119

Rapp, Rayna, 6–7

Reagan, Maureen, 173

La Realidad Médico-Social Chilena (The Chilean socio-medical reality; Allende), 28–29

redemocratization: and complexity of feminist strategy, 176–78; and demands for gender equity, 160; economic modernization, 198; fragmentation of feminist movement under, 167–70, 191, 194–95, 201; incomplete adoption of equal rights under, 194; increased political participation of women under, 199–200; legacy of military regime and, 167, 190, 193–94; ongoing feminist struggles under, 194–201; persistence of social conservatism, 198–99

The Regulation of Sexual Education (Office of Family Education), 27

reproductive rights of women: failure to consider, in birth control debate, 45–46, 47, 62, 68, 70; history of progress toward, 46; obstacles to, 245n115; as ongoing issue, 197, 198; UN recognition of, 166; women's demands for, 47

Requena, Mariano, 54, 56, 61, 107, 219n3

Responsible Parenthood (film), 147

Revista católica (periodical), 89

Revista fiducia (periodical), 223n65

Revista médica (periodical), 144

Revista mensaje (periodical), 84

Revolution in Liberty, 75, 76, 79, 100, 101

rights of women. *See* women's rights

right to health: obstacles to, under military regime, 188–89; ongoing struggle for, 191

Ríos Tobar, Marcela, 240n5

Rock, John, 67

Rockefeller, John D. III, 56, 65–66, 79–81, 82, 86

Rockefeller Foundation: and control of women, 15, 38, 40; left's accusations against, 106; support of fertility control programs, 7, 63, 67, 216n80; support of public health programs, 35–36

Rodríguez, Francisca, 170
Rojas Flores, Jorge, 22–23
Romero, Hernán: administrative duties, 63, 64; on Church's views on birth control, 93; on population control, 66; and reconstruction of meaning of family, 95–96; research by, 50–51; Rockefeller and, 79; on sex education, 92; support for family planning, 62; training of, 36
Roots (Raíces), 170
Rosemberg, David, 60
Rosemblatt, Karen, 40
Ruiz Tagle de Frei, María 77

Saa, María Antonieta, 199–200
Saavedra, Wilna, 122
Saf-t-coils, 98
Saint Jean, Heliette, 151
Salcedo Rojas, Lucy, 146–47
Salman, Ton, 238n119
Sanitary Code, on breastfeeding, 23
sanitary nurses, visiting (inspectoras visitadoras): and consolidation of gender roles, 40–41; control and management of women by, 39–41
Santa Cruz, Adriana, 183
Santiago: migration to, early twentieth century, 13–14, 15–16; migration to, mid-twentieth century, 49; population, 49; population control research in, 73, 80–83. See also shantytowns
Saporta Sternbach, Nancy, 176
saviors of the nation, women as, 10, 73, 91, 96–98, 100–101
School of Public Health (University of Chile), 36, 42
Schuster Cortes, Augusto, 144
Scott, Joan, 203n13
Second Vatican Council, 84, 87
Secretaría Nacional de la Mujer (the Woman's National Secretariat), 114, 138, 141
La segunda (newspaper), 185
selflessness, as essential quality of women, 39
SERNAM. See Servicio Nacional de la Mujer
Serrano, Elena, 155

Servicio Nacional de la Mujer (National Office for Women's Affairs; SERNAM), 169–70
sex, women's fear of, 151
sex education programs: avoidance of birth control information, 27–28; calls for, 27, 91–93, 209n49; lack of, and abortion crisis, 245n115; under military regime, 147–50, 161; under Unidad Popular, 121–22
sexual freedom, public opinion on, 145–46
sexuality, conceptions of: among pobladora women, 151; conservative women's defense of moral-religious paradigms, 150–51; under military regime, 151; moral-religious paradigms as basis of, 27–28; move from medicalized to human-based discourse, 147
sexuality and reproduction: culture of silence regarding, 50–53, 91–92; discussion of, under military regime, 136, 145–52, 161; discussion of, under Unidad Popular, 120–21; and double discourse system, 51
sexually transmitted diseases (STDs), education campaigns on, 150
sexual rights, double standard in, 99–100
shantytowns, 49, 76. See also campamentos
Shepard, Bonnie, 51
Sierra, Lucas, 24, 34
Siete Canchas campamento, 115
El siglo (newspaper), 106
The Silent Explosion (Appleman), 67
Silva, Clotilde, 158
Silva, Coti, 167–68, 195
Silva Henríquez, Raúl, 88, 154
Simon, Robert, 21
single mothers: in early twentieth century, 17; programs for, 27; as unfit mothers, 27, 206n35
Social Catholics, 23
social conservatism, persistence of, 198–99
Socialist Party, and election of 2006, 200
Socialist Republic (1931–1932), 18
social reform, calls for, 28–29
social welfare policies, of Popular Front governments, 18–19

social workers, female (*visitadoras*), control and management of women by, 38–41
Sociedad chilena de defensa de la tradición, familia, y propiedad, 223n54
Society of Pediatrics, 27
Soledad (*pobladora*), 152
solidarity groups: in Chile, 153; international, against Chilean human rights abuses, 164, 178, 191
"Song of Popular Power," 118
Spoerer, Alberto, 143
Statement on Population, 79–81
STDs. *See* sexually transmitted diseases
Stein, Oswald, 35
supermadres, and motherhood ideal, 31

Talpade Mohanty, Chandra, 241n37
Tatum, Howard, 66
teenage pregnancy: education programs, 149–50; as ongoing issue, 197
Teresa de los Andes (saint), 151
third-world women: disillusionment with North American feminist model, 171–72; as problematic term, 241n37
Tinsman, Heidi, 73, 219n3
Todaro, Rosalba, 155
Tomic, Radomiro, 106
Toribio Merino, José, 186
Tres Marías y una Rosa (Three Marys and a Rose; play), 152
Truth and Reconciliation Committee, 167
Tydings, Joseph, 67

Ugarte, José M., 50–51
UNDP. *See* United Nations Development Program
unfit mother concept: construction of, 14, 19–21, 29; and doctors' political power, 14, 41; equating of poverty with ignorance in, 21–22; and reinforcement of gender hierarchies, 15, 42–43; single mothers included under, 27, 206n35
Unidad Popular government: abortion policy, 122–23; art and culture under, 117–20; economic woes, 109–10, 125–26, 127, 129–30; and election of 1970, 105–9; family planning policies, 104, 107, 112–13, 123–24; health care and sexuality policies, 120–25; internal strife, 126; Mothers' Centers under, 79, 115–17; overthrow of, 110, 131–32; patriarchal politics in, 104; policies for/about women, 113–17; program, 104, 108, 109, 110, 117, 227n9; reproduction of old gender patterns in, 10, 117, 119, 131–32; requests for women's support, 126; supporters, *108, 109*, 131; women's anti-regime activism, 127–31; women's movement under, 110–13; women's participation in, 131–32. *See also* Peaceful Road to Socialism
union activism of women, 30
United Nations: CELADE and, 82; Decade for Women (1975–1985), 7, 164, 165–66, 183; and feminist ties to international groups, 164–66; International Women's Year (1975), 164–65; International Women's Year conference (1975), 165–66; recognition of reproductive rights, 166; World Conference on Human Rights (Vienna, 1993), 166; World Conference on Population and Development (Cairo, 1994), 166; World Conference on Women (Beijing, 1995), 166, 196
United Nations Development Program (UNDP), 82
United States: Chilean population control and, 79–81, 82; Good Neighbor Policy, 36; influence on Chilean health care, 35–36; interventions in Latin America, 47–48, 105; policy on population control, 67–68; undermining of Allende regime, 126. *See also* Cold War; Ford Foundation; Rockefeller Foundation
University of Chicago, and Pinochet economic policies, 137
University of Chile: abortion studies at, 50; birth control research at, 60; Department of Preventive Medicine, 54; Experimental Film Department education film, 96–97; Medical School, 5–6; National School of Sanitary Nurses, 39;

University of Chile: *(continued)*
population control research in, 81–82;
research grants, 97; School of Public
Health, 36, 42

U.S. Population Council: and family planning programs, 56, 63, 69, 82; research grants, 97; Rockefeller as leader
of, 65; and sex education, 92–93; and
Unidad Popular government, 107; and
U.S. foreign policy, 67; and women's
reproductive rights, 166

Valdés, Gabriel, 105
Valdés, Marina, 158
Valdés, Teresa, 132, 237n96
Valdivieso, Ramón, 79, 90, 93
Valenzuela, Maria Elena, 138, 150
Vargas, Virginia, 167, 177
Vekemans, Roger, 82, 83, 90, 93
Veldebenito, Ester, 116
Verba, Ericka, 3
Vergara, Marta, 31
Vicaria de Solidaridad (Vicariate of Solidarity), 154, 237n102
Vidal, Virginia, 112–13
Viel, Benjamín: and support of women's
autonomous access to birth control,
220n3; and birth control programs,
53, 61–62, 82; defense of family planning programs, 107, 228n21; departure from Chile, 107; international
support of, 35, 124; left's accusations
against, 106; *People's Magazine* profile,
147; on population control, 64–65,
66; postpartum care programs, 97–98,
228n25; rejection of Christian Democratic policies, 225n99; research by,
54, 97; on right to family planning, 149,
219n3; teenage pregnancy education
programs, 149–50; training of, 7, 36
Viera Altamirano, Napoleon, 82
voting rights of women: activism for, 30, 32;
granting of, 5, 31, 34, 43; voter registration, 75
Vuskovic, Pedro, 127

wage discrimination: early twentieth century,
17; outlawing of, 25; persistence of, 26

Week of the Chilean Child (1928), 26
Week of the Chilean Mother (1929), 26–27
Weisner, Monica, 187
"What women need to know in order to
raise their children well" (Congress for
the Protection of Childhood), 22
White Book of the Change, 233n11
Wolff, Eric, 119
Woman, What Is Your Mission (Catholic publica-
tion), 198–99
Woman's Emancipation (Vidal), 112–13
Woman's National Secretariat (Secretaría
Nacional de la Mujer), 114, 138, 141
Women and Their Bodies (workshop,
BWHBC), 184
Women Building the Future (Mujeres
Creando Futuro), 195
Women in Action (*Mujeres en Acción*; periodical),
184
women's activism: in *campamentos*, 102–3,
115, 134; combative assertion of
rights, 99, 131; conservative anti-
Allende activism, 104–5, 127–31; by
exiles from military regime, 178–81,
179, 180, 182–83; under military
regime, 153–61, 161–62; Mothers'
Centers and, 115–17; of *pobladoras,*
103, 157–59; Las Protestas (the
Protests), 158–59; union activism, 30.
See also beneficent materialism; *entries
under* feminist
Women's Citizenship Day, 196
women's rights: in Argentina, 8, 136; authoritarian regimes and, 136; in different political systems, 8; global legal
norms for, 166, 178, 191; under military regime, 136; under redemocratization, 194–201. *See also* gender
equity; reproductive rights of women;
voting rights of women
women's role: Allende (Salvador) on, 102,
104, 110, 113–15, 127; revived conservative view by Catholic Church on,
198–99; under military regime, 135,
138–39; under Unidad Popular,
110–11
Women's Studies Circle (Círculo de Estudios de la Mujer), 136, 154–57, 199

"Women's Voice" (pamphlet), 182
Workers' Compulsory Insurance Fund,
  24–25, 29
Workers' Compulsory Insurance Law of
  1924, 24–25
working women: feminist demands for support of, 50; opposition to Unidad Popular, 128; political engagement under
  Unidad Popular regime, 128, 131; protective legislation for, 25, 26, 34. *See
  also* employment for women; wage discrimination
World Conference of Solidarity with Chile
  (Madrid, 1978), 179
World Conference on Human Rights
  (Vienna, 1993), Declaration and Program of Action, 166
World Conference on Population and Development (Cairo, 1994), 166
World Conference on Women (Beijing,
  1995), 166, 196

World Leaders' Statement on Population,
  79–81
World Plan of Action (International Women's
  Year conference), 165–66

youth, and problem of unanswered questions
  about sex, 91–92; forum on sexuality
  for Chilean, 92; Hernán Romero
  on needs of open communication
  with, 92

Zambra, Gildo, 44, 45, 62, 124–25
Zañartu, Juan, 59–60
Zatuchni, Gerald I., 97–98
Zipper, Jaime, 56–59, 66, 68; and first
  unauthorized experiments with Zipper
  ring, 56–58; and first Family Planning
  Clinic, 58
Zipper ring, 57–59, 66
Zulawki, Ann, 9
Zwingel, Susanne, 240n6